Early Church Records

of

Monmouth County, New Jersey

Anna Miller Watring

HERITAGE BOOKS
2018

HERITAGE BOOKS
AN IMPRINT OF HERITAGE BOOKS, INC.

Books, CDs, and more—Worldwide

For our listing of thousands of titles see our website
at
www.HeritageBooks.com

Published 2018 by
HERITAGE BOOKS, INC.
Publishing Division
5810 Ruatan Street
Berwyn Heights, Md. 20740

Copyright © 2004 Anna Miller Watring

All rights reserved. No part of this book may be reproduced or transmitted in any form or by any means, electronic or mechanical, including photocopying, recording or by any information storage and retrieval system without written permission from the author, except for the inclusion of brief quotations in a review.

International Standard Book Number
Paperbound: 978-0-7884-5816-3

Old Tennent Presbyterian Church

OLD TENNENT SCOTCH PRESBYTERIAN CHURCH
Baptisms 1730-1800

Grace, d/o _, chr. 4 Aug. 1734.
John Murray, s/o _, chr. 19 Mar. 1738.
Yana, d/o _, chr. 19 Mar. 1738.
Mink_, s/o _, chr. 5 July 1741.
Kate, d/o _, chr. 14 Mar. 1742.
Hannah, d/o _, chr. 17 June 1744.
Tom, s/o _, chr. 28 Dec. 1746.
Nancy, d/o Yana, chr. 8 Mar. 1747.
Cyro, s/o Yana, chr. 8 Mar. 1747.
Mack, s/o Yana, chr.8 Mar. 1747.
Tony, s/o _, chr. 19 Apr. 1747
Jaef, s/o _, chr. 27 Sep. 1747.
Peter, s/o Mink, chr.18 Sep. 1748.
Moses, s/o _, chr. 18 June 1749.
Hagar, d/o _, chr. 14 Apr. 1751.
Ninus, s/o Mink, chr. Sep. 1751
Cube, s/o _, chr. 16 Oct. 1752.
Titus, s/o Cube, chr. 15 Apr. 1753.
Alice, d/o _, chr. 13 May 1753.
Diana, d/o _, chr. 13 May 1753.
Samson, s/o _, chr. 26 Oct. 1755.
Cofie, s/o _, chr. 17 Oct. 1756.
Samson, s/o Cube, chr. 8 May 1757.
James, s/o _, chr. 5 June 1757.
Peter, s/o _, chr. 25 June 1758.
Jack, s/o _, chr. 6 Aug. 1758.
Jaef, s/o _, chr. 7 Jan. 1759.
Rose, d/o _, chr. 7 Jan. 1759.
Simeon, s/o _, chr. 22 Feb. 1761.
George, s/o _, chr. 25 Oct. 1761.
Thomas, s/o _, chr. 2 Nov. 1766.
Mary, d/o _, chr. 2 Nov. 1766.
Hannah, d/o _, chr. 18 Oct. 1767.
Lewis, s/o _, chr. 9 Apr. 1786.
Mary, d/o Lewis and Hager, chr. 1787.
Rosay, d/o Lewis and Hager, chr. 1787.
Yaff, s/o Lewis and Hager, chr. 1787.

Pero, s/o _, chr. 7 Jan. 1787.
Simon, s/o _, chr. 16 Sep. 1787.
James, s/o _, chr. 6 Oct. 1787.
Hagar, d/o _, chr. 6 Oct. 1787.
Robert, s/o _, chr. 1788.
Kate, d/o _, chr. 1788.
Jane, d/o _, chr. 1788.
Agnes, d/o _, chr. 1789.
Margaret, d/o _, chr. 1789.
Diana, d/o _, chr. 1789.
Andrew, s/o _, chr. 1789.
Nero, s/o _, chr. 1789.
Rhoda, d/o _, chr. 1789.
Rachel, d/o _, chr. 1789.
Betty, d/o _, chr. 1789.
Samuel, s/o Lewis, chr. 1789.
Phebe, d/o _, chr. 1790.
Caesar, s/o _, chr. 1790.
Phebe, d/o _, chr. 1790.
Hester, d/o _, chr. 1790.
Broof, s/o _, chr. 1790.
Adam, s/o _, chr. 1790.
Flora, d/o _, chr. 1791.
Elizabeth, d/o _, chr. 1791.
Zebulon, s/o _, chr. 1791.
Rose, d/o _, chr. 1791.
Catharine, d/o _, chr. 1791.
Mary, spouse of David Cook, chr. 1791.
Elizabeth, d/o Jem and Flora, chr. 1 May 1791.
Susannah, d/o Jem and Flora, chr. 1 May 1791.
Pero, s/o Pero, chr. 24 Sep. 1791.
Lewis, s/o Pero, chr. 24 Sep. 1791.
Rose, d/o Yaf and Rose, chr. 23 Dec. 1791.
Yaf, s/o Yaf and Rose, chr. 23 Dec. 1791.
James, s/o Yaf and Rose, chr. 23 Dec. 1791.
Henry, s/o Yaf and Rose, chr. 23 Dec. 1791
Benjamin, s/o _, chr. 1792.
Susan, d/o _, chr. 1792.
Benjamin Harvey, s/o _, chr. 1792.
James, s/o Zebulon, chr. 1792.
Rachel, d/o Zebulon, chr. 1792.
Sampson, s/o Zebulon, chr. 1792.

Old Tennent Presbyterian Church

Zebulon, s/o Zebulon, chr. 1792.
Nathaniel, s/o Rachel (Relict of Ephraim Foster) chr. 1792.
Phebe, d/o Rachel (Relict of Ephraim Foster), chr. 1792..
William Alanson, s/o Rachel (Relict of Ephraim Foster), chr. 1792.
Ephraim, s/o Rachel (Relict of Ephraim Foster), chr. 1792.
Euphame, d/o Rachel (Relict of Ephraim Foster), chr. 12 Oct. 1792.
Rachel, d/o Rachel (Relict of Ephraim Foster), chr. 12 Oct. 1792.
Leah, d/o Rachel (Relict of Ephraim Foster), chr. 12 Oct. 1792.
Ursula, d/o Rachel (Relict of Ephraim Foster), chr. 12 Oct. 1792.
Jane, d/o Rachel (Relict of Ephraim Foster), chr. 12 Oct. 1792.
Jesse, s/o _, chr. 1793.
Lewis, s/o Zebulon, chr. 1793.
Ephraim, s/o _, chr. 1793.
Lewis, s/o Lewis, chr. 1793.
Phillis, d/o _, chr. 1793.
Hannah, d/o _, chr. 1 Oct. 1793.
Elizabeth, d/o _, chr. 1794.
Phebe, d/o _, chr. 1794.
Susannah, d/o _, chr. 1794.
Dora, d/o _, chr. 1794.
Diana, d/o _, chr. 1794.
Elizabeth, d/o _, chr. 1794.
Rachel, d/o _, chr. 1794.
Katey, d/o Lewis, chr. 3 Aug. 1794.
Anthony, s/o Diana, chr. 1795.
Mary, d/o _, chr. 1795.
Mary, d/o _, chr. 1795.
Lydia, d/o _, chr. 1795.
Hannah, d/o Lewis, chr. 1796.
Fortune, d/o _, chr. 1796.
Silas, s/o _, chr. 1796.
Flora, d/o _, chr. 1796.
Thomas, s/o _, chr. 1796.
Mary, d/o _, chr. 7 Oct. 1798.
Eliza, d/o Henry, chr. 1799.
Truey, d/o Rose, chr. 1799.
Jacob, s/o _, chr. 1800.
Clarissa, d/o _, chr. 1800.
Silas, s/o _, chr. 1800.
Mary, d/o _, chr. 1800.
Catherine, d/o _, chr. 1800.
Mc Ferrin, Elisabeth, d/o Hugh, chr. 6 Dec. 1730.

Williams, James, s/o George, chr. 6 Dec. 1730.
Zutphen, Aentije, d/o John, chr. 6 Dec. 1730.
Henderson, Jane, d/o John, chr. 26 Dec. 1730.
Weycof, Gerrit, s/o Gerrit, chr. 27 Dec. 1730.
Adams, Joseph, s/o Thomas, chr. 21 Jan. 1731.
Deboogh, Frances, d/o Frederick, chr. 21 Jan. 1731.
Brown, William, s/o Arthur, chr. 23 Jan. 1731.
Van Voorhees, child of Peter, chr. 7 Mar. 1731.
Barber, Sarah, d/o Edward, chr. 14 Mar. 1731.
Whitlock, Sarah, d/o Thomas, chr. 12 Mar. 1731.
Newal, Adam, s/o John, chr. 4 Apr. 1731.
Ker, Margaret, d/o William, chr. 18 Apr. 1731.
Mc Cay, Elisabeth, d/o Daniel, chr. 2 May 1731.
Mount, Brittan, s/o Humphry, chr. 2 June 1731.
Zutphen, Nealtije, d/o Derck, chr. 2 June 1731.
Lambertson, Roelph, s/o John, chr. 20 June 1731.
Watson, Richard, s/o Richard, chr. 25 July 1731.
Graham, Anne, d/o James, chr. 26 Jul. 1731.
Graham, Sarah, d/o James, chr. 26 Jul. 1731.
Wilson, Catharine, d/o John, chr. 1 Aug. 1731.
Wilson, Rachel, d/o Waltar, chr. Sep. 1731.
Tomson, John, s/o George, chr. 5 Sep. 1731.
Wilson, Rachel, d/o Waltar, chr. 12 Sep. 1731.
Rhe, Jonathan, s/o David, chr. 26 Sep. 1731.
Wall, Rebeca, d/o James, chr. 10 Oct. 1731.
Brown, John, s/o James, chr. 17 Oct. 1731.
Berry, Mary, d/o John, chr. 25 Nov. 1731.
Robinson, Mary, d/o James, chr. 5 Feb. 1732.
Mattison, Anne, chr. 11 Feb. 1732.
Hawkinson, Hannah, chr. 24 Feb. 1732.
Ker, Walter, s/o Samuel, chr. 12 Mar. 1732.
Jolley, David, s/o William, chr. 25 Apr. 1732.
Tomson, Rachel, chr. 25 Apr. 1732.
Tomson, Rachel, chr. 25 Sep. 1732.
Ker, Rebeca, d/o John, chr. 19 July 1732.
Mains, Andrew, s/o Andrew, chr. 19 Jul. 1732.
Nesmith, Anne, d/o Thomas, chr. 19 July 1732.
Nesmith, Thomas, chr. 19 July 1732.
Parent, Thomas, s/o Josiah, chr. 19 July 1732.
Adams, James, s/o Thomas, chr. 24 Sep. 1732.
Davison, child of, chr. 24 Sep. 1732.
Wilson, Hannah, d/o Cath., chr. 24 Sep. 1732.

Old Tennent Presbyterian Church

Anderson, Helena, d/o John, chr. 28 Jan, 1733.
Davison, Mary, d/o John, chr. 28 Jan. 1733.
Henderson, Elizabeth, d/o John, chr. 28 Jan. 1733.
Rue, Mary, d/o James, chr. 28 Jan. 1733.
Van Kerk, Alice, d/o John, chr. 28 Jan. 1733.
Van Delip, Baldwin, s/o Baldwin, chr. 25 Mar. 1733.
Ker, William, s/o Samuel, chr. 25 Mar.1733.
Wilson, Jane, d/o Waltar, chr. 25 Mar. 1733.
Redford, Thomas, chr. 29 Apr. 1733.
Wilson, Peter, chr. 29 Apr. 1733.
Sweetman, Jane, d/o Michael, chr. 1733.
Rogers, William, s/o William, chr. 29 Apr. 1733.
Wilson, Jane, d/o Waltar, chr. 25 Mar. 1733.
Ker, Margaret, d/o Joseph, chr. 4 June 1733.
Mc Connel, Eleazar, s/o John, chr. 1 Sep. 1733.
Glendinnen, John, chr. 16 Sep. 1733.
Robinson, James, s/o Margt., chr. 16 Sep. 1733.
Van Kerk, Elsie, d/o William, chr. 16 Sep. 1733.
Berry, Thomas, s/o John, chr. 4 Nov. 1733.
Ker, Mary, d/o William, chr. 4 Nov. 1733.
Laird, Alexander, s/o William, chr. 4 Nov. 1733.
Mc Ferrin, Jane, d/o Hugh, chr. 4 Nov. 1733.
Mc Cay, Daniel, s/o Daniel, chr. 2 Nov. 1733.
Newal, Agnos, d/o John, chr. 23 Dec. 1733.
Shaw, Sarah, d/o John, chr. 23 Nov. 1733.
Rhe, Nelley or Nealtije, d/o David, chr. 30 Dec. 1733
Deboogh, Sarah, d/o Frederick, chr. 8 Jan. 1734.
Mattison, Mary, d/o Jacob, chr. 8 Jan. 1734.
Hampton, Isabella, d/o William, chr. 24 Feb. 1734.
Hawkinson, Joseph, chr. 24 Feb. 1734.
Hawkinson, Thomas, chr. 24 Feb. 1734.
Robinson, Jane, d/o James, chr. 25 Feb. 1734.
Terry, Richard, s/o William, chr. 17 Mar. 1734.
Witlock, John, s/o Thomas, chr. 17 Mar. 1734.
English, Elizabeth, d/o James, chr. 23 Mar. 1734.
Mains, Charles, s/o Andrew, chr. 31 Mar. 1734.
Williams, Margaret, d/o George, chr. 14 Apr. 1734.
Adams, Hannah, d/o David, and Margaret, chr. 28 Apr. 1734.
Adams, David, s/o David and Margaret, chr. 28 Apr. 1734.
Adams, Sarah, d/o David and Margaret, chr. 28 Apr. 1734.
Errukson, Thomas, s/o Michael, chr. 5 May 1734.
Johnson, John, s/o Joseph, chr. 5 May 1734.

Ker, Joseph, s/o John, chr. 5 May 1734.
Mount, Dorcas, d/o Humphry, chr. 5 May 1734.
Laird, Moses, s/o Thomas, chr. 19 May. 1734.
Logan, Sarah, d/o William, chr. 19 May 1734.
Nesmith, Margaret, d/o Thomas, chr. 26 May 1734.
Reed, Jane, d/o John, chr. 26 May 1734.
Parent, Margaret, d/o Josiah, chr. 31 May 1734.
Brown, Thomas, s/o Arthur, chr. 21 July 1734.
Hutton, Mary, d/o John, chr. 6 Oct. 1734.
Ker, Mary, d/o Joseph, chr. 20 Oct. 1734.
Van Kerk, Peter, s/o John, chr. Nov. 1734.
Gordon, William, s/o Peter, chr. 3 Nov. 1734.
Gordon, Elizabeth, d/o Peter, chr. 3 Nov. 1734.
Anderson, Kenneth, s/o John, chr. 7 Nov. 1734.
Ker, Joseph, s/o Samuel, chr. 22 Nov. 1734.
Allen, Daniel, chr. 15 Dec. 1734.
Zutphen, John, d/o Abraham, chr. 15 Dec. 1734.
Davison, John, s/o Robert, chr. 29 Dec. 1734.
Ross, John, s/o Isaac, chr. 2 Feb. 1735.
Henderson, Anne, d/o John, chr. 9 Feb. 1735.
Pettit, James, s/o James, chr. 9 Feb. 1735.
Tomson, John, s/o John, chr. 5 Mar. 1735.
Van Kerk, Hannah, d/o William, chr. 23 Mar. 1735.
Van Scaiack, Elizabeth, d/o Francis, chr. 23 Mar. 1735.
Brown, Thomas, s/o Hannah Brown or Deboogh, chr. 6 Apr. 1735.
Dey, Hannah, d/o Isaac, chr. 4 May 1735.
Smith, Sarah, d/o John, chr. 1 June 1735.
Smith, Esther, d/o John, chr. 1 June 1735.
Smith, John, s/o John, chr. 1 June 1735.
Smith, Joseph, s/o John, chr. 1 June 1735.
Tomson, child of Rebeca, chr. 15 June 1735.
Mains, Jane, d/o Andrew, chr. 22 June 1735.
Rounay, Ruth, chr. 13 July 1735.
Johnson, Griffith, s/o Joseph, chr. 27 Jul. 1735.
Wall, James, s/o James, chr. 27 July 1735.
Logan, Soffel, s/o William, chr. 31 Aug. 1735.
Cowenhoven, William, s/o Wm., chr.28 Sep. 1735.
Applegate, child of Benjamin, chr. 5 Oct. 1735.
Applegate, Rebeca, d/o Benjamin, chr. 5 Oct. 1735.
Applegate, Jacob, s/o Benjamin, chr. 5 Oct. 1735.
Hampton, Timothy, s/o William, chr. 5 Oct. 1735.
Mc Cay, William, s/o Duncan, chr. 5 Oct. 1735.

Old Tennent Presbyterian Church

Mc Cay, Anne, sdo Duncan, chr. 5 Oct. 1735.
Mc Cay, Mary, d/o Duncan, chr. 5 Oct. 1735.
Mc Cay, Catharine, d/o Duncan, chr. 5 Oct. 1735.
Perrine, Daniel, s/o Daniel, chr. 5 Oct. 1735.
Laird, Moses, s/o William, chr. 19 Oct. 1735.
Wilson, Andew, s/o Joseph, chr. 19 Oct. 1735.
Wilson, Joseph, chr. 19 Oct. 1735.
Truax, Roelef, s/o John, chr. 25 Aug. 1735.
Van Voorhees, Jane, d/o Hendrick, chr. Nov. 1735.
Ker, Elizabeth, d/o Samuel, chr. 15 Nov. 1735.
Witlock, Mary, d/o Thomas, chr. 29 Feb. 1736.
King, Robert, s/o Richard, chr. 4 Mar. 1736.
Mc Connel, Marthar, d/o John, chr. 28 Mar. 1736.
Hawkinson, Aaron, s/o Joseph, chr. 4 Apr. 1736.
Abrams, James, s/o James, chr. 2 May. 1736.
Adams, James, d/o David, and Margaret, chr. 2 May. 1736.
Deboogh, Isaac, s/o Frederick, chr. 2 May 1736.
Sweetman, John, s/o Michael, chr. 2 May 1736.
Rogers, Elizabeth, d/o William, chr. 9 May 1736.
Rogers, Mary, d/o William, chr. 9 May 1736.
Ver Bryke, Aeltije, d/o Barnardus, chr. 9 May 1736.
Rhe, Janet, d/o David, chr. 16 May 1736.
Lowrey, Nathaniel, s/o John, chr. 29 May 1736.
Mount, Mary, d/o Humphry, chr. 7 June 1736.
Pittinger, Euphunea, d/o Richard, chr. 20 June 1736.
Morgan, Hannah, d/o Nathaniel, chr. 4 July 1736.
Anderson, Ursilla, d/o John, chr. 11 Jul. 1736.
Davison, William, s/o Robert, cnr. 11 July 1736.
Mc Ferrin, Margaret, d/o Hugh, chr. 11 July 1736.
Perrine, Mary, d/o Peter, chr. 11 July 1736.
Applegate, Elizabeth, d/o Thomas, chr. 8 Aug. 1736
Applegate, Hannah, d/o Thomas, chr. 8 Aug. 1736
Perrine, Elizabeth, d/o Daniel, chr. 8 Aug. 1736.
Addudel, William, s/o William, chr. 22 Aug. 1736.
Hawkins, Hugh, s/o Richard, chr. 29 Aug. 1736.
Smith, Moses, s/o Moses, chr. 29 Aug. 1736.
Smith, Dorothy, s/o Moses, chr. 29 Aug. 1736.
Smith, Eleanor, s/o Moses, chr. 29 Aug. 1736.
Ker, Nathan, s/o William, chr. 3 Oct. 1736.
Robinson, John, s/o James, chr. 3 Oct. 1736.
Van Kerk, William, s/o William, chr. 3 Oct. 1736.
Gordon, Catherine, d/o Peter, chr. 17 Oct. 1736.

Ammesley, Thomas, s/o William, chr. 20 Mar. 1737.
Cole, William, chr. 20 Mar. 1737.
English, Mary, d/o David, chr. 20 Mar. 1737.
Ker, Isbela, d/o Samuel, chr. 20 Mar. 1737.
Brown, Margaret, d/o Arthur, chr. 27 Mar. 1737.
Henderson, Stevens Nicholas, s/o John, chr. 24 Apr. 1737.
Williams, George, s/o George, chr. 24 Apr. 1737.
Cole, James, s/o Wm., chr. 29 May 1737.
Cole, Margaret, d/o Wm., chr. 29 May 1737.
Hibbets, James, s/o Charles, chr. 29 May 1737.
Huggon, Joseph, s/o William, chr. 29 May 1737.
Mc Ferrin, Daniel, s/o John, chr. 29 May 1737.
Pettit, Kezia, d/o James, chr. 29 May 1737.
Wind, John, s/o John, chr. 5 June 1737.
Mc Cay, James, s/o Duncan, chr. 12 June 1737.
Laird, Sarah, d/o William, chr. 10 July 1737.
Reed, James, s/o James, chr. 14 Aug. 1737.
King, James, s/o Richard, chr. 4 Sep. 1737.
Barclay, Robert, s/o John, chr. 16 Sep. 1737.
Addudel, Isabela, d/o William, chr. 6 Oct. 1737.
Hampton, Alice, d/o William, chr. 6 Nov. 1737.
Deboogh, Benjamin, s/o Frederick, chr. 13 Nov. 1737.
Preston, Rebeca, d/o Joseph, chr. 13 Nov. 1737.
Stuart, Stephen, s/o John, 20 Nov. 1737.
Hawkinson, William, s/o Joseph, chr. 27 Nov. 1737.
Logan, William, s/o William, chr. 18 Dec. 1737.
Tomson, James, s/o John, chr. 8 Jan. 1738.
Walker, Esther, d/o George, chr. 8 Jan. 1738.
Berry, Isabella, d/o John, chr. 22 Jan. 1738.
Weaver, Johannah, d/o Peter, chr. 16 Feb. 1738.
English, Jonathan, s/o James, chr. 19 Mar. 1738.
Ker, Elizabeth, d/o William, chr. 19 Mar. 1738.
Polhemus, John, s/o Tobias, chr. 19 Mar. 1738.
Service, Esther, d/o John, chr. 19 Mar. 1738.
Sweetman, Michael, s/o Michael, chr. 25 June 1738.
Wilson, Joseph, s/o Joseph, chr. 2 July 1738.
Anderson, Elizabeth, d/o John, chr. 4 July 1738.
Lee, Patience, d/o David, chr. 2 July 1738.
Ammesley, child of William, chr. 16 July 1738.
Dey, Gilbert, s/o Isaac, chr. 13 Aug. 1738.
Lowrey, Jane, d/o John, chr. 18 Sep. 1738.
Samuel, s/o W., chr. 24 Sep. 1738.

Old Tennent Presbyterian Church

English, Jane, d/o David, chr. 24 Sep. 1738.
Hughs, Silvester, chr. 24 Sep. 1738.
Perrine, Martha, d/o Peter, chr. 5 Nov. 1738.
Van Kerk, John, s/o William, chr. 19 Nov. 1738.
Mc Ferrin, Robert, s/o Hugh, chr. 26 Nov. 1738.
Benham, Benjamin, s/o John, chr. 17 Dec. 1738.
Ker, Jacob, s/o Samuel, chr. 17 Dec. 1738.
Henderson, Michael, s/o John, chr. 22 Jan. 1739.
Graham, Mary, d/o John, chr. 4 Mar. 1739.
Mc Ferrin, Elisabeth, d/o John, chr. 4 Mar. 1739.
Robinson, Charity, d/o James, chr. 4 Mar. 1739.
Hawkinson, Anne, s/o Joseph, chr. 11 Mar. 1739.
Wilson, Isabella, s/o Joseph, chr. 25 Mar. 1739.
Mc Cay, John, s/o Duncan, chr. 1 Apr. 1739.
Gordon, Alice, d/o Peter, chr. 15 Apr. 1739.
Pittinger, John, s/o Richard, chr. 22 Apr. 1739.
Perrine, Hannah, d/o Daniel, chr. 4 May 1739.
Mount, William, s/o Humphry, chr. 14 May 1739.
Pettit, Stephen, s/o James, chr. 3 June 1739.
Brown, Andrew, s/o Arthur, chr. 15 July 1739.
Errukson, Susanna, d/o Michael, chr. 19 Aug. 1739.
English, John, s/o James, chr. Sep. 1739.
Davison, Mary, d/o John, chr. 9 Sep. 1739.
Hibbets, Mary, d/o Charles, chr. 9 Sep. 1739.
Tennent, John, s/o William, chr. 15 Sep. 1739.
Carlile, William, s/o David, chr. 9 Dec. 1739.
Gaston, Mary, d/o John, chr. 9 Dec. 1739.
Weaver, Elizabeth, d/o Peter, chr. 9 Dec. 1739.
Davison, Alic, d/o Robert, chr. 13 Jan. 1740.
Hampton, John, s/o William, chr. 13 Jan. 1740.
Service, James, d/o John, chr. 13 Jan. 1740.
Chambers, William, s/o John, chr. 15 June 1740.
Chambers, James, s/o John, chr. 15 June 1740.
Gordon, Lydia, d/o John, chr. 15 June 1740.
Anderson, James, s/o John, chr. 6 July 1740.
Ker, Hannah, d/o William, chr. 31 Aug. 1740.
Rhe, David, s/o David, chr. 22 Sep. 1740.
Laird, Jane, d/o William, chr. 19 Oct. 1740.
Sweetman, Thomas, s/o Michael, chr. 19 Oct. 1740.
Ker, Samuel, s/o Samuel, chr. 6 Dec. 1740.
Mc Ferrin, Isabella, d/o Hugh, chr. 13 Dec. 1740.
Walker, James, s/o George, chr. 26 Feb. 1741.

Early Church Records of Monmouth County

Tennent, William, s/o William, chr. 15 Mar. 1741.
English, David, s/o David, chr. 17 Mar. 1741.
Weaver, Abigal, d/o Peter, chr. 26 Apr. 1741.
Dey, Isaac, s/o Isaac, chr. 10 May 1741.
Perrine, Margaret, d/o Peter, chr. 10 May 1741.
Berry, David, s/o John, chr. 18 May 1741.
Stout, Patience, chr. 18 May 1741.
Carswell, Sarah, d/o Janet Carswell or Reed, chr. 5 July 1741.
Carswell, Sarah, d/o Janet Carswell or Reed, chr. 12 July 1741.
Robinson, Henry or Heindrick, s/o James, chr. 12 July 1741.
Henderson, John, s/o John, chr. 3 Oct. 1741.
Hibbets, Charles, s/o Charles, chr. 1 Nov. 1741.
Ker, Ursula, d/o Joseph, chr. 1742.
Gordon, Charles, s/o David, chr. 31 Jan. 1742.
Ker, Lydia, d/o William, chr. 7 Feb. 1742.
Gaston, James, s/o John, chr. 28 Mar. 1742.
Pittinger, Rachel, d/o Richard, chr. 28 Mar. 1742.
Hawkins, Rachel, d/o Richard, chr. 2 Apr. 1742.
Tennent, Gilbert, s/o William, chr. May 1742.
Davison, Robert, s/o Robert, chr. 23 May 1742.
Combs, William, s/o Jonathan, chr. 11 June 1742.
Barclay, Catherine, d/o John, chr. 13 June 1742.
Hampton, Lewis, s/o William, chr. 13 June 1742.
Lloyd, Peter, s/o Timothy, chr. 20 June 1742.
Ker, Rachel, d/o Samuel, chr. 22 June 1742.
Laird, Elizabeth, d/o William, chr. 4 July 1742.
Sweetman, Catharine, d/o Michael, chr. 15 Aug. 1742.
Gordon, Robert, s/o John, chr. 17 Sep. 1742.
Benham, Nealtie, d/o John, chr. 2 Dec. 1742.
Lovell, Rachel, chr. 4 Dec. 1742.
Tone, Andrew, s/o John, chr. 17 Feb. 1743.
Tone, Thomas, s/o John, chr. 17 Feb. 1743.
Berry, John, s/o John, chr. 27 Feb. 1743.
Chambers, Margaret, d/o John, chr. 6 Mar. 1743.
Rhe, Anna, d/o David, chr. 6 Mar. 1743.
Mc Ferrin, Susanna, d/o Hugh, chr. 20 Mar. 1743.
Parent, Robert, s/o Samuel, chr. 27 Mar. 1743.
Stuart, Margaret, d/o John, 24 Apr. 1743.
Ward, William, s/o Michael, chr. 24 Apr. 1743.
Mount, John, s/o Matthias, chr. 5 June 1743.
Norcross, William, chr. 5 June 1743.
Buckalue, John, s/o Samuel, chr. 12 June 1743.

Old Tennent Presbyterian Church

Greeg, William, s/o Hugh, chr, 10 July 1743.
Van Kerk, Lydia, d/o William, chr. 10 July 1743.
Van Kerk, Sarah, d/o William, chr. 10 July 1743.
Dey, Sarah, d/o Isaac, chr. 21 Aug. 1743.
Combs, Joseph, s/o Thomas, chr. 28 Aug. 1743.
Henderson, Thomas, s/o John, chr. 28 Aug. 1743.
Gordon, John, s/o David, chr. 11 Sep. 1743.
Ker, Sarah, d/o William, chr. 18 Sep. 1743.
Tennent, Catharine, d/o William, chr. 26 Sep. 1743.
Benham, Joseph, s/o John, chr. 1744.
Gordon, Margaret, d/o Peter Gordon and Mary Craig, chr. 8 Jan. 1744.
Robinson, Joseph, s/o James, chr. 25 Mar. 1744.
Clark, Anne, d/o George Walker, chr. 15 Apr. 1744.
Ker, John, s/o Samuel, chr. 12 Feb. 1744.
Mc Conky, William, s/o Samuel, chr. 11 May 1744.
Laird, Mary, d/o William, chr. 15 Apr. 1744.
Perrine, Elizabeth, d/o Daniel, chr. 15 Apr. 1744.
Perrine, William, s/o Peter, chr. 15 Apr. 1744.
Combs, Robert, s/o Jonathan, chr. 24 Apr. 1744.
Brown, Thomas, s/o Patrick, chr. 6 May 1744.
Hibbets, Elizabeth, d/o Charles, chr. 6 May 1744.
Hawkins, Euphunia, d/o Richard, chr. 14 May 1744.
Anderson, Kenneth, s/o John, chr. 4 July 1744.
Ker, Sarah, d/o Joseph, chr. 8 July 1744.
Gaston, Hugh, s/o John, chr. 15 July 1744.
Boise, Cornelius, s/o Adam, chr. 22 July 1744.
Cowenhoven, Sarah, d/o Wm., chr. 5 Aug. 1744.
Hampton, Elizabeth, d/o William, chr. 15 Aug. 1744.
English, Margaret, d/o David, chr. 26 Aug. 1744.
Ammesley, William, s/o William, chr. 2 Sep. 1744.
Ammesley, Rebecca, d/o William, chr. 2 Sep. 1744.
Mackelwain, Margaret, d/o Daniel, chr., 2 Sep. 1744.
Sweetman, Margaret, s/o Michael, chr. 7 Oct. 1744.
Shaw, John, s/o John, chr. 13 Dec. 1744.
Shaw, Elizabeth, d/o John, chr. 13 Dec. 1744.
Shaw, Thomas, s/o John, chr. 13 Dec. 1744.
Shaw, Joseph, s/o John, chr. 13 Dec. 1744.
Shaw, Henry, s/o John, chr. 13 Dec. 1744.
Mc Knight, Sarah, chr. 16 Dec. 1744.
Lloyd, David, s/o Timothy, chr. 10 Feb. 1745.
Greeg, Hugh, s/o Hugh, chr, 16 June 1745.
Barclay, Richard, s/o John, chr. 30 June 1745.

Berry, Sidney, s/o John, chr. 30 June 1745.
Van Kerk, Catherine, d/o William, chr. 30 June 1745.
Tennent, Margaret, d/o William, chr. 7 Aug. 1745.
Clark, Peter, s/o Peter, chr. 11 Aug. 1745.
Ker, Waltar, s/o Joseph, chr. 11 Aug. 1745.
Crawford, Reyntie, s/o Samuel, chr. 25 Aug. 1745.
Crawford, Keturah, d/o Samuel, chr. 25 Aug. 1745.
Deveny, William, s/o William, chr. 1 Sep. 1745.
Mc Conky, Jacob, s/o Samuel, chr. 13 Sep. 1745.
Stuart, Hannah, d/o John, 13 Sep. 1745.
Ker, Nathaniel, s/o William, chr. 15 Sep. 1745.
Cole, Mary, d/o Wm., chr. 3 Nov.1745.
Gordon, Peter, s/o Peter, chr. 3 Nov. 1745.
Mc Knight, Robert, s/o William, chr. 3 Nov. 1745.
Van Kerk, Elshie, d/o Arthur, chr. 12 Jan. 1746.
Van Kerk, Hannah, chr. 12 Jan. 1746.
Hanse, Janatie or Jane, d/o Hendrick, chr. 2 Mar. 1746.
Ker, Catharine, d/o Samuel, chr. 16 Mar. 1746.
Henderson, Margaret, d/o John, chr. 27 Apr. 1746.
Laird, Margaret, d/o William, chr. 27 Apr. 1746.
Gordon, Elizabeth, d/o David, chr. 1 June 1746.
Combs, John, s/o Jonathan, chr. 1 June 1746.
Clayton, Abraham, s/o Abraham, chr. 26 June 1746.
Clayton, William, s/o Abraham, chr. 26 June 1746.
Boise, Molley or Mary, d/o Adam, chr. 10 Aug. 1746.
Rhe, Margaret, d/o Robert, chr. 24 Aug. 1746.
Greeg, James, s/o Hugh, chr, 27 Sept. 1746.
Rhe, Anna, d/o George, chr. 26 Sep. 1746.
Hawkinson, John, s/o Joseph, chr. 19 Oct. 1746.
Hawkinson, Joseph, s/o Joseph, chr. 19 Oct. 1746.
Mc Knight, Jane, s/o William, chr. 1747.
Sweetman, John, s/o Michael, chr. Feb. 1747.
Sweetman, Henderson, s/o Michael, chr. Feb. 1747.
Norcross, John, s/o William, chr. 11 Jan. 1747.
Gaston, Mary, d/o John, chr. 8 Mar. 1747
Gaston, Elizabeth, d/o John, chr. 8 Mar. 1747.
Chambers, Elizabeth, chr. 26 Apr. 1747.
Chambers, Bridget, d/o John, chr. 26 Apr. 1747.
Lloyd, Anna, d/o John, chr. 26 Apr. 1747.
Anderson, Ursilla, d/o John, chr. 3 June 1747.
Berry, Ebenezar, s/o John, chr. 19 July 1747.
Mc Conky, John, s/o Samuel, chr. 19 Jul. 1747.

Old Tennent Presbyterian Church

Mc Gallird, James, s/o Andrew, chr. 19 July 1747
La Conte, Thomas, s/o Peter, chr. 26 July 1747.
Parent, Samuel, s/o Samuel, chr. 26 July 1747.
Golden, John, s/o Elias, chr. 23 Aug. 1747.
Tone, Hannah, d/o John, chr. 23 Aug. 1747.
Van Kerk, Anne, d/o William, chr. 12 Sep. 1747.
Gordon, Archibald, s/o Peter, chr. 21 Feb. 1748.
Ker, Euphunea, d/o Joseph, chr. 13 Mar. 1748.
Gordon, William, s/o David, chr. 3 Apr. 1748.
Norcross, Aaron, s/o William, chr. 8 Apr. 1748.
Cuming, Catharine, d/o Robert Cuming and Mary Noble, chr. 1 May 1748.
Moorhead, William, s/o James, chr. 8 May 1748.
Laird, Bevan, s/o William, chr. 22 May. 1748.
Rhe, David, s/o George, chr. 26 June 1748.
Lloyd, Margaret, d/o John, chr. 3 July 1748.
Anderson, John, s/o John, chr. 28 Aug. 1748.
Rhe, David, s/o Robert, chr. 18 Sep. 1748.
Walker, Esther, d/o George, chr. 25 Sep. 1748.
Forman, Esther, chr. 29 Oct. 1748.
Weycof, Oakey, s/o Gerrit, chr. 4 Dec. 1748.
Gordon, Mary, d/o Charles and Gertrude, chr. 11 Dec. 1748.
Henderson, Anne, d/o John, chr. 18 Dec. 1748.
Ker, Waltar, s/o William, chr. 18 Dec. 1748.
Berry, Samuel, s/o John, chr. 5 Mar. 1749.
Mc Gallird, Jane, d/o Robert, chr. 26 Mar. 1749.
Sweetman, Anne, d/o Michael, chr. 26 Mar. 1749.
Chambers, John, s/o John, chr. 1 Apr. 1749.
Gaston, Daniel, s/o John, chr. 3 Apr. 1749.
Mc Conky, Anna, d/o Samuel, chr. 23 Apr. 1749.
Boise, Anne, d/o Adam, chr. 30 Apr. 1749.
Clark, Mary, d/o Benjamin, chr. 18 June 1749.
Tone, child of John, chr. 18 June 1749.
Mc Knight, Amie, d/o William, chr. July 1749.
Hampton, Samuel, s/o William Hampton and Gertrude Craig, chr. 2 July 1749.
Ker, Ursulla, d/o Joseph, chr. 6 Aug. 1749.
Eaton, Thomas, s/o John, chr. 20 Aug. 1749.
Anderson, Lewis, s/o John, chr. 27 Sep. 1749.
Norcross, Elisabeth, d/o William, chr. 31 Dec. 1749.
Mc Afie, Agnos, d/o Robert, chr. 18 Feb. 1750.
Gordon, Mary, d/o Peter, chr. 4 Mar. 1750.

Early Church Records of Monmouth County

Van Kerk, Joseph, s/o William, chr. 4 Mar. 1750.
Mills, William, s/o Richd., chr. 25 Mar. 1750.
Compton, Joseph, s/o Richard, chr. 6 May 1750.
Eagger, William, s/o George, chr. 6 May 1750.
Newman, Thomas, chr. 13 May 1750.
Cuming, Anna or Agnos, d/o Robert, chr. 27 May 1750.
Gordon, David, s/o David, chr. 27 May 1750.
Preston, Hannah, d/o William, chr. 27 May 1750.
Gordon, Ambrose, s/o Jonathan, chr. 1 July 1750.
Van Scaiack, John, s/o John, chr. 1 July 1750.
Eaton, Johannah, d/o John, chr. 5 Aug. 1750.
Eaton, Elizabeth, d/o John, chr. 5 Aug. 1750.
O Gallouchor, James, s/o Bryan, chr. 16 Sep. 1750.
Walker, Ursulla, d/o George, chr. 7 Oct. 1750.
Rhe, Mary, d/o George, chr. 28 Oct. 1750.
Craig, Catherine, d/o John, chr. 18 Nov. 1750.
Hampton, Gertrude, d/o William, chr. 1751.
Ker, Anna, d/o Joseph, chr. 1 Jan. 1751.
Van Hook, Lloyd, s/o Lawrence, chr. 12 Feb. 1751.
Mc Conky, Mary, d/o Samuel, chr.   Mar. 1751.
Rhe, Margaret, d/o Robert, chr. 17 Mar. 1751.
Ker, Stephen, s/o Samuel, chr. 28 Apr. 1751.
Mc Knight, John, s/o William, chr. 28 Apr. 1751.
Barklay, William, s/o David Barklay and Elizabeth Walker or Barklay, chr. 19 May 1751.
Cowenhoven, Mary, d/o Peter Cowenhoven, and Anne Davies, chr. 19 May 1751.
Henderson, Jane, s/o John, chr. 19 May 1751.
Van Matren, Ida, d/o Ryke, chr. 9 June 1751.
La Conte, Peter, s/o Peter, chr. 2 July 1751.
Chambers, James, s/o John, chr. 2 June 1751.
Gaston, Catherine, d/o John, chr. 2 June 1751.
Harvey, Thomas, s/o Samuel, chr. 24 June 1751.
Johnston, Peter, s/o Mihael, chr. 12 Aug. 1751.
Anderson, Margaret, d/o John, chr. 13 Oct 1751.
Laird, William, d/o William, chr. 22 Oct. 1751.
Craig, John, s/o Thomas, chr. 27 Oct. 1751.
Rhoades, Hester or Esther, d/o Charles, chr. 27 Oct. 1751.
Norcross, Abraham, s/o William, chr. 22 Dec. 1751.
Gordon, Sarah, d/o Peter, chr. 5 Jan. 1752.
Cuming, John, s/o Robert, chr. 5 Feb. 1752.
Craven, Peter, s/o Thomas, chr. 9 Feb. 1752.

Old Tennent Presbyterian Church

Craig, Samuel, s/o John, chr. 19 Feb. 1752.
Sweetman, Mary, d/o Michael, chr. 25 Mar. 1752.
Sweetman, John, s/o Michael, chr. 25 Mar. 1752.
Eagger, Daniel, s/o George, chr. 26 Apr. 1752.
Gordon, Priscilla, d/o Jonathan, chr. 26 Apr. 1752.
Robinson, Elizabeth, chr. 10 May 1752.
Rogers, Rebeca, d/o William, chr. 10 May 1752.
Drommond, Ruth, d/o John, chr. 25 May 1752.
Gordon, Hannah, s/o David, chr. 28 June 1752.
Davison, David, s/o Robert, chr. 15 Oct. 1752.
Cowenhoven, Lewis, s/o Peter, chr. 16 Oct. 1752.
Rhe, Margaret, d/o George, chr. 16 Oct. 1752.
Mills, David, s/o Richd., chr. 22 Oct. 1752.
Errickson, John, s/o Michael, chr. 3 Dec. 1752.
Van Scaiack, David, s/o John, chr. 17 Dec. 1752.
Van Voorhees, Hendrick, s/o John, chr. 1753.
Compton, Lucia, d/o William, chr. 25 Feb. 1753.
Johnston, Mary, s/o Mihael, chr. 18 Feb. 1753.
Cowenhoven, David, s/o John, chr. 4 Mar. 1753.
Mc Afie, Elizabeth, d/o Robert, chr. 18 Mar. 1753.
Barklay, George, s/o David, chr. Apr. 1753.
Clark, Elizabeth, d/o Benjamin, chr. 15 Apr. 1753.
Van Matren, Janatie or Jane, d/o Ryke, chr. 15 Apr. 1753.
Walker, Parthenia, d/o George, chr. 20 May 1753.
Forman, Catharine, d/o Samuel, chr. June 1753.
Mc Conky, Samuel, s/o Samuel, chr. 10 June 1753.
Chambers, William, s/o John, chr. 24 June 1753.
Mc Knight, Lewis, s/o William, chr. 24 June 1753.
Van Hook, Aaron, s/o Lawrence, chr. 12 Aug. 1753.
Johnson, James, s/o Hendrick, chr. 19 Aug. 1753.
Rhe, Anna, d/o Robert, chr. 9 Sep. 1753.
Wilson, Peter, chr. 30 Sep. 1753.
Wilson, Sarah, d/o Joseph, chr. 30 Sep. 1753.
Bennit, Abraham, s/o Ezekiel, chr. 18 Nov. 1753.
Kinman, Ealeanor, d/o Joseph, chr. 18 Nov. 1753.
Gaston, John, s/o John, chr. 20 Jan. 1754.
Craig, Archibald, s/o John, chr. 21 Apr. 1754.
Laird, Susanna, d/o William, chr. 21 Apr. 1754.
Applegate, Zebulon, s/o Zebulon, chr. 2 June 1754.
Van Kerk, Esther, d/o William, chr. 3 June 1754.
Boise, Matthias, s/o Adam, chr. 9 June 1754.
Boise, Elizabeth, d/o Adam, chr. 9 June 1754.

Clark, Alexander, s/o Benjamin, chr. 9 June 1754.
Gordon, Lewis, s/o Peter, chr. 7 July 1754.
Cuming, Margaret, d/o Robert, chr. 28 July 1754.
Van Kerk, John, s/o Matthias, chr. 28 July 1754.
Gordon, Ezekiel, s/o Jonathan, chr. 4 Aug. 1754.
Nichols, Elizabeth, d/o Joshua, chr. 4 Aug. 1754.
Zutphen, Joseph, s/o Derick, chr. 4 Aug. 1754
Newman, George, s/o Thomas Newman and Mary Wilkie, chr. 18 Aug. 1754.
Pittinger, Samuel, s/o Richard, chr. 18 Aug. 1754.
Norcross, Rebeca, d/o William, chr. 15 Sep. 1754.
Gordon, Alice, s/o David, chr. 21 Sep. 1754.
Ker, Ebenezar, s/o Joseph, chr. 25 Nov. 1754.
Wilson, Deborah, d/o Joseph, chr. 1755.
Craige, David, s/o Thomas, chr. 19 Jan. 1755.
Mc Knight, Mary, d/o William, chr. 26 Jan. 1755.
Johnston, John, s/o Mihael, chr. 2 Mar. 1755.
O Gallouchor, Ebenezar, s/o Bryan, chr. 2 Mar. 1755.
Van Scaiack, Janet, d/o John, chr. 22 Mar. 1755.
Hampton, Catharine, d/o William, chr. 13 Apr. 1755.
Compton, John, s/o William, chr. 11 May 1755.
Rhe, David, s/o Jonathan, chr. 11 May 1755.
Van Hook, Elizabeth, s/o Lawrence, chr. 18 May 1755.
Rhe, Elizabeth, d/o George, chr. 4 June 1755.
Nichols, Anne, d/o Joshua, chr. 22 June 1755.
Boise, Martha, d/o Adam, chr. 10 Aug. 1755.
Hill, Elizabeth, d/o James, chr. 24 Aug. 1755.
Van Matren, John, s/o Ryke, chr. 24 Aug. 1755.
Cowenhoven, Sarah, d/o David, chr. 26 Oct. 1755.
Craig, David, s/o William, chr. 6 Dec. 1755.
Forman, Aaron, s/o George, chr. 6 Dec. 1755.
Forman, Jonathan, s/o George, chr. 6 Dec. 1755.
Rhe, Mary, d/o Robert, chr. 6 Dec. 1755.
Van Voorhees, Aeltie, d/o John, chr. 7 Dec. 1755.
Riddel, Agnos, d/o George, chr. 21 Dec. 1755.
Laird, William, s/o Alexander, chr. 1756.
Laird, Lydia, chr. 1756.
Barclay, Catherine, d/o David, chr. 18 Jan. 1756.
Cowenhoven, Thomas, s/o Peter, chr. Feb. 1756.
Job, Catharine, d/o Geo., chr. 8 Feb. 1756.
Reed, Aaron, s/o James, chr. 21 Mar. 1756.
Mc Afie, Ealeanor, d/o Robert, chr. 22 Mar. 1756.

Old Tennent Presbyterian Church

Clark, Andrew, s/o Benjamin, chr. 18 Apr. 1756.
O Bryan, Margaret, d/o George, chr. 3 May 1756.
Chambers, Mary, d/o John, chr. 3 May 1756.
Applegate, Nathaniel, s/o Zebulon, chr. 23 May 1756.
Craig, Peter, s/o John, chr. 23 May 1756.
Bennit, Margaret, d/o Ezekiel, chr. June 1756.
Walker, George, s/o George, chr. 6 June 1756.
Weycof, Anne, d/o Jacob, chr. 27 June 1756.
Yateman, Margaret, d/o John Yateman and Margaret Gordon, chr. 27 June 1756.
Yateman, Lucia, d/o John Yateman and Margaret Gordon, chr. 27 June 1756.
Yateman, Elizabeth, d/o John Yateman and Margaret Gordon, chr. 27 June 1756.
Yateman, Peter, d/o John Yateman and Margaret Gordon, chr. 27 June 1756.
Yateman, Mary, s/o John Yateman and Margaret Gordon, chr. 27 June 1756.
Yateman, John, d/o John Yateman and Margaret Gordon, chr. 27 June 1756.
Zutphen, John, s/o Derick, chr. 4 July 1756.
Gaston, William, s/o John, chr. 18 July 1756.
Ker, Lydia, d/o Joseph, chr. 19 Sep. 1756.
Compton, Elizabeth, d/o William, chr. Oct. 1756.
Stevens, Jane, d/o Richard, chr. 5 Oct. 1756.
Van Scaiack, child of John, chr. 30 Jan. 1757.
Cowenhoven, Ealenor, d/o Joseph, chr. 13 Mar. 1757.
Davies, Catharine, d/o John, chr. 16 Apr. 1757.
Gordon, Jane, d/o Jonathan, chr. 17 Apr. 1757.
Rhe, Aaron, s/o Jonathan, chr. 5 May 1757.
Mc Knight, James, s/o William, chr. 8 May 1757.
Yateman, Manoah, s/o John, chr. 8 May 1757.
Rosabach, Aeltije, d/o Peter, chr. 27 May 1757.
Goodenough, Mary, d/o Samuel, chr. 5 June 1757.
O Gallouchor, John, s/o Bryan, chr. 5 June 1757.
Johnston, Mary d/o Mihael, chr. 22 June 1757.
Johnson, Mary, s/o Hendrick, chr. 12 June 1757.
Weycof, Catharine, d/o Jacob, chr. 21 Aug. 1757.
Brannan, Jane, d/o Andrew, chr. 2 Oct. 1757.
Clayton, Joseph, s/o John, chr. 6 Nov. 1757.
Clayton, Hannah, chr. 6 Nov. 1757.
Clayton, John, s/o Joseph and Hannah, chr. 6 Nov. 1757.

Hendrickson, John, s/o William, chr. 19 Nov. 1757.
Stevens, Anne, d/o Richard, chr. 25 Dec. 1757.
Laird, Robert, s/o Alexander, chr. 1758.
Pittinger, Jacob, d/o Richard, chr. 1 Jan. 1758.
Cowenhoven, John, s/o David, chr. 26 Mar. 1758.
Reed, John, s/o Andrew, chr. 26 Mar. 1758.
Combs, Solomon, s/o Thomas, chr. 9 Apr. 1758.
Rhe, Jonathan, s/o Robert, chr. 9 Apr. 1758.
Ker, Ezekiel, s/o Joseph, chr. 30 Apr. 1758.
Goodenough, Sarah, d/o Samuel, chr. 7 May 1758.
Craige, Samuel, s/o William, chr. 17 May 1758.
Mc Chesney, Robert, s/o John, chr. 14 May 1758.
Cowenhoven, Williamtije, d/o _, chr. 22 May 1758.
Boise, child of Adam, chr. 28 May 1758.
Forman, Jonathan, s/o David, chr. 4 June 1758.
Huggon, Elizabeth, d/o William, chr. 24 June 1758.
Van Schcaik, Josiah, s/o David, chr. 24 June 1758.
Van Matren, Mary, d/o Ryke, chr. 25 June 1758.
Van Matren, Catherine, d/o Ryke, chr. 25 June 1758.
English, Margaret, d/o David, chr. July 1758.
Clark, John, s/o Daniel, chr. Aug. 1758.
Riddel, Margaret, d/o George, chr. 20 Aug. 1758.
Erwing, Cornelius, s/o Cornelius, chr. 10 Sep. 1758.
Erwing, James, s/o Cornelius, chr. 10 Sep. 1758.
Erwing, _, s/o Cornelius, chr. 10 Sep. 1758.
Erwing, Phebe, d/o Cornelius, chr. 10 Sep. 1758.
Barklay, Esther, d/o David, chr. 19 Nov. 1758.
Bennit, Leah, d/o Ezekiel, chr. 25 Nov. 1758.
Mc Knight, Thomas, s/o William, chr. 10 Dec. 1758.
Scudder, Joseph, s/o Nathaniel Scudder and Isabella Anderson, chr. 1759.
Gaston, Jane, d/o John, chr. 25 Mar. 1759.
Gordon, Peter, s/o David, chr. 15 Apr. 1759.
O Gallouchor, Agnes, d/o Bryan, chr. 15 Apr. 1759.
Forman, Aaron, s/o George, chr. 6 May 1759.
Cowenhoven, Elizabeth, d/o Albert, chr. 13 May 1759.
Benham, Catherine, d/o Peter, chr. 31 May 1759.
Benham, Robert, s/o Peter, chr. 31 May 1759.
Benham, John, s/o Peter, chr. 31 May 1759.
Benham, Amey, d/o Peter, chr. 31 May 1759.
Benham, Peter, s/o Peter, chr. 31 May 1759.
Benham, Richard, s/o Peter, chr. 31 May 1759.

Old Tennent Presbyterian Church

Longstreet, Lydia, d/o Aaron, chr. 10 June 1759.
Brooks, Jonathan, s/o David, chr. 15 July 1759.
Clark, Elizabeth, d/o Peter, chr. 22 July 1759.
Rhe, Esther, d/o Jonathan, chr. 27 July 1759.
Denham, John, s/o James, chr. 5 Aug. 1759.
Huggon, Sarah, d/o William, chr. Sep. 1759.
Forman, Helena, d/o Peter, chr. 9 Sep. 1759.
Johnston, William Watson s/o Mihael, chr. 30 Sep. 1759.
Johnson, Mindert, s/o Hendrick, chr. 7 Oct. 1759.
Pittinger, Euphemia, d/o Richard, chr. 28 Oct. 1759.
Reed, Samuel, s/o Andrew, chr. 13 Mar. 1760.
Ker, Rachel, d/o Joseph, chr. 23 Mar. 1760.
Mc Chesney, James, s/o John, chr. 30 Mar. 1760.
Stevens, Nicholas, s/o Richard, chr. 30 Mar. 1760.
Craige, Mary, d/o William, chr. 25 Apr. 1760.
Zutphen, David, s/o Derick, chr. 25 Apr. 1760.
Compton, Joseph, s/o William, chr. 4 May 1760.
Van Kerk, Samuel, s/o Wm., chr. 4 May 1760.
Van Kerk, Elizabeth, d/o Wm.thias, chr. 4 May 1760.
Cahale, Ann, d/o William, chr.18 May 1760.
Gordon, Catharine, d/o Jonathan, chr. 1 June 1760.
Van Schcaik, Benjamin, s/o David, chr. 1 June 1760.
Heriot, Margaret, d/o Samuel, chr. 15 June 1760.
Laird, Richard, s/o Alexander, chr. 22 June 1760.
Van Matren, William, s/o Ryke, chr. 22 June 1760.
Cowenhoven, Gertrude, d/o Garrett, chr. 17 Aug. 1760.
Cowenhoven, Anne, d/o David, chr. 17 Aug. 1760.
Rhe, James, s/o Robert, chr. 28 Sep. 1760.
Pittinger, Richard, s/o John, chr. 5 Oct. 1760.
Mc Knight, Joseph, s/o William, chr. 10 Oct. 1760.
O Harra, Sarah, d/o John, chr. 12 Oct. 1760.
English, David, s/o David, chr. 24 Oct. 1760.
Walker, Lucretia, d/o George, chr. 26 Apr. 1761.
Johnston, Jane, d/o Michael, chr. 5 July 1761.
Riddel, John, s/o George, chr. 5 July 1761.
Brooks, Agnos, d/o David, chr. 6 Sept. 1761.
Gaston, William, s/o John, chr. 6 Sep. 1761.
Barklay, Lewis, s/o Robert, chr. 18 Oct. 1761.
Combs, Rachel, d/o Thomas, chr. 18 Oct. 1761.
Barklay, Rachel, d/o David, chr. 22 Nov. 1761.
Gordon, Lewis, s/o David, chr. 22 Nov. 1761.
Hendrickson, Elizabeth, d/o Coneraed, chr. 22 Nov. 1761.

Early Church Records of Monmouth County

Van Kerk, William Cox, s/o Thomas, chr. 22 Nov. 1761.
Yateman, Isabella, d/o John, chr. 22 Nov. 1761.
Henderson, Elizabeth, d/o John, b. 23 Dec. 1761 and chr. 4 Feb. 1762.
Gorden or Gorden, child of Charles, chr. 1762.
O Gallouchor, child of Bryan, chr. 24 Jan. 1762.
Forman, Lydia, d/o Peter, chr. 31 Jan. 1762.
Cowenhoven, Child of Albert, chr. 14 Feb. 1762.
Whitlock, William, s/o William, chr. 14 Feb. 1762.
Scudder, Joseph, s/o Nathaniel, chr. Mar. 1762.
Craig, Anne, d/o John, chr. 4 Apr. 1762.
Hawkinson, Margaret, d/o Thomas, chr. 4 Apr. 1762.
Rhe, John, s/o Jonathan, chr. 4 Apr. 1762.
Bennit, Cornelius, s/o Ezekiel, chr. 6 May 1762.
Reed, James, s/o Andrew, chr. 6 May 1762.
Van Schcaik, Robert, s/o David, chr. 16 May 1762.
Craige, John, s/o William, chr. 6 June 1762.
Van Kerk, William, s/o Wm., chr. 5 July 1762.
Laird, Amie, d/o Alexander, chr. 26 Sep. 1762.
Riddel, Elizabeth, d/o George, chr. 28 Nov. 1762.
Henderson, Anne, d/o John, b. 21 Jan. 1763 and chr. 27 Mar. 1763.
Van Matren, Nelly, d/o Ryke, chr. 13 Feb. 1763.
Rhe, David, s/o Robert, chr. 10 Mar. 1763.
Montier, Mary, chr. 27 Mar. 1763.
Cole, David, s/o William, chr. 1 May 1763.
Mattison, Sarah, chr. 1 May 1763.
Robinson, James, s/o David English, chr. 1 May. 1763.
Van Kerk, Mary, d/o Thomas., chr. 19 June 1763.
Cowenhoven, Eleanor, d/o Isaac, chr. 10 July 1763.
Cowenhoven, Sarah, d/o Isaac, chr. 10 July, 1763.
Johnston, Margaret, d/o Mihael, chr. 10 July 1763.
Gaston, Joseph, sd/o John, chr. 17 July 1763.
Rue, Matthew, s/o William, chr. 30 July 1763.
Stevens, Margaret, d/o Richard, chr. 30 July 1763.
Williamson, Amie, d/o Wm., chr. 18 Sep. 1763.
Whitlock, Lockhart, s/o William, chr. 29 Oct. 1763.
Scudder, Hannah, d/o Nathaniel, chr. Oct. 1763.
Johnston, Samuel, d/o Hendrick, chr. 15 Jan. 1764.
Gordon, Elizabeth, d/o Jonathan, chr. 22 Jan. 1764.
Brooks, David, s/o David, chr. 8 Apr. 1764.
Mc Chesney, John, s/o John, chr. 8 Apr. 1764.
Voorhees, Peter, s/o Hendrick, chr. 8 Apr. 1764.
Walker, Lydia, d/o George, chr. 8 Apr. 1764.

Old Tennent Presbyterian Church

Clayton, Thomas   s/o William, chr. 15 Apr. 1764.
Craig, William, s/o John, chr. 15 Apr. 1764.
Clayton, John, s/o Jonathan, chr. 6 May 1764.
Craige, Anne, d/o William, chr. 6 May 1764.
Ker, Sarah, d/o Walter, chr. 13 May 1764.
English, Margaret, d/o Jonathan, chr. 3 June 1764.
Van Schcaik, David, s/o David, chr. 3 June 1764.
Elliot, Alexander, s/o George, chr. 10 June 1764.
Combs, Esther, d/o Thomas, chr. 14 June 1764.
Cowenhoven, Eleanor, d/o Albert, chr. 14 June 1764.
Van Kerk, John, s/o Wm., chr. 22 July 1764.
O Gallouchor, James, s/o Bryan, chr. 5 Aug. 1764.
Forman, Samuel, s/o David, chr. 19 Sep. 1764.
Hults, Jane, d/o William, chr. 19 Sep. 1764.
Gordon, Hannah, s/o Charles, chr. 7 Oct. 1764.
Wilson, Hannah, d/o James, chr. 2 Dec. 1764.
Wilson, William, s/o James, chr. 2 Dec. 1764.
Wilson, Jane, d/o James, chr. 2 Dec. 1764.
Henderson, William, s/o John, b. 31 Mar. 1765 and chr. 2 June 1765.
Campbell, William, s/o John Campbell and Henritia Cowenhoven, chr. 14 Apr. 1765.
Errickson, Janet, d/o Thomas, chr. 14 Apr. 1765.
Gaston, John, s/o John, chr. 14 Apr. 1765.
Laird, Elizabeth, d/o Alexander, chr. 14 Apr. 1765.
Robinson, Charity, d/o Henry, chr. 15 Apr. 1765.
Van Scaiack, Peter, s/o John, chr. 2 June 1765.
Johnston, Michael, s/o Mihael, chr. 7 July 1765.
Brown, John, s/o Thomas, chr. 28 July 1765.
Riddel, David, s/o George, chr. Aug. 1765.
Cube, Mimbo, d/o _, chr. 18 Aug. 1765.
English, Robert, s/o Robert, chr. 22 Sep. 1765.
Weycof, Sarah, d/o Jacob, chr. 22 Sep. 1765.
Scudder, Kenneth Anderson, s/o Nathaniel, chr. 3 Nov. 1765.
Rue, Samuel, s/o William, chr. 24 Nov. 1765.
Rhe, Robert, s/o Robert, chr. 15 Dec. 1765.
Hughs, Margaret, d/o William, chr. 1766.
Hughs, Catherine, d/o William, chr. 26 Jan.1766.
Henderson, John, s/o Michael, chr. 17 Feb. 1766.
Cowenhoven, Elizabeth, d/o Isaac, chr. 23 Feb. 1766.
Cowenhoven, Garrett, s/o David, chr. 23 Feb. 1766.
Craig, Mary, d/o John, chr. 15 Mar. 1766.
Gordon, Lewis, s/o Jonathan, chr. 6 Apr. 1766.

Hults, Margaret, d/o William, chr. 13 Apr. 1766.
O Docherty, Hannah, d/o Bryan, chr. 13 Apr. 1766.
V Voorhees, Sarah, d/o Hendrick, chr. 13 Apr. 1766.
Anderson, Sarah, d/o Joshua, chr. 11 May 1766.
Mc Chesney, Eleanor, d/o John, chr. 11 May 1766.
O Gallouchor, Catharine, d/o Bryan, chr. 11 May 1766.
Stevens, Elizabeth, d/o Richard, chr. 11 May 1766.
Craige, Ursila, d/o William, chr. 18 May 1766.
Cole, Zilpah, d/o William, chr. 29 June 1766.
Craig, Mary, d/o John, chr. 29 June 1766.
English, Elizabeth, d/o Jonathan, chr. 29 June 1766.
Riddel, Mary, d/o George, chr. 13 July 1766.
Sweetman, John, s/o Thomas, chr. 24 Aug. 1766.
Bennit, John, s/o Ezekiel, chr. 24 Sep. 1766.
Newton, James, s/o Joseph and Eleanor, chr. 2 Nov. 1766.
Newton, Thomas, s/o Joseph and Eleanor, chr. 2 Nov. 1766.
Reynolds, Ealeanor, d/o William, chr. 2 Nov. 1766.
Walker, Elizabeth, d/o George, chr. 2 Nov. 1766.
Brooks, David, chr. 4 Jan. 1767.
William, s/o Hugh MackGill, chr. 28 June 1767.
Perine, Lydia, d/o Henry, chr. 5 Apr. 1736.
Campbell, Elizabeth, d/o John Campbell and Henritia Cowenhoven, chr. 12 Apr. 1767.
Gaston, Samuel, s/o John, chr. 12 Apr. 1767.
Gaston, James, s/o John, chr. 12 Apr. 1767.
Anderson, Sarah, d/o William, chr. 19 Apr. 1767.
Henderson, Jane, d/o John, b. 2 May 1767 and chr. 1 June 1767.
Laird, David, s/o Moses, chr. 10 May 1767.
Mount, Ezekiel, s/o Francis, chr. 7 June 1767.
Rue, William, s/o William, chr. 7 June 1767.
Van Scaiack, William, s/o John, chr. 7 June 1767.
Longstreet, Elias, s/o Peter, chr. 14 June 1767.
Brown, David, s/o Thomas, chr. 28 June 1767.
Anderson, James, s/o Michael, chr. 19 July 1767.
Truax, Sceytie, d/o Abraham, chr. 19 July 1767.
Cowenhoven, Thomas, s/o Isaac, chr. 13 Sep. 1767.
Van Arsdalen, Mary, d/o Jacob, chr. 20 Sep. 1767.
Voorhee, Jane, d/o William, chr. 11 Oct. 1767.
Robinson, Unice, chr. 18 Oct. 1767.
Robinson, Mary, d/o Joseph, chr. 18 Oct. 1767.
Rhe, Anne, d/o Jonathan, chr. 25 Oct. 1767.
Weaver, Peter, s/o Peter, chr. 25 Oct. 1767.

Old Tennent Presbyterian Church

Henderson, David, s/o Samuel, chr. 1 Nov. 1767.
Johnston, Thomas, s/o Mihael, chr. 22 Jan. 1768.
Thompson, John, s/o Moses, chr. 21 Feb. 1768.
Craig, James, s/o John, chr. 27 Mar. 1768.
Van Schcaik, David, s/o Isabella, chr. 8 May 1768.
Errickson, James, s/o Thomas, chr. 15 May 1768.
Cowenhoven, Phebe, d/o Peter, chr. 26 June 1768.
Cowenhoven, Elizabeth, d/o Peter, chr. 26 June 1768.
Rhe, Margaret, d/o Robert, chr. 26 June 1768.
English, James, s/o James, chr. 10 July 1768.
Walker, Elizabeth Rowena, d/o George, chr. 26 June 1768.
Mc Chesney, William, s/o John, chr. 10 July. 1768.
Scudder, Lydia, d/o Nathaniel, chr. 10 July 1768.
Clayton, Amie, d/o Jonathan, chr. 31 July 1768.
Cole, Benjamin, s/o Jacob, chr. 7 Aug.1768.
Cole, Rebekah, chr. 7 Aug. 1768.
Laird, Jane, d/o William, chr. 21 Aug. 1768.
Newton, Kenneth Anderson, s/o Joseph and Eleanor, chr. 23 Oct. 1768.
Craig, Margaret, d/o William, chr. 30 Oct. 1768.
Laird, William, s/o Moses, chr. 18 Jan. 1769.
Sweetman, Margaret, d/o Thomas, chr. 15 Apr. 1769.
English, David, s/o Jonathan, chr. 14 May 1769.
Hults, William, s/o William, chr. 14 May 1769.
Forman, Danuel, s/o David, chr. 11 June 1769.
Cowenhoven, Elizabeth, d/o David, chr. 25 June 1769.
Jewel, Jane, d/o John, chr. 9 July 1769.
Robinson, James, s/o Joseph, chr. 9 July 1769.
Anderson, William, s/o William, chr. 11 July 1769.
Mount, Anne, d/o Francis, chr. 16 July 1769.
Perine, Joseph, s/o Henry, chr. 23 July 1769.
Brown, William, s/o Thomas, chr. 13 Aug. 1769.
Craig, Charity, d/o John, chr. 20 Aug. 1769.
Napier, John, s/o Thomas, chr. 31 Oct. 1769.
O Gallouchor, Samuel, s/o Bryan, chr. 5 Nov. 1769.
Henderson, William, s/o Samuel, chr. 1770.
Henderson, Thomas, s/o John, b. 9 Feb. 1770 and chr. 15 Apr. 1770.
Longstreet, Anne, s/o Peter, chr. 29 Apr. 1770.
Bryson, Nancy, d/o James, chr. 3 June 1770.
Herbert, child of James, chr. 10 June 1770.
Sweetman, Michael, s/o Thomas, chr. 8 July 1770.
Mc Chesney, Samuel, s/o John, chr. 5 Aug. 1770.
Laird, Sarah, d/o William, chr. 28 Oct. 1770.

Van Voorhes, Cathrine, d/o Wm., chr. 24 Mar. 1771.
Laird, Lydia, d/o Alexander, chr. 7 Apr. 1771.
Errickson, Timothy, s/o Thomas, chr. 21 Apr. 1771.
Truax, Lyda, s/o Abraham, chr. 23 June 1771.
Covenhoven, Cathrine, d/o John, chr. 14 July 1771.
Hults, Peter, d/o William, chr. 28 July 1771.
Perine, Mary, d/o Henry, chr. 11 Aug. 1771.
Van Schcaik, Hannah, d/o David, chr. 4 Aug. 1771.
Combs, John, s/o John, chr. 25 Aug. 1771.
Anderson, Lewis, s/o John, chr. 1 Sep. 1771.
Sweetman, Michale, s/o Michale, chr. 1 Sep. 1771.
Brown, Catherine, d/o Thomas, chr. 1 Dec. 1771.
Covenhoven, Jane, d/o Wm., chr. 23 Feb. 1772.
Henderson, Mary, d/o John, b. 8 Mar. 1772 and chr. 26 Apr. 1772.
Craig, John, s/o John, chr. 26 Apr. 1772.
Johnston, Joseph, s/o Mihael, chr. 9 May 1772.
Anderson, Elleonar, d/o Joshua, chr. 7 June 1772.
Hawkinson, Keineth, s/o Keineth, chr. 7 June 1772.
Parent, Michale, s/o Samuel, chr. 1 Nov. 1772.
Laird, Elizabeth, d/o Moses and Catharine, chr. 17 Apr. 1773.
Laird, Catharine, chr. 17 Apr. 1773.
Mc Chesney, Joseph, s/o John, chr. 18 Apr. 1773.
Smith, Euphama, d/o David, chr. 30 May 1773.
Sweetman, Eleoner, d/o Michale, chr. 30 May 1773.
Cole, John, s/o Jacob, chr. 1 June 1773.
Covenhoven, Abigale, d/o John, chr. 13 June 1773.
Vancleif, Benjamin, s/o John, chr. 27 June 1773.
Combs, David, s/o Joseph, chr. 27 June 1773.
Craig, John, s.o Sammuel, chr. 27 June 1773.
Van Voorhes, Elloner, d/o Wm., chr. 27 June 1773.
Errickson, Sammuel, s/o Thomas, chr. 22 Aug. 1773.
Combs, Jonathan, s/o John, chr. 17 Oct. 1773.
Perine, Henry, s/o Henry, chr. 14 Nov. 1773.
Rue, Mary, d/o William, chr. 6 Dec. 1773.
Brown, Mary, d/o Thomas, chr. 13 Mar. 1774.
Henderson, John, s/o John, b. 18 Apr. 1774 and chr. 12 June 1774.
Covenhoven, Elshie, d/o Wm., chr. 24 Apr. 1774.
Hults, Jane, d/o William, chr. 8 May 1774.
Mc Knight, John, s/o Robart, chr. 8 May 1774.
Sweetman, Joseph, s/o Thomas, chr. 8 May 1774.
Davis, Jannet, d/o Aaron, chr. 5 June 1774.
Mount, Elizabeth, d/o Francis, chr. 5 June 1774.

Craig, Daniel, s/o John, chr. 12 June 1774.
Hawkinson, Lyidia, d/o Kieneth, chr. 19 June 1774.
Anderson, Elizabeth, d/o John, chr. 26 June 1774.
Covenhoven, William, s/o John, chr. 7 Aug. 1774.
Laird, Catharine, s/o Moses, chr. 31 Oct. 1774.
Smith, Moses, s/o Andrew, chr. 31 Oct. 1774.
Lane, Cathrine, d/o Danniel, chr. 27 Jan. 1775.
Lane, Lydia, chr. 27 Jan. 1775.
Loyd, Elias, s/o David, chr. 27 Jan. 1775.
Smith, Elizabeth, d/o Peter, chr. 27 Jan. 1775.
Smith, Peter, chr. 27 Jan. 1775.
Combs, Elizabeth, d/o Joseph, chr. 5 Feb. 1775.
Robinson, Elenor, d/o Abraham, chr. 19 Feb. 1775.
Craig, Lewis, s/o John, chr. 26 Feb. 1775.
Covenhoven, Cathrine, d/o Wm., chr. 7 Apr. 1775.
Sweetman, Michael, s/o Henderson, chr. 2 Apr. 1775.
Perine, William, s/o Henry, chr. 26 Mar. 1775.
Morris, Garret, s/o Ammariah, chr. 11 May 1775.
Morris, Wilson, s/o Robert, chr. 11 May 1775.
Calvert, William, s/o John, chr. 14 May 1775.
Jammison, William, s/o John, chr. 14 May 1775.
West, Thomas, chr. 14 May 1775.
West, Benjamin, s/o Thomas, chr. 14 May 1775.
Laird, Thomas, s/o William, chr. 28 May 1775.
Van Voorhes, Mary, d/o Wm., chr. 28 May 1775.
Davison, James, s/o John, chr. 9 July 1775.
Davison, Elizabeth, chr. 9 July 1775.
Lott, Mary, d/o Daniel, chr. 9 July 1775.
Laird, Susanna, d/o John, chr. 3 Sep. 1775.
Anderson, Anna, d/o John, chr. 26 Nov. 1775.
Covert, Peter, s/o Daniel, chr. 4 Feb. 1776.
Herbert, Cathrine, d/o Richard, chr. 4 Apr. 1776.
Nott, Cathrine, d/o David, chr. 4 Apr. 1776.
Gaston, John, s/o John, chr. 14 Apr. 1776.
Johnston, James Montgomery, s/o William, chr. 14 Apr. 1796.
Anderson, Cathrine, d/o Joshua, chr. 16 June 1776.
Clayton, Elizabeth, d/o Asher, chr. 23 June 1776.
Henderson, Charles Lee, s/o John, b. 27 July 1776 and chr. 7 Oct. 1776.
Lane, David, s/o Danniel, chr. 13 Oct. 1776.
Davis, Aaron, s/o Aaron, chr. 30 Mar. 1777.
Sweetman, Mary, d/o Michale, chr. 30 Mar. 1777.
Combs, Thomas, s/o Joseph, chr. 18 May 1777.

Smith, Mary, s/o Andrew, chr. 18 May 1777.
Errickson, Susanna, d/o Thomas, chr. 1 June 1777.
Sweetman, Forman, s/o Henderson, chr. 1 June 1777.
Freeman, Mary Howel, d/o John, chr. 29 June 1777.
Perine, Matthew Rue, s/o Henry, chr. 29 June 1777.
Loyd, Peter, s/o David, chr. 14 Sep. 1777.
Van Voorhes, William, s/o Wm., chr. 14 Sep. 1777.
Mc Clean, Phebe Ely, chr. 1787.
Calvert, Michael, s/o John, chr. 10 May 1778.
Vancleif, Peggy, d/o John, chr. 10 May 1778.
Laird, William, s/o Wm., chr. 10 May 1778.
Clayton, Joseph, s/o Joseph, chr. 17 Sep. 1778.
Covert, Mary, d/o Daniel, chr. 21 Sep. 1778.
Johnston, William, s/o William, chr. 14 Feb. 1779.
Henderson, Jane, d/o John, b. 21 Oct. 1778 and chr. Apr. 1779.
Breese, Samuel Byard, s/o Samuel e, chr. 2 May 1779.
Allwood, Joseph, s/o John, chr. 9 May 1779.
Smith, Michael Sweetman, s/o Andrew, chr. 9 May 1779.
Calvert, Mary, d/o John, chr. 20 June 1779.
Morris, Mary, d/o Ammariah, chr. 20 June 1779.
Morris, William, s/o Robert, chr. 20 June 1779.
Rue, Richard, s/o William, chr. 26 Sep. 1779.
Rue, Margaret, ds/o William, chr. 26 Sep. 1779.
Henderson, Mary, d/o Thomas, chr. 23 Oct. 1779.
Egburg, Polley, d/o Abraham, chr. 31 Oct 1779.
Rue, Joseph, s/o John, chr. 31 Oct. 1779.
Cole, Danniel, s/o Jacob, chr. 27 Feb. 1780.
Rue, Abigale, s/o Mathewm, chr. 9 Apr. 1780.
Henderson, Elizabeth, d/o John, b. 26 Oct 1781 and chr. 29 Apr. 1782.
Gollohan, Adam, s/o Wm. and Rebecca, b. 6 Sep. 1783 and chr. 8 May 1784.
Harbert, Ellen, d/o James and Elizabeth, b. 14 Feb. 1784 and chr. 20 June 1784.
Brewer, Thomas Hetfield, s/o Elizabeth, b. 10 Mar 1784, chr. 2 May 1784.
Forman, Jonathan, s/o Wm. and Francenes, chr. 2 May 1784.
Fry, Mary, chr. 2 May 1784.
Ogburn, Maria, d/o Rebeckah, chr. 2 May 1784.
H., John, s/o Dan. M. and Dorothy, chr. 30 May 1784.
Caldwell, Anna, d/o Wm. And Charity, chr. 20 June 1784.
Smally, Sarah, d/o James and Nelly, chr. 20 June 1784.
Voorhees, Hendrick, s/o Wm., chr. 27 June 1784.

Old Tennent Presbyterian Church

Combs, Hannah, d/o James, chr. 4 July 1784.
Gordon, Sarah, d/o David, chr. 4 July 1784.
Cook, Nancy, d/o George, chr. 11 July 1784.
Stevenson, Nancy, d/o James, chr. 18 July 1784.
Johnson, Elizabeth, d/o Wm., chr. 29 Aug. 1784.
Rue, Nathaniel Scudder, chr. 29 Aug. 1784.
Combs, Roberts, chr. 12 Sep. 1784.
Combs, Lydia, chr. 12 Sep. 1784.
Warner, George Rudolph, s/o Godfrey, chr. 12 Sep. 1784.
Warner, Deborah, d/o Godfrey, chr. 12 Sep. 1784.
Vanschiak, Mary, d/o Robert, chr. 24 Oct. 1784.
Vansciack, Sarah, chr. 24 Oct. 1784.
Covenhoven, Wikoff, s/o Wm. and Elenor, chr. 31 Oct. 1784.
Hawkenson, William, s/o Sarah, chr. 31 Oct. 1784.
Clayton, Joseph, s/o Jonathan, chr. 1785
Covenhoven, Ellen, d/o Garret, chr. 1785.
Pastedo, Pamela, d/o Mary, chr. 1785.
Pastedo, Lewis, s/o Mary, chr. 1785.
Coward, Alice, chr. 21 Mar. 1785.
Erickson, Sarah Franis, d/o Erick and Mary, chr. 1785.
Erickson, Mary, d/o Erick and Mary, chr. 1785.
Forman, Augustes, chr, 1785.
Gordon, William, s/o William, chr. 1785.
Matchet, Catherine, d/o John and Ann, chr. 1785.
Reid, Katey, d/o George, chr. 1785.
Reid, Joseph, s/o George, chr. 1785.
Sutton, Debby, d/o Richard and Rachel, chr. 1785.
Morford, John, s/o John and Hannah, chr. 8 Mar. 1785.
Morford, Margaret, d/o John and Hannah, chr. 8 Mar. 1785.
Morford, Catherine, d/o John and Hannah, chr. 8 Mar. 1785.
Johnson, Lydia, d/o Wm., b. 10 Mar. 1785 and chr. 8 Apr. 1785.
Jammison, Lydia, d/o John, chr. 20 Mar. 1785.
Tone, John, s/o William, chr. 20 Mar. 1785.
Zutphen, Polly Howell, d/o Joseph, chr. 20 Mar. 1785.
Hilyer, Elizabeth Dey, d/o John, chr. 21 Mar. 1785.
Hilyer, Lydia, d/o John, chr. 21 Mar. 1785.
Erickson, Mary, chr. Apr. 1785.
Henderson, Jane, d/o Thomas, chr. 3 Apr. 1785.
Voorhees, James, s/o James and Elinor, chr. 4 Apr. 1785.
Reid, George, chr. 7 Apr. 1785.
Starkey, Anna, chr. 7 Apr. 1785.
Johnson, John, s/o Peter and Rachel, chr. 17 Apr. 1785.

Early Church Records of Monmouth County

Forman, Mary Ann, d/o Jonathan, chr. 14 May 1785.
Gordon, Jonathan, s/o Ezekiel, chr. 29 May 1785.
Gordon, David, s/o Timothy, chr. 3 July 1785.
Schenck, Ruluff, s/o Ruluff, chr. 1 Oct. 1785.
Sweetman, Hilena, d/o Michael, chr. 6 Nov. 1785.
Forman, Emma Frisby, d/o David, chr. 18 Dec. 1785.
Parker, Anna, d/o David, chr. 1786.
Van Mater, Richard, s/o John, chr. 1786.
Holman, Catharine, d/o Joseph, chr. 4 Mar. 1786.
Craig, William, s/o James, chr. 19 Mar. 1786.
Friend, Bridget, d/o John, chr. 13 May 1786.
Morford, Joseph, chr. 13 May. 17865.
Hilyer, Sarah, chr. 10 July 1786.
Covenhoven, John, s/o Elias, chr. 6 Aug. 1786.
Covenhoven, Joseph, s/o Wm., chr. 10 Sep. 1786.
Matthews, Anna, d/o James, chr. 23 Sep. 1786.
Woodhull, John Tennant, chr. 24 Sep. 1786.
Abrams, David, s/o James, chr. 3 Dec. 1786.
Abrams, Sarah, d/o James, chr. 3 Dec. 1786.
Abrams, Anna, d/o James s, chr. 3 Dec. 1786.
Abrams, Jacob, s/o James, chr. 3 Dec. 1786.
Bower, David, s/o Anna, chr. 1787.
Combs, Hannah Smith, d/o Solomon, chr. 1787.
Covenhoven, Benjamin, s/o Garret, chr. 1787.
Dey, Harriot, d/o John, chr. 1787.
Dey, Lawrence, s/o John, chr. 1787.
Forman, John Burrows, s/o Jonathan, chr. 1787
Forman, Katey, d/o Wm., chr. 1787.
Gaston, Ellen, d/o Daniel, chr. 1787.
Jammison, Gertrude, d/o John, chr. 1787.
Laird, Anna, d/o William, chr. 1787.
Perine, Abighail, d/o Lewis, chr. 1787.
Rolfe, Moses, chr. 1787.
Sedam, John Rue, s/o Jacob, chr. 1787.
Colwell, Mary, d/o Wm., chr. 11 Mar. 1787.
Sedam, Lena, d/o Simon, chr. 18 Mar. 1787.
Sprouls, Elizabeth, d/o Moses, chr. 1 Apr. 1787.
Smally, Isaac, s/o James, chr. 8 Apr. 1787.
Conner, Rachel, chr. 12 Apr. 1787.
Edwards, Thomas, chr. 12 May 1787.
Henderson, Hope Burrowes, d/o Thos., chr. 12 May 1787.
Johnson, Joseph Ker., s/o Peter, chr. 27 May 1787.

Old Tennent Presbyterian Church

Ogburn, William, s/o Rebeckah, spouse of Wm., chr. 24 June 1787.
Forman, Eliza, chr. 8 July 1787.
Clayton, William, s/o John, chr. 31 Aug. 1787.
Story, John, s/o Wm., chr. 16 Sep. 1787.
Rolfe, Chitester, s/o Moses, chr. 22 Sep. 1787.
Rolfe, Jonathan, s/o Moses, chr. 22 Sep. 1787.
Rolfe, John, s/o Moses, chr. 22 Sep. 1787.
Rolfe, Ephraim, s/o Moses, chr. 22 Sep. 1787.
Rolfe, Isabel, d/o Moses, chr. 22 Sep. 1787.
Rolfe, Elizabeth, d/o Moses, chr. 22 Sep. 1787.
Gollohan, John, s/o Wm., chr. 6 Oct. 1787.
Robertson, Mary, chr. 6 Oct. 1787.
Carlisle, William, s/o Wm. chr. 4 Nov. 1787.
Anderson, Peggy, d/o John, chr. 18 Nov. 1787.
Wood, James English, s/o Miss Wood, chr. 25 Nov. 1787.
Barber, Sarah, d/o Thomas, chr. 8 Dec. 1787.
Tone, Rebeckah, d/o Wm., chr. 9 Dec. 1787.
Rue, Schuyler, s/o Matthew, chr. 30 Dec. 1787.
Applegate, Henry Perine, s/o Joseph, chr. 1788.
Colwell, Charity, d/o William., chr. 1788.
Erickson, Adonijah, s/o Miss Erickson, spouse of Erick, chr. 1788.
Forman, Rebeek, chr. 1788.
Gravat, Aaron, s/o Peter, chr. 1788.
Gravat, Robert, s/o Peter, chr. 1788.
Gravat, Peter, s/o Peter, chr. 1788.
Gravat, John, s/o Peter, chr. 1788.
Gravat, Richard, s/o Peter, chr. 1788.
Hulst, Elizabeth, d/o William, chr. 1788.
Parker, Hannah Scudder, d/o David, chr. 1788.
Colwell, Jenny Robinson, d/o William. chr. 1788.
Perine, Henry, s/o John, chr. 2 Jan. 1788.
Gordon, Betsy, d/o David, chr. 6 Jan. 1788.
Bailey, Peter, chr. 19 Jan. 1788.
Covenhoven, Lydia, d/o Wm. B., chr. 23 Mar. 1788.
Baird, Bedant, s/o John, chr. 5 Apr. 1788.
Baird, Zebulon, s/o John, chr. 5 Apr. 1788.
Baird, Mary, d/o John, chr. 5 Apr. 1788.
Baird, John, s/o John, chr. 5 Apr. 1788.
Abrams, Maria, d/o James, chr. 13 Apr. 1788.
Horn, Stephen, s/o William, chr. 2 May 1788.
Gordon, John Lloyd, s/o William, chr. 3 May 1788.
Sutphen, Phebe, d/o John, chr. 18 May 1788.

Frizehir, Katey, d/o Jacob, chr. 15 June 1788.
Campbell, John, s/o William, chr. 10 Aug. 1788.
Forman, Katey, d/o Jonathan, chr. 27 Sep. 1788.
Forman, Malvina, chr. 12 Oct. 1788.
Wikoff, Nathaniel Scudder, s/o Wm., chr. 19 Oct. 1788.
Clayton, Catherine, d/o John, chr. 1789.
Covenhoven, Eleanor, d/o Elias, chr. 1789.
Dey, John, s/o John L., chr. 1789.
Jammison, Joseph, s/o John, chr. 1789.
Ogburn, Sally Perine, d/o Rebeckah, spouse of Wm., chr. 1789.
Perine, Mary, d/o Catherine Perine (spouse of Henry), chr. 1789.
Reid, Joseph, chr. 1789.
Schenck, Peter, s/o Roeluff, chr. 1789.
Sutphen, Sally, d/o Joseph, chr. 1789.
Test, Anna, chr. 1789.
Wikoff, Sally, d/o William, chr. 1789.
Cook, Nicholas, s/o Mary, spouse of David Cook, chr. 27 Feb. 1789.
Craig, Anna, d/o John, chr. 15 Mar. 1789.
Laird, child of William, chr. 14 Mar 1789.
Craig, Sally, d/o James, chr. 22 Mar. 1789.
Johnson, Michael., s/o Peter, chr. 11 Apr. 1789.
Stevenson, Isaac, s/o James, chr. 26 Apr. 1789.
Morford, Elizabeth, d/o Joseph, chr. 9 May 1789.
Smally, Hannah, d/o James, chr. 9 June 1789.
Combs, Joseph, s/o James, chr. 26 July 1789.
Gordon, Alltia, d/o David, chr. 16 Aug. 1789.
Matthews, Phebe, d/o James, chr. 23 Aug. 1789.
Rue, Henry Perrine, s/o Matthew, chr. 30 Aug. 1789.
Low, Margaret, d/o Alexander, chr. 29 Nov. 1789.
Johnson, Euphame, d/o Michael, chr. 6 Dec. 1789.
Morrison, John, s/o James, chr. 13 Dec. 1789.
Tone, Elizabeth, d/o William, chr. 14 Dec. 1789.
Buck, Mary, chr. 1790.
Combs, Anna, chr. 1790.
Erickson, Anna, d/o Miss Erickson, spouse of Erick, chr. 1790.
Edbert, Katy Stryker, d/o Miss Egbert, chr. 1790.
Forman, Michael, s/o Samuel, chr. 1790.
Forman, Joseph, s/o Samuel, chr. 1790.
Forman, Molly, d/o Samuel, chr. 1790.
Forman, Peter, s/o Samuel, chr. 1790.
Gordon, Elsey, s/o Wm., chr. 1790.
Hervey, Margaret, chr. 1790.

Johnson, John Boram, s/o Corns., chr. 1790.
Scudder, Eliza Ann, d/o Joseph, chr. 29 Mar. 1790.
Perine, David Williamson, d/o John, chr. 2 May 1790.
Henderson, Eliza, d/o Thomas, chr. 8 May. 1790.
Abraham, Rebeckah, d/o James, chr. 16 May 1790.
Perine, Jeremiah Woolsey, d/o Lewis, chr. 20 June 1790.
Story, Mary English, d/o Wm., chr. 27 June 1790.
Covenhoven, Lidia, d/o Wm. B., chr. 26 Sep. 1790.
Combs, Jonathan, s/o Samuel, chr. 2 Oct. 1790.
Buckalue, Mary, d/o Fredk., chr. 17 Oct. 1790.
Craig, Ely, s/o David, chr. 21 Nov. 1790.
Voorhees, William, s/o Koert, chr. 28 Nov. 1790.
Anderson, Lewis, chr. 1791.
Anderson, Anna Lloyd, d/o Lewis, chr. 1791.
Colwell, Elizabeth, d/o William, chr. 1791.
Campbell, Hannah, s/o Benjamin, chr. 1791.
Covenhoven, Anna Rhea, d/o Garret, chr. 1791.
Forman, Rivine, chr. 1791.
Hunn, Phebe, chr. 1791.
Maxwell, Rachel, Chr. 1791.
Scudder, Phillip Johnson, s/o Joseph, chr. 1791.
Schenck, Peggy, d/o Ruluff, chr. 27 Mar. 1791.
Craig, Elizabeth, d/o James, chr. 10 Apr. 1791.
Laird, Sukey, d/o William, chr. 8 Apr 1791.
Johnson, William, s/o Peter, chr. 17 Apr. 1791.
Applegate, Lewis, s/o Joseph, chr. 16 May 1791.
Anderson, Lydia Hankinson, d/o James, chr. 10 June 1791.
Craig, Samuel, s/o John, chr.3 July 1791.
Maxwell, David, s/o David, chr. 31 July 1791.
Cole, Mary, d/o David, chr. 12 Aug. 1791.
Cole, Ebenezar, s/o David, chr. 12 Aug. 1791.
Morford, William Lane, s/o Joseph, chr. 12 Sep. 1791.
Schenck, Rebeekah, d/o John, chr. 18 Sep. 1791.
Tone, Elizabeth, s/o William, chr. 14 Dec. 1789.
Tone, Lydia, d/o William, chr. 2 Oct. 1791.
Sutphen, Mary Howel Burrows, d/o John, chr. 30 Oct. 1791.
Abraham, Jacob Sedam, s/o James, chr. 27 Nov. 1791.
Gordon, John, s/o Ezekiel, chr. 5 Dec. 1791.
Perine, Catherine, d/o John, chr. 5 Dec. 1791.
Reid, Jane, chr. 31 Dec. 1791.
Reid, Hanna, d/o George, chr. 31 Dec. 1791.
Reid, Nicholas, s/o George, chr. 31 Dec. 1791.

Reid, Nancy, d/o George, chr. 31 Dec. 1791.
Bown, Obadiah, chr. 1792.
Bown, Jane, d/o Obadiah, chr. 1792.
Bryan, John Lilly, s/o Miss Bryan, chr. 1792.
Colwell, Henry Robinson, s/o William, chr. 1792.
Clayton, John, s/o John, chr. 1792.
Clayton, Elizabeth, d/o John, chr. 1792.
Cole, William, s/o David, chr. 1792.
English, David, s/o James R., chr. 1792.
Erickson, Janet, d/o Miss Erickson, spouse of Erick, chr. 1792.
Foster, Rachel, chr. 1792.
Hendrickson, Dehart, chr. 1792.
Hendrickson, Daniel, chr. 1792.
Hubbard, Molly Jones, d/o Miss Hubbard, spouse of Jacob, chr. 1792.
Low, William, s/o Alexr., chr. 1792.
Maxwell, Molly, d/o Thomas, chr. 1792.
Mc Chesney, Elizabeth, d/o John, chr. 1792.
Mc Chesney, Robert, s/o Robt., chr. 1792.
Morrison, Mary Kirkpatrick, d/o James, chr. 1792.
Perine, Mary, d/o Lewis, chr. 1792.
Reid, Lydia, d/o Richard, chr. 1792.
Robinson, Elizabeth, chr. 1792.
Robinson, Joseph, chr. 1792.
Scudder, Charles, s/o John A., chr. 1792.
Taylor, Joseph Clayton, s/o Miss Taylor (spouse of Wm. Taylor), chr. 1792.
Van Der Veer, Anna, chr. 1792.
Van Der Veer, Joseph, s/o John, chr. 1792.
English, Oliver, s/o James R., chr. 30 Jan. 1792.
Sutphen, Jane Baldwin, d/o Joseph, chr. 8 Apr. 1792.
Story, William, s/o William., chr. 22 Apr. 1792.
Lena, d/o Garret, chr. 5 May 1792.
Anderson, Anna Lloyd, d/o John, chr. 3 June 1792.
Anderson, Kenneth, s/o Lewis, chr. 22 June 1792.
Carle, John Henry, s/o John, chr. 8 July 1792.
Wikoff, Matilda, s/o Wm., chr. 22 July 1792.
Hendrickson, Molly, d/o Danl. Hendrickson and Mary Rhea (spouse of Robt.), chr. 28 July 1792.
Hendrickson, Simon, s/o Danl. Hendrickson and Mary Rhea (spouse of Robt.), chr. 28 July 1792.
Hendrickson, Catherine, d/o Danl. Hendrickson and Mary Rhea (spouse of Robt.), chr. 28 July 1792.

Old Tennent Presbyterian Church

Hendrickson, William, s/o Danl. Hendrickson and Mary Rhea (spouse of Robt.), chr. 28 July 1792.
Campbell, Rachel, d/o Benj., chr. 20 Sep. 1792.
Matthews, James Burrows, s/o James, chr. 7 Oct. 1792.
Covenhoven, Alice, d/o Wm. B., chr. 28 Oct. 1792.
Reid, Rebeekah Story, d/o William, chr. 4 Nov. 1792.
V D Veer, Tunis, s/o John, chr. 2 Dec. 1792.
English, James, chr. 23 Dec. 1792.
Bryan, Thomas, s/o Elizh., chr. 1793.
Cook, Rachel, d/o Benjn., chr. 1793.
Craig, Hannah Anderson, d/o David, chr. 1793.
Forman, Samuel Rogers, s/o S. Foreman, chr. 1793.
Forman, David, s/o Jonathan, chr. 1793.
Lewis, Nathan, chr. 1793.
Meslar, Althay, d/o Oakey, chr. 1793.
Rue, Mary, d/o Henry, chr. 1793.
Rue, John, s/o Henry, chr. 1793.
Schenck, Jonathan, s/o Ruluff, chr. 1793.
Vanderveer, Eleanor, chr. 1793.
Voorhees, William, s/o James, chr. 1793.
Voorhees, Mary Johnson, chr. 20 Jan. 1793.
Wilson, Daniel, s/o Henry, chr. 1 Mar. 1793.
Rue, Theodorus, s/o Matthew, chr. 5 May 1793.
Lewis, Mary, d/o Nathan, chr. 11 May 1793.
Fenton, Robert, s/o William, chr. 9 June 1793.
Fenton, Ann, d/o William, chr. 9 June 1793.
Fenton, Margaret, d/o William, chr. 9 June 1793.
Fenton, Thomas, s/o William, chr. 9 June 1793.
Buckalue, Elizabeth, d/o Frederick, chr. 7 July 1793.
Gulick, Thomas Combs, s/o John, chr. 14 July 1793.
Hulst, Lydia, d/o William, chr. 23 July 1793.
Reid, Rebeekah Story, d/o William, chr. 4 Nov. 1792.
V D Veer, Sarah, d/o Ruluff, chr. 1 Sep. 1793.
V D Veer, John Lloyd, s/o Ruluff, chr. 1 Sep. 1793.
V D Veer, David, s/o Ruluff, chr. 1 Sep. 1793.
Anderson, Hannah, d/o Lewis, chr. 4 Oct. 1793.
Abrams, Charles, s/o James, chr. 6 Oct. 1793.
Scudder, John, d/o Joseph, chr. 12 Nov. 1793.
Wikoff, Ann, s/o William, chr. 12 Nov. 1793.
Colwell, William, s/o William, chr. 1794.
Covenhoven, James Bryson, s/o Lucas, chr. 1794.
Covenhoven, Elias, s/o Elias, chr. 1794.

Covenhoven, Anne, d/o Thomas, chr. 1794.
Covenhoven, Isaac, s/o Thomas, chr. 1794.
Erickson, Michael, s/o Miss Erickson, spouse of Erick, chr. 1794.
Gordon, William Tenent, s/o William, chr. 1794.
Morford, Lydia, d/o Joseph, chr. 1794.
Perine, Joseph, s/o John, chr. 1794.
Perine, Stephen, s/o Matthew, chr. 1794.
Schenck, Elizabeth, d/o John, chr. 1794.
Taylor, John, s/o Miss Taylor (spouse of Wm. Taylor), chr. 1794.
Van Der Veer, Catharine, d/o Ruluff, chr. 1794.
Van Der Veer, Amos Stout, s/o Ruluff, chr. 1794.
Henderson, Matilda, d/o Thomas, chr. 5 Jan. 1794.
Covenhoven, Vincentia, d/o Garret D., chr. 9 Feb. 1794.
Laird, Polly, d/o William, chr. 28 Feb1794.
Woodhull, Gilbert Smith, s/o John, chr. 10 May 1794.
English, Jane, d/o James R., chr. 20 Mar. 1794.
Story, David, s/o William., chr. 18 May 1794.
Sutphen, Nancy, d/o John, chr. 8 June 1794.
Craig, Daniel Logan, s/o John, chr. 15 June 1794.
Johnson, Anna Matilda, d/o Michael, chr. 22 June 1794.
Anderson, John Lloyd, s/o John L, chr. 29 June 1794.
Cole, Watson, s/o David, chr. 11 July 1794.
Gordon, Ezekiei, s/o Lewis, chr. 13 July 1794.
Gordon, William, s/o Lewis, chr. 13 July 1794.
Forman, child of Samuel, chr. 20 July 1794.
Bowne, Joseph, s/o Obadiah, chr. 31 Aug. 1794.
Scudder, Nathaniel, s/o John A., chr. 14 Sep. 1794.
Story, child of Joseph, chr. 26 Dec. 1794.
Barkelow, Daniel, s/o Wm., chr. 1795.
Combs, Margaret, d/o James, chr. 1795.
Covenhoven, William, s/o Saml., chr. 1795.
Cook, Thomas, s/o Benj., chr. 1795.
English, John, s/o James, chr. 1795.
Gordon, Hannah Lloyd, d/o David, chr. 1795.
Gordon, Joseph Combs, s/o Ezekiel, chr. 1795.
Johnston, Sarah, d/o Michael, chr. 1795.
Casler, Hannah, d/o Miss Casler, spouse of John, chr. 1795.
Mc Chesney, John Covenhoven, s/o John, chr. 1795.
Schenck, Daniel, s/o Ruluff, chr. 1795.
Stephenson, Polly Talman, d/o Miss Stephenson (spouse of James Stephenson) chr. 1795.
V D Veer, John, s/o John, chr. 1795.

Old Tennent Presbyterian Church

Voorhees, Daniel Slover, s/o Corns., chr. 1795.
Dey, Elizabeth, d/o William, chr. 15 Mar. 1795.
Dey, Daniel, s/o William, chr. 15 Mar. 1795.
Perine, William, s/o John, chr. 16 May 1795.
Robinson, Jane, d/o James, chr. 5 Apr. 1795.
Walton, Mary Forman, d/o Mary (spouse of P. Walton), chr. 20 June 1795.
Vanschiak, Joseph, s/o David, chr. 5 July 1795.
Johnson, Ebenezar, s/o Peter, chr. 20 Sep. 1795.
Smally, Mary, d/o James, chr. 25 Oct. 1795.
Covenhoven, Helena Anderson, d/o Lucus, chr. 1 Nov. 1795.
Campbell, Nelly, d/o Benjn., chr. 2 Dec. 1795.
Anderson, Phebe Rue, d/o John L., chr. 1796.
Bailey, Penelope, d/o Mary, chr. 1796.
Covenhoven, Mary Forman, d/o Garret B., chr. 1796.
Covenhoven, Sarah, d/o Richd., chr, 1796.
Covenhoven, Hannah, chr. 1796.
Craig, Mary, d/o John, chr. 1796.
Craig, Ellen, d/o James, chr. 1796.
Craig, Ann, d/o John, chr. 1796.
Craig, Anna, d/o James, chr. 1796.
Craig, Schenck, s/o John, chr. 1796.
Craig, John, s/o William, chr. 1796.
Craig, Peter, s/o John, chr. 1796.
Craig, Elizabeth, chr. 1796.
Hoover, John Lloyd, s/o Peter, chr. 1796.
Johnson, Sarah, d/o John, chr. 1796.
Laird, Joseph, s/o William, chr. 1796.
Perine, Lewis, s/o Lewis, chr. 1796.
Perine, Gertrude, d/o John, chr. 1796.
Rue, Abraham Schuyler, s/o Peter, chr. 1796.
Rue, Ellen, d/o Henry, chr. 1796.
Sutphen, Derick, s/o John, chr. 1796.
Sutfen, Getty, d/o David, chr. 1796.
Sutfen, Lydia, chr. 1796.
Voorhees, Elizabeth, d/o Johnson,   chr. 1796.
Scudder, Nancy, d/o John, chr. 13 Mar. 1796.
Rue, William, s/o Matthew, chr. 1 May 1796.
Scudder, Maria, d/o Joseph, chr. 2 May 1796.
Hubbard, Hannah, d/o Miss Hubbard, spouse of Jacob, chr. 14 May 1796.
Covenhoven, Hannah, d/o Saml., chr. 19 June 1796.

Barklay, Charles Ried, s/o D. Barklay, chr. 17 July 1796.
Craig, Phebe, d/o James, chr. 18 Sep. 1796.
Sutfen, Joseph Hasey, d/o Joseph, chr. 2 Oct. 1796.
Craig, David s/o David, chr. 9 Oct. 1796.
Smock, James, s/o Luke, chr. 21 Dec. 1796.
Smock, Elenor, s/o Luke, chr. 21 Dec. 1796.
Smock, Anne, s/o Luke, chr. 21 Dec. 1796.
Abraham, Stephen, s/o James, chr. 1797.
Cole, David, s/o David, chr. 1797.
Covenhoven, Peter, s/o William, chr. 1797.
Covenhoven, David, s/o Garret D., chr. 1797.
Covenhoven, Mary Dey, d/o William, chr. 1797.
Covenhoven, Phebe, d/o William, chr. 1797.
Dey, William, s/o John, chr. 1797.
Dey, Benjamin, s/o John, chr. 1797.
Dey, Edith, chr. 1797.
Dey, John ely, s/o William, chr. 1797.
Dey, Mary, d/o William, chr. 1797.
Erickson, Phebe Bird, d/o Miss Erickson, spouse of Erick, chr. 1797.
Fleming, James, chr. 1797.
Fleming, Joseph West, s/o James, chr. 1797.
Gordon, Matthew Rue, s/o John, chr. 1797.
Gordon, Charles, s/o William, chr. 1797.
Gulick, Peter, s/o John, chr. 1797.
Hawkinson, Anna, s/o Jos., chr. 1797.
Hilyer, Margaret, d/o John, 1797.
Morrison, Hannah Smith, d/o Catherine, chr. 1797.
Morrison, Eleanor, d/o Catherine, chr. 1797.
Perine, Elizabeth Anderson, d/o Miss Perine (spouse of Robt. Perine), chr. 1797.
Robinson, Hannah, d/o James, chr. 1797.
Taylor, Jonathan, s/o Miss Taylor (spouse of Wm. Taylor), chr. 1797.
Vanschiak, Davidh, s/o David, chr. 1797.
Vanderveer, Ruleef, s/o Ruluff, chr. 1797.
Walton, Ellen, d/o Mary (spouse of Peter Walton), chr. 1797.
Anderson, Kenneth, s/o James, chr. 16 Feb. 1797.
Anderson, Austin, s/o James, chr. 16 Feb. 1797.
Covenhoven, Eliza, d/o Elias, chr. 19 Mar. 1797.
English, William Covenhoven, s/o James R., chr. 2 Apr. 1797.
Schenck, William, s/o Ruluff, chr. 13 May 1797.
English, Hannah, chr. 28 May 1797.
Dey, Richard, s/o John, chr. 2 June 1797.

Old Tennent Presbyterian Church

Gordon, John Combs, s/o David, chr. 11 June 1797.
Scudder, Emma, chr. 25 June 1797.
Sloan, William Henry, chr. 22 July 1797.
Perine, Catherine Williamson, d/o John, chr. 6 Aug. 1797.
Lewis, William, s/o Martin, chr. 20 Aug. 1797.
Scudder, Louisa, d/o Joseph, chr. 11 Sept 1797.
Covenhoven, Idah, d/o Cornelius, chr. 24 Sep. 1797.
Hulst, Altie Covenhoven, d/o William, chr. 7 Oct. 1797.
Robinson, John, d/o James, chr. 27 Oct. 1797.
Applegate, Katey Longstreet, d/o Isaac, chr. 10 Nov. 1797.
Clayton, Matilda, d/o John, chr. 1798.
Covenhoven, William, chr. 1798.
Covenhoven, Robert, chr. 1798.
Covenhoven, John, s/o Saml., chr. 1798.
Covenhoven, Joseph, s/o Richd., chr. 1798.
Craig, Jane, d/o John, chr. 1798.
Deviney, Mary, chr. 1798.
Diviney, David Starkey, s/o Isaac, chr. 1798.
Hays, Sally, d/o Priscilla, chr. 1798.
Horn, Joseph V., chr. 1798.
Mc Chesney, William, s/o Wm., chr. 1798.
Mc Chesney, David Chambers, s/o Wm., chr. 1798.
Rue, Hannah, d/o Peter, chr. 1798.
Vanhorne, Ruth, d/o Joseph, chr. 1798.
Campbell, John, s/o Benjn., chr. 6 May 1798.
Craig, Samuel, s/o William, chr. 20 May 1798.
Dey, John Baird, s/o Daniel, chr. 20 May 1798.
Scudder, William, chr. 19 Aug. 1798.
V D Vear, Jane, d/o John, chr. 16 Sep.1798.
Laird, David, s/o David, chr. 7 Oct. 1798.
Covenhoven, John, s/o John, chr. 17 Nov. 1798.
Covenhoven, Leah, s/o John, chr. 17 Nov. 1798.
Covenhoven, Kenneth Anderson, s/o Lucus, chr. 1799.
Cotteral, James, s/o Miss Cotteral, spouse of James Cotteral, chr. 1799.
Craig, James, s/o James, chr. 1799.
Dey, John Woddhull, s/o John, chr. 1799.
Edbert, Anna, d/o William, chr. 1799.
Gordon, David, s/o John, chr. 1799.
Harvey, Catharine, chr. 1799.
Harvey, Catharine, d/o Benajah, chr. 1799.
Johnson, Letitia, d/o Cornelius, chr. 1799.
Lewis, Elizabeth, chr. 1799.

Longstreet, David, chr. 1799.
Schenck, John, s/o Ruluff, chr. 1799.
V D Veer, Tunis, s/o Ruluff, chr. 1799.
Voorhees, Sarah, chr. 1799.
Walton, Rebeekah, d/o Mary (spouse of P. Walton), chr. 1799.
Mc Chesney, Mary Stults, s/o John, chr. 28 Feb. 1799.
Anderson, Hannah Bowne, d/o John L., chr. 23 Apr. 1799.
English, Jeremiah Smith, s/o James R., chr. 28 Apr. 1799.
Craig, Mary Ann, d/o David, chr. 6 May 1799.
Gordon, David, s/o David, chr. 12 May 1799.
Rue, Ann, d/o Matthew, chr. 18 May 1799.
Wikoff, Lydia Scudder, s/o William, chr. 16 June 1799.
Bowne, Anna, d/o Obadh., chr. 23 June 1799.
Erickson, Margaret, d/o Miss Erickson, spouse of Erick, chr. 7 July 1799.
Abraham, William Gordon, s/o Lewis, chr. 14 July 1799.
Hawkinson, Maria, d/o Jos., chr. 4 Aug. 1799.
Dey, Sarah Perrine, d/o William, chr. 11 Oct. 1799.
Longstreet, Robert, s/o David, chr. 12 Oct. 1799.
Perine, Mary, d/o Matthew, chr. 25 Oct. 1799.
Scudder, Willaim Washington, s/o Joseph, chr. 10 Nov. 1799.
Abraham, Simon, s/o James, chr. 24 Nov. 1799.
Abraham, William, s/o James, chr. 24 Nov. 1799.
Craig, Catharine, d/o William, chr. 1 Dec. 1799.
Buckalew, Elizabeth, d/o Frederick, chr. 6 Dec. 1799.
Combs, Rebeekah, chr. 1800.
Combs, Elijah, chr. 1800.
Combs, Nancy, d/o Elijah, chr. 1800.
Covenhoven, James, s/o Richd., chr. 1800.
Covenhoven, Isaac, s/o Elias, chr. 1800.
Covenhoven, Elenor Forman, d/o Elias, chr. 1800.
Dey, Amey, d/o James, chr. 1800.
Dey, Stacey, d/o William, chr. 1800.
Gulick, Patty, d/o John, chr. 1800.
Hulst, Margaret, d/o William, 1800.
Laird, Nancy Covenhoven, d/o David, chr. 1800.
Low, Nancy, d/o William, chr. 1800.
V Pelt, Anna Anderson, d/o Benjn., chr. 1800.
Sutfin, Sally Woodhull, d/o John, chr. 23 Feb. 1800.
Covenhoven, Mary Vandorn, d/o Corns., chr. 6 Apr. 1800.
Mc Chesney, Elenor, s/o William, chr. 13 Apr. 1800.
Dey, Charlotte Watant, d/o Joseph W., b. 17 Apr. 1800.
Quay, Louisa, d/o John and Agnes, chr. 6 May 1800.

Old Tennent Presbyterian Church

Robinson, Eleanor, d/o James, chr. 10 May 1800.
Scudder, Kenneth Anderson, chr. 1 June 1800.
Patton, John, s/o Mary (spouse of S. Patton), chr. 8 June 1800.
Rue, Maria, s/o Peter, chr. 29 June 1800.
Covenhoven, William, s/o Lucus, chr. 31 Aug. 1800.
Rue, Lydia Kerr, d/o Henry, chr. 4 Oct. 1800.
Abraham, Lydia, d/o Lewis, chr. 12 Oct. 1800.
Cotteral, Cornelius Johnson, s/o Miss Cotteral, spouse of James Cotteral, chr. 9 Nov. 1800.
Covenhoven, Forman, s/o Tunis Forman, chr. 14 Dec. 1800.

Early Church Records of Monmouth County

Cemetery Records of Old Tennent

Samuel Twybill d. 13 Sept. 1799, in his 19th yr.
Hannah, w/o Wm. Crawford, d. 21 Jan. 1755, aged 51 yrs.
William, s/o Alex'r. and Ann Lowe, d. 10 Sept. 1799, aged 7-8-10.
Ann, w/o James Craig, d. 26 Aug. 1795, aged 30-5-3.
Lydia, d/o Joseph and Hannah Bowne, d. 14 Apr. 1799, aged 17-1-5.
Col___ Monkton d. 28 June 1778.
Thomas Smith d. 17 Oct. 1799, aged 56-4-25.
Jonathan Foreman d. 20 Mar. 1784, aged 37-2-19.
Helena, w/o Tunis Vanderveer, d. 23 Aug. 1784, aged 25 ys. and 25 days.
Caty, d/o Wm. and Frantje Forman, d. 28 Oct. 1788, aged 1-8-14.
Moses Laird d. 1798, in his 62nd yr.
Eliza, d/o Moses and Caty Laird, d. 31 Aug. 1794, aged 21-7-2.
Catherine, d/o Jacob and Sarah Wychoff, d. 21 Dec. 1782, aged 25 yrs.
Sarah, d/o Jacob and Sarah Wychoff, d. 2 June 1782, aged 17 yrs.
Mary, d/o Jacob and Sarah Wychoff, d. 17 May 1781, aged 22 yrs.
Rhoda, d/o Jacob and Sarah Wychoff, d. 12 Apr. 1783, aged 22.
Ann Wilson, 5th d/o Jacob and Sarah Wychoff, d. aged 27.
Sarah, d/o Peter and Ann Wilson, d. 21 Aug. 1784, aged 21 yrs.
Sarah, w/o Jacob Wychoff, d. 31 Aug. 1796, aged 64 yrs.
Nancy Dunham Hankinson, d/o James and Sarah, d. 15 Sept. 1791, aged 1 mo. and 25 dys.
Derrick Sutfin d. 27 June 1796, aged 84 yrs.
Mary, d/o Derrick & Mary Sutfin, d. 11 Sep. 1794, aged 73 yrs.
Phebe, d/o Derrick Sutfin, d. 5 Aug. 1777, aged 24 yrs.
David Combs d. 11 Jan, 1795, aged 21 yrs and 8 mo.
E. Combs d. 1777.
F. Combs d. 1777.
Ezekiel, s/o Lewis Gordon, d. 3 Sept. 1800, aged 6 yrs. and 5 mo.
John, s/o John and Rachel Campbell, d. 30 Mar. 1783, aged 32 yrs. and 7 dys.
Rachel Combs d. 10 Aug. 1777, in her 16th yr.
Campbell Combs d. 6 July 1778, aged 22 yrs.
Esther Combs d. 20 Mar. 1796, aged 33 yrs.
Rebecca, w/o David Baird, d. 6 Jan. 1778, aged 22 yrs.
Lydia, w/o Capt. David Baird, d. 15 Feb. 1791, aged 36 yrs.
Margaret, w/o Jon'n. R. Gordon, d. 28 Feb. 1792, aged 66 yrs.
Jonathan Rhea Gordon d. 1 Aug. 1800, aged 83 yrs.
John Craig d. 25 Sept. 1783, aged 73 yrs.
Archibald Craig d. 1 Aug. 1777, aged 24 yrs.

Old Tennent Presbyterian Church

Samuel Craig d. 6 July 1777, aged 26 yrs.
Sarah Dick d. 3 May 1763, aged 63 yrs.
John, s/o John and Mary Dey, d.13 June 1799, aged 18-11-13.
Joseph Johnston d. Feb. 1791, aged 21 yrs, 10 mo.
Henry, s/o Henry Perrine, d. 20 Feb. 1774, aged 5 mo.
Aaron, s/o Aaron Reid, d. 23 Sept. 1795, aged 1-11-3.
Rebecca, w/o Aaron Reid, d. 8 June 1796, aged 38 yrs.
Catherine, w/o John Perrine, d. 28 Apr. 1792, aged 83-5-15.
Jane, w/o John P. Covenhoven, d. 14 Aug. 1798, aged 49-6-21.
Eliz'h., d/o Wm. and Mary Huggen, d. 14 Sept. 1763, aged 5-3-20.
Sarah, w/o Wm. Huggen d. 3 Dec. 1753, aged 47 yrs.
Martha, w/o Benj'n. Vansehoie, d. 4 June 1791, aged 20-2-20.
John Loyd, Esq'r., d. 14 Oct. 1784, aged 61-3-21.
Sarah Mattison d. 23 Apr. 1774, aged 48-3-20.
James, s/o Aaron and Eliz'h. Mattison, d. 15 Oct. 1745, in his 10th yr.
John, s/o Aaron Mattison, d. 27 Oct. 1744, aged 23 yrs.
Aaron Mattison d. 26 Apr. 1762, in his 82nd yr.
Elizabeth, w/o Aaron Mattison, d. 3 Feb. 1773, aged 91 yrs.
Hugh McFerran d. 7 Mar. 1769, aged abt. 80 yrs.
Mary, w/o Conradt Hendrickson, d. 26 Oct. 1762, aged 26 yrs. and 3 dys.
Alce, w/o Leggget Smith, d. 14 Jan. 1759, aged 39 yrs.
Phebe, widow of Hartshorne White, d. 2 Jan. 1775, aged 39-1-18.
Hartshorne White d. 2 Apr. 1774, aged 37-2-14.
Elizabeth McGaliard d. 14 Aug. 1797, aged 76-5-7.
Robert McGaliard d. 31 Mar. 1782, aged 67 yrs.
Mary, w/o John McChesney, d. 20 May 1791, aged 56 yrs.
John McChesney d. 10 Mar. 1775, aged 45 yrs.
John Prest d. 12 Aug. 1773, aged 2 yrs., 6 mo.
Ruth Prest d. 24 June 1770, aged 1 yr., 7 mo.
Michael Johnston d. 9 Sept. 1785, aged 65 yrs., 9 mo.
Euphemia, w/o Mich. Johnston, d. 8 May 1770, aged 40-5-4.
Rebecca, w/o Vanhook DeBow, d. 19 June 1761, aged 26-5-3.
Frederick DeBow d. 19 Dec. 1757, aged 71 yrs, 3 mo.

The following are buried in Old Tennent Cemetery:
Thomas West, b. 8 March 1749 and d. 12 July 1833.
Ann West (w/o Thomas) b. 29 Sept. 1754 and d. 19 Apr. 1803.
Zilpha West (d/o Thomas) b.15 July 1779 and d. 15 July 1797.
Helena Conover (w/o Dan'l. West) b. 30 Mar. 1797 and d. 15 July 1828.
Tunis C. West b. 25 Apr. 1818 and d. 27 Oct. 1821.
Thomas West b. 14 Jan. 1820 and d. 1 Sept. 1824.
Elizabeth West b. 24 Mar. 1822 and d. 7 Oct. 1826.

Early Church Records of Monmouth County

The 7 above named are buried in front of the church, on the right hand side of the walk, as you go out of the middle door of the church, and about 50 feet from the middle door.

George Walker d. 2 Jan. 1791, aged 67 yrs.
William H., s/o Rev. J. Wood, d. 6 Sept. 1798, in his 20th yr.
Joseph Monford d. 20 Aug. 1760, aged 27 yrs.
Peter, s/o Peter Forman, d. 8 Sept. 1771, aged 15 yrs.
Margaret, d/o Peter Forman, d. 8 July 1767, aged 24-1-2.
Eleanor, w/o Peter Forman, d. 6 Nov. 1771, aged 51-1-13.
Peter Forman, Esq'r., d. 8 Sept. 1785, aged 66-8-10.
Michael Sweetman d. 28 Aug. 1766, aged 67 yrs.
Mary, w/o Michael Sweetman, d. 14 Aug. 1771, aged 66 yrs.
Jane, w/o Andrew Brannan d. 1 Sept. 1757, aged 24-4-29.
Jane, d/o Andrew Brannan, d. 6 Sept. 1766, aged 9 yrs., 14 dys.
James Anderson, Esq'r., d. 15 Sept. 1766, in his 27th yr.
Sarah M., w/o William G. Forman, d. 18 Jan. 1799, aged 26 yrs.
Joseph Forman d. 14 July 1775, aged 71 yrs.
Elizabeth, w/o Joseph Forman, d. 15 Oct. 1774, aged 64 yrs.
Robert Cumming d. 15 Apr. 1769, in his 68th yr.
Gilbert Tennent d. 6 Mar. 1770, aged 27-11-6
Catherine, d/o Wm. Tennent, d. 31 Aug. 1747, aged 4 yrs.
Mary, w/o Wm. P. Covenhoven, d. 30 Jan. 1777, aged 70 yrs.
Wm. P. Covenhoven d. 3 May 1777, aged 74 yrs.
William McKnight d. 21 Oct. 1761, aged abt. 45 yrs.
Charity, w/o Jas. Robinson, d. 23 Apr. 1762, aged 57-2-1.
James Robinson d. 22 Jan. 1773, aged 73 yrs., 4 mo.
David English, Jr., d. 13 Sept. 1762, aged 36 yrs.
Son of Robert English d. 25 Feb. 1764, aged 12 hours.
Robert English d. 25 Apr. 1768. aged 39-6-17.
John Anderson d. 19 July 1793, in his 90th yr.
Sarah, w/o John Anderson, d. 10 Aug. 1787, aged 82 yrs.
Nathaniel Scudder d. 19 Feb. 1797, aged 2 yrs., 8 mo.
Nathaniel Scudder d. 16 Oct. 1781, aged 48 yrs.
Isabella, w/o Nathaniel Scudder, d. 24 Dec. 1782, aged 45 yrs.
Elizabeth, d/o Geo. Walker, d. 3 June 1767, aged 9 mo.
Daniel, s/o David Forman, d. 8 Sept. 1772, aged 3-4-18.
Anna, w/o David Forman, d. 9 Sept. 1798, aged 63 yrs.
Henry, s.o Jas. Robinson, d. 3 Apr. 1768, aged 26-9-27.
David, s/o David English, d. 15 Feb. 1782, aged 23 yrs., 5 mo.
Jane, d/o David English, d. 26 May 1791, aged 35 yrs., 7 mo.
Charlotte, w/o Geo. W. Campbell, d. 4 July 1794, aged 24-11-28.

Old Tennent Presbyterian Church

Peter Gordon d. 21 Apr. 1770, aged 66-11-18.
Samuel, s/o Saml. Ker, d. 18 Nov. 1763, aged 23 yrs.
Elizabeth, d/o Saml. Ker, d. 31 Dec. 1755, aged 21 yrs.
Ann, w/o Samuel Forman, d. 27 Apr. 1793, aged 26 yrs.
Samuel Rogers, s/o Samuel Foreman, d. 27 Jan. 1793, aged 15 yrs.

Early Church Records of Monmouth County

QUAKER BIRTHS AND DEATHS
OF
SHREWSBURY MONTHLY MEETING
1657-1800

Children of ____ and ____ Lippincott:
John Lippincott b. __, at Shrewsbury.
Robert Lippincott b. __, at Shrewsbury.
____ Lippincott b. 15th of 7th mo., 16__, at Shrewsbury.
Mary Lippincott b. 4th of 11th mo., 167_, at Shrewsbury.
Ann Lippincott b. 17th of 4th mo., 1680 at, Shrewsbury.
Margaret Lippincott b. 7th of 3rd mo., 1683, at Shrewsbury.
Robart Lippincott b. 12th of 10th m0. 1685, at Shrewsbury.
Deborah Lippincott b. 30th of 3rd mo., 1690, at Shrewsbury.

____, s/o John Lippincott, d. 15th of 9th mo., 1684, in Shrewsbury.
Jenet, wife of John Lippincott, d. 1707, in Shrewsbury.
John Lippincott, the husband of Jenett, d. 16th of 2nd mo., 1720, at Shrewsbury.
Robart Lippincott, s/o John and Ann, d. abt. 1771/18, in Barbadoes.

Children of Isaac and Rachel Hance:
Timothy Hance b. 21st of 3rd mo., 1714. at night, 6th day of the week.
John Hance b. 6th of the 3rd mo., 1720, at 5;00 a.m., 5th day of the week.
Jacob Hance b. 3rd of Mar., 1723.

Children of Thomas and Ann Potter:
Mary Potter b. __, at Rhode Island.
Ephraim Potter b. 24th of 6th mo., __, at Shrewsbury.

Sarah Potter, wife of Ephraim Potter, b. 20th of 5th mo., 1669, in Shrewsbury, and d. 6th of 9th mo., 1715, in Shrewsbury.

Children of Ephraim and Sarah Potter:
Thomas Potter b. 18th of 12th mo., 1689, in Shrewsbury.
Mary Potter b. 8th of 12th mo., 1690.
Ann Potter b. 1st of 2nd mo., 1693, in Shrewsbury.
Ephraim Potter b. 30th of 9th mo.,1694, in Shrewsbury.
Mirobah Potter b. 19th of 6th mo., 1697, in Shrewsbury.
John Potter b. 24th of 1st mo., 1700, in Shrewsbury.
Cathorn Potter b. 23rd of 7th mo., 1702, in Shrewsbury.
Abraham Potter b. 1st of 8th mo., 1704, in Shrewsbury.

Shrewsbury Monthly Meeting

Amos Potter b. 23rd of 1st mo., 1705, in Shrewsbury.
Proseme and Hannah Potter b. 2nd of 1st mo., 1706/7, in Shrewsbury.

Leah Potter b. 6th of 1st mo., 1709, in Shrewsbury.
Joseph Potter b. 8th of 6th mo., 1710, in Shrewsbury.

Thomas Potter, husband of Sarah, d. 10th of 12th mo., 1703.
Amos Potter, s/o Ephraim and Sarah, d. 9th of 1st mo., 1705/6.
Sarah Potter, wife of Ephraim, d. 6th of 9th mo., 1715.
Ephraim Potter, husband of Mary, d. 11th mo., 1717.
Hannah Potter d. ___.

Children of Hugh Dirkman and Grace:
Elizabeth Dirkman b. 14th of __, at Lin.
Mary Dirkman b. 14th of 6th mo., __, at Rode Island.
Grace, wife of Hugh Dirkman, d. 23rd of 7th mo., 1678.
Hugh, husband of Grace, d. __ 1690.

Children of Jedidiah and Elizabeth Allen:
Maribah Allen b.   12th of 9th mo., 1686.
David and Jonathan Allen b.   16th of 8th mo., 1689.

Children of Richard Lippincott and Abigaill:
Rememberance Lippincott, son, b. 15th of __ mo., __ and d. 11th of "20" 1723.
John Lippincott b. 7th of 8th mo., 16__ and d. 16th of 2nd mo., 1720.
Restore Lippincott, son, b. 3rd of 5th mo., 165_.
Freedom Lippincott, son, b. 10th of 7th mo., 165_ and d. __ of 4th mo., 1697.
Increase Lippincott, daughter, b. 5th of 10th mo., 1657 and d. 29th of 9th mo., 1695.
Jacob Lippincott b. 11th of 3rd mo., 1660 and d. 6th of 12th mo., 1689.
Preserve Lippincott b. 25th of 12th mo., 1663.
____ Lippincott, son, b. 1st of __ mo., 1666.

Richard, husband of Abigail Lippincott, d. 25th of 9th mo., 1683.
Jacob, s/o Richard Lippincott, d. 6th of 12th mo., 1689.
Increase, d/o Richard Lippincott, d. 29th of 9th mo., 1695.
Freedom, s/o Richard Lippincott, d. __ of 4th mo., 1697.
Abigail, wife of Richard Lippincott, d. 22nd of 6th mo., 1697.
John, s/o Richard Lippincott, d. 16th of 2nd mo., 1720.

Early Church Records of Monmouth County

Remembrance, s/o Richard Lippincott, d. 11th of "25" 1723, aged 83 yrs.
Margaretta, his wife, was 73 at his death.
Richard, s/o Remembrance and Margaret Lippincott, d. 12th of 5th mo., 1723.

Children of Remembrance and Margaret Lippincott:
Josiah and Elizabeth b. 2nd ___.
Abigail b. 18th of 12th mo., 16__ and d. 9th of 7th mo., 1674.
Richard b. 19th of 1st mo., 167_.
Elizabeth b. 29th of 9th mo., 1677 and d. 7th of 11th mo., 1761/2.
Josiah b. 28th of 1st mo., 1680.
William b. 17th of 10th mo., 1682.
Abigail b. 17th of 9th mo., 1685.
Sarah b. 24th of 5th mo., 1688.
Ruth b. 6th of 8th mo., 1691.
Mary b. 6th of 7th mo., 1693.
Grace b. 13th of 2nd mo., 1695 and d. 3rd of 3rd mo., 1703.

Children of Wilber Lippincott and Frances:
Margaret Lippincott b. 17th of 10th mo., 1735.
Ann Lippincott b. 9th of 8th mo., 1737.
"Jediah" Lippincott b. 9th of 4th mo., 1740.

__ Lippincott, s/o Remembrance, d. 4th of 11th mo., 1671.

Children of William Worth and Faith:
Sarah Worth b. 27th of 12th mo., ____.
Hoxe Worth b. 26th of 11th mo., 16__.
Willmoth Worth b. 1st of 12th mo., 167_
William Worth b. 6th of 2nd mo., 1678.
Edward Worth b. 23rd of 2nd mo., 1679.
Patience Worth b. __ of 12th mo., 1681.

____ Worth, d/o William, d. 29th of 6th mo., 1674.
William Worth, s/o William, d. 1st of 8th mo., 1678.
Faith Worth, wife of William, d. 30th of 9th mo., 1693.
Mary Worth, wife of William, d. 16__.
William Worth, husband of Jane, d. 25th of 11th mo., 1710.
Jane Worth, widow of William, d. 15th of 7th mo., 172_.

Shrewsbury Monthly Meeting

Children of Thomas and Christian White:
Mary White b. 17th of 10th mo., 1716 and d. 3rd of 3rd mo., 1732.
Margaritt White b. 28th of 6th mo., 1718 and d. 29th of 5th mo., 1736.
Constant White b.29th of 1st mo., 1720.
Geoge White b.4th of 12th mo., 1721.
Jane White b.3rd of 2nd mo., 1722.
Anne White b.18th of 2nd mo., 1727.
Sarah White b.15th of 5th mo., 1729.
Thomas White b.18th of 1st mo., 1732.
Elizabeth White b. 8th of 5th mo., 1735.
John White b.28th of 11th mo., 1738.

Children of PterTillton and Reecka?:
Rebecka Tillton b. 6th of 7th mo., __.
John Tillton b. 11th of 1st mo., 1669.
Peter Tillton b. 10th of 2nd mo., 1672.
Mary Tillton b. 9th of 9th mo., 1675.
Thomas Tillton b. 20th of 7th mo., 1676.
Ester Tillton b. 5th of 6th mo., 1678.
Daniell Tillton b. 4th of 7th mo., 1679.
Marcy Tillton b. 2nd of 12th mo., 1681.
Cattorn Tillton b. 14th of 7th mo., 1684.
Henry Tillton b. 24th of 11th mo., 1686.
Samuel Tillton b. 17th of 1st mo., 1690.

__ Tillton, s/o Peter, d. __ 0f 3rd mo., 1677.
__ Tillton, d/o Peter, d. 31st of 6th mo., 1678.
Rebecka? Tillton, wife of Peter, d. 6th of 8th mo., 1700.
Peter Tilltpn, husband of Rebecka?, d. 15th of 1st mo., 1699/00.

Children of John Cleayton:
Rachel Cleaton b. 16th of 4th mo., __.
John __ of 9th mo., 167_.

Children of Jonathan and Sarah Marsh:
William Marsh b. 17th of 4th mo., 1685 and he is 22 yrs. old on 17th of 4th mo., 1707.

Children of John Chamberz:
John Chambers b. 21st of ___.
Richard b. 3rd of 11th mo., __.
Mary Chambers b. 5th of 4th mo., 167_.

William Chambers b. 21st of 7th mo., 167_.
Susannah Chambers b. 7th of 7th mo., 1780.
Thomas Chambers b. 18th of 8th mo., 1681.
Hannah Chambers b. 3rd of 3rd mo., 1684 and d. 13th of 7th mo., 1680 ?.

____ Chambers, s/o John, d. 22nd of 8th mo., 1679.

Children of Restore Lippincott and Hannah:
Samuel Lippincott b. 12 of 7th mo., __.
Abigaell Lippincott b. 16th of 12th mo., __.
Hannah Lippincott b. __ of 9th mo., 167_.
Hope Lippincott b. __ of 8th mo., 1681.
Rebena Lippincott b. 24th of 9th mon 1684.
James Lippincott b. 11th of 4th mo., 1787.
____ Lippincott b. 15th of 7th mo., 1690.
Jacob Lippincott b. __ of 6th mo., 1692.
Rachel Lippincott b. 8th of 11th mo., 1695.

Children of George and Johannah Williams:
Obadiah Williams b. 14th of 1st mo., 1710.
Hezekiah Williams b. 16th of 2nd mo., 1712/3.
George Williams b. 9th of 12th mo., 1714.
Hezekiah Williams b. 1st of 12th mo., 1715/6.
John Williams b. 20th of 1st mo., 1719.
Experience Williams b. 12th of 2nd mo., 1721.

____h Williams, s/o George and Johannah Williams, d. __ of 2nd mo., 1716.

Children of ffrances Borden and Jane:
Richard Borden b. 11th of 2nd mo., __.
ffrances Borden b. 1st of 8th mo., 16__.
Joyce Borden b. 4th of 7th? Mo., 168_.
Thomas Borden b. 4th of 12th mo., 1684.

Children of ffrances and Mary Borden:
Elizabeth Borden b. 6th of 5th mo., 1707.
Jane Borden b. 7th of 6th mo., 1708.
ffrances Borden b. 24th of 12th mo., 1709/10.
John Borden b. 3rd of 11th mo., 1711/12.
Amy Borden b. 6th of 12th mo., 1713/14.
Mary Borden b. 21st of 5th mo., 1717.

Shrewsbury Monthly Meeting

Thomas Borden b. 27th of 4th mo., 1719.
Jeams Borden b. 4th of 8th mo., 1722.

____ Borden, the husband of ----, d. 19th of 1st mo., 1705/6.

____ Tilton, wife of John Tilton, d. 15th of 10th mo., 1715.

Children of Nathaniel Camecks:
Mary Cammeck b. 8th of ___.
Andrey Cammeck b. 17th of 6th mo., __.
ffrances Cammeck b. 24th of 11th mo., 168_.
Ann Cammeck b. __ 169_.
Leah Cammeck b. 14th of 12th mo., 1692.

Children of Walter and Deborah Harbart:
Walter Harbart b. 25th of 11th mo., 1701.

Children of Walter and Sarah Harbart:
Rebecca Harbart b. 6th of 1st mo., 1704/5.
Deborah Harbart b. 1st of 12th mo., 1706.
Timothy Harbart b. 12th of 2nd mo., 1709.
Esther Harbart b. 18th of 1st mo., 1710.
Meribah Harbart b. 10th of 12th mo., 171/2?.
Paule Harbart b. 1st of 6th mo., 1715.
Sarah Harbart b. __ 171_.

Children of Henry Chamberlin:
John Chamberlin b. 14th of __.

Children of Ralph Allen and Margarett:
Aaron Allen b. 20th of 7th mo., 1708.
Ezekell Allen b. 17th of 3rd mo., 1710.
Miriam Allen b. 2nd of 10th mo., 1712.
Jedidiah Allen b. 17th of 10th mo., 1714.
James Allen b. 2nd of 10th mo., 1716.
Tabitha Allen b. 12th of 9th mo., 1718.

____ Allen, husband of Margaret Allen, d. 2nd of 8th mo., 1718.

Children of ffrances Jeffres and Ann:
Mary Jeffrey b. 29th of 7th mo., __.
ffrances Jeffrey b. 19th of 6th mo., 1__.

Early Church Records of Monmouth County

William Jeffrey b. 13th of 9th mo., 168_.

Children of Samuell Dennis and Increase:
Abigaill Dennis b. 25th of __.
Samuel Dennis b. 18th of 6th mo., 1__.
Jacob Dennis b. ___.
Zibah Dennis b. 25th of 10th mo., 1693.
Rachel Dennis b. 24th of 9th mo., 1695.

Children of Walter Herberts? and Deborah:
George Herberts b. 10th of 11th mo.,, 1729.
John Herberts b. 7th of 1st mo., 1731.
Timothy Herberts b. 16th of 9th mo., 1734.

Cease Denns, wife of Samuel, d. 29th of 9th mo., 1695.

Children of George Corlis and Exercise:
John Corlis b. 11th of 1st mo., _.
Hannah Corlis b. 25th of 8th mo., 16_.
Elizabeth Corlis b. 1st of 5th mo., 16_.
William Corlis b. 15th of 5th mo., 1689.
Mary Corlis b. 31st of 1st mo., 1692.
George Corlis b. 19th of 8th mo., 1694.

Children of George Corlis and Deborah:
Thomas Corlis b. 3rd of 9th mo., 1700.
Deborah Corlis b. 11th of 2nd mo., 1702.
Joseph Corlis b. 14th of 1st mo., 1704/5.
Banjaman Corlis b. 31st of 6th mo., 1707.
Timothy Corlis b. 10th of 2nd mo., 1710.
Dinah Corlis b. 17th of 11th mo., 1712.
Jacob Corlis b. 14th of 8th mo., 1715.

_____ Corlis, wife of George Corlis, d. 14th 0f 9th mo., 1695.
Thomas Corlis, s/o George and Deborah, d. 20th of 11th mo., 170_.
George Corlis, husband of Deborah, d. 10th of 7th mo., 1715.
Hannah Allen, 1st d/o George Corlis and wife of Henry Allen, d. 15th of
    1st mo., 1712.

Children of William Scott and Abigaill:
John Scott b. 9th of 11th mo., 1679.
William Scott b.8th of 8th mo., 1681.

Shrewsbury Monthly Meeting

William Scott b. 25th of 10th mo., 1683.
Samuel Scott b. 31st of 3rd mo., 1685.
Peter Scott b. 27th of 7th mo., 1787.
Hester Scott b. 6th of 10th mo., 1689.

Mary Warner, d/o Abigaill Scott by her 1st husband, d. - of 2nd mo., __.
Ralfe Warner, s/o Abigaill Scott by her 1st husband, d. _ of 4th mo., 167_.
____ Scott, s/o William and Abigaill, d. _ of 10th mo., 1682.
William Scott, s/o William and Abigaill, d. 8th of 11th mo., 1683.
Peter Scott, s/o William and Abigaill, d. 2nd of 8th mo., 1687.

Children of Benjamin Wooley and Ester:
Daniel Wooley b. 15th of 12th mo., 1717.
Mary Wooley b. 5th of 8th mo., 1719.
Sarah Wooley b. 6th of 8th mo., 1721.
Patience Wooley b. 9th of 6th mo., 1723.
Marcy Wooley b. 12th of 8th mo., 1725.
William Wooley b. 25th of 9th mo., 1728.
Elizabeth Wooley b. 9th of 4th mo., 1735.

John Eatton d. 11th of 2nd mo., 1750.

Children of Thomas Eaton and Jeru:
John Eaton b. 26th of 1ST mo., __.

__homas Eaton, s/o Thomas and Jerusha, d. 10th of 10th mo., 1686.
Thomas Eaton, husband of Jerusua, d. 26th of 9th mo., 1688.

Children of Thomas and Esther Vicars:
John Vicars b. 7th of 4th mo., __.
Thomas Vicars b. 11th of 6th mo., 16_.
Abraham Vicars b. 11th of 9th mo., 169_.
Isaac Vicars b. 31st of 6th mo., 1693.

Esther Vicars, wife of Thomas Vicars, d. 5th of 8th mo., 1693.
Thomas Vicars, husband of Esther Vicars, d. 21st of 11th mo.,, 1695/6.

Children of William and Hannah Lippincott:
Wilbur Lippincott b. 18th of 1st mo., 1710/1.
Sarah Lippincott b. 29th of 12th mo., 1212
Increase Lippincott b. 11th of 9th mo., 1714.
Abigaell Lippincott b. 1st of 2nd mo., 1716.

Early Church Records of Monmouth County

William Lippincott b. 25th of 2nd mo., 1718.
Phebe Lippincott b. 4th of 12 mo., 1719.
Samuel Lippincott b. 12th of 10th mo., 1720.
Remembrance Lippincott b. 9th of 9th mo., 1721.
Dorcas Lippincott b. 13th of 2nd mo., 1723/4.
Hannah Lippincott b. 2nd of 11th mo., 1725/6.
James Lippincott b. 17th of 1st mo., 1730.

Abiah Edwards, s/o Philip and Catherine, d. 26th of 3rd mo., 1723.
Naomi Edwards, d/o Philip and Catherine, b. 25th of 6th mo., 1728.

Children of Jacob Lippincott (d. 6th of 12th mo., 1689) and Grace:
Jacob Lippincott b. 18th of 7th mo., __, and d. 6th of 9th mo., 1687.
Ruth Lippincott b. 27th of 9th mo., __, anf d. 21st of 12th mo., 1689.

___ob Lippincott, s/o Jacob and Grace, d. 6th of 12th mo., 1689.
Jacob Lippincott, husband of Grace, d. 6th of 12th mo., 1689.
Ruth Lippincott, d/o Jacob and Grace, d. 21st of 12th mo., 1689.

Children of John and Naemy Corlies:
(None recorded)

Children of Jobe Jenkins (d. 11th of 7th mo., 1687) and Hannah:
Susanna Jenkins b. 15th of 9th mo., 1684.

Jobe Jenkins, husband of Hannah, d. 11th of 7th m0., 1687.

William Astin, husband of Janet, d. 14th of 6th mo., 1706.

Children of Philip and Catherine Edwards:
Elizabeth Edwards b. 25th of 3rd mo., 1714.
Abiah Edwards b. 14th of 4th mo., 1716.
Webley Edwards b. 29th of 3rd mo., 1718.
Mary Edwards b. 3rd of 9th mo., 1719.
Philip Edwards b. 28th of 11th mo. 1722.

Children of Ephraim Allen:
Ephraim Allen b. 29th of 5th mo., __.
Lidia Allen b. 13th of 2nd mo., 168_.
John Allen b. 29th of 7th mo., 1688.
Ephraim Allen b. 13th of 5th mo. 1691.

Shrewsbury Monthly Meeting

Ephraim Allen, s/o Ephraim Allen and Margaret, d. 2nd of 6th mo., 1684.
Ephraim Allen, husband of Margaret Allen, d. 29th of 11th mo., 1691.

Children of Thomas Hillborn and Elizabeth:
Samuel Hillborn b. 20th of 8th mo., 1689.
Robart Hillborn b. 31st of 5th mo., 1692.
Mary Hillborn b. 7th of 10th mo., 1794.
Elizabeth Hillborn b. 2nd of 1st mo., 1697/8.
Katheron Hillborn b. 30th of 1st mo., 1799.
Deborah Hillborn b. 25th of 3rd mo., 1701.

Children of Thomas and Mary fforman:
Rebeca fforeman b. 7th of 4th mo., 8, in Freehold.
Elizabeth fforeman b. 3rd of 2nd mo., 1702, in Freehold.
Benjamin fforeman b. 3rd of 10th mo., 1795, in Freehold.

Children of Nathaniel and Lydia Parker:
Nathaniel Parker b. 22nd of 2nd mo., 1708, 5th day of the week.
Meribah Parker b. 20th of 10th mo., 1710, 4th day of the week.
Ephraim Parker b. 18th of 2nd mo., 1715, 2nd day of the week.
Lydia Parker b. 5th od 9th mo., 1717, 3rd day of the week.

Children of John Tooker:
Elizabeth Tooker b. 9th of 10th mo., __.
James Tooker b. 26th of 6th mo., 169_.

Children of Henry Allen and Hannah:
Jacob Allen b. 15th of 7th mo., 1704.
Exercise Allen b. 18th of 8th mo., 1705.
Moses Allen b. 22nd of 7th mo., 1707.
Zephaniah Allen b. 1st of 10th mo., 1709.
Patience Allen b. 27th of 11th mo., 1711/2.

Hannah Allen, wife of Henry Allen, d. 15th of 1st mo., 1712.

Children of Henry Allen and Abigaell:
Hannah Allen b. 21st of 11th mo., 1714/5.
Gabriell Allen b. 25th of 5th mo., 1716.
Meribah Allen b. 18th of 2nd mo., 1718.
Cattron Allen b. 24th of 7th mo., 1719.
Zerviah Allen b. 13th of 3rd mo., 1721.
Samuel Allen b. 29th of 4th mo., 1723.

Michael Allen b. 20th of 12th mo., 1726/7.

Elizabeth Tooker, d/o John Tooker and Ruth, d. 6th of 11th mo., 1689.

Children of Nathaniel and Hannah Slocom:
Samuel Slocom b. 11th of 12th mo., __.
Sarah Slocom b. 16_.
Meribah Slocom b. 7th of 9th mo., 1686.
Elizabeth Slocom b. 15th of 11th mo., 1689.
Naomy Slocom b. 12th of 5th mo., 1692.
John Slocom b. 14th of 9th mo., 1694.
Mary Slocom b. 1st mo., 1697.

Children of Peter and Elizabeth Parker:
Sofias Parker b. 13th of 12th mo., 1708/9.
Hannah Parker b. 3rd of 6th mo., 1712.
Heinrich (?) b. 23rd of 2nd mo., 1716.
John Parker b. 27th of 8th mo., 1719.
Peter Parker b. 4th of 9th mo., 1722.
Margaret Parker b. 25th of 11th mo., 1725/6.
Elizabeth Parker b. 27th of 12th mo., 1732/3.

Nathaniel Slocom, husband of Hannah Slocom, d. 31st of 6th mo., 1702.

Children of John Wooley:
Thomas Wooley b. 1st of __.
Ruth Wooley b. 24th of 5th mo., __.
William Wooley b. 17th of 6th mo., 16_.
John and Joseph Wooley b. 31st of 10th mo., 1690.
Binjaman Wooley b.25th of 12th mo., 1692.
James Wooley b. 6th of 6th mo., 1695.
Elizabeth Wooley b. 23rd of 2nd mo., 1697.
Leah Wooley b. 15th of 12th mo., 1698.
Elizabeth Wooley b. 17th of 2nd mo., 1700.
Ann Mary Wooley b. 3rd of 12th mo., 1702.

____ Wooley, d/o John and Mary Wooley, d. 14th of 7th mo., 1687.
Elizabeth Wooley, d/o John and Mary Wooley, d. 8th mo., 1699.
Joseph Wooley, s/o John and Mary Wooley, d. 1st of 12th mo., 1705.
James Wooley, s/o John and Mary Wooley, d. 17th of 12th mo., 1716/7.

Shrewsbury Monthly Meeting

Children of Thomas and Patience Wooley:
Joseph Wooley b. 21st of 11th mo., 1708/9.
John Wooley b. 27th of 7th mo., 1710.
Content Wooley b. 11th of 12th mo., 1712/3.
Lydia Wooley b. 11th of 11th mo., 1714/5.
Abigaell Wooley b. 17th of 3rd mo., 1717.
Hannah Wooley b. 19th of 6th mo., 1719.
Meribah Wooley b. 16th of 9th mo., 1721.
Thomas Wooley b. 24th of 7th mo., 1725.

Joseph Wooley, s/o Thomas and Patience, 12th of 3rd mo., 1715.

Children of Richard Lippincott and Mary:
Richard Lippincott b. 6th of 1st mo.,__ and d. 9th of 3rd mo., 1715, in Shrewbury.
Remembrance Lippincott b. 27th of 1st mo., 170_, and d. 3rd of 2nd mo., 1701, in Shrewbury.
Jacob Lippincott b. 27th of 2nd mo., 1702.
David Lippincott b. 31st of 8th mo., 1704.
My first dau. b. in Springfield, 19th of 7th mo., 1696 and d. in Springfield, 21st of 7th mo., 1696.
My second dau. b. in Springfield, 7th of 4th mo., 1697 and d. in Springfield, 7th of 4th mo., 1697.
My third dau. b. in Shrewsbury, 28th of 12th mo., 1698 and d. in Shrewsbury, 28th of 12th mo., 1698.
Abigail Lippincott b. 29th of 4th mo., 1707.
Nathan Lippincott b. 13th of 1st mo., 1709/10.
Remembrance Lippincott b. 13th of 6th mo., 1712.
Ruth Lippincott b. 4th of 11th mo., 1716/7.

Marty Lippincott, wife of Richard, d. at Shrewsbury, 8th of 12th mo., 1721/2. b.

Children of John and Elizabeth Worthley:
John Worthley b. 22nd of 10th mo., __.
Lydia Worthley b. 11th of 2nd mo., 16_.
Elizabeth Worthley b. 16th of 7th mo., 170_ and d. at Shrewsbury, 7th of 2nd mo., 1715.
Deborah Worthley b. 12th of 4th mo., 1703.
Sarah Worthley b. 11t of 7th mo., 1706.
Joseph Worthley b. 6th of 5th mo., 1709 and d. in Shrewsbury, 5th mo., 1709.

May Worthley b. 27th of 7th mo., 1710.
Richard Worthley b. 22nd of 8th mo., 1712.

John Worthley, husband of Elizabeth, d. 3rd of 10th mo., 1715.

Children of Josiph and Margarett Parker:
Josiph Parker b. 28th of 6th mo., 16_.
Mary Parker b. 1st of 12th mo., 167_ and d. 1676/7.
Nathaniel Parker b. 20th of 5th mo., 1679.
Peter Parker b. 4th of 8th mo., 1681.
Margaret Parker, wife of Joseph, d. 6th of 11th mo., 1783.
Joseph Parker, husband of Margaret, d. 18th of 8th mo., 1684.

Children of Joseph and Elizabeth Parker:
Margaret Parker b. 20th of 1st mo., 1699/1700.
Joseph Parker b. 24th of 11th mo., 1701.
George Parker b. 24th of 10th mo., 1703.
Benjamin Parker b. 22nd of 1st mo., 1705/6.
Peter Parker b. 10th of 6th mo., 1708 and d. in Sgrewsbury, 27th of 6th mo., 1708.
William Parker b. 13th of 6th mo., 1709.
James Parker b. 30th of 10th mo., 1714.
Elizabeth and Meribah Parker b. 11th of 11th mo., 1716/7.
Phebe Parker b. 1st of 1st mo., 1718/9.

Children of Joseph and Deborah Parker:
Joseph Parker b. 17th of 4th mo., 1727.
John Parker b. 7th of 2nd mo., 1731.
Joseph Parker, 2nd, b. 24th of 8th mo., 1833.
John Parker, 2nd, b. 15th of 5th mo., 1735.
William Parker b. 7th of 9th mo., 1736.

Children of John ns Sar__ Lippincott:
Thomas Lippincott b. 19th of 3rd mo., 16_.
Jacob Lippincott b. 7th of 5th mo., 1695.
Joseph Lippincott b. 8th of 7th mo., 1697.
John Lippincott b. 18th of 12th mo., 1699.
Margert Lippincott b. 22nd of 10th mo., 1702.
Mary Lippincott b. 3rd of 1st mo., 1704/5.
ffrances Lippincott b. 23rd of 7th mo., 1707.
Deborah Lippincott b. 17th of 1st mo., 1711.
Ann Lippincott b. 1712.

Shrewsbury Monthly Meeting

Sarah Lippincott b. 5th of 11th mo., 1720.

Ffaith Huett, widow, d. in Shrewsbury, 30th of 11th mo., 1710/1.

Children of Edward Wooley:
Elizabeth Wooley b. 28th of 3rd mo., __.
Hannah Wooley b. 8th of 5th mo., __.
Adam Wooley b. 4th of 12th mo., 169_.
Edward Wooley b. 16th of 11th mo., 1692.
Content Wooley b. 9th 0f 9yth mo., 1694.
George Wooley b. 14th of 10th mo., 1697.
William Wooley b. 22nd of 12th mo., 1698.
Ruth Wooley b. 8th of 4th mo., 1701.
Lydia Wooley b. 23rd of 1st mo., 1702/3.

Children of of George and Hannah Allen:
William Allen b. 7th of 9th mo., 1704.
Lydia Allen b. 19th of 7th mo., 1708.
Mary Allen b. 14th of 9th mo., 1710.
Abigaell Allen b. 12th of 6th mo., 1712.
Daniel Allen b. 4th of 7th mo., 1715.
Richard Allen b. 17th of 10th mo., 1717.
Matthew Allen b. 6th of 8th mo., 1719 and d. at Srewsbury, 1st mo., 1719/20.
Joseph Allen b. 10th of 5th mo., 1723.
James Allen b. 7th of 12th mo., 1725/6.

Children of Thomas Lippincott:
Sarah Lippincott b. 17th of 6th mo., 171_.
Elizabeth Lippincott b. 3rf 3rd mo., 1717.
Mary Lippincott b. 17th of 11th mo., 1719/20.
Zerviah Lippincott b. 23rd of 1st mo., 1723.
Rachel Lippincott b. 23rd of 5th mo., 1726.
Uriah Lippincott b. 10th of 4th mo., 1728.

Children of Thomas and Hannan Lippincott:
Thomas Lippincott b. h of 9th mo., 1742.

Children of George and Deborah Hance Corlies:
Thomas Corlies b. 3rd of 2nd mo., 1700.
Deborah Corlies b. 11th of 2nd mo., 1702.
Joseph Corlies b. 14th of 1st mo., 1704/5.

Benjamin Corlies b. 31st of 6th mo., 1707.
Timothy Corlies b. 10th of 2nd mo., 1710.
Dinah Corlies b. 17th of 11th mo., 1712.
Jacob Corlies b. 14th of 8th mo., 1715.

Thomas Corlies, s/o George and Deborah, d. 1700.
George Corlies d. 10th of 7th mo., 1715.
Timothy Corlies, s/o George and Deborah, d. 23rd of 1st mo., 1733.
Benjamin Corlies, s/o George and Deborah, d. 11th of 8th mo., 1739.
Deborah Corlies, d/o George and Deborah, d. 3rd of 2nd mo., 1757.

Children of George and Joanna Bills Williams:
Obediah Williams b. 14th of 1st mo., 1710.
Hezekiah Williams b. 16th of 2nd mo., 1713.
George Williams b. 6th of 10th mo., 1714.
Hezekiah Williams b. 18th of 10th mo., 1716.
John Williams b. 20th of 1st mo., 1719.
Experience Williams, a dau., b. 12th of 2nd mo., 1721.
Elihu Williams b. 3rd of 3rd mo., 1726.

Hannah Williams, d/o George and Lydia Williams, b. 22nd of 3rd mo., 1743.

John Williams, father of George Williams, d. 22nd of 12th mo., 1719.
Thomas Bills d. 2nd of 2nd mo., 1721.
Joanna Bills, his wife, d. 4th of 4th mo., 1723.
Experience Williams, d/o John and Elizabeth, d. 4th of 4th mo., 1709.
Hezekiah Williams, s/o George and Joanna, d. 3rd of 2nd mo., 1716.
Experience Williams d. 9th of 2nd mo., 1723.
Joanna Williams, wife of George Williams, d. 1st of 2nd mo., 1728.
Mary Williams, wife of George Williams, d. 6st of 2nd mo., 1739.
George Williams d. 15th of 1st mo., 1744.
Obadiah Williams d. 25th of 1st mo., 1748.

Children of John and Elizabeth Williams:
James Williams b. 12th of 10th mo., 1743.
"Daliel" Williams b. 23rd of 11th mo., 1745.
Lydia Williams b. 5th of 2nd mo., 1749.
Elizabeth Williams b. 10th of 6th mo., 1751.
George Williams b. 25th of 8th mo., 1753.
Joanna and Odediah Williams b. abt. 10:00 a.m., 24th of 5th mo., 1758.
Joseph Williams b. 14th of 7th mo., 1760.

Shrewsbury Monthly Meeting

Hannah Williams b. 17th of 12th mo., 1762, at abt. 11:00 p.m.
Mary Williams b. 13th of 9th mo., 1765.

John Williams, s/o George and Joanna, d. 16th of 10th mo., 1768.
Lydia Williams d. 24th of 2nd mo., 1768.
Daniel Williams d. 25th of 10th mo., 1770.
John Williams d. 3rd of 1st mo., 1779.
Obediah Williams d. 19th of 9th mo., 1780.

Children of George and Elizabeth (Abbott) Williams:
Tyla Williams b. 23rd of 12th mo., 1738/9.
Edmond Williams b. 8th of 8th mo., 1740.
George Williams b. 5th of 4th mo., 1743.
Joanna Williams b. 8th of 8th mo., 1745.
Obediah Williams b. 23rd of 12th mo., 1747/8.

George Williams, Jr., d. 23rd of 2nd mo., 1750.

Children of Hezekiah and Sarah (Abbott) Williams:
Samuel Williams b. 8th of 3rd mo., 1741.
Mary Williams b. 16th of 8th mo., 1743.
Abbott Williams b. 20th of 4th mo., 1746.

Sarah Williams d. 2nd of 5th mo., 1746.

Children of Joseph and Margaret Corlies:
Lydia Corlies b. 21st of 6th mo., 1731.
Timothy Corlies b. 5th of 11th mo., 1735.
Deborah Corlies b. 17th of 10th mo., 1739.
Hannah Corlies b. 9th of 7th mo., 1741.
Margaret Corlies b. 5th of 2nd mo., 1746.

Lydia Corlies, wife of Timothy Corlies, b. 4th of 9th mo., 1755.
Joseph Corlies d. 26th of 1st mo., 1784.
Margaret Corlies d. 26th of 2nd mo., 1798, aged abt. 89 yrs.

Children of Jacob and Sarah Corlies:
Britan Corlies b. 27th of 9th mo., 1738.
Elizabeth Corlies b. 8th of 2nd mo., 1740.
Benjamin Corlies b. 2nd of 3rd mo., 1742.
Abegil Corlies b. 2nd of 3rd mo., 1744.
John Corlies b. 2nd of 12th mo., 1745/6.

Early Church Records of Monmouth County

Peter Corlies b. 23rd of 5th mo., 1747.
George Corlies b. 18th of 2nd mo., 1749.
Jacob Corlies b. 24th of 4th mo., 1751.
Jacob Corlies b. 1st of 4th mo., 1755.
Sarah Corlies b. 20th of 6th mo., 1758.

John Corlies, s/o Jacob and Sarah, d. 30th of 4th mo., 1746.
Jacob Corlies, s/o Jacob and Sarah, d. 13th of 6th mo., 1751.
Jacob Corlies, the father, d. 8th of 12th mo., 1767.

Children of Benjamin and Deborah Corlies:
Mary Corlies b. 18th of 5th mo., 1774.
Sarah Corlies b. 19th of 10th mo., 1775.
William Corlies b. 30th of 3rd mo., 1777.
Jacob Corlies b. 15th of 7th mo., 1779.
Elizabeth Corlies b. 25th of 5th mo., 1781.
Deborah Corlies b. 7th of 11th mo., 1783.
Phebe Corlies b. 3rd of 9th mo., 1786.
Abigail Corlies b. 25th of 1st mo., 1793.

Children of Timothy and Rebecca Hance:
Rachel Hance b. 27th of 1st mo., 1738.
David Hance b. 18th of 9th mo., 1739.
Isaac Hance b. 3rd of 2nd mo., 1741.
Jeremiah Hance b. 14th of 7th mo., 1746.
Mary Hance b. 11th of 9th mo., 1749.
Elizabeth Hance b. 22nd of 4th mo., 1751.

Rebecca Hance, wife of Timothy, d. 23rd of 10th mo. 1759.

Children of Isaac and Increase Tilton:
Mary Tilton b. 11th of 7th mo., 1736.
Catherine Tilton b. 10th of 11th mo., 1737.
Phebe Tilton b. 2nd of 8th mo., 1739.
William Tilton b. 14th of 6th mo., 1741.
Anne Tilton b. 9th of 9th mo., 1743.
Nathan Tilton b. 24th of 2nd mo., 1749.

Nathan Tilton, Sr., d. 30th of 3rd mo, 1788.
William Tilton d. 12th of 3rd mo., 1797.

Children of Jedediah and Phebe Allen:

Shrewsbury Monthly Meeting

William Allen b. 17th of 8th mo., 1739.
Ralph Allen b. 25th of 4th mo., 1741.
Miriam Allen b. 15th of 1st mo., 1744.
Jedediah Allen b. 8th of 7th mo., 1750.

Children of Brittain and Dinah (Corlies) White:
Deborah White b. 22nd of 7th mo., 1735.
Elizabeth White b. 25th of 6th mo., 1740.
Rachel White b. 4th of 2nd mo., 1744.
Hannah White b. 4th of 7th mo, 1745.
Britain White b. 2nd of 7th mo., 1747.
Margaret White b. 21st of 2nd mo., 1751.
Joseph White b. 5th of 4th mo., 1753.

Rachel White d. 3rd of 4th mo., 1745.
Joseph White d. 8th of 11th mo., 1755.
Brittain White d. 26th of 12th mo., 1760.

Children of John na Elizabeth Worthley:
John Worthley b. 22nd of 10th mo., 1696.
Lydia Worthley b. 11th of 2nd mo., 1699.
Elizabeth Worthley b. 16th of 7th mo., 1701.
Deborah Worthley b. 12th of 4th mo., 1703.
Sarah Worthley b. 11th of 7th mo., 1706.
Joseph Worthley b. 6th of 5th mo., 1709.
Mary Worthley b. 27th of 7th mo., 1710.
Richard Worthley b. 22nd of 8th mo., 1712.

Joseph Worthley, s/o John and Elizabeth Worthley, d. 5th mo., 1709.
Elizabeth Worthley d. 7th of 2nd mo., 1715.
John Worthley d. 3rd of 10th mo., 1715.
John Worthley d. 8th of 4th mo., 1729.
Sarah Apelgate, d/o John and Elizabeth Worthley, d. 29th of 4th mo., 1741.
Elizabeth Worthley, d/o John and Elizabeth Worthley, d. 9th of 3rd mo., 1749.
Lydia Williams, d/o John and Elizabeth Worthley, d. 18th of 8th mo., 1780.

Children of Levi and Ann White:
Thomas White b. 30th of 9th mo., 1734.
Elizabeth White b. 2nd of 7th mo., 1739.

John White b. 1st of 11th mo., 1745.
Joseph White b. 27th of 6th mo., 1749.

Elizabeth White, d/o Levi and Ann White, d. 20th of 10th mo., 1767.

Children of Thomas and Faith Tilton:
Sarah Tilton b. 10th of 7th mo., 1718.
Rebecca Tilton b. 4th of 5th mo., 1720.
Esther Tilton b. 10th of 3rd mo., 1722.
Elizabeth Tilton b. 26th if 1st mo., 1724.
Hannah Tilton b. 24th of 4th mo., 1726.
Mary Tilton b. 16th of 2nd mo., 1728.
Rachel Tilton b. 14th of 5th mo., 1730.
Thomas Tilton b. 14th of 2nd mo., 1732.
Patience Tilton b. 3rd of 11th mo., 1735/6.
Lydia Tilton b. 5th of 1st mo., 1738.
John Tilton b. 5th of 3rd mo., 1739.
Deborah Tilton b. 21st of 10th mo., 1740.
Joseph Tilton b. 24th of 10th mo., 1741.

Thomas Tilton d. 4th of 1st mo., 1763, aged 78 yrs.

William Cook b. 7th of 3rd mo., 1721; mar. 3rd mo., 1744.
Elizabeth Cook, his wife, b. 7th of 12th mo., 1725/6.
Their children:
Jacob Cook b. 23rd of 10th mo., 1744.
Job Cook b. 22nd of 2nd mo., 1750.

William Cook and Lydia Corlies mar. 4th mo., 1752.
Their children:
Margaret Cook b. 5th of 2nd mo., 1753.
William Cook b. 22nd of 4th mo., 1755.
Lydia Cook b. 17th of 6th mo., 1757.
Phebe Cook b. 30th of 6th mo., 1759.
Joseph Cook b. 23rd of 11th mo., 1761.
Hannah Cook b. 11th of the 11th mo., 1761 at 7:00 p.m.

Elizabeth White, wife of William Cook, d. 10th of 7th mo., 1750.
William Cook, the father, d. 22nd of 9th mo., 1767.

Shrewsbury Monthly Meeting

Children of Thomas and Elizabeth (Borden) White:
Elizabeth White b. 7th of 12th mo., 1725/6.
Samuel White b. 6th of 12th mo., 1727/8.
Mary White b. 19th of 2nd mo., 1730.
Hannah White b. 10th of 2nd mo.,1734.
Thomas White b. 17th of 7th mo., 1736.
Lydia White b. 6th of 4th mo., 1739.
Sarah White b. 3rd of 5th mo., 1741.
Rachel White b. 5th of 9th mo., 1743.
Jacob White b. 9th of 5th mo., 1746.
Zilpah White b. 29th of 11th mo., 1748/9.

Elizabeth Cook, d/o Thomas and Elizabeth White, d. 10th of 7th mo., 1750
Samuel White, s/o Thomas and Elizabeth White, d. 27th of 9th mo., 1759.
Elizabeth White, wife of Thomas White, d. 6th of 3rd mo., 1760.

Thomas White, s/o Samuel and Anne White, b. 26th of 11th mo., 1756.
Curtis White, s/o Samuel and Anne White, b. 8th of 6th mo., 1758.
Meribah White (twin with above), s/o Samuel and Anne White, b. 8th of
    6th mo., 1758.

Children of John and Elizabeth Burden:
Mary Burden b. 4th of 1st mo., 1739.
John Burden b. 1st of 7th mo., 1742.
Joel Burden b. 6th of 8th mo., 1744.
Elisabeth Burden b. 2nd of 2nd mo., 1746.
Anna Burden b. 30th of 9th mo., 1749.
Joan Burden b. 24th og 3rd mo., 1753.
Hannah Burden b. 15th of 8th mo., 1755.
Lydia Burden b. 30th of 11th mo., 1759.

Lydia Burden, d/o John and Elizabeth Burden, 22nd of 4th mo., 1763.

Children of Joseph and Katharine Mitton:
Israel Mitton b. 4th of 9th mo., 1761.
Margaret Mitton b. 24th of 6th mo., 1765.
Abigail Mitton b. 9th of 10th mo., 1769.

John Hance, of Rumson, and Catherine Wapels mar. 13th of 1st mo.,
    1760.
Their children:
Wapels Hance.

John Hance.
Isaac Hance.
Rachel Hance, mar. Asher Corlies, of Rumson.
Elizabeth Hance, mar. George Wooley.

John Hance, above, b. 20th of 8th mo., 1762 and mar. Ann Borden, d/o James and Susan (Robins) Borden. She was b. 17th of 6th mo., 1778.

Children of James and Leah (White, widow of Wilber) Tucker:
John Tucker b. 25th of 5th mo., 1718.
Ruth Tucker b. 16th of 2nd mo., 1722.
Elizabeth Tucker b. 25th of 5th mo., 1724.
James Tucker b. 30th of 8th mo., 1727.
Hannah Tucker b. 9th of 1st mo., 1730.
Samuel Tucker b. 8th of 8th mo., 1735.

James Tucker, s/o James and Leah, d. 25th of 3rd mo., 1755.
Hannah Wardell, d/o James and Leah, d. 25th of 12th mo., 1757.
Ruth Wooley, d/o James and Leah, d. 17th of 10th mo., 1759.
Leah Tucker wife of James Tucker, d. 18th of 2nd mo., 1767, aged 73 yrs.

Children of John and Phebe Tucker:
Leah Tucker b. 11th of 12th mo., 1745.
Elisabeth Tucker b. 13th of 1st mo., 1750.
Margaret Tucker b. 20th of 8th mo., 1755.

Elisabeth Tucker, d/o John and Phebe Tucker, d. 13th of 9th mo., 1764.
John Tucker d. 6th of 9th mo., 1793.

Children of James Tucker, Jr,. And Margaret:
Hannah Tucker b. 16th of 3rd mo., 1752.
Elizabeth Tucker b. 17th of 12th mo., 1753.

Elizabeth Tucker, d/o James Tucker, Jr., and Margaret, d. 27th of 2nd mo., 1758.

Children of Samuel and Elizabeth Tucker:
James Tucker b. 6th of 11th mo., 1761.
Brittain Tucker b. 3rd of 10th mo., 1763.

Shrewsbury Monthly Meeting

Children of Robert and Miriam Tilton:
Miriam Tilton b. 18th of 9th mo., 1733.
Deborah Tilton b. 31st of 11th mo., 1734.
Valariah Tilton b. 4th of 6th mo., 1736.
Obediah Tilton b. 18th of 10th mo., 1738.
Dinah Tilton b. 31st of 11th mo., 1740.
Miriam Tilton b. 28th of 5th mo., 1743.
Robert Tilton b. 18th of 10th mo., 1745.
David Tilton b. 20th of 7th mo/.749.
Jedediah Tilton b. 24th of 7th mo., 1752.
Robert Tilton b. 31st of 5th mo., 1756.

Robert Tilton, s/o Robert and Miriam Tilton, d. 4th of 10th mo. 1754.
Robert Tilton, s/o Robert and Miriam Tilton, d. 29th of 12th mo., 1756.
Valariah Tilton, d/o Robert and Miriam Tilton, d. 2nd of 8th mo., 1763.
Margaret Tilton, d/o Robert and Miriam Tilton, d. 31st of 8th mo., 1762.
Robert Tilton, the father, d. 23rd of 10th mo., 1762.
Miriam Lowrie, the mother, d. 7th of 3rd mo., 1787.

Children of Elihu and Ann Wady Williams:
Humphry Wady Williams b.   7th of 4th mo., 1751.
Mary Williams b. 31st of 7th mo., 1753.
Hunphrey Williams b. 29th of 4th mo., 1756.
Amos Williams b. 24th of 4th mo., 1758.
Israel Williams b. 13th of 5th mo., 1760.
Samuel Williams b. 26th of 6th mo., 1762.
Sarah Williams b. 1st of 7th mo., 1764.

Humphry Wady Williams, s/o Elihu and Ann Wady Williams, d. 6th mo., 1751.
Humphrey Wady, father of Ann Wady, d. 2nd of 10th mo., 1759, aged abt. 70 yrs.
Amos Williams, s/o Elihu and Ann Williams, d. 17th of 8th mo., 1763.

Children of Isaac and Rachel Hance:
Timothy Hance b. 21st if 3rd mo., 1714.
John Hance b. 6th of 3rd mo., 1720.
Jacob Hance b. 3rd of 3rd mo., 1729.

Rachel Hance d. 30th of 6 mo., 1734.
Contant Hance d. ____.
Isaac Hance, husband of the above named woman, d.5th of 9th mo., 1764.

Children of Jacob and Ann Hance:
Rachel Hance b. 23rd of 12th mo., 1751.
Thomas Hance b. 30th of 10th mo., 1753.
Sarah Hance b. 14th of 10th mo., 1755.

Children of Jacob and Elizabeth Hance:
William Hance b. 20th of 5th mo., 1760.
Deborah Hance b. 5th of 10th mo., 1762.

Elizabeth Corlies Hance, wife of Jacob Hance, d. 16th of 10th mo., 1736.
Ann Hance, wife of Jacob, d. 22nd of 8th mo., 1757.
Jacob Hance d. 21st of 6th mo., 1798.

Children of Ebenezer and Sarah (Tilton) Cook:
Hannah Cook b. 15th of 3rd mo. 1742.
Faith Cook b. 18th of 1st mo., 1747.
Mary Cook b. 21st of 5th mo., 1752.
Thomas Cook b. 26th of 9th mo., 1757.
William Cook b. 28th of 3rd mo., 1759.

Children of Obediah ad Hannah Tilton:
Robert Tilton b. 16th of 2nd mo., 1764.
Margaret Tilton b. 26th of 10th mo., 1768.
Miriam Tilton b. 2nd of 3rd mo., 1772.
Joseph Tilton b. 18th of 10th mo., 1775.
Hannah Tilton b. 12th of 9th mo., 1781.

Hannah Tilton, d/o Obediah and Hannah Tilton, b. 30th of 3rd mo., 1786.

Children of John and Patience Lippincott:
James Lippincott b. 9th of 10th mo., 1732/3.
Dinah Lippincott b. 12th of 11th mo., 1734/5.
Elizabeth Lippincott b. 1st of 10th mo., 1736.
Sarah Lippincott b. 27th of 9th mo., 1738.
Hannah Lippincott b. 8th of 1st mo., 1760/1.
Huldah Lippincott b. 13th of 5th mo., 1743.
Mary Lippincott b. 2nd of 8th mo., 1745.
Henry Lippincott b. 22nd of 10th mo., 1750
Joseph Lippincott b. 14th of 7th mo., 1753.
Patience Lippincott b. 27th of 3rd mo., 1757.

Shrewsbury Monthly Meeting

Patience Lippincott d. 14th of 6th mo., 1793.

Children of Joseph and Hannah Allen:
Abagail Allen b. 28th of 9th mo., 1759.
Miriam Allen b. 27th of 3rd mo., 1761.
Joseph Allen b. 15th of 4th mo., 1763.
Jedediah Allen b. 5th of 3rd mo., 1765.

Abigail Allen d. 4th of 12th mo., 1763.
William Lippincott d. 6th of 1st mo., 1765, aged abt. 83 yrs.

Children of Joseph and Rebecca Potter:
Jacob Potter b. 23rd of 2nd mo., 1737.
James Potter b. 20th of 9th mo., 1738.
Catherine Potter b. 28th of 11th mo., 1740/1.
Peter Potter b. 20th of 3rd mo., 1743.
Abigail Potter b. 20th of 3rd mo., 1745.
Rebecca Potter b. 18th of 9th mo., 1747.
Sarah Potter b. 30th of 10th mo., 1749.

Daniel Potter, s/o Joseph and Abigail Potter, b. 25th of 5th mo., 1756.
Lydia Potter, d/o Joseph and Abigail Potter, b. 2nd of 2nd mo., 1758.
Joseph Potter, s/o Joseph and Abigail Potter, b. 27th of 4th mo., 1760.

Children of Peter and Lydia Tilton:
Abigail Tilton b. 22nd of 7th mo., 1723.
Daniel Tilton b. 5th of 9th mo., 1725.
Amos Tilton b. 6th of 8th mo., 1727.
Lydia Tilton b. 15th of 3rd mo., 1731.
Hannah Tilton b. 27th of 8th mo., 1735.

Amos Tilton d. 15th of 10th mo., 1765.

John Lippincott b. 20th of 2nd mo., 1725.
Mary Hulet b. 7th of 2nd mo., 1727.

Their children:
Diana Lippincott b. 17th of 6th mo., 1751.
William Lippincott b. 15th of 1st mo., 1753.
Jacob Lippincott b. 15th of 9th mo., 1755.
Lydia Lippincott b. 2nd of 3rd mo., 1758.
Margreat Lippincott b. 3rd of 12th month, 1760.

Early Church Records of Monmouth County

John Lippincott b. 21st of 3rd mo., 1763.

Diana Lippincott, d/o John and Mary, d. 12th of 8th mo., 1751.
John Lippincott d. 28th of 12th mo., 1764.

Children of John and Elizabeth Brinly:
William Brinly b. 21st of 10th mo., 1745.
John Brinly b. 13th of 9th mo., 1748.
Lydia Brinly b. 3rd of 6th mo., 1751.
Joseph Brinly b. 25th of 12th mo., 1754.
Deborah Brinly b. 18th of 3rd mo., 1758.
Reap Brinly b. 4th of 10th mo., 1759.
Jacob Brinly b. 4th of 12th mo/, 1763.

Children of Brittain and Ann Corlies:
David Corlies b. 9th of 9th mo., 1765 at 9:00 p.m.
Lydia Corlies b. 9th of 9th mo., 1765 at 9:00 p.m.
Sarah Corlies b. 28th of 8th mo., 1767.

Children of Benjamin and Rebecca Jackson:
Elizabeth Jackson b. 14th of 7th mo., 1763.
Rebecca Jackson b. 1st of 10th mo., 1765.
Lydia Jackson b. 3rd of 1st mo., 1768.
Ann Jackson b. 5th of 11th mo., 1770.
Benjamin Jackson b. 13th of 2nd mo., 1773.

Elizabeth Jackson, d/o Benjamin and Rebecca, d. 25th of 1st mo., 1780.
Rebecca Jackson, wife of Benjamin, d. 21st of 1st mo., 1791, aged 53 yrs., 10 dys.

Children of Edman and Elizabeth (Scott) Lafretra:
Edman Lafetra b. 27th of 9th mo., 1767.
Hannah Lafetra b. 27th of 9th mo., 1767.
Anna Lafetra b. 12th of 3rd mo, 1769.
Elizabeth Lafetra b. 29th of 1st mo., 1771 and mar. Daniel Allen.

Children of Edmund and his 2nd wife, Sarah (Potter) Lafetra.
Jacob Lafetra b. 1777.
Lydia Lafetra b. 1779.
Rebecca Lafetra b. 1782.
Sarah Lafetra b. 1787 and d. 1794.

Shrewsbury Monthly Meeting

Children of Richard and Alice Lawrence:
Sarah Lawrence b. 26th of 9th mo., 1763.
Richard Lawrence b. 3rd of 4th mo., 1765.
Mary Lawrence b. 16th of 1st mo., 1767.
Elizabeth Lawrence b. 11th of 11th mo., 1769.
Margaret Lawrence b. 29th of 3rd mo., 1772.
Philadelphia Ann Lawrence b. 1st of 5th mo., 1775.

Philadelphia Ann Lawrence d. 23rd of 8th mo., 1789.
Mary Lawrence d. 7th of 6th mo., 1791.

Children of Hugh and Mary Jackson:
Mary Jackson b. 13th of 6th mo., 1746.
Benjamin Jackson b. 2nd of 10th mo., 1748.
Isaac Jackson b. 18th of 6th mo., 1750.
William Jackson b. 22nd of 6th mo., 1752.
Hugh Jackson b. 25th of 3rd mo., 1754.
Mary Jackson b. 14th of 6th mo., 1756.
Peter Jackson b. 19th of 7th mo., 1758
Joseph Jackson b. 21st of 9th mo., 1760.

Children of Thomas and Maraget Curtis:
Joseph Curtis b. 5th of 2nd mo., 1769.
Meribah Curtis b. 25th of 2nd mo., 1770.
Elihu Curtis b. 18th of 7th mo., 1772.
John Curtis b. 17th of 7th mo., 1775.

Margaret Curtis d. 10th of 11th mo., 1779.

Hugh Jackson, s/o Hugh and Mary Jackson, b. 2nd of 10th mo., 1754.
Rebecca Jackson, his wife, b. 10th of 10th mo., 1763.

Their children:
Deborah Jackson b. 2nd of 11th mo., 1782.
Morris Jackson b. 1st of 4th mo., 1786.
Rebecca Jackson b. 31st of 8th mo., 1788.
Hugh Jackson b. 9th of 10th mo., 1790.
Peter Jackson b. 23rd of 4th mo., 1792.
William Jackson b. 26th of 3rd mo., 1794.
Isaac Jackson b. 9th of 10th mo., 1795.
James M. Jackson b. 11th of 9th mo., 1797.
Mary Jackson b. 19th of 3rd mo., 1799.

Anne Jackson b. 25th of 2nd mo., 1801.
Benjamin Jackson b. 3rd of 11th mo., 1803.
Nathan Jackson b. 15th of 8th mo., 1805.

The 2nd son died at birth.
Rebecca Jr. died aged 6 yrs, 4 mo.
Isaac died aged 2 mo.

Children of Jacob and Ann Laing:
David Laing b. 20th of 10th mo., 1759.
Margaret Laing b. 0th of 9th mo., 1761.
Ann Laing b. 20th of 3rd mo., 1764.
Jacob Laing b. 20st of 9th mo., 1766.
Isaac Laing b. 21st of 2nd mo., 1769.
Rebecca Laing b. 20th of 3rd mo., 1771.
Abraham Laing b. 2nd of 11th mo., 1772.

Ann Laing d. 23rd of 6th mo., 1775.

Children of William and Hannah Jackson:
Ann Jackson b. 15th of 2nd mo., 1758.
Sarah Jackson b. 6th of 6th mo., 1759.
Mary Jackson b. 24th of 10th mo., 1761.
Elizabeth Jackson b. 22nd of 8th mo., 1763.
William Jackson b. 12th of 11th mo., 1765.
Deborah Jackson b. 25th of 1st mo., 1768.
Rebeccah Jackson b. 10th of 8th mo., 1769.
Deborah Jackson b. 1st of 5th mo., 1771.
Meribah Jackson b. 18th of 6th mo., 177_ .

Sarah Jackson d. 22nd of 8th mo., 1777.

Thomas Tilton, s/o William and Hester Tilton, b. 14th of 4th mo., 1771.
Amos Tilton, s/o William and Hester Tilton, b. 7th of 10th mo., 1774.

Joseph Wardell b. 26th of 3rd mo., 1724.

Children of Joseph and Hannah Wardell:
Daniel Wardell b. 23rd of 8th mo., 1754.
James Wardell b. 10th of 7th mo., 1756.
John Nicholson Wardell b. 10th of 2nd mo., 1763.
Charles Wardell b. 10th of 9th mo., 1766.

Shrewsbury Monthly Meeting

Margaret Wardell b. 23rd of 9th mo., 1768.
Alice Wardell b. 2nd of 11th mo., 1770.
Joseph Wardell b. 7th of 8th mo., 1776.
Hannah Maragret Wardell b. 27th of 4th mo., 1778.

George Wardell, s/o Daniel Wardell of Middletown, b. 25th of 12th mo., 1786.
Joseph Wardell d. 28th of 11th mo., 1776.
Alica Wardell d. 29th of 3rd mo., 1777.
Margaret Wardell d. 21st of 4th mo., 1777.
Daniel Wardell d. 5th of 8th mo., 1787.

Jacob Burdg b. 5th of 4th mo. 1743, OS.
Judith Burdg b. 9th of 5th mo., 1751, OS

Their children:
Lydia Burdg b. 23rd of 8th mo., 1770, NS.
Joseph Burdg b. 31st of 3rd mo., 1772, NS.
Anthony Burdg b. 12th of 10th mo., 1774, NS.

Peter White b. 19th of 6th mo., 1746.
Payience White b. 12th of 8th mo., 1757.

Their children:
Amos White b. 15th of 1st mo., 1777.
Mary White b. 10th of 11th mo., 1778.
Jean White b. 1st of 8th mo., 1780.
Sarah White b. 25th of 10th mo., 1780.
Hannah White b. 4th of 7th mo., 1783.
Phebe White b. 19th of 4th mo., 1785.
Abigail White b. 29th of 8th mo., 1787.
Peter White b. 26th of 3rd mo., 1789.
Samuel White b. 2nd of 4th mo., 1791.
Allen White b. 8th of 10th mo., 1793.
Elizabeth White b. 18th of 2nd mo., 1796.
Jane White b. 31st of 10th mo., 1798.

Jean White d. 5th of 8th mo., 1780.
Abigail White d. 26 th of 11th mo., 1789.
Samuel White d. 27th of 8th mo., 1793.
Peter White, the father, d. 26th of 3rd mo., 1798.

Children of Edmond and Miriam (Tilton) Williams:
Elizabeth Williams b. 18th of 8th m., 1763.
Margaret Williams b. 5th of 12th mo., 1765.
Tylee Williams b. 30th of 1st mo., 1768.
Phebe Williams b. 16th of 5th mo., 1771.
Anne Williams b. 8th of 6th mo., 1774.
Mary Williams b. 31st of 12th mo., 1776.
Miriam Williams b. 29th of 1st mo., 1781.

Elizabeth Williams mar. Joseph Allen.
Tylee Williams mar. Elizabeth Hartshorn 10th of 1st mo., 1792.
Margaret Williams mar. Joseph Throckmorton.
Phebe Williams mar. Henry Burr.
Anne Williams mar. Nimrod Woodward.
Mary Williams mar. Samuel W. Tenbrook, M. D.
Miriam Williams mar. Seth Lippincott.

Children of Tylee and Elizabeth Williams:
Elizabeth Williams b. 1792 and mar. Joseph Parker.
Edmond Williams b. 1795.
Miriam Williams b. 1797 and mar. Benjamin Corlies.
Hannah Williams b. 1800 and mar. Joseph Wooley.

Children of James and Rebecca Williams:
Champlis Williams b. 29th of 2nd mo., 1768.
John Williams b. 27th of 10th mo., 1769.
Daniel Williams b. 4th of 7th mo., 1771.

Daniel Williams, s/o James and Rebecca Williams, d. 18th of 3rd mo., 1772.
Rebecca Williams, d/o James and Rebecca Williams, d. 13th of 4th mo., 1774.

Robert White b. 24th of 11th mo., 1753.
Esther Crawford, his wife, b. 3rd of 2nd mo., 1762.
They mar. 13th of 1st mo., 1780.
Their children:
Crawford White b. 4th of 6th mo., 1782.
Catharine White b. 25th of 3rd mo., 1784.
Tylee White b. 29th of 10th mo., 1786.
Robert Bowne White b. 17th of 10th mo., 1788.
Lydia Grover White b. 20th of 12th mo., 1791.

Shrewsbury Monthly Meeting

William C. White b. 8th of 9th mo., 1794.

Esther White, wife of Robert, d. 10th of 5th mo., 1797.

Children of George and Martha Parker;
James Parker b. 25th of 2nd mo., 1764.
John Parker b. 7th of 6th mo., 1766.
Elizabeth Parker b. 4th of 4th mo., 1769.
George Parker b. 25th of 10th mo., 1772.
Susannah Parker b. 19th of 4th mo., 1775.
Jacob Parker b. 23rd of 4th mo., 1778.
Phebe Parker b. 22nd of 5th mo., 1781.
Martha Parker b. 27th of 7th mo., 1784.
Children of David and Sarah Tilton:
William Tilton b. 4th of 7th mo., 1773.
David Tilton b. 8th of 1st mo., 1885.

Children of Peter and Margaret (Tucker) Corlis:
John Corlies b. 4th of 11th mo., 1775.
Peter Corlies b. 30th of 7th mo., 1778.
Jacob Corlies b. 15th of 8th mo., 1781.
Phebe Corlies b. 1st of 4th mo., 1783.
Leah Corlies b. 27th of 11th mo., 1786.
Sarah Corlies b. 2nd of 8th mo., 1789.
Edward Pentington Corlies b. 22nd of 4th mo., 1793.

Jacob Corlies d. 5th of 3rd mo., 1782.

Children of Benjamin and Hannah Jackson:
Hugh Jackson b. 22nd of 9th mo., 1778.
Joseph Jackson b. 24th of 11th mo., 1780.
Elizabeth Jackson b. 26th of 3rd mo., 1782.
Mary Jackson b. 12th of 8th mo., 1784.
Mercy Jackson b. 10th of 11th mo., 1785.
Micajah Jackson b. 22nd of 8th mo., 1789.
Jesse Jackson b. 1st of 5th mo., 1795.
Benjamin Jackson b. 7th of 10th mo., 1797.

Mary Jackson d. 22nd of 9th mo., 1769.
Elizabeth Jackson b. 19th of 4th mo., 1795.

Children of Jacob and Elizabeth (Tucker) Wooley:

Benjamin Wooley b. 10th of 9th mo., 1785.
Catherine Wooley b. 7th of 5th mo., 1787.
Jacob Wooley, Jr., b. 23rd of 5th mo., 1789.
Elizabeth Wooley b. 5th of 9th mo., 1793.
Eden Wooley b. 1st of 3rd mo., 1801.
Emeline Wooley b. 9th of 5th mo., 1808.

Children of Elihu and Mary (Jackson) Wooley:
Deborah Wooley b. 2nd of 12th mo., 1776.
Samuel Wooley b. 19th of 9th mo., 1778.
Ruth Wooley b. 13th of 11th mo., 1781.
Mary Wooley b. _ of 5th mo., 1785.
Elihu Wooley b. 16th of _ mo., 1788.
Tylee Wooley b. 20th of 7th mo., 1781.
William Wooley b. 27th of 6th m., 1793.

Mary Wooley mar. a Conover of Middletown and moved to Ohio.
Elihu Wooley moved to Shelby Co., Ohio.
Tylee Wooley mar. a Conover and moved to Ohio.
William Wooley resided at Mattawan.

Goerge Parker d. 15th of 11th mo., 1798.

Joseph Jackson b. 20th of 12th mo., 1724.
Children of Joseph and Sarah (Wooley) Jackson:
Lydia Jackson b. 15th of 11th mo., 1752.

Meribah Jackson b. 15th of 6th mo., 1754.

Benjamin Wooley b. 15th of 12th mo., 1755.
John Wooley b. 11th of 5th mo., 1757.

{Sarah Jackson b. 20th of 8th mo., 1759.}
{Phebe Jackson b. 20th of 8th mo., 1759.}

Children of Joseph Jackson and his 2nd wife, Sarah:
Sarah Jackson b.11th of 12th mo., 1765.
Ann Jackson b. 20th of 2nd mo., 1767.
Deborah Jackson b. 14th of 7th mo., 1769.
Joseph Jackson b. 22nd of 1st mo., 1772.
William Jackson b. 2nd of 3rd mo., 1774.
Jonathan Jackson b. 6th of 10th mo., 1776.

Shrewsbury Monthly Meeting

Lawrence Jackson b. 8th of 11th mo., 1778.
{George Jackson b. 22nd of 2nd mo., 1780.}
{Rebeckah Jackson b. 22nd of 2nd mo., 1780.}
Elizabeth Jackson b. 14th of 8th mo., 1784.
Esther Jackson b. 29th of 3rd mo., 1788.
Joseph Jackson d. 9th of 11th mo., 1799.
Sarah Jackson, wife of Joseph, mother of 6 children, d. 20th of 8th mo., 1759.
Sarah Jackson, d/o Joseph and Sarah, d. 16th of 12th mo., 1759.
Willaim Jackson, father of Joseph, d. 10th of 3rd mo., 1776.
Meribah Jackson, d/o Joseph and wife of Nathan Jackson, d. 19th of 3rd mo., 1777.
Ann Jackson, mother of Joseph, d. 7th mo., 1777.
Jonathan Jackson, s/o Joseph, d. 7th mo., 1777.
Joseph Jackson, s/o Joseph, d. 7th of 10th mo., 1781.
Esther Jackson, d/o Joseph, d. 20th of 9th mo., 1793.

Children of William and Acsah Hance:
Achsah Hance b. 9th of 11th mo., 1765.
Revo Hance b. 9th of 11th mo., 1790.

Children of George and Patience Corlies:
Benjamin Corlies b. 19th of 8th mo., 1775.
Jacob Corlies b. 8th of 4th mo., 1778.
Joseph Corlies b. 21st of 2nd mo., 1780.
Sarah Corlies b. 14th of 10th mo., 1781.
Joseph Corlies b. 5th of 10th mo., 1784.
Mary Corlies b. 2nd of 2nd mo., 1787.

Joseph Corlies, s/o George, d. 5th of 9th mo., 1781.

Children of William and Ruth (Wooley) Jackson:
Samuel Jackson b. 5th of 4th mo., 1778.
James Jackson b. 20th of 4th mo., 1780.
Mary Jackson b. 14th of 5th mo., 1783.
Brittain Jackson b. 1st of 8th mo., 1785.
Willaim Jackson b. 4th of 10th mo., 1787.
Leah Jackson b. 18th of 1st mo., 1791.
Hartshorn Jackson b. 26th of 11th mo., 1795.
Rebeckah Jackson b. 7th of 9th mo., 1799.

Children of Peter and Lydia Wolcott:

Joseph Wolcott b. 6th of 8th mo., 1778.
John Wolcott b. 22nd of 3rd mo., 1780.
Abigail Wolcott b. 31st of 3rd mo., 1782.
Clementine Wolcott b. 28th of 8th mo., 1784.
Lydia Wolcott b. 7th of 8th mo., 1786.
Hannah Wolcott b. 11th of 11th mo., 1788.
Peter Tilton Wolcott b. 27th of 5th mo., 1791.
Benjamin Wolcott b. 15th of 8th mo., 1793.
{Daniel Wolcott b. 31st of 5th mo., 1795.}
{Abigail Wolcott b. 31st of 5th mo., 1795.}
Samuel Potter Wolcott b. 7th of 11th mo., 1796.
Henry Wolcott b. 22nd of 5th mo., 1799.

Peter Wolcott, father of the above children, b. 28th of 9th mo., 1753.
Lydia Wolcott, mother of the above children, b. 2nd of 2nd mo., 2758.
Abigail Wolcott, d/o Peter and Lydia, d. 22nd of 2nd mo., 1787, aged 4-10-22.
Benjamin Wolcott, s/o Peter and Lydia, d. 22nd of 3rd mo., 1794, aged 7 mo., 7 dys.
Abigail Wolcott, 2nd d/o Peter and Lydia, d. 29th of 8th mo., 1795.
Daniel Wolcott, sd/o Peter and Lydia, d. 21st of 9th mo., 1795.

Manuel Pearce b. 9th of 6th mo., 1758.
Elizabeth Pearce, his wife, b. 12th of 5th mo., 1761.
Their children:
Mirabah Pearce b. 3rdof 10th mo., 1790.
Jeremiah Pearce b. 24th of 9th mo., 1791.
Benjamin Pearce b. 9th of 3rd mo., 1793.
Nathan Allen Pearce b. 5th of 1st mo., 1795.
Elizabeth Pearce b. 1st of 4th mo., 1796.
Elizabeth Pearce b. 4th of 1st mo., 1801.
Ann Pearce b. 23rd of 9th mo., 1802.
Lydia Pearce b. 19th of 12th mo., 1803.

Jeremiah Pearce, s/o Manuel and Elizabeth, d. 8th of 12th mo., 1791.

Children of Samuel and Elizabeth (Allen) Lafetra:
Elizabeth Lafetra b. 5th of 7th mo., 1793.
Nathan Lafetra b. 19th of 11th mo., 1797.
Rilee Lafetra b. 27th of 9th mo., 1800 and mar. Mirabah Wolcott.

Shrewsbury Monthly Meeting

William Penn Lafetra b. 8th of 5th mo., 1803 and mar. Elizabeth Wooley.
James Lafetra b. 19th of 3rd mo., 1808 and mar. Sarah Wolcott.
Henry Lafetra b. 9th of 9th mo., 1810.

Elizabeth Lafetra, d/o Samuel and Elizabeth (Lippincott) Lafetra, d. 7th of 3rd mo., 1795.

Children of James and Elizabeth Lafetra:
Samuel Lafetra b. 17th of 3rd mo., 1768 and mar. Elizabeth Allen.
John Lafetra b. 3rd of 6th mo., 1769 and mar. Hannah Card.
Joseph Lafetra b. 19th of 2nd mo., 1776 and mar. Ruth Wooley.
Deborah Lafetra b. 22nd of 3rd mo., 1778 and mar. Hugh Jackson.
Nathan Lafetra b. 17th of 4th mo., 1780 and mar. ____ Wolcott.

George Wolcott Lafetra, s/o James and Meribah Lafetra, b. 30th of 5th mo., 1793, and mar. Elizabeth Throckmorton.
Tylee W. Lafetra, s/o James and Meribah Lafetra, b. 23rd of 1st mo., 1795, and mar. Catherine Herring.
Benjamin Jackson Lafetra, s/o James and Meribah Lafetra, b. 2nd of 5th mo., 1798, and mar. Rebecca Wainwright.
Robert Erilman Lafetra, s/o James and Meribah Lafetra, b. 28th of 12th mo., 1799 and mar. Mary Carter.
Elizabeth Lafetra d. 26th of 10th mo., 1784.

Children of Ruben and Mary Shreve:
Elizabeth Shreeve b. 9th of 9th mo., 1796.
Sarah Shreeve b. 26th of 9th mo., 1799.
Susannah Shreeve b. 13th of 7th mo., 1801.
Mary Shreeve b. 14th of 7th mo., 1803.
Martha Shreeve b. 21st of 9th mo., 1805.
Phebe Ann Shreve b. 16th of 12th mo., 1807.

Mary Hartshorne, d/o William and Sarah Hartshorne, d. 8th of 4th mo., 1799.

Children of Joseph and Elizabeth (Williams) Allen:
Hannah Allen b. 22nd of 6th mo., 1786.
Edmond W. Allen b. 14th of 8th mo., 1783.
Phebe Allen b. 22nd of 11th mo., 1791.
Miriam Allen b. 23rd of 9th mo., 1793.
Joseph W, Allen b. 15th of 6th mo., 1796.
Elizabeth Allen b. 22nd of 10th mo., 1799.

Caroline Allen b. 20th of 5th mo., 1802.
Jane Allen b. 19th of 10th mo., 1806.

Children of Jedediah and Ann Allen:
George Allen b. 1st of 12th mo., 1789.
John Allen b. 18th of 9th mo., 1791.
Elihu Allen b. 24th of 12th mo., 1793.
Phebe Allen b. 21st od 1st mo., 1797.
Samuel Allen b. 25th of 11th mo., 1799.
Joseph Allen b. 31st off 8th mo., 1802.
Charles W. Allen b. 29th of 10th mo., 1805.

Hannah Allen d. 16th of 1st mo., 1787, aged 6 mo., 24 dys.

Children of Tylee and Elizabeth Williams:
Elizabeth Williams b. 19th of 11th mo., 1792.
Edmund Williams b. 19th of 7th mo., 1795 and d. 1st of 8th mo., 1800.
Miriam Tilton Williams b. 8th of 10th mo., 1797 and d. 11th of 10th mo., 1797.
Hannah Hartshorne Williams b. 4th of 8th mo., 1800.
Phebe Williams b. 30th of 12th mo., 1802.
Edmond Tylee Williams b. 30th of 10th mo., 1804.
Esek Hartshorne Williams b. 1st of 5th mo., 1807.

Children of William and Elizabeth Parker:
Mary Parker b. 16th of 6th mo., 1788.
Joseph Parker b. 16th of 5th mo., 1790.
Willaim Parker b. 10th of 9th mo., 1793.
Benjamin Parker b. 23rd of 4th mo., 1795.
Hannah Parker b. 22nd of 7th mo., 1798.
Robert W. Parker b. 31st of 8th mo., 1801.
Elizabeth Parker b. 15th of 11th mo., 1804.

Children of Briton and Sarah Corlies:
Ann Corlies b. 16th of 7th mo., 1781.
Elizabeth Corlies b. 3rd of 1st mo., 1783.
Briton Corlies b. 12th of 7th mo., 1784 and d. 22nd of 5th mo., 1788, aged 3-10-10.
Deborah Corlies b. 7th of 4th mo., 1787 and d. 16th of 7th mo., 1790, aged 3-3-9.
Joseph W. Corlies b. 3rd of 7th mo., 1791.
Jacob W. Corlies b. 20th of 3rd mo., 1793.

Shrewsbury Monthly Meeting

Benjamin W. Corlies b. 9h of 2nd mo., 1797.

Brittain White, the father, b. 2nd of 7th mo., 1747.
Elizabeth White, the mother, b. ___ and d. 5th of 12th mo., 1795.
Their children:
George Allen White b. 1st of 12th mo., 1775.
Brittain White b. 29th of 6th mo., 1778.
Joseph White b. 25th of 1st mo., 1781.
Lydia White b. 10th of 9th mo., 1783 and d. in New York, 25th of 1st mo., 1785, aged 1-4-15.
Samuel White b. 16th of 3rd mo., 1787.
Lydia White b. 14th of 10th mo., 1788.
Thomas Chalkley White b. 25th of 9th mo., 1790.
Elizabeth White b. 12th of 10th mo., 1792.
Rebeckah Wryte White b. 8th of 10th mo., 1794.

Thomas Cook, s/o Ebenezer and Sarah Cook, 26th of 9th mo., 1757.
Rachel Borden Cook, his wife, b. 16th of 2nd mo., 1763.
Their children:
Richard Cook b. 27th of 2nd mo., 1784.
Ebenezer Cook b. 26th of 7th mo., 1786.
{Sarah Cook b. 21st of 9th mo., 1787.}
{Hannah Cook b. 21st of 9th mo., 1787.}
Thomas Cook b. 6th of 12th mo., 1790.
Thomas Cook b. 11th of 6th mo., 1793.

Children of Israel and Bathsheba Williams:
John Williams b. 21st of 2nd mo., 1782 and d. 18th of 9th mo., 1800, aged 18-6-24.
Daniel Williams b. 2nd of 2nd mo., 1784.
Hannah Williams b. 1st of 1st mo., 1786.
George Williams b. 10th of 6th mo., 1787 and d. 13th of 2nd mo., 1792, aged 4-8-3.
Mary Williams b. 24th of 12th mo., 1789.
Israel Williams b. 1st of 8th mo., 1793 and d. 21st of 9th mo., 1800, aged 7-1-20.
Amy Williams b. 7th of 8th mo., 1797.

Bathsheba Williams, 1st wife, d. 12th of 9th mo., 1800.

Children of Richard and Hannah Borden:
Sarah Borden b. 11th of 4th mo., 1759.
Thomas Borden b. 6th of 11th mo., 1760.
Rachel Borden b. 16th of 2nd mo., 1763.
Benjamin Borden b. 22nd of 12th mo., 1766

Children of Benjamin and Mary Borden:
John L. Borden b. 30th of 11th mo., 1794.
Richard Borden b. 27th of 10th mo., 1796.
William L. Borden b. 29th of 3rd mo., 1798.
Thomas T. Borden b. 24th of 6th mo., 1800.

Lydia Worden, wife of James Worden, d. 16th of 1st mo., 1786.
William Jackson d. 10th of 3rd mo., 1776.
Ann Jackson, his wife, d. 20th of 7th mo., 1777.
Mosher Maxson b. 6th of 3rd mo., 1730 and d. 24th of 12th mo., 1787.
John Hartshoren b. 6th of 8th mo., 1725, OS.
John Merton b. 8th of 4th mo., 1762.

Shrewsbury Monthly Meeting

Shrewsbury Monthly Meeting
Marriages

Restore Lippincott, s/o Richard and Abigaill Lippincott and Hannah Shattock, d/o William Shattock-6th of 9th mo., 1674, at William Shattock's house.

Francis Borden and Jane Vicars-12th of 4th mo., 1677, at Francis Borden's house.

John Tooker of the town of Shrewsbury, county of Monmouth, Province of East New Jersey, and Ruth Wooley of the same place, d/o John Wooley [Error: d/o Emmanuel Wooley]-25th of 2nd mo., 1688, at the house of Judah Allen.

Francis Jeffryes of Shrewsbury and Ann Worth of the same place-2nd of 12th mo., 1680, at the house of Eliakim Wardell.

John Hamton of Middletown and Martha Brown of Shrewsbury-3rd of 1st mo., 1686/7.

John Sterkyes of Shrewsbury and Mary Chamelhouse of Shrewsbury, widow of Addam Chamelhouse, deceased 27th of 8th mo., 1684.

Ephraim Allen of Shrewsbury, Monmouth County, and Margaret Wardell, Province of East New Jersey-29th of 1st mo., 1681 at the house of Eliakim Wardell.

George Curtis of Shrewsbury and Exersise Shattock of Shrewsbury-10th of 10th mo., 1680, at Shrewsbury at the house of William Shattock.

Thomas Hillborn of Shrewsbury and Elizabeth Hutton of Shrewsbury-12th of 10th mo., 1688, at the house of Elizabeth Hutton..

Robert Ray of Shrewsbury and Jennett Hamton of Shrewsbury-9th of 11th mo., 1689, at the house of John Hampton.

John Cheshire of Shrewsbury and Ann Sutton of Shrewsbury-14th of 2nd mo., 1692.

William Astin of Shrewsbury and Jennett Mill of Shrewsbury-10th of 1st mo., 1692.

John Lippincott of Shrewsbury and Sarah Huett of Shrewsbury-7th of 5th mo., 1692.

Abraham Brown of Shrewsbury and Leah Clayton of Middletown-29th of 7th mo., 1692, at the house of John Clayton.

Thomas Garwood of Burlington, East Jersey, and Jane White of Shrewsbury-28th of 7th mo., 1693.

John Addams of the county of Burlington and Esther Allen of Shrewsbury- 2nd of 7th mo., 1695.

Richard Lippincott of Shrewsbury and Mary White of Shrewsbury-12th of 10th mo., 1695.

John Worthley of Shrewsbury and Elizabeth Hance, Jr., of Shrewsbury-12th of 1st mo., 1695.

James Antrom of Burlington County and Mary Hance-14th of 3rd mo., 1696.

Thomas French, Jr., of West Jersey, near Burlington, and Mary Allen of Shrewsbury-3rd of 10th mo., 1696.

Thomas Hooton of West Jersey and Mary Lippincott of Shrewsbury-28th of 8th mo., 1697.

Joseph Parker of Monmouth County and Elizabeth Lippincott of Shrewsbury-7th of 2nd mo., 1699, at the house of Remembrance Lippincott.

Robert Bonell of Philadelphia and Esther Wardell of Shrewsbury-4th of 8th mo., 1699, at the house of Eliakim Wardell.

George Corlies of Shrewsbury and Deborah Hance of Shrewsbury-23rd of 9th mo., 1699.

Samuel Lippincott of Burlington and Ann Hulitt of Shrewsbury-3rd of 5th mo., 1700.

Seth Hill of Burlington and Elizabeth White (widow) of Shrewsbury-5th of 10th mo., 1700.

Josiah Wing of Shrewsbury and Ann Lippincott of Shrewsbury-2nd of 5th mo., 1701.

Josiph Lippincott of Shrewsbury and Elizabeth White of Shrewsbury-14th of 8th mo., 1701, at the house of Mary White.

Henry Allen, of Shrewsbury and Hannah Corlies, of the same place-18th of 11th mo., 1702.

John Tilton, of Monmouth County, and Margrett Lippincott, of the same place-29th of the 5th mo., commonly called July, 1703.

Walter Harbart, living in Shrewsbury, and Sarah Tillton, of Shrewsbury-2nd of the 4th mo., 1704, at the house of Rebeca Tillton.

William B__ley and Elizabeth Corlies, both of Shrewsbury-25th of 11th mo., 1704.

Samuel Tillton and Patience Allen, both of the county of Monmouth, 5th day of 4th mo., 1705.

John Williams and Sarah Lippincott, both of Shrewsbury-2nd of 3rd mo., 1706, at the house of Remembrance Lippincott.

Nathaniel Fitzrandolph of Woodbridge and Jane Hampton of Freehold-12th of 4th mo., 1706, at the house of Jane Hampton.

Thomas Wooley of Shrewsbury and Patience Tucker of Shrewsbury-3rd of 7th mo., 1707, at the house of Meribah Slocom.

George Williams of Shrewsbury and Joanna Bills of Shrewsbury-27th of 11th mo., 1708.

Shrewsbury Monthly Meeting

Amos White of Shrewsbury and Hannah Mills of Shrewsbury-2nd of 12th mo., 1708, at the house of Jennet Astins.

William Thorn of Nottingham, Burlington County, yeoman, and Meribah Allen of Shrewsbury-21st of 12th mo., 1708.

Isaac Hance of Shrewsbury and Rachell White of Shrewsbury-5th of 8th mo., 1710.

John Lippincott of Shrewsbury and Jenet Astin (Aston?) of Shrewsbury-6th of 12th mo., 1710, at the house of John Lippincott.

Abell Preston of Philadelphia and Meribah Slocum of Shrewsbury-8th of 8th mo., 1712, at the house of Meribah Slocom.

Thomas Lippincott of Shrewsbury and Elizabeth White of Shrewsbury-7th of 8th mo., 1714.

James Tucker of Shrewsbury and Leah Wilbur of Shrewsbury-3rd of 8th mo., 1717.

Jacob Lippincott of Shrewsbury and Mary White of Shrewsbury-17th of 8th mo., 1717.

Daniel Tillton of Monmouth County and Elizabeth Powell of Monmouth County-6th of 9th mo., 1717.

John Wooley of Shrewsbury and Patience Lippitt of Middletown-16th of 11th mo., 1717/8, at the house of Sarah Lippitt..

Anthony Woodward of Freehold and Constant Williams of Shrewsbury-2nd of 10th mo., 1718, at the house of John Williams.

Joseph Wardell, Jr., of Shrewsbury and Margaret Parker of Shrewsbury-16th of 10th mo., 1718, at the house of Joseph Parker.

William Lawrence of Monmouth Co. and Easter Tillton of Monmouth Co.-5th of 8th mo., 1719, at the house of Peter Tillton.

Jacob Lippincott of Shrewsbury and Dinah Allen of Shrewsbury-28th of 9th mo., 1723.

John Mattocks Denn of Salem County, New Jersey, and Leah Wooley of Shrewsbury -5th of 1st mo., 1723/4, at the house of John Wooley.

Walter Harbert, Jr., of Shrewsbury and Deborah Corlies, Jr., -12th of 10th mo., 1728.

James Irons of Shrewsbury and Martha Burchom of Shrewsbury -4th of 3rd mo., 1730, at the house of Nathaniel Buchom.

John Wooley of Shrewsbury and Rachel Clark of Shrewsbury -12th of 6th mo., 1730, at the house of John Wooley.

Eliakim Haeger of Stonybrook and Margaret Lippincott of Shrewsbury - 17th of 10th mo., 1730.

William Corlies of Shrewsbury and Sarah Wing of Shrewsbury-13th of 11th mo., 1731, at the house of Sarah Wing.

Robert Tilton of Middletown and Mirioum Allen of Shrewsbury-6th of 11th mo., 1731.

Ezekiel Allen of Shrewsbury and Amey Wooley of Shrewsbury-10th of 12th mo., 1731, at the house of William Wolley.

John Wooley, Jr., of Shrewsbury and Sarah Rundels of Shrewsbury-4th of 3rd mo., 1732, at the house of Thomas Wooley

Francis Borden, Jr., of Shrewsbury and Lydia Wooley of Shrewsbury-4th of 3rd mo., 1732, at the house of Thomas Wooley.

Zebulon Dickason of Shrewsbury and Joyce Hance of Shrewsbury-5th of 3rd mo., 1732, at the house of Francis Borden.

John Lippincott of Shrewsbury and Patience Allen of Shrewsbury-23rd of 1st mo., 1732.

Benjamin Corlis of Shrewsbury and Mary Jackson of Shrewsbury-24th of 3rd mo., 1732, at the house of Deborah Corlies.

Levi White of Shrewsbury and Ann Lippincott of Shrewsbury-13th of 11th mo., 1733.

James Irons of Shrewsbury and Esther Herbert of Shrewsbury-_ of 4th mo., 1733, at the house of Walter Herbert.

David Corlies of Shrewsbury and Meribah Herbert of Shrewsbury-_ of 4th mo., 1734, at the house of Walter Herbert.

Britton White of Shrewsbury and Dinah Corlies of Shrewsbury-19th of 10th mo., 1734.

John Corlis, Jr., of Shrewsbury and Zilpah Wilbe? of Shrewsbury-24th of 12th mo., 1734, at the house of James Tucker.

Wilber Lippincott of Shrewsbury and Francis Stout of Shrewsbury-6th of 11th mo., 1734.

William Bills of Shrewsbury and Mary Bordin of Shrewsbury-22nd of 3rd mo., 1735, at the house of Francis Bordin.

Philip Edwards of Shrewsbury and Elizabeth Eatton of Shrewsbury-4th of 6th mo., 1735.

Richard Randolph of Woodbridge, New Jersey, and Elizabeth Corlis of Shrewsbury-25th of 7th mo., 1735, at house of John Corlis.

William Scott of Shrewsbury and Mary Runnels of Shrewsbury-27th of 9th mo., 1735.

Thomas White of Shrewsbury and Elizabeth Lippincott of Shrewsbury-18th of 10th mo., 1735.

Nathan Tilton of Middletown and Increase Lippincott of Shrewsbury-25th of 9th mo., 1735.

Thomas Middletown of Nottingham and Patience Tilton of Middletown-15th of 11th mo., 1735.

Francis Hance of Shrewsbury and Elizabeth Roggers of Shrewsbury-4th of 5th mo., 1735, at house of Isaac Hance.

Samuel Scott of Shrewsbury and Almy Bordin of Shrewsbury-11th of 2nd mo., 1736, at the house of Francis Bordin.

Shrewsbury Monthly Meeting

William Folwell of Chesterfield, Burlington County, New Jersey, and Elizabeth Edwards of Shrewsbury-22nd of 2nd mo., 1736.

Stephen Cook of Shrewsbury and Sarah Lippincott of Shrewsbury-22nd of 2nd mo., 1736.

Isaak Hance of Shrewsbury and Content Bills of Shrewsbury-27th of 3rd mo., 1736.

Joseph Potter of Shrewsbury and Rebekah Champlice of Shrewsbury-12th of 6th mo., 1736.

Timothy Hance of Shrewsbury and Rebekah Allen of Shrewsbury-9th of 10th mo., 1736.

William Brinley, Jr., of Shrewsbury and Keziah Wooley [also of Shrewsbury] -6th of 11th mo., 1736, at the house of Emmanuel Wooley.

Jacob Corlies of Shrewsbury and Sarah White of Shrewsbury-22nd of 10th mo., 1737.

Jedediah Allen of Shrewsbury and Phebe Lippincott of Shrewsbury-30th of 9th mo., 1738.

James Lefetra of Shrewsbury and Hannah Brewer of Shrewsbury.-27th of 4th mo., 1739, at the house of Adam Brewer.

William Brinley of Shrewsbury and Elizabeth Lippincott of Shrewsbury-19th of 7th mo., 1739, at the house of Daniel Lippincott.

William Morris of Middletown, New Jersey, and Elizabeth Brewer of Shrewsbury-19th of 8th mo., 1739, at the house of Adam Brewer.

George Nicholson [Nickerson] of Chesterfield, county of Burlington, and Hannah Wooley of Shrewsbury-5th of 1st mo., 1739, at the house of Thomas Wooley.

Ephraim Parker of Shrewsbury and Constant White of Shrewsbury-27th of 5th mo., 1740.

Joseph Potter of Shrewsbury and Abigail Tilton of Middletown-20th of 12th mo., 1753.

Thomas Lippincott of Shrewsbury and Hannah Wooley of Shrewsbury-19th of 10th mo., 1740, at the house of Thomas Lippincott.

John Woodmaney [Woodmance, Woodmancey] of Shrewsbury and Bathsheba Allen of Shrewsbury-8th of 12th mo., 1740, at the house of Jonathan Allen.

Isaac Hance, Jr., of Shrewsbury and Joanna Bills of Shrewsbury-(date omitted from register, permission given at M. M. 3rd of 4th mo., 1741), at house of Isaac Hance.

George Williams of Shrewsbury and Lidya Hewlet of Shrewsbury-25th of 1st mo., 1742.

Thomas Bordin, Jr., of Shrewsbury and Mary Edwards of Shrewsbury-29th of 5th mo., 1742, at the house of Francis Borden.

Richard Worthley of Shrewsbury and Elizabeth Williams of Shrewsbury-23rd of 10th mo., 1742.
John Williams of Shrewsbury and Elizabeth Tucker of Shrewsbury-29th of 10th mo., 1742, at the house of James Tucker.
Benjamin Lawrence of Shrewsbury and Patience Worth of Shrewsbury-13th of 11th mo., 1742, at the house of Edward Worth.
Josiah Parker of Shrewsbury and Margaret Wooley of Shrewsbury-30th of 1st mo., 1743, at the house of William Wooley.
Benjamin Swain of Shrewsbury and Catherine Rulon [Rolon] of Shrewsbury-10th of 9th mo., 1743, at the house of David Rulon.
Amos White of Shrewsbury and Jane White of Shrewsbury-12th of 11th mo., 1743,
Isaac Van Dike of Shrewsbury and Surviah [Survier] Lippincott of Shrewsbury-15th of 1st mo., 1743/4.
William Cook of Shrewsbury [cordwinder] and Elizabeth White of Shrewsbury- 16th of 3rd mo., 1743, at the house of Thomas White.
Benjamin Wooley of Shrewsbury and Cattron Cook of Shrewsbury-19th of 7th mo., 1744, at the house of Cattron Cook.
John Brinley of Shrewsbury and Elizabeth Hulet [Hewlet] of Shrewsbury-17th of 11th mo., 1744.
John Tucker of Shrewsbury and Phebe Parker of Shrewsbury-13th of 12th mo., 1744, at the house of Joseph Parker.
Stephen West of Shrewsbury and Sarah Lippincott of Shrewsbury-31st of 10th mo., 1745, at the house of William Lippincott.
William Lippincott [Junr.] of Middletown and Estor [Esther] Tilton of Middletown-31st of 10th mo., 1745, at the house of Samuel Tilton.
Peter Wolcott of Shrewsbury and Lydia Potter-27th of 6th mo., 1777.
Stephen Wooley of Shrewsbury and Ruth Tucker of Shrewsbury-28th of 6th mo., 1746, at the house of James Tucker.
Thomas Wooley of Shrewsbury and Rachel White of Shrewsbury-15th of 8th mo., 1746, at the house of Amos White.
William Cook of Shrewsbury and Rebekah Howland of Shrewsbury-1st of 11th mo., 1746.
Amos Middletown of Upper Freehold, New Jersey, and Elizabeth Chamblis of Shrewsbury-18th of 1st mo., 1746/7, at the house of Robert Tilton.
Richard Stoute of Shrewsbury and Hannah Wooley of Shrewsbury-23rd of 2nd mo., 1747.
Richard Worthey of Shrewsbury and Mary White of Shrewsbury-17th of 4th mo., 1747, at the house of Thomas White.
William Lawrence [joyner] of Middleton and Margaret Tilton of Middleton-5th of 3rd mo., 1748, at the house of Daniel Tilton.

Shrewsbury Monthly Meeting

Isaac Hance of Shrewsbury and Mary Allen of Shrewsbury-8th of 2nd mo., 1750, at the house of Lidia Williams.

John Lippincott of Shrewsbury and Mary Hewlet of Shrewsbury-5th of 2nd mo., 1750, at the house of Lydia William.

Elihue Williams of Shrewsbury. and Ann Wadey of Shrewsbury-27th of 4th mo., 1750, at the house of Humphrey Wady.

Joseph Jackson of Shrewsbury and Sary Wooley of Shrewsbury-7th of 4th mo., 1750.

Jacob Hance of Shrewsbury and Ann White of Shrewsbury-6th of 10th mo., 1750, at the house of Christian White

James Tucker, Jr., of Shrewsbury and Margaret Parker of Shrewsbury-31st of 11th mo., 1750, at the house of Elizabeth Parker.

Thomas Wooley of Shrewsbury and Elizabeth Jackson of Shrewsbury-9th of 4th mo., 1752, at the house of William Jackson.

William Cook of Shrewsbury and Lydia Corlis of Shrewsbury-22nd of 4th mo., 1752, at the house of Joseph Corlis.

Samuel White of Shrewsbury and Ann Curtis of Shrewsbury-26th of 11th mo., 1755, at the house of David Curtis.

William Parker, Jr., of Shrewsbury and Mary White of Shrewsbury-10th of 12th mo., 1755, at the house of Amos White.

Herbert Curtis of Shrewsbury and Lydia Tilton of Shrewsbury-22nd of 4th mo., 1756, at the house of Thomas Tilton.

David Curtis, Jr., of Shrewsbury and Lydia White of Shrewsbury-19th of 5th mo., 1756, at the house of Thomas White.

John Curtis, Jr., of Shrewsbury and Patience Tilton of Shrewsbury-18th of 11th mo., 1756, at the house of Thomas Tilton.

Benjamin Bordin of Shrewsbury and Rebecah Tilton of Shrewsbury-29th of 12th mo., 1757, at the house of Thomas Tilton.

Richard Borden of Shrewsbury and Hannah Tilton of Shrewsbury-22nd of 6th mo., 1758.

Jacob Hance of Shrewsbury and Elizabeth Corlies of Shrewsbury-8th of 2nd mo., 1759.

Joseph Allen of Shrewsbury and Hannah Lippincott of Shrewsbury-8th of 3rd mo., 1759.

Thomas Kirby of Burlington, New Jersey, and Rachel Hance of Shrewsbury-7th of 3rd mo., 1759, at the house of Timothy Hance.

Joseph Mitten of Shrewsbury and Catherine Michel of Shrewsbury-20th of 11th mo., 1760.

Samuel Tucker of Shrewsbury and Elizabeth White of Shrewsbury-22nd of 1st mo., 1761.

Joseph Shotwell of Woodbridge, New Jersey, and Phebe Allen of Shrewsbury-13th of 8th mo, 1761.

Amos White of Shrewsbury and Ester Borden of Shrewsbury-17th of 12th mo., 1761.

Obadiah Allen of Shrewsbury and Hannah Woodmansey of Shrewsbury-28th of 1st mo., 1762.

David Hance of Shrewsbury and Hannah Cook of Shrewsbury-23rd of 6th mo., 1762.

George Middleton of Nottingham, New Jersey, and Dinah Tilton of Shrewsbury-25th of 11th mo., 1762.

Obadiah Tilton of Middleton and Hannah Corlis of Shrewsbury-20th of 1st month, 1763.

Isaac Hance of Shrewsbury and Deborah White, of Shrewsbury-16th of 2nd mo., 1763, at the house of Thomas White.

Francis Borden of Shrewsbury and Elizabeth Parker of Shrewsbury-24th of 2nd mo., 1763.

Thomas Tillton of Shrewsbury and Katherine Potter of Shrewsbury-12th of 5th mo., 1763.

Joseph Jackson of Shrewsbury and Sarah Lawrence of Shrewsbury-11th of 10th mo., 1764.

Brinton Corlis of Shrewsbury and Anne White of Shrewsbury-10th of 1st mo., 1765, at the house of David Curtis.

James Haydock of Middlesex County, New Jersey, and Phebe Tilton, d/o Nathan, of Monmouth County, New Jersey-14th of 2nd mo., 1765.

Jacob Shotwell of Woodbridge, New Jersey, and Catherine Tilton of Middletown-11th of 9th mo., 1766.

John Lippincott, s/o Nathaniel Lippincott of Chester, New Jersey, Yeoman, and Hannah Tilton, d/o Peter Tilton (dec'd) of Middletown, New Jersey-4th of 11th mo., 1766.

Edmund Lafetra of Shrewsbury and Elizabeth Scott of Shrewsbury-11th of 12th mo., 1766.

James Lafetra of Shrewsbury and Elizabeth Lippincott of Shrewsbury - 14th of 5th mo., 1767.

Thomas Curtiss of Monmouth County, New Jersey, and Margaret Corlis of Monmouth County, New Jersey,-21st of 5th mo., 1767.

James Williams of Shrewsbury and Rebekah Potter of Shrewsbury-13th of 8th mo., 1767, at Shrewsbury.

William Corliss of Shrewsbury and Mary Wooley of Shrewsbury-17th of 9th mo., 1767, at Shrewsbury.

John Wooley, minor (Jr.?), of Shrewsbury and Rebekah Borden of Shrewsbury-14th of 10th mo., 1767, at Amos White's in Shrewsbury.

Joseph Hahurst of Middletown and Deborah Lawrence of Shrewsbury-9th of 12th mo., 1767, at Manasquam.

Shrewsbury Monthly Meeting

David Cutler of Pennsylvania and Ann Lawrence of Shrewsbury-1st of 5th mo., 1769.
Joseph White of Shrewsbury and Sarah Parker, d/o Ephraim, of Shrewsbury-13th of 12th mo., 1770.
Peter Parker of Shrewsbury and Sarah White, d/o George, of Shrewsbury-17th of 1st mo., 1771.
Samuel Middleton, s/o Thomas Middleton, of Nottingham, Burlington County, N. J., and Ann Tilton of Middleton-11th of 4th mo., 1771, at Shrewsbury.
Thomas Smith of Shrewsbury and Deborah Laing of Shrewsbury-11th of 12th mo., 1771, at George Parker's in "Sqaauem".
Isaiah Shotwell of Plainfield and Constant Lippincott of Shrewsbury-27th of 2nd mo., 1772.
Benjamin Corlies of Shrewsbury and Deborah Parker of Shrewsbury-20th of 5th mo., 1773.
Brittain White of Shrewsbury and Elizabeth Allen of Shrewsbury-22nd of 4th mo., 1773.
Robert Bowne of New York, s/o John Bowne, (dec'd) of Flushing, and Elizabeth Hartshorne, d/o Robert of Middletown,-18th of 11th mo., 1773, at Shrewsbury.
Jonathan Pickering of Buckingham, Pennsylvania, and Mary Williams of Shrewsbury-7th of 12th mo., 1773.
Joshua Morris of Abington, Penna. and Lydia Wardell of Shrewsbury-6th of 1st mo., 1774, at Shrewsbury.
Jonathan Wright of Chesterfield, New Jersey, and Elizabeth Williams of Shrewsbury-9th of 3rd mo., 1774..
Peter Corlis of Shrewsbury and Margaret Tucker of Shrewsbury-14th of 4th mo., 1774.
Jeremiah Hance of Shrewsbury and Phebe Woodmansea of Shrewsbury-15th of 12th mo., 1774.
Elihu Wooley of Shrewsbury and Mary Jackson of Shrewsbury-12th of 4th mo., 1755, at Squaneum.
Nathan Jackson of Shrewsbury and Meribah Jackson of Shrewsbury-21st of 12th mo., 1775, at Shrewsbury.
Edmond Lafetra of Shrewsbury and Sarah Dotter of Shrewsbury-17th of 10th mo., 1775.
Jacob Laing of Shrewsbury and Leah Brindley of Shrewsbury-22nd of 1st mo., 1777, at Shrewsbury.
George Williams of Shrewsbury and Margaret Cook of Shrewsbury-13th of 3rd mo., 1777.
Humphrey Williams of Shrewsbury and Meribah Curtis of Shrewsbury-12th of 6th mo., 1777.

William Jackson of Shrewsbury and Ruth Wooley of Shrewsbury-15th of 5th mo., 1777.
Thomas White of Shrewsbury and Meribah Parker of Shrewsbury-4th of 12th mo., 1777, at Thomas White's house in Shrewsbury.
Nathan Jackson of Shrewsbury and Mary Setson of Shrewsbury-15th of 10th mo., 1778.
Thomas Earle of Springfield, New Jersey, and Leah Tucker, d/o John Tucker of Shrewsbury,-4th of 5th mo., 1779.
Robert White of Shrewsbury and Hester Crawford of Middletown, New Jersey,-13th of 7th mo., 1780.
Nathan Tilton, Jr., of Middletown, New Jersey, and Abigail Birdsall of Middletown, New Jersey-15th of 1st mo., 1784.
Jacob Wooley of Shrewsbury and Elizabeth Tucker, d/o Samuel of Shrewsbury,-16th of 9th mo., 1784.
Daniel Wardell, s/o Joseph Wardell of Shrewsbury, and Alice Elizabeth Nicholson, d/o George Nicholson (dec'd) late of Princeton-17th of 3rd mo., 1785.
Joseph Allen, Jr., s/o Joseph of Shrewsbury and Elizabeth Williams, d/o Edmond of Shrewsbury-16th of 6th mo., 1785.
James Morris of Shrewsbury and Ann Jackson of Shrewsbury- 22nd of 3rd mo., 1786, at Shrewsbury.
John Barrow of New York, s/o John and Abigail Barrow of Lancaster, Great Britain, and Mary Lawrence, d/o Richard and Alice Lawrence of Shrewsbury-9th of 12th mo., 1790, at Shrewsbury.
Henry Bourn(?), Jr., of Burlington County, New Jersey, and Phebe Williams of Shrewsbury-12th of 5th mo., 1791, at Shrewsbury.
Joseph Byrd of New York, s/o Thomas and Hannah of Uffculm in Great Brittain, and Elizabeth Lawrence, d/o Richard and Alice of Shrewsbury-17th of 11th mo., 1791, at Shrewsbury.
Trlee Williams of Shrewsbury and Elizabeth Hartshorne, d/o Esek Hartshorne of Middletown,-10th of 1st mo., 1792, at Esek Hartshorne's house.
Samuel Lafetra of Shrewsbury and Elizabeth Allen of Shrewsbury-17th of 5th mo., 1792.
James Lafetra, Jr., of Shrewsbury and Meribah Wolcott of Shrewsbury-12th of 7th mo., 1792, at Shrewsbury.
John Rively, s/o John (dec'd) and Dorothy of Kingsessing, Philadelphia County, Penna., and Sarah Corlies, d/o Jacob and Sarah Corlies (dec'd) of Shrewsbury-3rd of 9th mo., 1794, at Shrewsbury.
William Hartshorne of Middletown, New Jersey, s/o Robert and Sarah, and Sarah Lawrence, d/o Richard and Alice Lawrence-14th of 12th mo., 1797, at Shrewsbury.

Shrewsbury Monthly Meeting

Peter Jackson of Shrewsbury and Mary Cox of Shrewsbury-9th of 11th mo., 1797, at Shrewsbury.

James Morris of Shrewsbury, s/o Job and Mary, and Elizabeth Curtis, d/o David and Lydia Curtis, all of Shrewsbury-10th of 10th mo., 1798, at Sqaun.

Dennis Hurley of Middlesex County, New Jersey, and Deborah Wooley, d/o Elihu and Mary of Shrewsbury-7th of 9th mo., 1799, at Shrewsbury.

Amos Tilton of Middletown, s/o William ans Esther, and Elizabeth White, d/o Benjamin and Mary of Shrewsbury-12th of 9th mo., 1799, at Shrewsbury.

William Hance, s/o Sarah and Elizabeth of Shrewsbury, and Margaret Tilton, d/o Obadiah and Hannah of Shrewsbury-19th of 12th mo., 1799, at Shrewsbury.

George Parker, s/o George and Martha Parker of Shrewsbury, and Hannah Tilton, d/o Thomas and Sarah Tilton of Shrewsbury-12th of 2nd mo., 1800, at Squan.

Early Church Records of Monmouth County

SHREWSBURY MONTHLY MEETING MINUTES

Only those marriages not reported in the register are noted here.

4th of 4th mo. 1733 - Application made for a certificate for Ebeneazer Wardell.

7th of 11th mo. 1733 - At this meeting Timothy Harbort and Sarah Bills did declare their intentions of marriage, this being the first time. Also at this meeting David Johnson and Sarah Laurence declared their intentions to marry, this being the first time.

7th of 1st mo. 1734 - The two young couples allowed to publish their intentions of marriage at our Monthly Meeting 11th mo. 1733 are married contrary to good order.

5th of 2nd mo. 1734 - Daniel Shotwell and Elizabeth Parker declare their intentions to marry, this being the first time.

8th of 4th mo. 1734 - Friends appointed to attend the marriage of Daniel Shotwell and Elizabeth Parker report it was orderly accomplished. James Irons and Esther Horbert did declare that they continue their intentions of marriage, this being for the second time.

1st of 5th mo. 1734 - Friends appointed to attend the marriages of James Irons and Esther Horbert reported that things were decently carried out.

6th of 11th mo. 1734 - Application being made for a certificate for George Parker.

3th of 12th mo. 1734 - Application being made for Benjamin Carter.

3th of 1st mo. 1734/5 - Application being made for a certificate for Joseph Gardner.

2nd of 4th mo. 1736 - Walter Harbers testification - Inasmuch as Walter Harber hath for many years welked in communion with us the people called Quakers and hath appeared in Publick in our meetings with whom we had unity but contrary to the rules of our Society he hath taken to wife a woman not of our Society and one which we have good ground to believe is ... another man and has had a child by him. We do therefore disown the sd. Walter Harbourt as a minister of our Society and a member ...

16th of 7th mo. 1735 - A certificate is received from Woodbridge for Richard Randels

3rd of 3rd mo. 1736 -.Gersham Bills and Sarah Gardner declare their continued intentions of marriage. Joseph Wardell brought a certificate for Thos. Hance and it was received and approved. A certificate to be drawn for Tobithorn Allen.

Shrewsbury Monthly Meeting

4th of 4th mo. 1736 - It was reported that the marriage of Gersham Bills and Sarah Gardner was orderly accomplished. A certificate for Tobyther Allen was received.

2nd of 5th mo. 1736 - The person appointed to inspect into Joseph Lawrence Jnr. life and conversations reports it to be orderly and ...

6th of 10th mo. 1736 - It is reported that George Parker's life and conversation are orderly.

7th of 12th mo. 1736. To visit Eliz. Edwards to deal with her about the report between her and William Exceen and also her having a child too soon according to the time of her being married.

4th of 2nd mo. 1737 - James Irons has given his reasons for his wrong proceedings in marrying a wife out of the unity.

2nd of 3rd mo. 1737 - Elizabeth Edwards disowned, she having a child too soon after marriage and also being seen with Willm. Exceen in an unseemly manner and refusing to make satisfaction.

4th of 5th mo. 1737 - Application was made for a certificate for Walter Herbert Jnr.

5th of 7th mo. 1737. Received 25 shillings which our worthy Friend Meribah Slocum gave to this meeting in her will.

6th of 12th mo. 1737. Persons appointed to receive the legacies of Lewis Morrises which his uncle Cornel Lewis Morris gave to this meeting.

3rd of 2nd mo. 1738 - Persons appointed inspect into Thomas Hartshorne's clearness and into his conversation and to report to next monthly meeting [nothing found to obstruct his having a certificate]. Persons also appointed to inspect into George Williams Junr's clearness on account of marriage and into his conversation [certificate approved]. Also to inspect into Stephen Burchums clearness and into his conversation.

5th of 4th mo. 1738 - Persons appointed to inspect into Richard Gardiner's and his wife's conversation [certificate is delayed].

3rd of 5th mo. 1738 - A certificate was requested for Ruth Courtre (?) and Susan Hudson.

3rd of 10th mo. 1739 - A certificate to be drawn for Sarah Wiles and Richard Gardiner and his wife. James Tucker appointed treasurer.

7th of 2nd mo. 1740 - The widow Tolmon paid 14 shillings? to the repairing the fence about our buring ground.

3rd of 9th mo. 1740 - William Lawrence brought a certificate from Philadelphia Monthly Meeting for himself and wife.

5th of 11th mo. 1740 - Application was made for a certificte for Benjamin Hanch.

2nd of 12th mo. 1740 - Jerediah Allen has been dealt with fo marrying out of unity of Friends and he gave no satisfaction. A certificate is to be drawn for Benjamin Hanch.

6th of 2nd mo. 1741 - Ebenezar Cook and Sarah Tilton, both of the town afsd. declared their intentions of marriage this bing the first time.

4th of 3rd mo. 1741 - EbenezerCook and Sarah Tilton declared their intention of marriage the second time. The Friends appointed to inspect into the lives and conversation of Judah Williams and his family report they are orderly and a certificate is approved.

1st of 4th mo. 1741 - The marriage of Ebenezer Cook and Sarah Tilton are reported as orderly accomplished.

3rd of 6th mo. 1741 - Joseph Lawrence junr. and Esther Parke of the town of Shrewsbury declared their intentions of marriage with each other this being the first time.

7th of 1st mo. 1742/3 - Certificate to be drawn for Leah Denard.

2nd of 3rd mo. 1743 - Adam Brewer has sent in a paper of condemnation of his action [fornication]. John Corleis to be warned to refrain from drinking to excess.

1st of 6th mo. 1743 - Joseph Wardell, James Tucker and William Jackson are appointed to settle bounds with Thomas Holmes above our farm yard.

5th of 10th mo. 1743 - Application was made for a certificate for John Tilton. [Approved]

5th of 1st mo. 1743/4 - The overseers report that some time ago Daniel Tilton complained to them that his brother Samuel Tilton had got some of his ground in his inclosure and made use of it. [On 3rd of 10th mo. 1744 it was reported that their difference had ended.]

4th of 2nd mo. 1744 - A certificate was received from Philadelphia for Samuel and Mary Lippincott.

9th of 3rd mo. 1744 - Benjamin and Cattron Swain sent in a paper stating that they should be guilty of such folly as to have a child so soon after their marriage for which they are truly sorry. An application was made for a certificate for William Lawrence, blacksmith. [Approved]

7th of 8th mo. 1745 - An application was made for a certificate for Benjamin Lawrence and his wife.

2nd of 10th mo. 1745 - A certificate was received from South Kingston Monthly Meeting for James Scriven who is on a religious visit among Friends in these parts. Also a certificate from Deakmouth(?) Monthly Meeting signifying their consent and unity with Stephen Wilcock in going on a religious visit in these parts.

3rd of 3rd mo. 1746 - Jeremiah Borden and Ester Tilton, both of the town of Shrewsbury, declared their intentiosn of marriage, this being the first time.

Shrewsbury Monthly Meeting

7th of 5th mo. 1746 - The marriage of Jeremiah Bordin and Ester Tilton was reported as orderly accomplished.

6th of 8th mo. 1746 - Application was made for a certificate for Hezekiah Williams. [Approved]

32nd of 1st mo. 1746/7 Amos Middleton brought a certificate from Chesterfield Monthly Meeting.

4th of 3rd mo. 1747 - A certificate for Elizabeth Midelton was requested.

7th of 7th mo. 1747 - Certificate prepared for Friend Nicklos Davis who visited our meetings.

7th of 10th mo. 1747 - Selvester Tilton asks to come under the care of Friends. [Approved]

1st of 12th mo. 1747/8 - Richard and Hannah Stout sent a paper signifying their sorrow for their misconduct before marriage.

2nd of 3rd mo. 1748 - William Lawrence requests a certificate as he is moving to Philadelphia.

7th of 9th mo. 1748 - Certificates of Benjamin Farris and David Akins were approved.

5th of 12th mo. 1749/50 - John Wardell sent in a paper signifying that he wsa sorry tht he had broken the rules of our Society in marrying which was accepted.

1st of 8th mo. 1750 - A certificate was received from Burlington Monthly Meeting for Hugh Harthorn and his wife. Approved.

2nd of 7th mo. 1751 - Certificate received from Chesterfield Monthly Meeting recommending William Kinnison and his wife Elizabeth to the care of Friends.

4th of 7th mo. 1751 - The meeting to demand the legacy that Lewis Morris dec'd. gave to this meeting.

1st of 6th mo. 1752 - Jeremiah Pears made application to come under the care of Friends [continued for some time and by 3rd of 12th mo. he had dropped his request].

1st of 11th mo. 1752 - Jos. Wardell Junr. and Hannah Tucker declared their intentions of marriage for the first time. A certificate is requested for Daniel Wardell.

5th of 3rd mo. 1753 - The marriage of Joseph Wardell Junr. and Hannah Tucker is reported as orderly accomplished.

7th of 5th mo. 1753. The request of Elizabeth Allen by the report of the women Friends can not be complied with for she married one that was near of kin and contrary to the rules of our Society.

4th of 6th mo. 1753 - Friends in Salem to be written to let them know how the said Elizabeth Allen behaved herself when she lived with us. Certificate for Marcey Field to be prepared.

5th of 10th mo. 1753 - Wilber Lippincott requested a certificate for himself and family.

1st of 4th mo. 1754 - A certificate for Hugh Hartshorn and his wife is approved.

1st of 7th mo. 1754 - A complaint was made by Jerediah Allen against William Brinley. [It is the opinion that William Brinley is wrong in endeavoring to wrong the estate of Ralf Allen dec'd and for saying of things that did not appear to be true.]

2nd of 12th mo. 1754 - William Kineson [Kinerson] is to be notified that he must give the meeting satisfaction fo rhis misbehaviour in drinking and gaming and ... into trade beyond his ability to the hurt of many people. [continued] Certificate to be prepared for Lydia Tilton. Benjamin Wilcott made application to come under the care of this meeting.

2nd of 6th mo. 1755 - Joseph Hewhit, James Lippincott, Obediah Lippincott, George White, John Borden, Uriah Lippincott, Thomas White, Derious Lippincott, Thomas Brinley, Derious Lippincott, Thomas Brinley, Selvester Brinley and Peter Parker and Uriah Lippincott brought in a paper in which he [sic] condemns his scanderlous conduct. James Lippincott brought in a paper condemning his conduct in marrying contrary to our discipline. The meeting allows him to be under their care.

7th of 7th mo. 1755 - John Woodmancey and his wife brought in a paper setting forth their sorror for their misconduct before marriage. George White and his wife brought n a paper signifying their sorrow for breaking the rule of our society in marriage. Derious Lippincott sent in a paper setting forth his sorrow for his misconduct in several things.

4th of 8th mo. 1755 - David Johnston and his wife sent in a paper condemning their former conduct respecting marriage.

6th of 10th mo. 1755 - Benjamin Wooley Junr brought in a paper condemning his marrying contrary to the good order used amongst Friends. Hugh Jackson requested to come under the care of Friends.

3rd of 11th mo. 1755 - Hugh Jackson to become under the care of Friends. Joel White brought in a paper condemning his conduct in marrying contrary to the rules of our Society.

1st of 12th mo. 1755 - Joseph Hulet to be notified that satisfaction is expected of him for his wrong condition in marriage and other ways.

Testifications:

Thomas Brinley [a Friend by birthright] has transgressed the rules of our Society in marriage and neglected religious meetings and lived a

Shrewsbury Monthly Meeting

corrupt life and is disowned.

Thomas White, cordwinder, was suffered to marry amongst Friends and was in some degree under their care but has been guilty of drinking to excess and has lived a corrupt life. Disowned.

Selvester Brinley's testification is in the same words as Thomas Brinley. Discowned.

5th of 1st mo. 1756 - Joseph Hewlit brought in a paper condemning his behaviour. Jacob Lippincott Junr and Obediah Lippnicott brought in papers condemning their marrying contrary to the rules of our Society.

2nd of 2nd mo. 1756 - James Lawrence brought in a paper condemning his marrying contrary to the rules of our Society.

1st of 3rd mo. 1756 - Antoney Woodward Junr. of Chesterfield and Deborah Tilton of Midelton declare their intentions of marriage. David Allen, John Curtis, David Curtis Junr. and Peter Parker brought in papers condemning their wrong proceedings in marriage. Humprey Wadey, Amos White and David Curtis, Justices of the Peace being under dealing for administering of oaths and marrying by lysence did appear and have promised to lay down their commissions as soon as opportunity presents.

5th of 4th mo. 1756 - Benjamin Bordin made application to come under the care of Friends. [Approved]

3rd of 5th mo. 1756 - The marriage of Anthony Woodward and Deborah Tilton report it was orderly accomplished. William Parker and his wife Mary brought in a paper condemning their proceedings before marriage [having a child too soon after marriage]. Joseph Corleis complained of Lovey White.

- of 6th mo. 1756 - Remembrance Lippincott brought a paper signifying his sorrow for breach of discipline in marriage. A certificate is requested for Deborah Woodward.

Testification of William Brinley: whereas William Brinley wronged the estate of Ralf Allen dec'd. and for more, saying of things that did not appear to be true and other offenses. Disowned.

5th of 7th mo. 1756 - A report has been brought against Remembrance Lippincott in having a child by a woman which is not his wife. James Lippincott, son of John Lippincott, has given a paper wherein he greatly condemns his crimes of having two children by two different persons and afterwards marrying the third.

2nd of 8th mo. 1756 - The dispute between Joseph Corlis and Leny White regarding boundaries of their lands is resolved. Informed that John Allen has taken a wife contrary to good order of Friends. Anis

Fisher, Neomy Treadwell, Sarah West, Elizabeth Mount and Elizabeth Wardil are disowned - for breach of discipline in marriages and a neglect of meetings for worship. Samuel White is expected to make satisfaction for not making application for a certificate before removal.

Shrewsbury Monthly Meeting

Shrewsbury Monthly Meeting
Minutes 1786-1800

6th of 2nd mo. 1786 - John Hartshorne Jun'r, for his offence in paying a fine in lieu of military service, is disowned.

6th of 3rd mo. 1786 - Elizabeth Hartshorne is received in membership. Thomas Woolley Jun'r hath been treated with for marrying a woman not of our society.

3rd of 4th mo 1786 - Elisha Lawrence hath been treated with for horse racing and fighting.

5th of 6mo 1786 - Samuel Williams acknowledges that he attended a marriage contrary to our rules, fought with his neighbor and whilst under dealing for the above offenses married a young woman not of our Society by the assistance of a priest, contrary to advice from his parent. Rebekah Harris acknowledges keeping company with a man not of our society and marrying him with the assistance of a magistrate, without consent of her parents. Jacob Corlies expresses sorrow for giving way to passions much that he has been guilty of fighting. John Wardell hath been treated with for marrying a woman not of our society with the assistance of a magistrate. A certificate is requested for Tylee Williams to the Monthly Meeting of New York, he being placed in apprentice to Tho's Pearsall of that place.

3rd of 7th mo. 1786 - A certificate for Tylee Williams to the Monthly Meeting at New York was approved. George Williams requests a certificate of removal for himself, his wife and three children, Elizabeth, Lydia and Phebe, to Upper Springfield. A certificate is requested for George Parker, son of Peter, to New York Monthly Meeting, who is placed an apprentice to George Fox of that place.

7th of 8th mo. 1786 - A certificate was produced to The New York Monthly Meeting for George Parker, placed apprentice to George Fox. A certificate to Chesterfield was produced for Sarah Debow, wife of John Debow, and her 4 children, who have removed with him within the verge of that meeting.

4th of 9th mo. 1786 - A certificate to Springfield on behalf of George Williams, Margaret his wife and children Elizabeth, Lydia and Phebe was approved. John Wardell handed in a paper wherein he acknowledges his wrong doing in marrying a woman not of our society with the assistance of a magistrate and without the consent of his parents, with whom he has made up. A certificate to New York Monthly Meeting on behalf of George Parker, who is placed apprentice to George Fox, was approved. A certificate to New York

Monthly Meeting on behalf of Sarah Dubois was approved. A certificate is requested for Isaac Laing, who is placed an apprentice to Cowperthhwait Copeland of Rahway Monthly Meeting. A certificate for Jane Scot, who has removed from Flushing Monthly meeting on Long Island was read and accepted.

1st of 10th mo. 1786 - A certificate from Little Eggharbour on behalf of Margery Grant, wife of James Grant, and her 3 children, Liddia, John and Anthony, being in their minority, was read and accepted.

6th of 11th mo. 1786 - A testification against Elisha Lawrence, whereas he hath been guilty of horse-racing and fighting and being profane in his conversation, was published but with no signs of amendment showing he is disowned. A certificate to Rahway Monthly Meeting for Isaac Laing, placed apprentice to Couperthwait Copeland, was approved. A certificate to New York for Hannah Lippincott was approved. Sarah Corlies Jun'r gave in a paper wherein she acknowledges attending a marriage solemnized contrary to the rules of discipline, for which she expresses sorrow. John White requests a certificate for his son George who is placed under the care of John White of New York.

4th of 12th mo. 1786 - A certificate to New York on behalf of George White, who is placed under the care of John White, was approved. It appears that John Tucker Jun'r hath been treated with for committing fornication with the woman who is now his wife and also for accomplishing his marriage by the assistance of a priest. Ebenezer Hance hath been treated with for paying fines in lieu of military service. John Borden requests that his children may be taken under the care of Friends, which request appears also to be with by his wife. The clerk is appointed to draw a certificate to New York Monthly Meeting for Jane White.

1st of 1st mo. 1787 - A certificate on behalf of Jane White to New York Monthly Meeting is approved. Hannah Jackson and Sarah Hartshorne are approved as Elders.

5th of 2nd month 1787 - John Tucker Jun'r expresses sorrow for having married a woman that was not in unity with us and having committed fornication with her. He has obtained reconciliation with his parents. The children of John Borden, Zilpha, Elizabeth, Lydia, Mary, John Richard, Francis, Jeremiah and Samuel, are taken under the care of friends.

5th of 3rd mo. 1787 - Sam'l Williams hath been treated with for committing fornication with the woman who is now his wife. Dav'd Hance hath been treated with on a complaint from Mary Worthley for not paying a debt due to her as Executrix of her husbands estate.

Shrewsbury Monthly Meeting

- 2nd of 4th mo. 1787 - Thomas Wilson of Pennsylvania and Margaret Knight declared their intentions of marriage, having he consent of his parents. Ebenezer Hance is disowned. Friends appointed have treated with David Hance and Mary Worthley and report the business is so well settled that the complaint is withdrawn. Charity White hath been tenderly and repeatedly treated with for her evil and ill conduct in going to places of diversion and being active in dancing, and that she also appears to be with child by fornication for which she has been treated with and seems insensible of her misconduct. John Hawthorne is appointed to draw a testification against her.
- 7th of 5th mo. 1787 - Thomas Wilson produced a certification from Middletown Monthly Meeting in Bucks County, Pennsylvania, then he, with Margaret Knight, declared the continuation of their intentions of marriage. They are now left to consummate the same. Sam'l Williams published a paper in which he condemns and expresses sorrow for committing fornication with her that is now his wife.
- 4th of 6th mo. 1787 - The Friends appointed report that Thomas William's marriage was orderly accomplished. A certificate to Rahway and Plainfield Monthly Meeting for Mary Matson was read and approved. It again appears that Ann Stevenson is again in necessitous circumstances.
- 2nd of 7th mo. 1787 - Charity White is disowned for frequenting places of diversion and being active in dancing, and is now by appearance with child by fornication. The committee appointed brought in a report that Ann Stevenson is the widow of John Stevenson of Middletown in the county of Monmouth, state of New Jersey, and a member of this meeting. At the decease of her husband she was left on a valuable farm, well stocked with cattle, sheep, & c. A great part of the stock, at divers times during the late troubles, was taken from her by parties of armed men under pretense of their becoming forfeity reason that her eldest son had joined the British, and finally the farm confiscated and sold and she turned out of possession by the sheriff, which hath reduced her from a comfortable and plentiful living to a state truly necessitous, which, in her advance age and the unhappiness of having a daughter not endowed with common understanding, renders her condition really deplorable. It further appears that the said Ann Stevenson, having entered into arbitration bonds with the person now in possession of her right, and that the sum of fifty pounds was awarded to be paid by her, on which payment she is to be put into possession of her dower and probably

thereby enabled to maintain herself comfortably during the reminder of her life. The clerk is directed to send a copy of the said report and this minute, with a desire to be informed whether the sufferings of the above mentioned Friend doth not entitle her to part of the Irish Donation, should any thereof yet remain unappended. Edm'd Williams is appointed to draw a certificate of removal for Margaret Wilson and Miriba Wardele to the monthly meeting of Middletown in Bucks County, Pennsylvania.

6th of 8th mo. 1787 - A certificate for Margaret Wilson and Miriba Wardell to the monthly meeting of Middletown, Bucks County, Pennsylvania, was read and approved. Britain Tucker has been treated with for committing fornication with the woman who is now his wife and also for being married with the assistance of a priest. Britain, being present, produced a paper of condemnation which is accepted.

3rd of 9th mo. 1787 - Brittain Woolley hah been treated with for drinking to excess and quarreling. Humphrey Williams has been treated with for quarreling, fighting and drinking to excess. A paper of condemnation from Mary Lippincott was read and is accepted.

1st of 10th mo. 1787 - A paper of condemnation from Britain Tucker was published wherein he expresses sorrow for committing fornication with her that is his wife and having married by a priest without the consent of his parents, with whom he has been reconciled. Britain Woolley produced a paper of condemnation which is accepted. Humphrey Williams delivered a paper of condemnation which not being satisfactory is returned to him. A paper from Mary Lippincott was published in which she expresses sorrow for keeping company with a man not in unity with Friends and against the advice of her mother, with whom she has obtained forgiveness, and for committing fornication with him and for marrying with the assistance of a priest. Application was made for a certificate for Mary Pintard and her daughter Ann Pintard to New York Monthly Meeting. A condemnation of Tacy Miller in which she expresses sorry for marrying one not belonging amongst us, unknown to and without the consent of her parents, with the assistance of a priest, was accepted.

5th of 11th mo. 1787 - A certificate to New York Monthly Meeting for Mary Pintard and her daughter Ann was read and approved. A paper of condemnation from Britain Woolley in which he acknowledges and expresses sorrow for drinking spiritous liquors to access, quarreling and being concerned in military service.

3rd of 12th mo. 1787 - Asher Corlies has been treated with for profane

Shrewsbury Monthly Meeting

swearing and fighting and being concerned in military service, horse racing and frolicking. Lydia, the wife of Joseph Corlies, has been married by a priest and had a child by fornication.

7th of 1st mo. 1788 - A paper from Humphrey Williams was published in which he expresses sorrow for quarreling and fighting with his neighbors and drinking spiritous liquors to excess. Lydia Brewer requests a certificate for her son George who is placed with Samuel Clark of Philadelphia. A paper of condemnation from Jonathan Manson, wherein he acknowledges marrying one not belonging amongst Friends, unknown to his parents and without their consent, was read and approved. Stephen West stands in need of assistance.

4th of 2nd mo. 1788 - A certificate to Friends in Philadelphia for George Brewer, a youth, placed under the care of Samuel Clark, was read and approved. The Friends appointed report they have made some inspection into Stephen West's circumstances and supplied him with sundry necessities. Robert Hartshorne is appointed to draw a certificate for Tacy Miller to the monthly meeting at Rahway.

3rd of 3rd mo. 1788 - Benjamin Stevenson has been treated with for training, being corrupt in conversation and neglect of attending meetings.

7th of 4th mo. 1788 - A certificate to Rahway Monthly Meeting for Tacy Miller was read and approved. Job Smith has been treated with for profane swearing, non attendance of our religious meetings and neglecting to pay a debt owed to Obadiah Williams. Anthony Smith requests a certificate for himself, his wife and son, John, to Little Eggharbour. A certificate requested for Elihu Curtis who is placed apprentice to Thomas Smith in Burlington.

5th of 5th mo. 1788 - Lydia, wife of Joseph Corlies, guilty of fornication and being married by a priest, is disowned. A certificate to Burlington for Elihu Corlies, placed apprentice with Thomas Smith, was read and approved.

2nd of 6th mo. 1788 - A certificate to the monthly meeting at Little Eggharbour on behalf of Anthony Smith, his wife and son John, was read and approved.

7th of th mo. 1788 - Benjamin Stevenson is disowned for training, being corrupt in his conversation and neglect in attending our meetings. Nathan Jackson has been treated with for not attending our meetings, drinking spiritous liquors to access and neglect in paying a debt. A certificate from the monthly meeting held at Chesterfield on behalf of Hannah Lippincott, widow, was read and accepted.

4th of th mo. 1788 - A certificate to the monthly meeting at Greenwich, new Jersey, on behalf of Hannah Reeve and Deborah Bassett, on a religious visit, was approved. A certificate for William Bradway, accompanying he above mentioned women Friends, is approved. A certificate to Salem, New Jersey, for Deborah Bassett was approved. A paper from Stephen Manson wherein he expresses sorrow for marrying one not belonging among Friends by a magistrate and without the consent of his mother, was read. A paper from Thomas Borden Jun'r condemns his drinking spiritous liquors. Mary Holmes is disowned for marrying a man not of our society and without the consent of her parent.

1st of 9th mo. 1788 - Jonathan Manson and his wife request that their son David, an infant, come under the care of friends. Deborah, wife of Benjamin Wardell, hath been treated with for being guilty of fornication and marrying a man not in unity with us by the assistance of a priest. Also, attending places of diversion and being active in dancing. A certificate from Mount Holly Monthly Meeting on behalf of Lydia Tilton was read and accepted.

6th of 10th mo. 1788 - Jonathan Maxson's request that his son David might come under the care of Friends is granted. It appears that Sarah Ustick has married a man not professing with us and declines making satisfaction.

3rd of the 11th mo. 1788 - Sarah Ustick, wife of William Ustick of New York, having with the assistance of a priest married a man not of our religious society, is disowned.

1st of 12th mo.1788 - A certificate from New York Monthly Meeting on behalf of Tylee Williams, who is returning home, is accepted. Philip Borden hath been treated with for drinking spiritous liquors to excess, training and the neglect of attending our religious meetings. David Hance has removed from us sometime since without a certificate and left his business unsettled and that he hath been treated with for the same. George Corlies Jun'r hath removed from us without a certificate and neglects settling his business to satisfaction.

5th of 1st mo. 1789 - Nathan Jackson is disowned for drinking spiritous liquors to excess and neglecting the attendance of our religious meetings. Job Smith is disowned, having been guilty of profane swearing, non attendance of our religious meetings and neglect in paying a debt. Deborah, the wife of Benjamin Wardell, is disowned, being guilty of fornication and marrying a man not in unity with us by the assistance of a priest, also frequented places of diversion and was active in dancing. A paper from Rachel Salter wherein she expresses sorrow for having twice been married to men not of our society was read and accepted. Abigail Morris is accepted into

Shrewsbury Monthly Meeting

membership. Manuel Pearce requests be taken under the care of Friends. John Scott hath been treated with for neglect of attending our religious meetings and being concerned in training. It also appears that William Parker Jun'r hath been treated with for being married contrary to the rules of discipline and by a priest.

2nd of 2nd mo. 1789 - Rachel Parker is disowned, having been married by a priest to a man not in unity with us, and who was her former husband's sister's husband - and notwithstanding she hath given in a paper of acknowle-dgment, yet it not appearing to this meeting that her mind was humbled by real contrition and sorrow. A certificate to Evesham Monthly Meeting on behalf of Rachel Saltar is approved. A paper from Abigail Morris in which she expresses shame and sorrow for being guilty of fornication with he who is now her husband and also imposed so much on another man as to keep his company and also publish my intentions of marriage with him.

2nd of 3rd mo. 1789 - William Parker produced a paper of condemnation, being read and accepted, in which he is sensible he has done wrong in marrying contrary to good order by a priest an without the consent of his father and father-in-law, who are both willing to pass by his offense. A paper of acknowledgment from Rachel Parker, in which she expresses sorrow for marrying contrary to good order by a priest and without the consent of her parents, was read and accepted.

6th of 4th mo. 1789 - A testification against Phebe Chambers, who hath been guilty of fornication, having married with the assistance of a priest, was published and she is disowned. Alice Leonard and Zilpha Dennis have been dealt with for going out in marriage. Brittain White requests a certificate to New York Monthly Meeting for himself, wife and family.

4th of 5th month. 1789 - James Lawrence hath been dealt with for neglect in attending meetings and for training. Ann Hulet is received into membership.

1st of 6th mo. 1789 - It appears by our former minutes that Philip Borden hath been already disowned, therefore his case is discontinued. Alice Leonard and Zilpha Dennis are disowned, both having married men not in religious profession with us. Brittain White requests this meeting not to proceed with his certificate as he expects to return here again. Margaret Davis, wife of Rich'd. Davis, is disowned, having married a man not of our society and by the assistance of a magistrate. John Hartshorne sent in a paper condemning his paying a fine in lieu of military services and requesting to be reinstated among Friends.

6th of 7th mo., 1789 - Stephen Maason requests a certificate of removal to Redstone Monthly meeting. Jediah Allen produced a paper condemning his breach of our discipline in going out in marriage by the assistance of a priest. Jacob Corlies produced a paper condemning his breach of our discipline in going out in marriage and frequenting places of diversion.

6rd of 8th mo., 1789 - John Scott, Jr., is disowned, having trained for military service. Alice Lawrence, Miriam Williams and Patience Corlies are appointed Elders. Richard Hulet has been treated with for going out in marriage with the assistance of a priest and also for being concerned in military services.

7th of 9th mo., 1789 - Benjamin Woolley and Hannah Jackson declared their intentions of marriage. David Hance, having moved from amongst us without a certificate and left his business and affairs much unsettled, is disowned. A certificate to Red Stone Monthly Meeting for Stephen Maason was read and approved. A certificate to Red Stone Monthly Meeting for Lydia Pearce was read and approved. A certificate to Red Stone Monthly Meeting for Avis Duly, wife of Joshua Duly, was read and approved. A paper from Anne Allen condemns her having married a man without the consent of her mother and by the assistance of a priest.

5th of 10th mo., 1789 - Benj'n. Wooley and Hannah Jackson declare their intentions to marry for the second time. Mary Hance sent in a paper condemning her being too far off her guard as to go to places of diversion without the consent of her parents and also being active in dancing. A letter from Little Eggharbour informs this meeting that Anthony Smith had not produced to that meeting the certificate of removal for himself and his family which was given by this meeting. Friends are appointed to forward a copy of said certificate to Little Eggharbour. This meeting is informed that Stephen West stands in need of assistance.

2nd of 11th mo., 1789 - A paper from Sarah Hulet wherein she expresses sorrow for having accomplished her marriage with the assistance of a priest, and having been guilty of fornication with the man who is now her husband was published. The friends appointed report that Stephen West stands in need of some necessaries, which they are desired to supply him with and apply to the treasurer for payment. A certificate to Red Stone Monthly Meeting for Mercy Johnson, about to remove with her husband, was read and approved. A certificate is requested for John Corlies who is placed apprentice to Joseph Field of Springfield Monthly Meeting.

Shrewsbury Monthly Meeting

7th of 2th mo., 1789 - A certificate to Buckingham Monthly Meeting for Meribah Jackson, daughter of William and Hanna, who is in her infant state and now lives with Amos File, a member of that meeting. A paper of condemnation from James Lawrence wherein he acknowledges having been active in training and too much neglected attending meetings was read and accepted. A certificate to Springfield Monthly Meeting for John Corlies, a youth, placed and apprentice to Joseph Field was read and signed.

4th of 1st mo., 1790 - Jacob Lawrence has been treated with for fornication with the woman now his wife and likewise for horse racing and training. Sylvanus Smith has been treated with for taking and oath and also for being at a training. A certificate requested for the sons of David Hance who removed with their father within he verge of Chesterfield Monthly Meeting. Also for Hannah, the wife of David Hance, and her three daughters. Sarah, the wife of Brittain Corlies, with the approbation of her husband, requests that her four children Ann, Elizabeth, Deborah and Brittain, may be received into membership with us.

1st of 2nd mo., 1890 - Rebeckah, the wife of Samuel Wardell, having been guilty of fornication and marrying a man not in unity with us, is disowned. A certificate to Chesterfield Monthly Meeting on behalf of Hannah, the wife of David Hance, and their children, (viz) Sarah, a young woman clear o marriage, David, Jeremiah, Hannah and Lydia, was read and approved. Dav'd Curtis, Jun'r, hath been treated with for going to a training.

1st of 3rd mo., 1790 - Sylvanus Smith produced a paper of condemnation whereas he expresses sorrow for taking an oath and likewise being at training. Henry Wolcott expresses sorrow for having been guilty of fornication with the woman who is now his wife and accomplishing his marriage by the assistance of a magistrate. David Curtis, Jun'r. Produced a paper acknowledging that he attended a training and has also been at places of diversion. Israel Williams has been treated with for the neglect of attending our meetings and offering for sale a beef, a creature that was found dead in his field.

5th of 4th mo., 1790 - A letter was received from the monthly meeting at Little Eggharbour, inclosing Antho' Smith, his wife and son John's certificate, informing that said certificate was not accepted.

3rd of 5th mo., 1790 - A certificate to New York Monthly Meeting on behalf of Gorge Corlies, Jun'r., was read and approved. A paper from Elizabeth Wolcott wherein she expresses sorrow for having committed fornication with the man who is now her husband and accomplishing her marriage by the assistance of a magistrate.

5th of 7th mo., 1790 - Samuel Williams has been treated with for drinking spiritous liquors to excess, fighting with his neighbor, neglect of attending meetings and not paying his debts. George Williams has been treated with for drinking to excess and neglect of attending meetings.

2nd of 8th mo., 1790 - Elizabeth Knott, having married a man not of our religious society by the assistance of a magistrate, is disowned.

6th of 9th mo., 1790 - Content Francis, having married a man not of our religious profession, is disowned. A certificate to Rahway Monthly Meeting for Britain Tucker is requested.

4th of 10th mo., 1790 - Jacob Corlies produce a paper of condemnation wherein he professes sorrow for marrying a woman not in unity and by the assistance of a magistrate and for having frequented taverns and places of diversion. A paper from Jacob Williams condemns his neglect of attending meetings, attending horse races and once suffering his mare to run, being active in training and committing fornication with the woman he has since married. A paper from Israel Williams expresses sorrow for offering for sale as beef a creature he found dead in his field and for his neglect in attending meetings. Margaret Throckmorton, wife of Jos'h. Throckmorton, Jun'r., having kept company with and admitted the addresses of a man not of our religious profession and has been guilty of fornication, and also contributed to the support of an hireling ministry by being married to the same man by the assistance of a priest, is disowned. A certificate from the monthly meeting at New York for Mary Pintard and her daughter Ann was read and accepted.

1st of 11th mo., 1790 - John Barrow of New York and Mary Lawrence of Shrewsbury declared their intentions to marry. A certificate to Friends at Plainfield and Rahway on behalf of Brittain Tucker was approved and ordered to be signed.

6th of 12th mo., 1790 - John Barrow produced a certificate from the monthly meeting at New York and the said John Barrow and Mary Lawrence then declared the continuation of their intentions to marry. George Williams produced a paper acknowledging that he has been guilty of drinking spiritous liquors to excess and has also neglected the attendance of our religious meetings. Samuel Williams produced two papers in which he condemns his being guilty of drinking spiritus liquors to excess, fighting with his neighbour, neglecting the attendance of our religious services and his slackness in paying towards the expenses of the meeting. Jacob Corlies complains that Peter Walcot, as Administrator to Dan'l Potter's estate, refuses paying him a debt. Will'm Hartshorne is pointed to draw a certificate

Shrewsbury Monthly Meeting

to New York Monthly Meeting for Mary Lawrence.

3rd of 1st mo., 1791 - The Friends appointed report that John Barrows marriage was orderly accomplished. A certificate to New York Monthly Meeting for Mary Lawrence, now Mary Barrow, was approved.

7th of 2nd mo., 1791 - James Parker sent in a paper wherein he acknowledges he has been guilty of fornication with her that is now his wife and has been married by the assistance of a magistrate. Champless Williams has been treated with for neglect of our religious meetings and also for running a footrace. A certificate from the monthly meeting at New York on behalf of Jane White, who came recommended in the year 87 and is now returning, was read and accepted. Esek and Elizabeth Hartshorne request that their daughter Hannah, who is in her childhood, be accepted into membership.

7th of 3rd mo., 1791 - Jediah Allen requests a certificate to Buckingham Monthly Meeting for himself, his wife and son George. A letter of acknowledgment from Rachel Hance wherein she empresses sorrow for having accomplishing her marriage by the assistance of a Justice of the Peace and to a man not in unity.

4th of 4th mo., 1791 - Henry Burr, of Mount Holly, and Phebe Williams, d/o Edm'd Williams, declare their intentions to marry. A paper from Champlis Williams wherein he acknowledges that he has been in neglect of attending meetings and has run a foot race. A paper from Patience Parker acknowledges that she has been guilty of fornication with him that is now her husband and has been married contrary to good order.

2nd of 5th mo., 1791 - Henry Burr produced a certificate from the monthly meeting at Mount Holly, which being satisfactory, he and Phebe Williams declared the continuation of their intentions to marry. A certificate to Buckingham Monthly Meeting for Jediah Allen, his wife Ann and son George, was read and approved. Jeremiah Pearce requests to be to be joined in membership with Friends.

6th of 6th mo., 1791 - David Laing produced a paper condemning his going out in marriage and neglect of attending our religious meetings. David Curtis Jun'r has been treated with for being guilty of fornication with her that is now his wife and for being married contrary to good order. James Lawrence has been treated with for being guilty of fornication with her that is now his wife and for being married contrary to good order.

4th of 7th mo., 1791 - A paper from Lydia Corlies, w/o Joseph Corlies, wherein she condemns being guilty of fornication by marrying a man not in unity with Friends and with the assistance of a priest, and also requests to again be received into membership, was read and approved. Hannah Wikoff, having married a man not of our society, with the assistance of a priest, is disowned. Margaret Hance, being guilty of fornication, is disowned. A paper from Britton Woolley, wherein he condemns his having run a race and for quarreling and fighting with his neighbor, was read. The certificate granted to Mercy Johnson, dated 2nd of 11th mo., 1789, was this day returned- she having returned to live among us. The said certificate not having reached her in time to be delivered to Redstone Monthly Meeting.

1st of 8th mo., 1791 - A certificate to Mount Holly Monthly Meeting on behalf of Phebe Burr was read and ordered to be signed. Elihu Smith has removed to a considerable distance from this meeting without a certificate and has been guilty of fornication and marrying another woman contrary to our society.

5th of 9th mo., 1791 - Rachel White and Ann and Elizabeth Allen have requested to come under the care of Friends. Request for a certificate for John Curtis, placed apprentice to Sam'l Rogers of Burlington, for Sam'l Tucker, Jun'r, placed apprentice to Sam'l Earl of Burlington, and for Lawrence Jackson, placed apprentice to Joseph Hahurst of Middletown Monthly Meeting in Pennsylvania. George Williams has been treated with for seizing and selling the property of Jacob Corlies.

3rd of 10th mo., 1791 - Joseph Byrd of New York and Elizabeth Lawrence, daughter of Rich'd and Alice Lawrence, declared their intentions of marriage. A certificate on behalf of Tacy Maxson, widow, to Redstone Monthly Meeting in Pennsylvania. Rachel White and Ann and Elizabeth Allen are received as members. Elizabeth Hartshorne, Jr, is received into membership. A certificate to Middletown Monthly Meeting in Pennsylvania for Lawrence Jackson, placed apprentice to Joseph Hahurst.

7th of 11th mo., 1791 - Joseph Byrd produced a certificate from New York Monthly Meeting, then the said Joseph Byrd and Elizabeth Lawrence declared the continuation of their intentions to marry. They are now left to accomplish the same. A certificate to Mount Holly on behalf of Samuel Tucker, Jun'r, placed apprentice to James Earl was read and approved A certificate to Burlington Monthly Meeting on behalf of John Curtis, placed apprentice to Sam'l Rogers was read and approved.

5th of 12th mo., 1791 - Friends report that Joseph Byrd's marriage was orderly accomplished. David Curtis, Jun'r, being guilty of fornication with her that is now his wife and marrying contrary to

Shrewsbury Monthly Meeting

good order, is disowned. Sam'l Williams has been treated with for drinking strong drink to excess.

2nd of 1st mo., 1792 - Elihu Smith, being guilty of fornication, has since married the woman contrary to good order and having also removed a considerable distance beyond the limits of this meeting without applying for a certificate, is disowned. David Laing requests a certificate to the monthly meeting at Rahway and Plainfield. Through mistake, the certificate for Sam'l Tucker Jun'r was directed to Burlington Monthly Meeting instead of Mount Holly. The clerk is directed to make the necessary alteration.

6th of 2nd month, 1792 - James Lawrence acknowledges being guilty of fornication with her that is now his wife and having married contrary to good order. Lydia Lawrence, likewise, acknowledges being guilty of fornication with him that is now her husband and having married contrary to good order by a magistrate A certificate to Rahway and Plainfield on behalf of David Laing was read and approved. John Hartshorne laid before this meeting his prospect of attending our friend Thomas Scattergood to some meetings in West Jersey.

5th of 3rd mo., 1792 - A certificate to Friends in New York on behalf of Elizabeth Byrd was read and approved.

2nd of 4th mo., 1792 - Samuel Lafetra and Elizabeth Allen declared their intentions to marry. Ann Little, being guilty of fornication and marrying a man not of our society, is disowned. A certificate is desired for Joseph Jackson to the Falls Meeting in Pennsylvania, he living with Wm Jackson.

7th of 5th mo., 1792 - Samuel Lafetra and Eliz'a Allen declare the continuation of their intentions to marry and are left to accomplish the same. The difference between Geo. Williams and Jacob Corlies is settled. Geo. Williams produced a paper wherein he acknowledges having given out a landlords warrant whereby his brother in membership's property was seized and sold. Achsah Hance is received into membership. A certificate is requested for Benj'n Corlies, son of George, who is placed apprentice to Robt White, a member of Chesterfield Monthly Meeting. Certificates are requested for Asher and Daniel Parker to New York Monthly Meeting. A certificate for George White from New York, Monthly Meeting was read.

4th of 6th mo., 1792 - Sam'l Lafetra's marriage was orderly accomplished. Ebenezer Hance acknowledges being guilty of paying fines in lieu of military service. A certificate to the Falls in Bucks County, Pennsylvania for Joseph Jackson who is gone to live with his brother Wm Jackson was read and approved. A certificate to the monthly meeting at Chesterfield for Benj'n Corlies, son of George, who is placed an apprentice to Robert White, was read and approved. A certificate is requested for Abigail Parker and her daughters. A certificate from Buckingham on behalf of Jediah Allen, Anne his wife and son George, not long since recommended to them and now returning, was read and accepted.

6th of 8th mo., 1792 - Jacob Laing, Jun'r, having married a wife not in unity with us and neglected attending our religious meetings, is disowned. A certificate to New York Monthly Meeting on behalf of Abigail Parker and her 6 children, Asher, Daniel, Margaret, Sarah, Elizabeth and Margery, all being in heir nonage, was approved.

3rd of 9th mo., 1792 - Ann Pintard has been treated with for neglecting our religious meetings and having joined herself with another profession. Brittain Tucker complains that James Williams neglects paying him a just debt.

5th of 11th mo., 1792 - A certificate for Ann Loyd, removed with her husband William Loyd, from the monthly meeting at Philadelphia, held for the Northern District, was read and accepted. A certificate for Mary Loyd, removed with her parents and clear of debt and marriage engagement, from the monthly meeting at Philadelphia, held for the Northern District, was read and accepted. Elizabeth Allen acknowledges having married a man not in unity with us, accomplishing the same with the assistance of a magistrate, without the consent of her parents.

3rd of 12th mo., 1792 - George Williams has been treated with for neglect of attending our religious meetings and for drinking spiritous liquors to access. George Parker requests a certificate for his son George who is placed apprentice to Jesse Farrington of Rahway and Plainfield Monthly Meeting. A certificate from New York on behalf of George White who is returning to us after serving an apprenticeship with a Friend from that city, was read and accepted. It appears that Jerem'h Pearce stands in need of the immediate attention of his friends.

7th of 1st mo., 1793 - Samuel Williams, being in the practice of drinking spiritous liquors to excess, is disowned. Ann Pintard, having neglected the attendance of our religious meetings and joining herself in membership with another society, is disowned. A certificate to Rahway and Plainfield Monthly Meeting on behalf of George Parker, Jun'r, who is placed apprentice to Jesse Farrington, was read and approved. Samuel Tucker has been treated with for refusing to settle a demand of James Williams (Administrator to his brothers estate).

Shrewsbury Monthly Meeting

4th of 3rd mo., 1793 - John Parker acknowledges having kept company with a young woman not of our society and married her with the assistance of a Justice, contrary to the advice of his parents, and having kept his seat in a public meeting when one of our members went to prayer. Jacob Corlies acknowledges having fell into company and drinking spiritous liquors to excess. Daniel Woodmansee requests a certificate to Upper Springfield Monthly Meeting for himself, his wife and children, viz: William, Tylee and Ann.

1st of 4th mo., 1793 - Friends appointed on Brittain Tucker's complaint report the matter is settled. Silvanus Smith hath married a woman not of our society, neglects th attendance of our religious meetings, has been at a place of gaming and is profane in his language. A certificate requested for Hannah White, daughter of Peter and Patience, who is in her childhood and is put out to Robert White, a Friend of Chesterfield Monthly Meeting.

6th of 5th mo., 1793 - A certificate to Chesterfield Monthly Meeting on behalf of Hannah White, being in her childhood, who has become a resident with Robert and Hannah White of Stony Brook, was read and approved George Williams, guilty of drinking spiritous liquor and going out in marriage by a priest to a woman not of our society, is disowned. John Lippincott acknowledges accomplishing his marriage by the assistance of a magistrate. Elizabeth Lippincott acknowledges the same, without the consent of her mother.

3rd of 6th mo., 1793 - A request for a certificate to Springfield Monthly Meeting on behalf of Miriam Woodmansee and her 3 children, to wit, William, Tylee and Ann.

1st of 7th mo., 1793 - A certificate to Springfield Monthly Meeting for Miriam Woodmansee and her three children, William, Tylee and Ann, all in their nonage, was read and approved. Thomas Cook acknowledges having gone contrary to good order in paying a fine for not turning out in the militia and marrying his cousin by a priest. Rachel Cook acknowledges marrying her first cousin by a priest.

2nd of 9th mo., 1793 - A certificate to New York Monthly Meeting for Elizabeth Riker, who is clear of marriage, was read and approved. Henry Woolcott has been treated with for committing fornication with a woman who is not a member of our society who is now his wife.

7th of 10th mo., 1793 - Mary Pintard has been treated with for omitting the attendance of our religious meetings and joining herself to another society. Elizabeth Jackson desires to be admitted into membership.

4th of 11th mo., 1793 - Sylvanus Smith, having married a woman not of our religious society, neglected attending our religious meetings, being at a place of gaming and being profane in his language, is disowned. Elizabeth Jackson, wife of Peter Jackson, is received into membership. Ann Jackson condemns having paid a fine.

2nd of 12th mo., 1793 - Joseph Jackson acknowledges having let out his affections to a young woman not in membership with us, and with the assistance of a magistrate has married her. Mary Pintard has not only omitted the attendance of our religious meetings but joined herself in membership with another society. Peter Jackson requests that his two sons, Isaac and William, who are in their nonage, be received into membership. Hannah Robinson, wife of Thomas, is taken under the care of Friends. Request for a certificate to the monthly meeting at New Cornwall on behalf of Ann Jackson.

6th of 1st mo., 1794 - Peter Jackson's two sons, Isaac and William are received into membership. As a similar request was made for his daughters Elizabeth, Margaret and Mary, who are also in their childhood, they too are accordingly received.

3rd of 2nd mo., 1794 - A certificate on behalf of Ann Jackson, who is clear of marriage engagements, to the monthly meeting at New Cornwall ib the state of New York was read and approved. Henry Wollcott denies the charge of fornication. Hester Hance requests to be taken into membership. There is a difference between John Parker and Joseph Parker. Jeremiah Pearce stands in need of immediate care.

3rd of 3rd mo., 1794 - The difference between John Parker and Joseph Parker appears to be settled. Benjamin Wolcott requests that his sons, William and Benjamin, may come under the care of Friends. Champlys Williams has been treated with for fighting and drinking spiritous liquors to excess. Jonathan Maxson requests a certificate for himself and his sons David and Nathan to Redstone Monthly Meeting.

7th of 4th mo., 1794 - Britton Corlies, who acknowledges his guilt in quarreling with his neighbor and carrying the same to a reproachful length, is reinstated into society and received into membership. Esther Hance is received into membership. A certificate is requested for Jonathan Maxson, his wife and children, to Redstone Monthly Meeting. Benj. White complains of Abraham Parker for not paying a debt due to him.

5th of 5th mo., 1794 - A certificate to Redstone Monthly Meeting on behalf of Jonathan Maxson, his wife Mary Magdalene and their two children, was read and approved. Thomas Curtis, Jun'r, has been treated with for fighting. There is a difference subsisting between

Shrewsbury Monthly Meeting

Thom's Tilton and Hugh Jackson. Ann Wolcott, wife of Benjamin, requests to be taken into membership.

4nd of 6th mo., 1794 - Henry Wolcott has married a woman not of our society and has also been accused of committing fornication with her, and notwithstanding he denies the charges, the circumstances are so strong appearing to confirm it we think it right to disown him. Benjamin White's complaint is settled. Amos Wolcott condemns his having accomplished his marriage contrary to discipline and without the consent of parents. The difference between Thomas Tilton and Hugh Jackson is settled. Daniel Woodmansee has conducted in such a way to give occasion for scandalous reports respecting his being too familiar with a woman who lived in his house. He has equivocated and told falsehoods and also there is sufficient reason to believe that he has been disrespectfully concerned in gambling and has drunk spiritous liquors to excess. John Lafetra has been treated with for accomplishing his marriage contrary to discipline. Benjamin White's complaint is not yet settled. Anne Wolcott, the wife of Benjamin, and her children, William, Benjamin, Anne, Elizabeth and Hannah, all within childhood, are received into membership. Nathan Woolley has been accused of being guilty of adultery. David Corlies has been charged with being guilty of fornication and marrying with another woman not a member, and also for being in neglect of attending our religious meetings.

4th of 8th mo., 1794 - Champlys Williams, being guilty of drinking spiritous liquors to excess, and also of quarreling and fighting with his neighbor, is disowned. Benjamin White withdraws his complaint against Abraham Parker. John Lafetra condemns having fixed his affection on a woman and marrying her, who has not a right amongst Friends, without the consent of parents.

1st if 9th mo., 1794 - A certificate from Burlington Monthly Meeting on behalf of Thomas Haywood was produced. A certificate on behalf of Margaret Grant and such of her children shall be found to have a right of membership, is requested.

6th of 10th mo., 1794 - A certificate to West Land in Pennsylvania on behalf of Margery Grant, wife of John Grant, and her children, John, Anthony, Lydia, Annzube, and Judith, being in heir minority, was read and approved.

3d of 11th o., 1794 - A certificate from Burlington Monthly Meeting on behalf of Thomas Haywood was read and approved. Request for a certificate to Chesterfield Monthly Meeting on behalf of Sarah Robbins. A minute against Elizabeth Borden and Esther Borden, daughters of the late Sam'l Borden, to be prepared. A certificate requested for Sarah Rively to Darby Monthly Meeting. John Hartshorne, Jun'r, to accompany our friend Joseph Cloud on his religious visits to the eastward.

1st of 12th mo., 1794 - A certificate to Darby Monthly Meeting on behalf of Sarah Rivley.

5th of 1st mo., 1795 - William Hance acknowledges having been concerned with training and appearing with a gun in order to learn warlike exercises. A letter from Nathan Woolley demanding an appeal from the judgement of this meeting was produced. Benjamin Jackson the 4th has been treated with for going to a marriage accomplished contrary to discipline.

2nd of 2nd mo., 1795 - Thomas Curtis, Jun'r, having been guilty of fighting, is disowned. Benjamin Borden has been treated with for committing fornication with the woman he has since married.

2nd of 3rd mo., 1795 - Lydia Little has been treated with for going out in marriage and being guilty of fornication. A certificate to West Land Monthly Meeting on behalf of Patience Jewell, wife of Hopewell Jewell, was read and approved. Daniel Woodmansee, having been too familiar with woman who lived in his house, for which he equivocated and told falsehoods, and who hath also been concerned in gambling and has drunk spiritous liquors to excess, is disowned. Ben'j. Jackson the 4th acknowledges having accomplished his marriage contrary to discipline. A certificate is requested on behalf of Will'm. Tilton, son of Thomas, to Chesterfield Monthly Meeting. William Lloyd and his son Joseph Lloyd request to be received into membership.

6th of 4th mo., 1795 - George White and Elizabeth Borden declare their intentions to marry. Charity Tallman acknowledges being guilty of fornication with him that is now her husband. Elizabeth Croxson acknowledges having been guilty of fornication with the man who is now her husband and has also obtained the forgiveness of her parents. Benjamin Borden acknowledges having committed fornication with her that is now his wife. William Lloyd is accepted into membership but as his son, Joseph Lloyd is but a youth, we think a farther time for him to be more fully acquainted with Friends principles and rules. Brittain White requests a certificate to New York Monthly Meeting for his son Brittain. Also, a certificate for John Lippincott to New York Monthly Meeting.

4th of 5th mo., 1795 - George White and Elizabeth Borden declared the continuation of their intentions to marry and are now left to accomplish the same. Nathan Wooley, being guilty of adultery, is disowned. A certificate to Haddonfield Monthly Meeting on behalf

Shrewsbury Monthly Meeting

of Benjamin Swett, who, with his companion Job Whitall, was on a religious visit with us, was read and approved. A certificate to Woodbury Monthly Meeting on behalf of Job Whitall, who, in company with Benjamin Swett, was on a religious visit with us, was also read and approved. A certificate to New York Monthly Meeting on behalf of Brittain White, son of Brittain, who is placed an apprentice to Joseph Hopkins. Lydia Woolcott acknowledges accomplishing her marriage contrary to discipline, without the consent of her parents and with the assistance of a magistrate.

11th of 6th mo., 1795 - Thomas Cook requests that his children, Richard and Sarah, being in their nonage, may be taken under the care of Friends. George Parker requests a certificate for his son Jacob, who is placed an apprentice to Isaac Vail, a Friend of Rahway and Plainfield Monthly Meeting. Content Parker requests to be received into membership. George White's marriage was orderly accomplished.

6th of 7th mo., 1795 - A certificate to Rahway and Plainfield Monthly Meeting on behalf of Jacob Parker, son of George, placed apprentice with Isaac Vail. A certificate to New York Monthly Meeting on behalf of John and Elizabeth Lippincott was read and approved..Thomas Cook's children, Richard and Sarah, are received into membership. Jacob Lawrence has been treated with for fighting and neglecting the attendance of our religious meetings. Content Parker is received into membership.

3rd of 8th mo., 1795 - It being a time of great fall of rain and but a small number of Friends present, the meeting is adjourned to 2nd day next.

10th of 8th mo., 1795 - Thomas Wooley acknowledges his drunkenness, corruptness in life and conversation and neglect in the attendance of religious meetings. Mary Borden acknowledges being guilty of fornication with the man that is now her husband and accomplishing her marriage by a magistrate.

7th of 9th mo., 1795 - Lydia Little, having committed fornication with the man she hath since married, is disowned.

5th of 10th mo., 1795 - David Corlies, being guilty of fornication and since married another woman who has not a right among us and also in the neglect of our religious meetings, is disowned.

2nd of 11th mo., 1795 - John Tucker has been treated with for drinking spiritous liquors to excess, in which he shot a gun into his neighbors window, and also for neglecting the attendance of our religious meetings. William Jackson, Jun'r, has been treated with for training and for drinking spiritous liquors to excess, and also for the neglect in attending of our religious meetings. Elizabeth Lafetra, the wife of

Early Church Records of Monmouth County

William Lafetra, is received into membership.

7th of 12 th mo., 1795 - Jacob Lawrence, who hath been guilty of fighting and neglects the attendance of our religious meetings, is disowned Sarah Jackson acknowledges having been guilty of fornication. Will'm Tilton has married one not in membership with us.

4th of 1st mo., 1796 - Benj. Jackson the 4th has been treated with for going out in marriage with one not a member, and for neglecting the attendance of our religious meetings. A certificate is requested for James Jackson, son of William, to Mount Holly Monthly Meeting, who is placed apprentice some time since to Samuel Earl.

1st of 2nd mo., 1796 - A certificate to Mount Holly Monthly Meeting on behalf of James Jackson, son of Will'm Jackson, who was some time ago placed apprentice to Samuel Earl. Will'm Tilton acknowledges having married a woman not a member of our religious society and by the assistance of a magistrate. A certificate from Rahway and Plainfield Monthly Meeting on behalf of George Parker Jun'r was read and approved.

7th of 3rd mo., 1796 - Rich'd Borden, Jun'r, has been treated with for fighting and attending places of diversion, and neglecting the attendance of our religious meetings. William Tilton, son of Thomas, requests to be united in membership.

4th of 4th mo., 1796 - John Tucker, who hath been guilty of drinking spiritous liquors to excess, and while in a state of intoxication fired a gun into his neighbors window, and has also neglected the attendance of our religious meetings, is disowned. William Tilton, son of Thomas, is received into membership.

2nd of 5th mo., 1796 - Benj'n Jackson the 4th acknowledges having married a wife contrary to his parents advice, and not a member of our society, and at time having neglected attending meetings.

6th of 6th mo., 1796 - William Tilton, son of Thomas, requests a certificate to Chesterfield Monthly Meeting. William Lafetra requests to be received into membership. Mary Tenbrook has married a man not in membership with us. Phebe White, having married a man not in membership with us, is disowned.

4th of 7th mo., 1796 - William Jackson, Jun'r, having appeared at training for military purposes, and also being guilty of drinking spiritous liquors to excess and neglecting the attendance of our religious meetings, is disowned. John Williams requests a certificate to New York Monthly Meeting.

1st of 8th mo., 1796 - A certificate to New York Monthly Meeting on behalf of Wil'm Tilton, son of Thomas, clear of marriage engagements, was read.

Shrewsbury Monthly Meeting

5th of 9th mo., 1796 - Ann Woodward is disowned.

3rd of 10th mo., 1796 - The certificate to New York Monthly Meeting on behalf of Wil'm Tilton, son of Thomas was again read and is approved.

7th of 11th mo., 1796 -Benjamin Parker requests to be taken into membership with Friends. Elizabeth Vanpelt, who hath been guilty of fornication, is disowned. Jeremiah Hance has been treated with for neglect of our religious meetings and for marrying a woman not of our society. Sidney Parker requests a certificate to New York Monthly Meeting. Ann White, wife of Esek White, requests to be received into membership. Mary Cox requests to be received into membership.

5th of 12th mo., 1796 - Meribah Little, guilty of the gross sin of fornication, is disowned. Lydia Morris, guilty of fornication and marrying a man not in unity with us, is disowned. A certificate to New York Monthly Meeting for Sydney Parker, clear of marriage engagements, was read and approved. Ann White is received into membership. Mary Cox is received into membership.

2nd of 1st mo., 1797 - Benjamin Parker is received into membership.

6th of 2nd mo., 1797- Thomas Borden has been treated with for neglect in the attendance of our religious meetings, frequenting taverns and drinking spiritous liquors to excess.

6th of 3rd mo., 1797 - William White has been treated with for marrying one not a member of our society.

3rd of 4th mo., 1797 - Timothy Corlies, who acknowledges that some years past he did marry a woman who was his mothers first cousin and was married by a Justice of the Peace, is received into membership. William Hance requests that his son, Revo, being in his childhood, might be received into membership. Thomas Haywood has been treated with for being guilty of fornication with the woman he has since married.

5st of 6th mo., 1797 - Jeremiah Hance, having been in neglect of attending our religious meetings and marrying a woman not of out religious profession, is disowned. Ebenezer Curtis has been treated with for going out in marriage with one not a member.

3rd of 7th mo., 1797 - Thomas Haywood acknowledges having been guilty of fornication and having since married the woman.

7th of 8th mo., 1797 - Thomas Borden acknowledges frequenting taverns, drinking strong liquors to excess and the neglect of attending meetings. Will'm White acknowledges marrying a young woman not a member of our society and contrary to the advice of his parents.

4th of 9th mo., 1797 - A certificate from the monthly meeting at Little Eggharbour on behalf of Stephen Eayres, his wife Elizabeth and their two minor children, viz.: Jonathan and Jacob Eayres, was read and accepted. Tho's Haywood requests a certificate to Little Eggharbour. Edmund Williams has been treated with for levity of behavior to women.

2nd of 10th mo., 1797 - A certificate to Little Eggharbour for Thomas Haywood was read and approved.

6th of 11th mo., 1797 - Ebenezer Curtis acknowledges marrying his mothers first cousin, who is not in membership, by a magistrate. A certificate to Westland Monthly Meeting on behalf of Judith Burdge, who is clear of marriage engagements, and her daughter Mariam, who is in her childhood. Lucy Hartshorne has deceased since last monthly meeting.

4th of 12th mo., 1796 - Francis Borden has been treated with for going out in marriage with a woman not of our society.

5th of 2nd mo., 1798 - Amos Tilton, son of Thomas, requests to come under the care of Friends.

5th of 3rd mo., 1798 - Francis Borden, having accomplished his marriage contrary to the rules of discipline, is disowned.

2nd of 4th mo., 1798 - Margaret Odell, being guilty of fornication and married a man not of our religious society, is disowned.

7th of 5th mo., 1798 - Walter Curtis acknowledges having taken an active part in the war and Militia exercise, and is accordingly received into membership. Mary Dennis, having married contrary to our discipline and been present at a marriage accomplished contrary thereto, is disowned. Dav'd Curtis, son of Walter, requests a certificate to Chesterfield Monthly Meeting. Walter Curtis requests a certificate for his son William who is placed apprentice to a Friend within the compass of Rahway Monthly Meeting.

Th of 6th mo., 1798 - Amos Tilton, son of Thomas, is received into membership. A certificate to rahway Monthly Meeting on behalf of William Curtis, placed apprentice to Hugh Davids, was read and approved.

6nd of 8th mo., 1798 - A certificate to the Monthly Meeting at Chesterfield for David Curtis, son of Walter, was read and approved. Elizabeth White is received into membership. A certificate is requested for Sarah Debow.

3rd of 9th mo. 1798 - James Morris and Elizabeth Curtis declared their intentions to marry. A certificate to Chesterfield Monthly Meeting on behalf of Sarah Debow was read and approved. Hannah Wooley requests a certificate for her son Mahlon Jackson, who is placed an

Shrewsbury Monthly Meeting

apprentice to Jesse Betts, a Friend of Buckingham Monthly Meeting.

1st of 10th mo., 1798 - James Morris and Elizabeth Curtis are clear to marry. A certificate to Buckingham Monthly Meeting on behalf of Mahlon Jackson, who is placed apprentice to Jesse Betts was read and approved. A certificate from Haddonfield Monthly Meeting on behalf of Nathan Middletown was read and accepted.

5th of 11th mo., 1798 - Brittain Tucker has some time since had a certificate from our Monthly Meeting to the Monthly Meeting at Rahway which hath not been given in.

3rd of 12th mo., 1798 - Brittian White has informed Friends that the certificate granted him by this meeting is lost, having received it after his return from Rahway. He now resides within the compass of our Monthly Meeting.

7th of 1st mo., 1799 - A certificate from the monthly meeting of Mount Holly, dated 4th of 10th mo., 1798, for Samuel Tucker, Jun'r, was read and accepted. Mary Emley, late Hance, hath, after being pre-cautioned, married a man not of our religious society.

4th of 2nd mo., 1799 - Mary Emley, late Hance, having accomplished her marriage with a man not of our religious society, is disowned. Hugh Jackson, Jun'r, has been treated with for frequenting places of diversion and being active in dancing.

4th of 3rd mo., 1799 - Sarah Thompson, being guilty of fornication and marrying a man not in unity with us, is disowned.

5th of 4th mo., 1799 - Hugh Jackson, Jun'r, acknowledges being guilty of being at places of diversion and being active in dancing. Rachel Parker requests a certificate for her son Thomas Borden, son of Amos Borden, deceased, who is placed an apprentice to Samuel Rogers, a Friend of Burlington Monthly Meeting.

6th of 5th mo., 1799 - A certificate to Burlington Monthly Meeting on behalf of Thomas Borden, son of the late Amos Borden, who is placed an apprentice to Samuel Rogers, was read and approved. Jacob White has been treated with for going out in marriage with a woman not in membership with us and accomplishing his marriage with the assistance of a priest. Jonathan _____ has been treated with for going out in marriage with a woman not in membership with us and accomplishing his marriage with the assistance of a priest and for the neglect of attending our religious meetings. A certificate to Chesterfield Monthly Meeting on behalf of John Hartshorne, Jun'r, in order for marriage, was read and approved.

3rd of 6th mo., 1799 - Abraham Laing, being guilty of fornication, is disowned.

5th of 7th mo., 1799 - Joseph Burg has been treated with for removing from this place to Redstone without a certificate and has been charged with being guilty of fornication and vain in conversation. It appears that Anthony Burg has left his master before his time was out, and this place without a certificate. Lydia Corlies, widow of Joseph Corlies, requests her two sons be received into membership, and also her daughters. It being satisfactory to this meeting, the said Lydia Corlies children, Brittain, Timothy, Ann, Hannah, Deborah, Lydia and Meribah Corlies are received into membership. Wm Lafetra requests his son and daughter, who are in their childhood, be received into membership, which being considered, Wm Lafetra's children, Jesse and Grace are accordingly received into membership. Deborah Jackson has been treated with for committing fornication.

2nd of 9th mo., 1799 - Dennis Hurley produced a certificate from the monthly meeting at Rahway and Plainfield. Jacob White acknowledges having married a woman not of our society, by the assistance of a priest, and having attended a marriage accomplished contrary to the rules of Friends. Jonathan Ares, having married a woman out of unity with us, by the assistance of a priest, and also neglecting attending our religious meetings, is disowned. A certificate for Elizabeth Hartshorne from the monthly meeting of Chesterfield is accepted.

7th of 10th mo., 1799 - Deborah Jackson, having committed the shameful crime of fornication, is disowned. Jacob Corlies requests that his son, Edward Garigues Corlies, be taken into membership. Jacob Parker produced a certificate from the monthly meeting of Rahway and Plainfield which being read, is accepted. A certificate requested for Hannah and Lydia Corlies. Elizabeth Curtis's request to be taken into membership is approved.

4th of 11th mo., 1799 - Benj'm Morris, having acknowledged paying a fine in lieu of military service is reinstated into society. Edward G. Corlies is received into membership. A certificate is requested for Jacob Corlies. A certificate to Chesterfield Monthly Meeting on behalf of Hannah and Lydia Corlies, being in their childhood, Hannah being placed with Ann, the wife of Daniel Hendrickson and Lydia with Joseph Hendrickson. A certificate is requested for Deborah Harley.

2nd of 12th mo., 1799 - A certificate to the monthly meeting at Rahway and Plainfield on behalf of Deborah Hurley, wife of Dennis Hurley, was read and approved. A certificate to the monthly meeting at Rahway and Plainfield on behalf of Jacob Corlies Jun'r, clear of marriage engagements, was read and approved. Fanny Hart, having

Dutch Reformed Church - Freehold and Middletown

married a man not of our religious society, is disowned.

6th of 1st mo., 1800 - Mary Bessonnet, having married a man contrary to good order, is disowned. Samuel Curtis has been treated with for training and learning military exercises. Hugh Jackson Jun'r has been treated with for going out in marriage.

3rd of 2nd mo., 1800 - Anne Morris, late Wolcott, having married a man not a member o our society, is disowned.

3rd of 3rd mo., 1800 - Samuel Curtis, having been active in training in order to learn war like exercises, is disowned. A certificate to New York Monthly Meeting on behalf of Amy Lefetra, clear of marriage engagements, was read and approved.

7th of 4th mo., 1800 - It appears that Benj'm Jackson the Fourth has gone out in marriage with a woman not in membership with us. A certificate requested for Elizabeth Jackson.

5th of 5th mo., 1800 - Benjamin Jackson the Fourth, having married a woman contrary to good order, is disowned. A certificate to Middletown, in Pennsylvania, on behalf of Elizabeth Jackson, who is in her minority and is placed with Joseph and Ann _____, was read and approved. It appears that Richard Worthly hath married a woman not in membership with us

2nd of th mo., 1800 - Richard Worthly, having married a woman not in membership with us, is disowned.

7th of 7th mo., 1800 - Joseph Parker has been treated with for _____ evil report. Brittain Corlies has been treated with for refusing to pay a debt to Timothy Corlies agreeable to an award made by arbitration of their own choosing.

4th of 8th mo., A certificate requested on behalf of Richard Cook, son of Thomas Cook, who is placed an apprentice with Wm Cook, a Friend of the same meeting.

1st of 9th mo., 1800 - Hugh Jackson, Jun'r, acknowledges having gone out in marriage without the consent of his parents, who he has since obtained forgiveness. Rebeckah Brewer is received into membership. A certificate to Chesterfield on behalf of Thomas Tilton, son of Thomas, who is placed an apprentice with Jacob Middletown was accepted. A certificate to Chesterfield Monthly Meeting on behalf of Richard Cook, son of Thomas, who is placed apprentice with Wm. Cook. Hannah Chandler, having married a man not in membership with us, is disowned. John Corlis produced a certificate from the monthly meeting at Chesterfield which was read and accepted. A certificate from he monthly meeting at Upper Springfield on behalf of Deborah Woodward, wife of Anthony Woodward, was read an accepted.

- 6th of 10th mo., 1800 - Zilpha Newberry, having married a man not in membership with us, is disowned. Joseph Tilton has been treated with for drinking spiritous liquors to excess and also for the neglect of attending our religious meetings. A minute was signed and approved for Joseph Allen who requested a few lines for his son, Edmund William Allen, who he expects to send to the boarding school of Friends at Nine Partners.
- 3rd of 11th mo., 1800 - The complaint that Timothy Corlies made against William Corlies is settled. Sarah Jackson acknowledges having accomplished her marriage contrary to good order

Dutch Reformed Church - Freehold and Middletown

UPPER FREEHOLD QUARTERLY MEETING (Baptist)

March 6, 1778: Mr. Pitman, not giving satisfaction, was forbid preaching in the meeting-house and warned to go out of the dwelling house and he left them and moved to Allintown. The church appointed Brother William Tapscott and Thomas Cox to let out the dwelling house.

September 4, 1778: Whereas it is reported that Brother Caleb Carmon is unsound in the doctrines of grace-the church doth appoint Brother Thomas Cox to sight him to appear here at our next quarterly meeting in order to satisfy the church respecting his principles. Our Sister Elizabeth Mason giving satisfaction to the church, is restored to her place.

December 4, 1778: Whereas our Brother Jacob Burge hath not attended us a long time, appointed Brother Thomas Cox to write to him and request his attendance with us. Our Brother Edward Taylor is appointed to visit our Sisters Jerusa James, Anna Stricland, Sarah Everngham and Rebecah Clayton and admonish them to their duties.

May 24, 1781: Brother Caleb Carmon attended and gave the church satisfaction respecting his faith as to the doctrines of Grace. Brother Thomas Cox reported that he had written to Jacob Burge. And Brother Edward Taylor that he had visited our Sister Rebecca Clayton and her resaon for not attending with us is bodily infirmity.

September 3, 1781: Brother Edward Taylor reported that he had visited Jaruska James, now Parker, that her reason for not attending with us is her local distance.

December 3, 1781: The Rev. John Blackwell, being conversed with upon the subject of coming and settling among us as our minister, by Brother Thomas Cox, and signified his willingness if he were the choice of the church. Therefore the church does unanimously to give him a call and invite him to come and settle with us as our minister. Brother Thomas Cox is hereby appointed to acquaint him therewith.

March 4, 1782: Mr. Blackwell has accepted our call of him to be our minister.

September 2, 1781: Whereas Mr. John Blackwell has accepted our call and has removed among us. The church chose Brother Arthur Cox Deacon, in room of his brother Thomas, deceased.

March 3, 1783: Whereas our brethren about Jacob'stown requested to be a branch of this church and to have the Ordinances administered there, and that Mr. Blackwell should attend there every first Lordsday in the month for that purpose, which was granted.

September 6, 1784: Brother Thomas Stow has removed his residence to Wilmington in Pennsylvania, has requested a letter of dismission. It was granted.

December 6, 1784: Requested Brother Arthur Cox to provide window-glass for the meeting house and dwelling houses.

March 7, 1785: Prince, a black man, formerly a member of this church was excommunicated for disregarding the admonitions of the church, and other malconduct.

October 8, 1785: The brethren living about Jacob'stown presented a petition for a letter of dismission that they might be constituted into a church at Jacobstown. We granted their request and dismissed the following persons-Peter Sexton, Arthur Cox, Caleb Carmon, James Cox, Samuel Sexton, Richard Sexton, James Sexton, William Snowden, Samuel Cox, Joseph Emley, James Tilton, Mary Cox, Ann Cox, Precilla Cox, Mary Eaton, Elizabeth Harbert, Rebecca Sexton, widow, Rebecca Sexton, Elizabeth Sexton, Sarah Sexton, Mary Potts, Elizabeth Potts, William Potts, Euphany Stevens, Sarah Brown, Catherine Reed, Mary Jacaway, Bersheba Jabs, Rebecca McGilliard, Mary Oliver, Esther Ewing, Phoebe Emley, to be constituted in a church at Jacobstown.

March 6, 1786: Appointed Brothers Edward Taylor and James Tapscott to settle with James Cox and Arthur Cox respecting what they have belonging to this church in their hands.

September 4, 1786: Mr.'s John Blackwell, John Lawrence, Esq., Richard Cox, Esq., Richard Kinnan, Forman Mount and William Lloyd were unanimously chosen as Trustee's of this Society. Likewise requested Nathaniel Davison to draw a letter to the Association. Appointed Mr.'s Blackwell and Taylor messengers to the same.

Dutch Reformed Church - Freehold and Middletown

September 3, 1787: Appointed our Brethren John Blackwell and Edward Taylor as messengers to the Association and the clerk to draw up a letter for that purpose.

March 29, 1788: Mr. Blackwell gave up the church book, resigning his ministerial office among us, requested a letter of dismission, which was granted. He promised to remove from the Parsonage as soon as he conveniently could.

The Church of Christ at Upper Freehold being destitute of a Minister, unanimously gave the Rev'd. Joseph Stevens a call to supply them in the ministry one half of the Lords days during the term of one year. The Rev'd. Joseph Stevens after due consideration accepted the call of the church.

April 4, 1789: Nancy Wardle and Elizabeth Herbert were approved of by the church. Immediately proceeded to the ordinance of baptism. The next day they were cordially received by the church as members within the same body.

May 3, 1789: After devine service Phebe Dye, Elizabeth Hendrickson, Elizabeth James, James Herbert, and Rebekah Herbert gave into the church their life of faith.

July 4, 1789: Richard Kinnan related to the church his experience for near 20 years back, which was much approved by the church. He was baptized the 19th of July and on the 4th day in October received into the church.

September 19, 1789: The church unanimously gave the Rev'd. Joseph Stevens a further call to supply them in the ministry another year. Appointed Bro. Joseph Stevens to write the letter to the Association. Appointed Bro. Edward Taylor and Bro. John Morford messengers.

October 3, 1789: After service, James Parine and Mary Cook gave in their experience to the church. They were approved off, were baptized, and the next day were added to the church.

October 4, 1789: The Rev'd. Joseph Stephens was received as a member of the church by a letter from the church in North Carolina, Caswell County, at the head of flat river, and signed in behalf of the church

by James Jay, Aaron Parker and Samuel Neely. As Bro. John
Morford could not conveniently leave his family, Bro. Joseph
Stephens was appointed messenger in his place. After Communion,
the church heard the experience of Rebekah Hendrickson, which was
satisfactory; the 15th Dec. she was baptized & accordingly receiv'd a
member of the church. Isbel Parine rec'd a member 4th April 1790. 2
Jan'y 1790-After sermon, Sarah Primmer, Richard James and Mary
Bazil were rec'd as candidates for baptism. The next day were added
to the church. 4th April 1790-John Meclen & Isbel_B_woman joined
ye church.

April 3, 1790: As Sister Mercy Cox appears to have left her seat in ye
church for near two years ye church appoints Bro. Richard Kinan
and Bro. Edward Taylor to enquire into ye cause. Also, Bro.
Lawrence Kale and Bro. James Herbert to enquire into ye cause of
Sister Achsah Harker and bring in their reports at our next meeting.
Bro. James Parine made known to the church his dissatisfaction in
joining the church without the imposition of hands and requested
that hands should be laid upon him. Accordingly, Bro. Stephens was
appointed to request a minister of the faith to attend our meeting ye
first opportunity for ye purpose. Elizabeth Cox and Catherine
Meclen revealed their experiences to ye church and were approved
off; ye same day were baptized; on day following were received as
members of ye church. June 20, 1790-Bro. James Parine dismissed
by letter to ye church at Middletown.

July 3, 1790: After devine service ye church heard ye experiences of Ann
Allen, Rebecca Barcalow and Abia Davidson; ye same day they
were baptized and on ye day ensuing were received into ye church.
Hester Clayton received, and also Rebecca Chumard, by letter.

October 2, 1790: Continued to call our Bro. Stephens to supply us in our
ministry. Appointed Bro. Stephens to write ye letter to ye
Association. Bro. Stephens and Bro. Edward Taylor were appointed
messengers. Jane Wilson and Susannah Ellis dismissed by to letter
ye church at New Mills. 3rd. Oct'r.-David Barcalow baptiz'd. 25th
July Wm Black_man, Sarah Clayton and Hannah Johnston were
rec'd members of ye church.

October 23, 1790: Bro. Edward Taylor settled with ye church. Appointed
Bro. Morford to talk with Jacob Burgh who is supposed to have
embraced ye quaker sentiments. Appointed our brethren Ed'd

Dutch Reformed Church - Freehold and Middletown

Taylor, Richard James and David Barcalow to circulate subscriptions and to collect that which may be subscribed at Upp-Freehold, and Bro. James Tapscot and J'n Morford collectors for Lower Freehold in the year 1791.

January 3, 1791: The church appoints Brethren Jos'h Stephens and Edw'd Taylor to talk with Sist'r Maisy Cox, as she has absented herself from communion some time. Appointed Bro. Stephens to enquire into ye truth of a report with respect to ye immoral conduct of Sist'r McClasky. Appointed Bro. Tapscot to buy a new tablecloth for the use of communion at ye expense of ye church; also to purchase cloth for a coat, to get it made, and give it to Bro. Lawrence Cale, at ye expense of ye church.

March 30, 1791: Church concluded to call Achsah Harker to give an account for ye immoral conduct done in her house. 2 Apr'l Thomas Herbert and Rich'd Steepe gave a relation of ye work of grace upon their hearts and ye next day they were baptized and rec'd as members of ye church. Also Obadiah Baird joined ye church 22nd oct. 1790.

May 26, 1791: Breth'n Stephens and Taylor brought in their report, after enquiring into ye conduct of Sis'r Mcclasky. The ch'h considered and concluded to write her a friendly letter. Bro. Stephens appointed to write it. Bro. Stephens accus'd J'n Meclen of viz. He deny'd any cause of repentance after confessing his fault before brethren E. Taylor and Rich'd Kinan. Leaving his seat in ye church he desired ye ch'h would exclude him, he refused to appear when called by ye ch'h. He threatened to sue his minister & c. After ye ch'h considered ye charge they concluded to wait with him until our next meeting. And as Sis'r Meclan acquiesced in ye conduct of her husband, ye ch'h considered her in ye same light as they did him & both are to appear at our next meeting, but in the meantime ye ch'h were to use their influence to bring them to a proper sense of their duty. Upon report of Bro. Morford in respect had to ye conduct of Bro. Jacob Burgh _ he had joined ye Quakers & expected to continue with them, Ye ch'h consider'd him _inore of them.

June 29, 1791: The ch'h considered ye conduct of J'n & Caty Meclen & as they utterly rejected ye counsel of ye ch'h ye ch'h unanimously concluded to disown them.

September 28, 1791: Mr & Mrs Meclen acknowledged their faults to ye ch'h and were restored.. Sister Massy Cox who formerly was dissatisfied with ye conduct of ye ch'h towards Rev'd Blackwell-she acknowledged that she had been in darkness-with respect to Mr B'ssins & his acknowledgment-she was sorry that she had absented herself from communion & from this time to take her seat again with consent of ye church. The ch'h appointed brethren James Tapscot & Edw'd Taylor as members in ye Association & bro. Stephens to write ye letter. The church continues to call Elder Joseph Stephens to preach. The ensuing day Rebecca Cox was rec'd into ye ch'h, baptiz'd 24th Sep'r.

December 31, 1791: J'n Shumar baptiz'd; 1 Jan'r 1792 rec'd into ye church.

March 28, 1792: Sarah Rainair dismissed by letter.

September 26, 1792: The ch'h continued to call Elder Stephens until next spring 1793.

January 2, 1793: Ye ch'h considered ye conduct of William Blackman and concluded to disown him for lying, swearing, drunkenness & c.

April 8, 1793: At the request of our Brother Joseph Stephens and Sister Mercy Cox, the church granted them letters of recommendation and dismission.

July 22, 1793: The church met by special appointment. Took under consideration the case of Br. Joseph Stephens and after examining the accusation against him prior to the convention of the church, and receiving a letter from him when met, in which he declares his sentiment in favor of universal salvation, do agree he be suspended from communion of the Church until he gives satisfaction. Appointed Brethren Edward Taylor, James Tapscot and Nathaniel Davisson a committee to wait upon Mr Stephens to admonish him and site him to attend upon the Church at our next meeting of business to answer for himself.

January 1, 1794: Rev. David Loofbourrow proposed to join himself a member of this church and producing sufficient testimonials of his good character and standing in the church from whence he came. was by the unanimous voice of the church received.

Dutch Reformed Church - Freehold and Middletown

August 9, 1794: The church met by special appointment. Appointed Brethren David Barcalow and John McLean to endeavor to procure bricks and repair the back-wall and hearth of the Payton house. Brother James Tapscott to admonish Brethren Richard Steepy and Thomas Harber for their neglect of duty in not attending upon devine worship. Agreed to call Mr. Loofbourrow to the pastoral care of the church an other year.

January 1, 1795: First attended to an accusation against Br. James and having no proof and otherwise receiving satisfaction from our Brother we agreed to acquit him of the charge. Secondly, we took notice of a charge brought into the church against Sister Hannah Parmir by Sister Rebecah Hendrickson. Agreed to suspend her from Communion untill the matter be further inquired into and she be cited to make her appearance at our next meeting in prder to confute the accusation.

August 9, 1796: Brother Tapscott reported to the church that the ministering Brethren who attended at Haights town Q meeting advised the church at Upper Freehold te receive Brother Andrew Harpending as their supply to preach for them till next spring. The church unanimously agreed.

September 27, 1796: Voted that Brother Barcalow visit our Brother Thomas Harbor and know of him his reason for neglecting his place in the church. Voted that our Sister Kiurby(?) Visit our Sister Ose(?) Clasky to have information why she so neglects her duty and privledges in the church. Unanimously agree to have Mr. Harpending ordained on the 29 March and agree to call to our assistance the following Brethren-Runey Runyan, William van Horn, Benjamin Bennett, James Ewing, Burgiss Allison, Alexander McGown and Petter Willson.

March 29, 1797: Met according to the above appointment and ordained Mr Andrew Harpending pastor of the Church at upper freehold. Mr. Wilson preached the ordination sermon.

June 28, 1797: Maria Harpending offered for baptism and was received and baptised. Mary Furman, now Green, applied for a Dismission and it was granted but afterward did not take it for certain reasons.

DUTCH REFORMED CHURCH
FREEHOLD AND MIDDLETOWN
1709-1800

Kowenoven, Trijnke, d/o Jan and Jacoba, chr. 1709.
Kowenoven, Aelke, d/o Albert Kowenoven and Nelke Schenk, chr. 1709.
Goulder, Maria, d/o Joseph Goulder and Anneke Daws, chr. 1709.
Van Derventer, child of Peter, chr. 1709.
Van Kerk, William, s/o Jan and Allicia, chr. 1709.
Putinger, Daniel, s/o Richard, chr. 8 Jan. 1709.
Kowenoven, Nelke, d/o Peter Kowenoven and Patience Daws, chr. 22 Jan. 1709.
Van Doorn, Allicia, d/o Cornelius Van Doorn and Anneke Golder, chr. 5 Feb. 1709.
Romeyn, Elizabeth, d/o Jan Romeyn and Geertie Van Dijk, chr. 19 Feb. 1709.
Schenk, Rachel, d/o Jan Schenk and Sara Kowenoven, chr. 5 Mar. 1709.
Van Doorn, Abraham, s/o Jacob Van Doorn, chr. 20 Oct. 1709.
Laen, Jacob, s/o Jacob Laen and Elizabet Barkelo, chr. 30 Oct. 1709.
Hendricksen, Willem, s/o Daniel Hendricksen and Nelke Van Dijke, chr. 6 Nov. 1709.
Langstraet, Katrijnke, d/o Aurie__, chr. 27 Nov. 1709.
Bennet, child of Abraham, chr. 1710.
Lane, Castijnke, d/o Cornelius Laan, chr. 1710.
Polhemus, Elizabeth, d/o Johannes Polhemus, chr. 1710.
Wijkof, Anna, d/o Peter and Willempe, chr. 18 Feb. 1710.
Wijkof, Sara, d/o Jacob, chr. 4 Mar. 1710.
Schenk, Rachel, d/o Geret and Nelke, chr. 2 Apr. 1710.
Wijkof, child of Simon, chr. May 1710.
Van Matra, Joseph, s/o Krijn Jansen Van Matra and Nelke V. Cleve, chr. 13 Aug. 1710.
Jansen, Petrus, s/o Andres, chr. 29 Sep. 1710.
Barkelo, Aelke, d/o Derrick Barkelo and Janeke Aesda or Aesdale, chr. 1 Oct. 1710.
Borum, Johannes, s/o Aurie_ Borum and Sara Smack, chr. 12 Nov 1710.
Langstraet, Sara Gisbert Aurie, d/o Stoffel, chr. 26 Nov. 1710.
Kowenhoven, Maria, d/o Cornelius Kowehoven and Marg. Schenk, chr. 24 Dec. 1710.
Guyluck, Katelijnke, d/o Hendrick Guyluck and Kautie Ammerman, chr. 1711.
Langstraet, Jan, d/o Adrian, chr. 1711.

Dutch Reformed Church - Freehold and Middletown

Romeyn, Geertie, d/o Jan Romeyn and Giertie Van Dijk, chr. 1711.
Ammerman, Paulus, s/o Albert, chr. 13 Jan. 1711.
Putinger, Abraham, s/o Richard, chr. 20 Jan. 1711.
Van Doorn, Joseph, s/o Cornelis Van Doorn and Anneke Golder, chr. 1711.
Bennet, Mattenke, d/o Adrian and Barbara, chr. 10 Feb. 1711.
Court, Zacherias, s/o Johannes, chr. 1 Apr. 1711.
Potman, Cornelia, d/o David, chr. 29 Apr. 1711.
Van Cleve, Johannes, s/o Benjamin Van Cleve and Hank_ Sutphen, chr. 3 June 1711.
Tijs, Evert, s/o Jan, chr. 29 July 1711.
Van Doorn, Petrus, s/o Jacob Van Doorn and Marika Ben or Bennet, chr. 2 Sep. 1711.
Van Dijk, Martin, s/o Thomas Van Dijk and Meyke Wijkof, chr. 23 Sep. 1711.
Leffertsen, Leffert, s/o Ouke, chr. 14 Oct. 1711.
Sutphen, Jan, s/o Jan Sutphen and Engelke Bennet, chr. 18 Nov. 1711.
Wijkof, Johannes, s/o Jan Wijkof and Nelke Kouwenhoven, chr. 16 Dec. 1711.
Hendricksen, Annake, d/o Daniel Hendricksen and Katrijnke Van Dijk, chr. 30 Dec. 1711.
Kowenhoven, Margareta, d/o Albert Kowenhoven and Nelke Schenk, chr. 1712.
Kouenhoven, Cornelis, s/o Jan and Jacoba, chr. 1712.
Kowenhoven, Rachel, d/o Cornelis Kowenhoven and Margaret Schenk, chr. 1712.
Laen, Maria, d/o Cornelis Laen, chr. 1712.
Sutphen, Derick, s/o Derick chr. 1712.
Van Dijk, d/o Thomas, chr. 1712.
Romeyn, Maria, d/o Jacobus Romeyn, chr. 11 Jan. 1712.
Foreman, Nelke, d/o Marga, chr. 8 Feb. 1712.
Potman, Fyke, d/o David, chr. 22 Feb. 1712.
Race, Hanna, d/o Andres, chr. 23 Mar. 1712.
Kouenhoven, Peter, s/o Peter Kouenhoven and Patience Daws, chr. 6 Apr, 1712.
Keemer, Annake, d/o Benjamin, chr. 13 Apr. 1712.
Barkelo, Elizabeth, d/o Derick Barkelo and Janneke Aesdale, chr. 11 May 1712.
Tijs, Johannes, s/o Peter, chr. 22 June 1712.
Schenk, Maria, d/o Jan Schenk and Sara Kowenhoven, chr. 7 Sep. 1712.
Goulder, Patience, d/o Joseph Goulder and Anneke Daws, chr. 28 Sep. 1712.

Schenk, Gerret, s/o Garret Schenk and Nelke Court Voorhees, chr. 2 Nov. 1712.
Laen, Mattheus, s/o Jacob Laen and Elizabeth Barkelo, chr. 16 Nov. 1712.
Van Kerk, Sara, d/o Jan and Alicia, chr. 14 Dec. 1712.
Smith, Elizabeth, d/o Thomas, chr. 28 Dec. 1712.
Guyluck, child of Hendrick Guyluck and Cautie Ammerman, chr. 1713.
Leffertsen, Aelke, d/o Ouke, chr. 1713.
Verwye, Hendrickus, s/o Hendrick Verwye and Engelke Van Dijk, chr. 16 Feb. 1713.
Kouwenhoven, Rolaph, s/o Jacob Kouwenhoven and Sara Schenk, chr. 22 Mar. 1713.
Bown, Maria, d/o Obadiah Bown and Elizabeth Langevelt, chr. 30 Mar. 1713.
Van Cleve, Derick, s/o Benjamin Van Cleve and Hank_ Sutphen, chr. 3 May 1713.
Tijs, Johannes, s/o Jan. chr. 10 May 1713.
Wijkof, Femke, d/o Jacob, chr. 14 June 1713.
Sutphen, Ananeke, d/o Jan Sutphen and Angelke Bennet, chr. 2 Aug. 1713.
Romeyn, Christoffel, s/o Jan Romeyn and Geertie Van Dijk, chr. 16 Aug. 1713.
Hooglandt, Nelke, d/o Jan Hooglandt, chr. 25 Aug. 1713.
Wijkof, child of Peter, chr. 30 Aug. 1713.
Van Derventer, child of Jan, chr. 18 Oct. 1713.
Van Doorn, Diedelo, s/o Cornelis, chr. 22 Nov. 1713.
Ritsman, Jacob, s/o Harmanus Ritsman and Miss Lucas, chr. 4 Dec. 1713.
Langstraet, Stoffel, s/o Stoffel, chr. 25 Dec. 1713.
Kouwenhoven, Margareta, d/o Cornelis Kouwenhoven, chr. 1714.
Langstraet, child of Adrian, chr. 1714.
Moor, Willem, s/o Willem, chr. 1714.
Polhemus, Cornelis, s/o Johannes Polhemus, chr. 1714.
Sutphen, Isaac, s/o Jan, chr. 1714.
Barkelo, Willem, s/o Derrick Barkelo and Janneke Aesdale, chr. 16 Jan. 1714.
Schenk, Lea, d/o Jan Schenk and Sara Kouenoven, chr. 30 Jan. 1714.
Foreman, Samuel, s/o Jonathan Foreman and Margaret Wijkof, chr. 13 Feb. 1714.
Van Doorn, Isaac, s/o Jacob Van Doorn and Marike Bennet, chr. 13 Mar. 1714.

Dutch Reformed Church - Freehold and Middletown

Emans, Daniel, s/o Abraham Emans and Margaret Willemsen, chr. 11 Apr. 1714.
Laen, Cornelis, s/o Cornelis Laen, chr. 7 May 1714.
Bennet, Katrijnke, d/o Adrian and Barbara, chr. 9 May 1714.
Van Noortwijk, Volkert, s/o Simon Van Noortwijk, chr. 30 May 1714.
Jansen, Jan, s/o Andres, chr. 6 June 1714.
Smith, child of Thomas Smith and Deborah Buys, chr. 27 June 1714.
Putinger, Sijke, d/o Richard, chr. 4 July 1714.
Soy, s/o Joost, chr. 28 Aug. 1714.
Potman, child of David, chr. 24 Oct. 1714.
Van Hoeck, Francijke, d/o Laurens Van Hoeck, chr. 31 Oct. 1714.
Kouwenhoven, child of Peter Kouwenhoven, chr. 7 Nov. 1714.
Jansen, Andres, s/o Jan, chr. 21 Nov. 1714.
Kouwenhoven, Peter, s/o Jan Kouwenhoven, chr. 5 Dec. 1714.
Hendricksen, Francijnke, d/o Daniel Hendricksen and Nelke Van Dijk, chr. 19 Dec. 1714.
-- Janneke, d/o Frederick, chr. 1715.
Laen, child of Mathijs, chr. 1715.
Van Dijk, child of Thomas Van Dijk and Mayke Wijkof, chr. 1715.
Verwie, Karel, s/o Hendrick Verwie and Engelke Van Dijk, chr. 1 Jan. 1715.
Golder, Sara, d/o Joseph and Anna, chr. 27 Mar. 1715.
Schenk, child of Gerret, chr. 17 Apr. 1715.
Barber, child of Edward Barber and Marike Tijs, chr. 24 Apr. 1715.
Sutphen, Aert, s/o Derick, chr. 15 May. 1715.
De Hert, Katelijnke, d/o Elias De Hert and Katie Laen, chr. 8 Sep. 1715.
Wijkoff, Cornelius, s/o Peter Wijkoff and Willempe Schenk, chr. 11 Sep. 1715.
Van Kleve, Marike, d/o Benjamin Van Kleve and Hank Sutphen, chr. Oct. 1715.
Wijkof, Jacobus, s/o Jacob, chr. 6 Nov. 1715.
Romeyn, Giertie, d/o Jacobus Romeyn and Marie Foreman, chr. 4 Dec. 1715.
Barber, Peter, s/o Edward Barber and Marike Tijs, chr. 11 Dec. 1715.
Doorn, child of Cornelis Doorn and Anke_ Golder, chr. 18 Dec. 1715.
Kouwenhoven, Peter, s/o Albert Kouwenhoven and Nelke Schenk, chr. 1716.
Le Fever, child of Mijndert Le Fever and Katrijnke Van Blerke, chr. 1716.
Sutphen, Derrick, s/o Gijsbert Sutphen and Geertrye Van Pelt, chr. 1716.
Soy, d/o Joost, chr. 16 Jan. 1716.
Van Kerk, Alicia, d/o Jan and Alicia, chr. 21 Jan. 1716.

Smack, Lendert, s/o Lendert, chr. 11 Feb. 1716.
Amack, Janeke, d/o Jan Amack and Marike Jans, chr. 11 Mar. 1716.
Romeyn, Peter, s/o Jan Romeyn and Gertie Van Dijk, chr. 8 Apr. 1716.
Hagewout, child of Ouke, chr. 3 May 1716.
Langstraet, Mayka, d/o Stoffel, chr. 6 May 1716.
Beys, child of Johannes, chr. 26 Aug. 1716.
Tijs, child of Derick, chr. Aug. 1716.
Van Kelder, child of Hendrick, chr. 11 Oct. 1716.
Hendricksen, child of Tunke Hendricksen, chr. 28 Oct. 1716.
Wijkof, child of Cornelius Wijkof and Adrianke Leyster, chr. 28 Oct. 1716.
Laen, Gerret, s/o Matijs Laen and Anke_ Schenk, chr. 25 Nov. 1716.
Kouwenhoven, Gerret, s/o Jacob Kouwenhoven and Sara Schenk, chr. 23 Dec.1716.
Van Kelder, Ephraim, s/o Hendrick, chr. 11 Oct. 1716.
Polhemus, child of Johannes Polhemus, chr. 14 Oct. 1716.
Raes, Anna Marike, d/o Andres Raes and Miss Higby, chr. 1717.
Sutphen, Jacob, s/o Jan Sutphen and Engelke Bennet, chr. 1717.
Emans, Maria, d/o Abraham Emans and Margaret Willemsen, chr. 20 Jan. 1717.
Bennet, Isaac, s/o Adrian and Barbara, chr. 14 Apr. 1717.
Foreman, Jan, s/o Jonathan Foreman and Margaret Wijkof, chr. 28 Apr. 1717.
Schenk, Katrijnke, d/o Roleph Schenk and Ghesie Hendricksen, chr. 19 May 1717.
Petersen, Barbara, d/o Matijs Petersen and Ghesie Hendricksen, chr. 26 May 1717.
Barkelo, child of Derrick Barkelo and Janeke Aesdale, chr. 17 Nov. 1717.
Kouwenhoven, child of Cornelis Kouwenhoven and Margreet Schenk, chr. 28 Nov.1717.
__, Aicia chr. 1718.
Coegert, child of Tunis Coegert and Miss Verscheur, chr. 1718.
Holsaert, child of Benjamin, chr. 1718.
Laen, child of Mattijs Laen and Anke_ Schenk, chr. 1718.
Nefies, child of Peter, chr. 1718.
Schenk, Willem, s/o Jan Schenk and Sara Kowenhoven, chr. 1718.
Schenk, Katrijnke, d/o Roeleph Schenk and Ghesie Hend or Hendricksen, chr. 1718.
De Hart, child of Elias, chr. Feb. 1718.
Van Cleve, Derick, s/o Benjamin Van Cleve and Hank_ Sutphen, chr. 1718.

Dutch Reformed Church - Freehold and Middletown

Wijkiof, Peter, s/o Jacob, chr. 1718.
Schenk, Jan, s/o Geret Schenk and Nelke Voorhuys, chr. 9 Feb. 1718.
Laen, child of Cornelis Laen, chr. 6 Mar. 1718.
Smith, child of Thomas Smith and Deborah Buys, chr. 16 Mar. 1718.
Hagewout, child of Ouke, chr. 23 Mar. 1718.
Sutphen, Aert, s/o Gisbert, chr. 13 Apr. 1718.
Smack, Femmeke, d/o Johannes, chr. 1 June 1718.
Hendricksen, d/o Daniel Hendricksen and Nelke Van Dijk, chr. 21 June 1718.
Buys, child of Johannes, chr. 27 July 1718.
Sutphen, child of Jan Sutphen and Angelke Bennet, chr. 10 Aug. 1718.
Golder, Wilhelmus, s/o Joseph, chr. 24 Aug. 1718.
Van Metra, Krijm, s/o Jan, chr. 28 Sep. 1718.
Van Dijk, Isaac, s/o Jan and Rebecca, chr. 7 Nov. 1718.
Van Dijk, Abram, s/o Jan and Rebecca, chr. 7 Nov. 1718.
Van Kerk, Aert, s/o Jan and Alicia, chr. 9 Nov. 1718.
Petersen, Peter, s/o Mattijs Petersen and Gesie Hendricksen, chr. 23 Nov. 1718.
Kouwenhoven, child of Jacob Kouwenhoven, chr. 21 Dec.1718.
Verwie, Elizabet, d/o Hendrick Verwie and Engeke Van Dijk, chr. 1719.
Wamsley, Willem, s/o Christopher Wamsley and Jannek Hendricksen, chr. 1719.
Kouwenhoven, Jan, s/o Jan and Jocoba, chr. 12 Apr.1719.
Schenk, Gerret, s/o Roeleph Schenk and Engelke Van Doorn, chr. 3 May 1719.
Sutphen, Derick, chr. 25 Dec. 1719.
Holsaert, Aleke, d/o Benjamin, chr. 1720.
Le Feffer, Mettie, d/o Mijndert Le Feffer and Katrijnke Van Blerke, chr. 1720.
Romeyn, Janneke, d/o Jan Romeyn and Geertie Van Dijk, chr. 1720.
Sutphen, Willem, chr. 1720.
Van Metra, Krijm, child of Jan, chr. 1720.
Verwie, Jacob, s/o Hendrijck Verwie and Engelke Laen, chr. 1720.
Voorhees, Janneke, d/o Peter Voorhees and Miss Nefies, chr. 1720.
Barkelo, Daniel, s/o Derick Barkelo and Janeke Aesdale, chr. 1 Jan. 1720.
Luyster, Cornelis, s/o Johannes Luyster and Miss Brower, chr. 15 Jan. 1720.
Sutphen, Jan, s/o Derrick Sutphen and Margaret Van Pelt, chr. 29 Jan.. 1720.
Davis, child of Thomas, chr. 12 Feb. 1720.
Laen, Mattheus, s/o Matijs Laen and Anke_ Shenk, chr. 26 Feb. 1720.

Early Church Records of Monmouth County

Van Cleve, Janneke, d/o Isbrant and Janneeke, chr. 8 Mar. 1720.
Schenk, Jan, s/o Roeleph Schenk and Ghesie Hendricksen, chr. 12 Mar. 1720.
Van Hoorn, child of Abram Van Hoorn and Anke_ Kouwenhoven, chr. 1 May 1720.
Foreman, Peter, s/o Jonathan Foreman and Margaret Wijkof, chr. 8 May 1720.
Voorhees, Gerret, s/o Hhendrick Voorhees, chr. 15 May 1720.
Buys, Willem, s/o Johannes, chr. 22 May 1720.
Kouwenhoven, Peter, s/o Jacob Kouwenhoven and Sara Schenk, chr. 29 May 1720.
Kouwenhoven, Catrina, d/o Cornelis Kouwenhoven and Margret Schenk, chr. June 1720.
Schenk, Marike, d/o Roeleph Schenk and Engelke Van Doorn, chr. 17 July 1720.
Nefies, child of Peter, chr. Aug. 1720.
Nefies, Willempe, d/o Martin, chr. 4 Sep 1720.
Brower, Anke, d/o Hans Brower and Nelke Golder, chr. 11 Sep. 1720.
Willemson, Nelke, d/o Aert Willemson and Miss Kouwenhoven, chr. 16 Oct.1720.
Sutphen, Jacob, chr. 6 Nov. 1720.
Holms, Daniel, s/o Tuntie, chr. 1721.
Jansen, child of Mijndert, chr. 1721.
Lake, Jacobus, s/o Nicolas, chr. 1721.
Potman, child of David, chr. 9 Apr. 1721.
Van Cleve, Benjamin, s/o Benjamin Van Cleve and Hendricke_ Sutphen, chr. 1721.
Kestner, Barbara, d/o Coenrad and Rebecca, chr. 7 May 1721.
Schenk, Albert, s/o Gerret Schenk and Nelke Voorhees, chr. 18 May 1721.
Kouwenhoven, Gerret, s/o Albert Kouwenhoven and Nelke Schenk, chr. 16 July 1721.
De Hert, child of Elias De Hert and Miss Laen, chr. 20 Aug. 1721.
Romeyn, Christophel, s/o Jacobus, chr. 8 Oct. 1721.
Smith, Joseph, s/o Thomas Smith and Deborah Buys, chr. 15 Oct. 1721.
Sutphen, Grietie, d/o Abraham and Mayke_, chr. 29 Oct. 1721.
Buys, Frans, s/o Johannes, chr. 3 Dec. 1721.
Bennet, Geertie, d/o Willem, chr. 21 Dec. 1721.
Benham, Jan, s/o Jan Benham and Giertie Van Dijck, chr. 1722.
De Boog, child of Frederick De Boog and Miss Van Hoeck, chr. 1722.
Swart, child of Jacobus Swart and Jannek Lane, chr. 1722.
Van Metra, Gisbert, s/o Jan, chr. 4 Feb. 1722.

Dutch Reformed Church - Freehold and Middletown

Voorhees, Willempe, d/o Hendrick Voorhees, chr. 18 Feb. 1722.
Doorn, child of Cornelis Doorn and Anke_ Golder, chr. 4 Mar. 1722.
Lambertson, Anke, d/o Jan Lambertson and Mayke_ Van Kerk, chr. 18 Mar. 1722.
Davis, child of Thomas, chr. 26 Mar. 1722.
Van Hoorn, child of Abraham Van Hoorn and Anke_ Kouwenhoven, chr. 8 Apr. 1722.
Sutphen, Elizabeth, d/o Jan Sutphen and Angelke Bennet, chr. 15 Apr. 1722.
Lawrence, William, s/o Jan Lawrence and Miss Van Cleve, chr. 22 Apr. 1722.
Verbrijk, child of Barnardus Verbrijk and Janneke Schenck, chr. 17June 1722.
Van Hoeck, child of Rickus Van Hoeck amd Miss Parent, chr. 8 July 1722.
Kouwenhoven, child of Jacob Kouwenhoven and Sara Schenk, chr. 15 July 1722.
Schenk, Jan, s/o Jan Schenk and Sara Kouwenhoven, chr. 22 July 1722.
Holms, Jonathan, s/o Jonathan Holms and Tuntie Hendricksen, chr. 29 July 1722.
Verbrijk, Gerret, s/o Gerret Verbrijk and Miss Wijkof, chr. 14 Oct. 1722.
Sutphen, Jan, s/o Jacob Sutphen and Nelke Bennet, chr. 18 Oct. 1722.
Amak, Janneke, d/o Jan Amak and Helena Laen, chr. 1723.
Brower, child of Willem, chr. 1723.
Kouwenhoven, child of Willem Kouwenhoven, chr. 1723.
Kip, child of Hendrik, chr. 1723.
Nefies, Janneke, d/o Peter and Aeltie, chr. 1723.
Poling, child of Samuel, chr. 1723.
Sutphen, Elizabeth, d/o Abram and Marijke_, chr. 1723.
Peterson, Willem, s/o Mattijs Peterson and Gesie Willemsen, chr. 13 Jan. 1723.
Brower, child of Hans Brower and Miss Golder, chr. 27 Jan. 1723.
Sutphen, Margaret, d/o Gisbert Sutphen and Geertrie Van Pelt, chr. 17 Mar. 1723.
Kouwenhoven, Jan, s/o Albert Kouwenhoven and Nelke Schenk, chr. 24 Mar.1723.
De Vier, child of ____, chr. 21 Apr. 1723.
Lawrence, Ruth, s/o Jan Lawrence and Miss Van Cleve, chr. 22 Apr. 1723.
Hendricksen, Daniel, s/o Daniel Hendricksen and Trijnke Van Dijk, chr. 5 May 1723.

Van De Vere, child of Cornelis Van De Vere and Miss Wijkof, chr. 12 May 1723.
Van Pelt, child of Tunis Van Pelt and Miss Bennet, chr. 24 May 1723.
Schenk, Daniel, s/o Roeleph Schenk and Gesie Hendricksen, chr. 26 May 1723.
Luyster, child of Johannes Luyster and Miss Brower, chr. 23 June 1723.
Langstraet, child of Adrian, chr. 3 Oct. 1723.
Verwie, child of Hendrick Verwie and Englke Van Dijk, chr. 3 Oct. 1723.
Sutphen, child of Derick Sutphen and Miss Van Pelt, chr. 20 Oct.. 1723.
Van Voorhees, Garet, s/o Hendrick Van Voorhees, chr. 24 Nov. 1723.
De Wit, child of Lucas, chr. 8 Dec. 1723.
Barkelo, child of Derick Barkelo and Janeke Aesdale, chr. 22 Dec. 1723.
Birdsal, Rebecka, d/o Abram Birdsal and Katrijne Emans, chr. 1724.
Brower, child of Jan Brower and Miss Van Kleve, chr. 1724.
Kouwenhoven, child of Jan and Jacoba, chr. 1724.
Kouwenhoven, child of Willem Kouwenhoven and Elisabeth Van Cleve, chr. 1724.
Jansen, child of Myndert, chr. 1724.
Le Feffer, child of Myndert Le Feffer and Katryntje Van Blerka, chr. 1724.
Laen, Margaret, d/o Gisbert Laen and Hanna Loveridge, chr. 1724.
---- Smith, child of Thomas Smith and Deborah Buys, chr. 1724.
Verbrijk, Jan, s/o Barnardus Verbrijk and Janneke Schenck, chr. 1724.
Wamsley, child of Christopher Wamsley and Jannek Hendricksen, chr. 1724.
Schenk, Nelke, d/o Roeleph Schenk and Engelke Van Doorn, chr. 17 Jan. 1724.
Lambertsen, Jan, d/o Jan Lambertsen and Mayke_ Van Kerk, chr. 19 Jan. 1724.
Romeyn, child of Jacobus, chr. 29 Jan. 1724.
Jansen, Hendricus, s/o Court Jansen and Churtie Laen, chr. 9 Feb. 1724.
Antonides, Vincentius, s/o Johannes Antonides and Johanna Kouwenhoven, chr. 16 Feb. 1724.
Willemson, Elbert, d/o Elbert Willemson and Jackamynke Kouwenhoven, chr. Mar.1724.
Sutven, child of Jan Sutven and Engelke Bennet, chr. 24 May 1724.
Van Kleve, child of Isbrant, chr. 7 June 1724.
Bennet, child of Jan Bennet and Eyke_ Van Metra, chr. 14 June 1724.
Davis, child of Thomas, chr. 21 June 1724.
De Boogh, Maryke, d/o Frederick De Boogh and Hanna Van Hoeck, chr. 26 July 1724.

Dutch Reformed Church - Freehold and Middletown

Holsart, child of Benjamin, chr. 2 Aug. 1724.
Van Hoeck, Jacob, s/o Arent Van Hoeck, chr. 6 Sep. 1724.
Kouwenhoven, child of Cornelis Kouwenhoven and Margaret Schenk, chr. 25 Oct.1724.
Van Kerk, Jan, s/o Hendrick Van Kerk and Dorothy Morgan, chr. 1 Nov. 1724.
Van De Vere, child of Tunis Van De Vere and Aelke Schenk, chr. 8 Nov. 1724.
Van Metra, Jannetie, d/o Jan and Eytie, chr. 22 Nov. 1724.
Amack, child of Teunis Amack and Lena Laen, chr. 1725.
Benham,___, s/o Jan Benham, chr. 1725.
Brower, child of Hans Brower and Nelke Golder, chr. 1725.
Foreman, child of Jonthan Forman and Margretie Wykof, chr. 1725.
Jemmy, James, s/o Frank and Maria, chr. 1725.
Mackenny, child of Mordicai, chr. 1725.
Verbryk, child of Barnardus Verbryk and Jannek Schenck, chr. 1725.
Niefies, child of Peter, chr. 1 Jan 1725.
Willemsen, child of Willem Willemsen and Janneke Kouwenhoven, chr. 1725.
Van Doorn, Jacob, s/o Christiaen Van Doorn and Aelke Schenk, chr. 31 Jan. 1725.
Verbryk, Samuel, s/o Gerret Verbryk and Miss Wykof, chr. 26 Mar. 1725.
Smak, Katryntie, d/o Hend... and Marya, chr. 29 Mar. 1725.
Schenk, Nelke, d/o Roeleph Schenk and Gheesie Hendricksen, chr. 16 May 1725.
Luyster, Antie, d/o Johannes and Lucretia, chr. 23 May 1725.
Teunisen, child of Cornelis, chr. 8 Aug. 1725.
Sutven, child of Abraam, chr. 29 Aug. 1725.
Swart, Femmetie, d/o Teunis and Geertie, chr. 5 Sep. 1725.
Sutven, child of Gisbert, chr. 17 Nov. 1725.
Schenk, Geret, s/o Coert Schenk and Marike Kouwenhoven, chr. 12 Dec. 1725.
Putinger, Richard, s/o Richard Putinger and Rachel Reynolds, chr. 19 Dec. 1725.
Van Meteren, Serynus, s/o Gysbert and Mayken, chr. 25 Dec. 1725.
Kouwenhoven, child of Willem Kouwenhoven and Miss Collier, chr. 1726.
Golder, Joseph, s/o Joseph Golder and Adrianke Laan, chr. 1726.
Laan, child of Mattys Laan and Antie_ Schenk, chr. 1726.
Langstraat, child of Adrian, chr. 1726.
Schenk, child of Roleph Schenk and Engelke Van Doorn, chr. 1726.

Schenk, child of Roleph Schenk and Engelke Van Doorn, chr. 1726.
Sutven, child of Jan Sutven and Katrine Langstraat, chr. 1726.
Sutven, Petrus, s/o Derick Sutven and Miss Van Pelt, chr. 1726.
Van Cleve, child of Isaac, chr. 1726.
Van Kerk, Jan, s/o Jan Van Kerk and Cornelia Brakel, chr. 1726.
Voorhees, child of Hendrick Voorhees and Miss Nefies, chr. 1726.
Voorhees, child of Peter Voorhees and Adrianke Nefies, chr. 23 Jan. 1726.
Bennet, Kryjans, s/o Jan Bennet and Eyke_ Van Metra, chr. 27 Feb. 1726.
Kouwenhoven, child of Willem Kouwenhoven, chr. 13 Mar.1726.
Sutven, child of Jan Sutven and Engelke Bennet, chr. 20 Mar. 1726.
Van De Bilt, child of Hendrick Van De Bilt and Nelke Van Cleve, chr. 27 Mar. 1726.
De Wit, child of Lucas, chr. 1 Apr. 1726.
Hendricksen, Trynke, d/o Hendrick Hendricksen and Nelke Schenk, chr. 3 Apr. 1726.
Brouwer, child of Jan Brouwer and Helelna Van Cleve, chr. 11 Apr. 1726.
Smith, Ezekiel, s/o Thomas Smith and Deborah Buys, chr. 24 Apr. 1726.
Lawrence, child of Jan Lawrence and Miss Van Cleve, chr. 1 May 1726.
Swart, Teunis, s/o Jacob and Jannetie, chr. 19 June 1726.
Holms, child of Jonathan Holms and Teunke Hendricksen, chr. Aug. 1726.
Antonides, Petrus, s/o Johannes Antonides and Johana Kouwenhoven, chr. 21 Aug. 1726.
Barkelo, Janneke, d/o Derick Barkelo and Janneke Aesdale, chr. 1727.
De Wit, Elyas, s/o Lucas and Engeltie, chr. 1727.
Lambertsen, Joseph, d/o Jan Lambertsen and Mayke_ Van Kerk, chr. 1727.
Schenk, child of Coert Schenk and Maryke Kouwenhoven, chr. 1727.
Willemson, Aert, s/o Elbert Willemson and Jackumynke Kouwenhoven, chr. 1 Jan.1727.
Benham, Anke_, d/o Jan Benham and Geertie Van Dyck, chr. 29 Jan.1727.
Kouwenhoven, Cornelis, s/o Joris and Altie, chr. 2 July 1727.
Brouwer, Pieter, s/o Jan and Hilletie, chr. Aug. 1727.
Luyster, Lucretia, d/o   Joh. and Lucretia, chr. Aug. 1727.
Truax, Johannes, s/o Johannes Truax and Syke Van Kerk, chr. 27 Aug. 1727.
Barber, child of Edward Barber, chr. 1 Oct. 1727.
Kip, Willemtie, d/o Hendr. and Willemptie, chr. 5 Nov. 1727.

Dutch Reformed Church - Freehold and Middletown

Amack, child of Steven, chr. 1728.
Kouwenhoven, child of Willem Kouwenhoven, chr. 1 Jan. 1728.
Van Metra, Jannetie, child of Jan, chr. Aug. 1728.
Davids, Moses, s/o Thomas, chr. 1730.
Furman, Willem, s/o Jonathan Furman and Grietje Wykof, chr. 1730.
Janssze, Petus, s/o Hendrik and Ariaantje, chr. 1730.
Van Noortstrant, Aart, s/o Hans Van Noortstrant and Helena Willemsz, chr. 1730.
Schenk, Catharina, d/o Roelof Schenk and Engeltje Van Dooren, chr. 1730.
Smit, Mattheus, s/o Jan and Barentje, chr. 1730.
Sutfen, Neeltje, d/o Gysbert Sutphen and Geertruy Van Pelt, chr. 1730.
Van D Vere, Maria, d/o Cornelis Van D Vere and Matje Smak, chr. 1730.
Smak, Saartje, d/o Barend Smak and Annatje Luister, chr. 22 May 1730.
Sutfen, Isaac, s/o Jacob Sutfen and Antje Bennet, chr. 24 May 1730.
Bennet, Mayke, s/o Willem, chr. 1731.
Bennit, Willem, s/o Hendereck Bennet and Jannetke Couwenhoove, chr. 1731.
Couwenhoven, Marya, d/o Elias Couwenhoven, chr. 1731.
Couwenhoven, Geurtry, d/o Willem Couwenhoven and Arrejantie Bennet, chr. 1731.
Ellisson, Metje, d/o Seth and Metje, chr. 1731.
Hendrick, Hendreck, s/o Handrick Hendrick and Altie Couhoven, chr. 1731.
Hooems, Elsie, d/o Jonnatan Hooems and Tryntje Hendraekse, chr. 1731.
Schenk, Neeltie, d/o Coert Schenk and Marytie Couwenhoven, chr. 1731.
Swart, Johannes, s/o Tunus, chr. 1731.
Van Cleef, Johannes, s/o Josep, chr. 1731.
Van Derventer, Margrita, d/o Isack Van Derventer and Sartie Couwenhooven, chr. 1731.
Van Metere, Neeltie, d/o Benjemen Van Metere and Elisabet Laan, chr. 1731.
Van Meterea, Maarya, d/o Jan Van Meterea and Ydaa Sedam, chr. 1731.
Van Metere, Crynjans, s/o Cerynis Van Metere and Abigail Lefferse, chr. 1731.
Van Kerck, Cnelyaa, d/o Jan, chr. 20 Jan. 1731.
Van Kerk, Matemus, s/o Jan, chr. 20 Jan. 1731.
Van Der Bilt, Benjamin, s/o Hendrik Van Der Bilt and Neeltie Van Cleeff, chr. 1731.
Van Dooren, Jacop, s/o Jacop Van Dooren and Maryaa Schenck, chr. 1731.

Van Dooren, Maryaa, d/o Arry Van Dooren and Antie_ Schenck, chr. 1731.
Van Meteren, Jan, s/o Gysbert Van Meteren and Mayke_ Hendrikse, chr. 1731.
Couwenhoven, Pieter, s/o Joris and Aeltie, chr. 31 Mar. 1731.
Van Cleef, Jacob, s/o Lourens Van Cleef and Jannite Laan, chr. 31 Mar. 1731.
Holzaert, Gerrit s/o Benjamin Holzaert and Johanna Luyster, chr. 8 Aug. 1731.
Goolder, Antie, d/o Joseph Goolder and Ariaantie Laan, chr. 22 Aug. 1731.
Schenk, Willemtie d/o Pieter Schenk and Jannetie Van Noortstrant, chr. 29 Aug. 1731.
Suydam, Marytie, d/o Hendrik Suydam and Marytie Van Siggelen, chr. 23 Sep. 1731.
Stoergjes, Jacobus, s/o Pieter Stoergjes and Marytie Burger, chr. 10 Oct. 1731.
Couwenhoven, Aelbert, s/o Roelof Couwenhoven and Aeltie_ Strykers, chr. 24 Oct. 1731.
De Wit, Engeltie, d/o Lucas and Engeltie, chr. 31 Oct. 1731.
Schenk, Hendrik, s/o Roelof Schenk and Geesje Hendriksen, chr. 7 Nov. 1731.
Bayrt, Alexander, s/o Willem Bayrt and Elsje Van Cleeff, chr. 21 Nov. 1731.
Brouwer, Jan, s/o Hans Brouwer and Neeltie Goolder, chr. 28 Nov. 1731.
Van Cleeff, Martha, d/o Joh. Van Kleef and Maria Kraffert, chr. 19 Dec. 1731.
Everse, Margrita, d/o Nicholaes Everse and Susanna Roeters, chr. 1732.
Hendrikse, Aelbert, s/o Hendrik Hendrikse and Aeltie Couwenhove chr. 1732.
Hendrikse, Catrina, d/o Willem Hendrikse and Maria Langestraat, chr. 1732.
Nevius, Johanna, d/o Pieter Nevius and Aaltie Ten Nyk, chr. 1732.
Sutphen, Jan, s/o Dirk Sutphen and Marytie Couwenhoven, chr. 1732.
Sutphen, Benjamin, s/o Jan Sutphen and Engeltie Bennit, chr. 1732.
Voorhees, Petrus, s/o Pieter Voorhees and Arriaentie Nevius, chr. 1732.
Haeghoort, Hester, d/o Gerard Haeghoort and Catharina De Loy, chr. 30 Jan. 1732.
Hoffmeier, Isaak, s/o Samuel Hoffmeie and Maria Badlou, chr. 5 Mar. 1732.
Davids, child of Thomas and Annetie, chr. 19 Mar.1732.

Dutch Reformed Church - Freehold and Middletown

Fasigk, Hendrik, s/o Valentyn Fasigk and Katryntie Hosman, chr. 9 Apr. 1732.
Wykhoff, Jannetie, d/o Jan Wykhoff and Aeltie Borkelo, chr. 1732.
Van Derventer, Pieter, s/o Abram Van Derventer and Aeltie Couwenhooven, chr. 16 Apr. 1732.
Wamsley, child of Christoffel Wamsley and Jannetie Hendrikse, chr. 16 Apr. 1732.
Van Brunt, Engeltie, d/o Nicolaes Van Brunt and Geesje Hendrikse, chr. 23 Apr. 1732.
Sutphen, Maria, d/o Jan Sutphen and Catryntie Langstraet, chr. 21 May 1732.
De Nys, Tryntie, d/o Teunis De Nys and Fransyntie Hendrikse, chr. 4 June 1732.
Gerritse, Petrus, s/o Gerrit Gerritse and Maria Wykhoff, chr. 18 June 1732.
Swart, Adrian, s/o Jacobus Swart and Jannetie Laan, chr. 19 June 1732.
Sutphen, David, s/o Jacob Sutphen and Antie_ Bennit, chr. 16 July 1732.
Willemse, Jannetie, d/o Elbert Willemse and Jacomyntie Kouwenhoven, chr. 3 Aug. 1732.
Smak, Cornelis, s/o Barent Smak and Annatie Luyster, chr. 6 Aug. 1732.
Bryk, Jannetie, d/o Bernardus V. Bryk and Jannetie Schenk, chr. 27 Aug. 1732.
Barber, Jannetie, d/o Edwaerd Beerber and Mary Tysen, chr. 10 Sep. 1732.
Wilson, Jannetje, d/o Jan Wilson and Antie_Van Cleeff, chr.15 Oct. 1732.
Heyer, Gysbert, s/o Joh. Heyer and Antie_ De Hart, chr. 22 Oct. 1732.
Borkelo, Maria, d/o Dirk Borkelo and Jannetie Van Aersdael, chr. 5 Nov. 1732.
Wykhoff, Samuel, s/o Gerrit Wykhoff and Aeltie Borkelo, chr. 19 Nov. 1732.
Hanse, Antie, d/o Jan Hanse and Lena Willemse, chr. 3 Dec. 1732.
Bennit, Gerrit, s/o Hendrik Bennit and Jannetie Couwenhoven, chr. 17 Dec. 1732.
Van Der Bilt, Margrietje, d/o Aris Van Der Bilt and Jannetie Couwenhoven, chr. 24 Dec. 1732.
Bayrt, Madalena, d/o Willem Bayrt and Elsje Van Cleeff, chr. 1733.
Van Cleeff, Femmetie, d/o Laurens Van Kleef and Jannetie Laan, chr. 1733.
Couwenhoven, Petrus, s/o Elias Couwenhoven and Willemptie Wale, chr. 1733.

Couwenhoven, Joris, s/o Abraham Couwenhoven and Antie_ Goolder, chr. 1733.
Couwenhoven, Theodorus, s/o Willem Couwenhoven and Maryke Coljer, chr. 1733.
Pieterse, Marritie, d/o Gerbrant Pieterse and Antie_ Bennit, chr. 1733.
Schenk, Jan, s/o Pieter Schenk and Jannetie Van Noortstrant, chr. 1733.
Smit, Margrietje, d/o Jan Smit and Barendyna Melling, chr. 1733.
Truwexs, Elsje, s/o Johannes Truwexs and Sytie V. Kerk, chr. 1733.
Van Der Bilt, Hendrik, s/o Hendrik Van Der Bilt and Neeltie Van Cleeff, chr. 1733.
Van Der Vere, Catryna, d/o Corn. Van Der Vere and Marytie Smak, chr. 21 Jan. 1733.
Smak, Hendrikus, s/o Hendr. Smak and Anti_ Van Duyn, chr. 28 Jan. 1733.
Low, Sara, d/o Corn. Low and Johanna Gouverneur, chr. 4 Feb. 1733.
Van Doorn, Jan, s/o Jacob Van Doorn and Maria Schenk, chr. 11 Feb. 1733.
Haeghoort, Petrus, s/o Gerard Haeghoort and Catharina De Loy, chr. 25 Feb. 1733.
Van Meteren, Yda, d/o Jan Van Meteren and Ytie Sudam, chr. 4 Mar. 1733.
Couwenhoven, Jan, s/o Roelof Couwenhoven and Aeltie_ Stryker, chr. 11 Mar 1733.
Heyer, Thys, s/o Willem Heyer and Marytie Van De Ryp, chr. 25 Mar. 1733.
Van Cleeff, Gerrit, s/o Joseph Van Kleef and Sytie Van Wikkelen, chr. 8 Apr. 1733.
Hendrikse, Johannes, s/o Johannes Hendrikse and Sara Mesier, chr. 15 Apr. 1733.
Willemse, Peysiens, d/o Willem Willemse and Aeltie Couwenhoven, chr. 4 May 1733.
Pieterse, Maria, d/o Thys Pieterse and Geesje Hendrikse, chr. 10 June 1733.
Antonides, Johannes, s/o Joh. Antonides and Johanna Couwenhoven, chr. 24 June 1733.
Voorhees, Petrus, s/o Hendrik Voorhees and Jannetie Andriese, chr. 8 July 1733.
Amak, Elisabeth, d/o Teunis Amak and Helena Laan, chr. 5 Aug. 1733.
Couwenhoven, child of Willem Couwenhoven and Lybetie Van Cleef, chr. 16 Sep. 1733.
Wykhoff, Maria, d/o Willem Wykhoff and Agnitie Van Doorn, chr. 28 Oct. 1733.

Dutch Reformed Church - Freehold and Middletown

Teunisse, Cornelis, s/o Jan Teunisse and Aeltie Smak, chr. 4 Nov. 1733.
Eversen, George Roeterse, s/o Nicolaes Eversen and Susanna Roeters, chr. 11 Nov. 1733.
Sudam, Eyda, d/o Hendrik Sudam and Marytie Van Siggelen, chr. 25 Nov. 1733.
Hopmoejer, Samuel, s/o Sameul Hopmoejer and Marytie Bedlo, chr. 16 Dec. 1733.
Benhem, Elisabbeth, d/o Jan Benhem and Geertie Van Dyck, chr. 1734.
Haeghoort, Johanna, d/o Gerard Haeghoort and Catharina De Loy, chr. 1734.
Hendrikse, Elisabeth, d/o Johannes Hendrikse and Sara Mosier, chr. 1734.
Van Doorn, Jacob, s/o Ary Van Doorn and Antie_ Schenk, chr. 1 Jan. 1734.
Van Der Vere, Neeltie, d/o Teunis Van Der Vere and Aeltie Schenk, chr. 20 Jan. 1734.
Jsanse, Jacobus, s/o Jan Jsanse and Mayke_ V. Kerk, chr. 3 Mar. 1734.
Tyse, Barbara, d/o Abraham Tyse and Sara Willemse, chr. 17 Mar. 1743.
Hendrikse, Neeltje, s/o Hendrik Hendrikse and Neeltie Schenk, chr. 24 Mar. 1734.
Wykhoff, Petrus, s/o Gerrit Wykhoff and Aeltie Gerritse, chr. 31 Mar. 1734.
Schenk, Petrus, s/o Coert Schenk and Marya Couwenhoven, chr. 14 Apr. 1734.
Schank, Agnitie, d/o Roelof Schank and Engeltie Van Doorn, chr. 5 May 1734.
De Nys, Neeltje, d/o Teunis De Nys and Francyntie Hendrikse, chr. 24 May 1734.
Sutphen, Abraham, s/o Dirk Sutphen and Grietje Van Pelt, chr. 14 July 1734.
Sutphen, Jannetie, d/o Jan Sutphen and Catryntie Langstraet, chr. 25 Aug. 1734.
Jones, Elisabeth, s/o Caleb Jones and Elisabet Romeyn, chr. 8 Sep. 1734.
Holzaert, Marya, d/o Corn. Holzaert and Saertie Sloover, chr. 5 Oct. 1734.
Couwenhoven, Johannes, s/o Johannes Couwenhoven and Styntie Laan, chr. 27 Oct. 1734.
Shermerhoorn, Peter, s/o Lucas Shermerhorn and Sara Thyse, chr. 3 Nov. 1734.
Nevius, Sara, d/o Pieter and Aaltie, chr. 17 Nov. 1734.
Beert, Elisabeth, d/o Willem Beert and Elsje Van Cleeff, chr. 1735.

Couwenhoven, Maria, d/o Willem Couwenhoven and Arriaentie Bennit, chr. 1735.
Schenk, Willemtie, s/o Pieter Schenk and Jannetie Van Noortstrant, chr. 1735.
Van Metere, Neeltie, d/o Syrynus Van Metere and Abigail Lefferse, chr. 1735.
Van Der Bilt, Aris, s/o Hendrik Van Der Bilt and Neeltie Van Cleeff, chr. 1735.
Emans, Abraham, s/o Corn. Emans and Corn_ Holzaert, chr. 6 Apr. 1735.
Hun, Judith, d/o Adriaan Hun and Pheby Smit, chr. 13 Apr. 1735.
Hanse, Willemptie, d/o Johannes Hanse and Lena Willemse, chr. 11 May 1735.
Van Pelt, Petrus, s/o Teunis Van Pelt and Geertruy Bennit, chr. 22 June 1735.
Amak, Aphie, d/o Teunis Amak and Lena Laan, chr. 17 Aug. 1735.
Brouwer, Henrikus, s/o Jan Brouwer and Hilletje Van Kleef, chr. 25 Dec. 1735.
Bennit, Hendrik, s/o Hendrik Bennit and Jannetje Couwenhoven, chr. 1736.
Dusberry, Antje, d/o Hindrik Dusberry and Cathrina Hindrikse, chr. 1736.
Emans, Maria, d/o Benjamin Emans and Rachel Fenton, chr. 1736.
Emans, Margrietje, d/o Cornelius Emans and Cornelia Holsaart, chr. 1736.
Hansen, Maria, d/o Hindrik Hansen and Jannetje Laan, chr. 1736.
Hun, Thomas, s/o Adriaan Hun and Phebi Smit, chr. 1736.
Loos, Maria Elisabeth, d/o Johannes Loos and Elisabeth Miller, chr. 1736.
Zeedam, Cathrina, d/o Hendrik Zeedam and Maria Van Sikkele, chr. 1736.
Zeedam, Elizabeth, d/o Ryk Zeedam and Elizabeth Borkloo, chr. 1736.
Wilmze, Lena, d/o Wilm Wilmze and Aaltje Couwenhove, chr. 1736.
Zechels, Zacharias, s/o Hendrik Zechels and Maria Stilwel, chr. 1736.
Zechels, Maria, d/o Gerrit Zechels and Arriaantje Lammerze, chr. 1736.
Voorhese, Petrus, s/o Pieter Voorhese and Ariaantje Nevius, chr. 10 Mar. 1736.
Fasi, Johannes, s/o Felton Fasi and Cathrina Harsman, chr. 20 June 1736.
Van Mettere, Neeltje, d/o Joseph Van Mettere and Sara Schenk, chr. 20 June 1736.
Heggens, Barbara, d/o Petrec Heggens and Jannetie Tyse, chr. 23 June 1736.

Dutch Reformed Church - Freehold and Middletown

Thysse, Barbara, d/o Abraham Thysse and Sara Wilmze, chr. 26 Sep. 1736.
Smit, Benjamin, s/o John Smit and Barentje Melling, chr. 20 Nov. 1736.
Hendrikse, Daniel, s/o Wilm Hendrikse and Maria Langstraat, chr. 19 Dec. 1736.
Hindrikse, Wilm, s/o Jan Hindrikse and Sara Moesier, chr. 25 Dec. 1736.
Bennit, Johannes, s/o Johannes Agnietje, chr. 1737.
Van Cleeff, Jannetje, d/o Laurens Van Kleef and Jannetje Laan, chr. 1737.
Couwenhove, Maria, d/o Roelof Couwenhove and Sara Voorhees, chr. 1737.
Doorn, Jacobus, s/o ____ Doorn and Elsje Golder, chr. 1737.
Hanssen, David, s/o Johannes Hanssen and Helena Wilmse, chr. 1737.
Holsart, Johanna, d/o Cornleius Holsart and Sara Slovers, chr. 1737.
Langstraat, Petrus, s/o Jan Langstraat and Antje Couwenhove, chr. 1737.
Langstraat, Aaron, s/o Jan Langstraat and Anna Couwenhove, chr. 1737.
Schenk, Roelef, s/o Roelof Schenk and Engeltje Van Doorn, chr. 1737.
Schenk, Neeltje, d/o Gerrit Schenk and Jannetje Couenhove, chr. 1737.
Van Kerk, Jacobus, s/o Jan Van Kerk and Cornelia Van Brakele, chr. 1737.
Van Mettere, Joseph, s/o Gysbert Van Mettere and Mayke_ Hindrikze, chr. 1737.
Van Mettere, Annie, d/o Jan Van Mettere and Eyda Zedam, chr. 1737.
Van Meteren, Cyrenius, s/o Benjamin Van Meteren and Elisabeth Laan, chr. 1737.
Voorheze, Johannes, s/o Pieter Voorheze and Ariaantje Nevius, chr. 1737.
Voorheese, Antje, d/o Pieter Voorheese and Ariaantje Nevius, chr. 1737.
Zutveen, Christopher, s/o John Zutveen and Cathrina Langstraat, chr. 1737.
Zutveen, Abraham, s/o Abraham Zutveen and Maria Borkloo, chr. 1737.
Schenk, Antje, d/o Coert Schenk and Maria Kouwenhove, chr. 1 Jan. 1737.
Smak, Hindrik, s/o Barent Smak and Johanna Luister, chr. 21 Jan. 1737.
Van Doorn, Wilm, s/o Jacob Van Doorn and Maria Schenk, chr. 6 Mar. 1737.
Couwenhove, Daniel, s/o Wilm Couwenhove and Antje Hindrikse, chr. 27 Mar. 1737.
Couwenhove, Daniel, s/o Wilm Couwenhove and Antje Hindrikse, chr. 30 Mar. 1737.
Van Kerk, Maria, d/o John Van Kerk and Cornelia Van Brakel, chr. 3 Apr. 1737.

Antonides, Barbara, d/o Johannes Antonides and Johanna Kouwenhove, chr. 23 Apr. 1737.
Homes, Jacobus, s/o Jonathan Homes and Teuntje Hindrikse, chr. 1 May 1737.
Van Der Bilt, Eyda, d/o Hindrik Van Der Bilt and Neeltje Van Kleef, chr. 8 May 1737.
Leffertse, Maria, d/o Leffert Leffertse and Jannetje Willemse, chr. 22 May 1737.
Van Cleeff, Laurens, s/o Laurens Van Kleef and Jannetje Laan, chr. 29 May 1737.
Hendrikse, Hindrik, s/o Hendrick Hendrikse and Neeltje Schenk, chr. 30 May 1737.
Sutveen, Maria, d/o Gysbert Sutveen and Geertruid Van Pelt, chr. 5 June 1737.
Nevius, Maria, d/o Pieter Nevius and Aaltje D_Neik, chr. 19 June 1737.
Homes, Samuel, s/o Jonathan Homes and Teuntje Hindrikse, chr. 8 July 1737.
Schenk, Sara, d/o Pieter Schenk and Jannetje Hanssen, chr. 17 July 1737.
Van Mettere, Cornelius, s/o Jan Van Mettere and Eyda Zedam, chr. 25 July 1737.
Everzon, George Roeters, s/o Niclaas and Susanna, chr. 29 July 1737.
Everzon, Susanna, d/o Niclaas and Susanna, chr. 29 July 1737.
Everzon, Jacob Roeters, s/o Niclaas and Susanna, chr. 29 July 1737.
Everzon, Elisabeth, d/o Niclaas and Susanna, chr. 29 July 1737.
Van Doorn, Isaak, s/o Jacob Van Doorn and Maria Schenk, chr. 12 Aug. 1737.
Heyer, Jannetje, d/o Wilm Heyer and Maria Van De Ryp, chr. 14 Aug. 1737.
Van Pelt, Maria, d/o Teunis Van Pelt and Geertruid Bennit, chr. 26 Aug. 1737.
Van Der Bilt, Maria, d/o Aart Van Der Bilt and Jannetje Couwenhove, chr. 26 Aug. 1737.
Van Metteren, Hindrik, s/o Gysbert Van Metteren and Mayke_ Hindrikse, chr. 28 Aug. 1737.
Van Der Bilt, Derk, s/o Hindrik Van Der Bilt and Neeltje Van Kleef, chr. 9 Sep. 1737.
Heyer, Thomas, d/o Johannes Heyer and Elisabeth Van Dyk, chr. 11 Sep. 1737.
Erickson, Wilm, s/o Reinhart Ericksoin and Maria Provoost, chr. 18 Sep. 1737.
Hindrikze, Tryntje, d/o Hindrik Hindrikze and Neeltje Schenk, chr. 30

Dutch Reformed Church - Freehold and Middletown

Sep. 1737.
Hindrikze, Neeltje, d/o Hendrick Hindrikze and Neeltje Schenk, chr. 30 Sep. 1737.
Lammerze, Maria, d/o Jan Lammerze and Mayke_ Van Kerk, chr. 7 Oct. 1737.
Stout, Pieternella, chr. 9 Oct. 1737.
Couwenhove, Jacob, s/o Wilm Couwenhove and Antje Hindrikse, chr. 14 Oct. 1737.
Van Mettere, Aaltje, d/o Cyrenius Van Mettere and Abigael Lefferse, chr. 27 Oct. 1737.
Wykhof, Isaak, s/o Wilm Wykhof and Agnitje Van Doorn, chr. 4 Nov. 1737.
Wilmse, Aart, d/o Wilm Wilmse and Aaltje Kouwenhove, chr. 2 Dec. 1737.
Swart, Rebecca, d/o Teunis Swart and Geertje Luister, chr. 9 Dec. 1737.
Bennit, Ariaantje, d/o Hindrik Bennit and Jannetje Couwenhove, chr. 23 Dec. 1737.
Bennit, Jacob, s/o Johannes and Agnietje, chr. 29 Dec. 1737.
Brouwer, Benjamin, s/o Jan Brouwer and Hilletje Van Kleef, chr. 1738.
De Neis, Neis, s/o Teunis De Neis and Fransyna Hindrikse, chr. 1738.
Emans, Elisabeth d/o Benjamin Emans and Rachel Fenton, chr. 1738.
Emans, Elias, s/o Cornelius Emans and Cornelia Holsart, chr. 1738.
Hindrikze, Jacob, s/o Jan Hindrikze and Antje Couwenhov, chr. 1738.
Jansen, Maria, d/o Petrus Jansen and Antje Coevert, chr. 1738.
Laan, Helena, d/o Jacob Laan and Maria Romein, chr. 1738.
Shermerhoorn, Barbara, d/o Lucas Shermerhorn and Sara Tiesse, chr. 1738.
Smak, Barent, s/o Hindrik Smak and Maria Schenk, chr. 1738.
Tysse, Antje, d/o Johannes Tysse and Sara Goolder, chr. 17 Mar. 1738.
Kouwenhove, Petrus, s/o Pieter Kouwenhove and Lea Schenk, chr. 12 Feb. 1738.
Wykhof, Wilm, s/o Wilm Wykhof and Agnietje Van Doorn, chr. 19 Feb. 1738.
Thysse, Jannaetje, d/o Mathias Thysse and Maria Baart, chr. 26 Feb. 1738.
Van Metteren, Roelef, s/o Joseph Van Metteren and Sara Schenk, chr. 19 Mar. 1738.
Fabryk, Wilhelmus, s/o Bernardus Fabryk and Jannetje Schenk, chr. 23 Apr. 1738.
Couwenhove, Lydia, d/o Elias Couwenhove and Antje Hindrikse chr. 30 Apr. 1738.
Voorhees, Wilm, s/o Hendrik Voorhees and Sara Schenk, chr. 22 May

1738.
Fasie, Harmen, s/o Felten Fasie and Cathrina Horsman, chr. 4 June 1738.
Wykhof, Jacob, s/o Niclaas Wykhof and Maria Waal, chr. 11 June 1738.
Emans, Cornelia, d/o Abraham Emans and Annatje Luister, chr. 18 June. 1738.
Hindrikse, Coenrad, s/o Johannes Hindrikse and Sara Mosier, chr. 30 July 1738.
Zeedam, Ryk, s/o Ryk Zeedam and Elizabeth Borkloo, chr. 27 Aug. 1738.
Hun, Phoebi, d/o Adriaan Hun and Phoebi Smit, chr. 10 Sep. 1738.
Borkloo, Jannetje, d/o Wilm Borkloo and Aaltje Wilmse, b. 11 Sep. 1738 and chr. 24 Sep. 1738.
Wilmse, Wilhelmus, s/o Johannes Wilmse and Agnietje Sutveen, chr. 5 Nov. 1738.
Van Der Veer, Johannes, s/o Corn.Van Der Veer and Marretje Smak, chr. 3 Dec. 1738.
Dusberry, Anna, d/o Hindrik Dusberry and Cathrina Hindrikse, chr. 24 Dec. 1738.
Amak, Jan, s/o Teunis Amak and Helena Laan, chr. 1739.
Hanssen, Cornelius, s/o Hindrik Hanssen and Jannetje Laan, chr. 1739.
Hervie, Petrus, s/o Robert Hervie and Jannetje Amak, chr. 1739.
Zutveen, Christoffer, s/o Jan Zutveen and Cathrina Langstraat, chr. 1739.
Tiesse, Maria, d/o Abraham Tiesse and Sara Wilmse, chr. 25 Feb. 1739.
Smak, Catrina, d/o Barent Smak and Anna Luister, chr. 18 Mar. 1739.
Van Doorn, Antje, d/o Arie Van Doorn and Antje Schenk, chr. 25 Mar. 1739.
Schenk, Wilm, s/o Gerrit Schenk and Jannetje Couwenhove, chr. 15 Apr. 1739.
Van Der Veer, Teunis, s/o Teunis Van Der Veer and Aeltje Schenk, chr. 19 Apr. 1739.
Leffertse, Aart, s/o Leffert Leffertse and Jannetje Wilmse, chr. 22 Apr. 1739.
Pieterson, Daniel, s/o Ties Pieterson and Geesje Hindrickson, chr. 10 June 1739.
Zutveen, Jacob, s/o Abraham Zutveen and Maria Borkloo, chr. 17 June 1739.
Borkloo, Aart, s/o Wilm Borkloo and Aaltje Wilmse, chr. 1740.
De Neis, Jannetje, d/o Teunis De Neis and Francyntje Hindrikson, chr. 1740.
Emans, Maria, d/o Cornelius Emans and Cornelia Holsart, chr. 1740.
Emans, Petrus, s/o Daniel Emans and Altje Holsart, chr. 1740.
Heyer, Maria, d/o Wilm Heyer and Maria Van De Ryp, chr. 1740.

Dutch Reformed Church - Freehold and Middletown

Schenk, Petrus, s/o Pieter Schenk and Annetje Van Noortstrant, chr. 1740.
Shermerhoorn, Matthias, s/o Lucas Shermerhorn and Sara Pieterson, chr. 1740.
Erickson, David, s/o Reinhart Ericksoin and Maria Provoost, chr. 13 Jan. 1740.
Berkaar, Hendrikjen, s/o __ Berkaar and Maria Van Kleef, chr. 20 Jan. 1740.
Schenk, Jan, s/o Roelof Schenk and Engeltie Van Doorn, chr. 3 Feb. 1740.
Van Noorstrant, Jannetje, s/o Johannes Van Noorstrant and ____ Wilmse, chr. 24 Feb. 1740.
Kouwenhove, Jannetje, d/o Elias Kouwenhove and Wilmtje Waal, chr. 2 Mar. 1740.
Kouwenhove, Jan, s/o Pieter Kouwenhove and Lea Schenk chr. 9 Mar. 1740.
Van Der Bilt, Sara, d/o Aart Van Der Bilt and Jannetje Couwenhove, chr. 23 Mar. 1740.
Thiesse, Sara, d/o Johannes Thiesse and Sara Goolder, chr. 26 May 1740.
Heyer, Annetje, d/o Pieter Heyer and Aaltje Van Pelt, chr. 1 June 1740.
Voorhees, Hendrik, s/o Hendrik Voorhees and Sara Schenk, chr. 15 June 1740.
Janse, Margrietje, d/o Pieter Janse and Antje Koevert, chr 29 June 1740.
Laan, Elisabeth, d/o Matthias Laan and Cathrina Polhemus, chr. 11 July 1740.
Kouwenhove, Cornelis, s/o Roelef Kouwenhove and Sara Voorhees, chr. 10 Aug. 1740.
Van Mettere, Cyrenius, s/o Joseph Van Mettere and Sara Schenk, chr. 14 Sep. 1740.
Heyer, Johannes, s/o Joh. Heyer and Elisabeth Van Dyk, chr. 21 Sep. 1740.
Couwenhove, Anna, d/o Pieter Couwenhove and Pieternella Polhemus, chr. 2 Oct. 1740.
Doorn, Jacob, s/o Joseph Doorn and Femmetje Wykhof, chr. 12 Oct. 1740.
Boun, Phoebi, d/o Cesgem Boun and Elisabeth Lement, chr. 23 Nov. 1740.
Van Der Veer, Cornelius, s/o Teunis Van Der Veer and Aeltie Schenk, chr. 1741.
Wykhof, Margarita, d/o Wilm Wykhof and Agnietje Van Doorn, chr. 1741.

Voorhees, Lea, d/o Pieter Voorhees and Ariaantje Nefius, chr. 1 Jan. 1741.
Theunisse, Femmetje, d/o Jan Theunisse and Antje Smak, chr. 15 Feb. 1741.
Couwenhove, Elisabeth, d/o Wilm Couwenhove and Elisabeth Van Cleef, chr. 22 Feb. 1741.
Van Doorn, Sarah, d/o Jacob Van Doorn and Maria Schenk, chr. 12 Apr. 1741.
Leffertse, Antje, d/o Leffert Leffertse and Jannetje Wilmse, chr. 26 Apr. 1741.
Heyer, Geertje, d/o Pieter Heyer and Aaltje Van Pelt, chr. 24 May 1741.
Smak, Roelelf, s/o Hendrik Smak and Maria Schenk, chr. 31 May 1741.
Hindrikson, Gysbert, sd/o Johannes Hindrikson and Sara Moesier, chr. 28 June 1741.
Van De Bilt, Neeltje, d/o Hindrik Van De Bilt and Neeltje Van Cleef, chr. 12 July 1741.
Van Emburg, Peregrinus, s/o Peregrinus Van Emburg and Cornelia Provoost, chr. 26 July 1741.
Amak, Mattheus, s/o Theunis Amak and Helena Laan, chr. 2 Aug. 1741.
Schenk, Antje, d/o Gerrit Schenk and Jannetje Couwenhove, chr. 9 Aug. 1741.
Sutveen, Cornelius, s/o Abraham Sutveen and Maria Borkloo, chr. 10 Sep. 1741.
Sutphen, Jan, s/o Jan Sutphen and Pieternelle Stout, chr. 25 Oct., 1741.
Hindrikson, Maria, d/o Hindrik Hiendrikson and Neeltje Schenk, chr. 25 Dec. 1741.
Brouwer, Aafje d/o Samuel Brouwer and Aaffje Kienie, chr. 1742.
Emans, Cornelis, s/o Cornelis Emans and Cornelia Holsart, chr. 1742.
Holsart, Antje, d/o Mattheus Holsart and Antje Martae, chr. 1742.
Heyer, Maria, d/o Pieter Heyer and Aaltje Van Pelt, chr. 1742.
Heyer, Walter, s/o Wilm Heyer and Maria Van De Ryp, chr. 1742.
Laan, Johannes, s/o Mattheus Laan and Cathrina Polhemus, chr. 1742.
Schenk, Roelef, s/o Jan Schenk and Jacomyntje Couwenhove, chr. 1742.
Van Cleef, Benjamin, s/o Benjamin Van Cleef and Helena Kouwenhove, chr. 1742.
Van Matre, Cathrina, d/o Gysbert Van Matre and Mayke_ Hindrikson, chr. 1742.
Van Doorn, Neeltje, d/o Arie Van Doorn and Antje Schenk, chr. 1742.
Wykhof, Jan, s/o Niclaas Wykhof and Maria Waal, chr. 1742.
Wilmson, Elbert, s/o Wilm Elb. Wilmson and Antje Voorhees, chr. 3 Jan. 1742.

Dutch Reformed Church - Freehold and Middletown

Couwenhove, Sara, d/o Roelef Couwenhove and Jannetje Hindrickson, chr. 21 Feb. 1742.
Van Kerk, Sara, d/o Jan Van Kerk and Cornelia Van Brakele, chr. 28 Feb. 1742.
Thiesse, Jannetje, d/o Abraham Thiesse and Sara Wilmson, chr. 14 Mar. 1742.
Schenk, Maria, d/o Pieter Schenk and Jannetje Van Oostrande, chr. 4 Apr. 1742.
Couwenhove, Patiens, d/o Pieter Couwenhove and Lea Schenk, chr. 25 Apr. 1742.
Bennit, Hendrik, s/o Johannes and Agnietje, chr. 16 May 1742.
Van Der Veer, Sinai, s/o Cornelius Van Der Veer and Marretje Smak, chr. 6 June 1742.
Van Oostrand, Maria, d/o Joh. Van Oostrand and Helena Wilmse, chr. 1 Aug. 1742.
Emans, Henricus, s/o Daniel Emans and Aaltje Holsart, chr. 15 Aug. 1742.
Van Noortwyk, Antje, d/o Adriaan Van Noortwyk and Rachel Unjert, chr. 19 Sep. 1742.
Voorhees, Roelef, s/o Hindrik Voorhees and Sara Schenk, chr. 26 Sep. 1742.
Clerk, Cornelis, s/o Jan Clerk and Antje Doorn, chr. 10 Oct. 1742.
Van Cleef, Isaac, s/o Laurens Van Cleef and Jannetje Laan, chr. 24 Oct. 1742.
Swart, Elizabeth, d/o Theunis Swart and Geertje Luister, chr. 12 Dec. 1742.
Couwenhove, Wilm, s/o Wilm Couwenhove and Elisabeth Van Cleef, chr. 19 Dec. 1742.
De Neis, Femmetje, d/o Teunis De Neis and Francyntje Hendrikson, chr. 1743.
Doorn, Cornelius, s/o Joseph Doorn and Femmetje Wykhof, chr. 1743.
Hervie, Jacob, s/o Robert Hervie and Jannetje Amak, chr. 1743.
Heyer, Gerard, s/o Johannes Heyer and Elisabeth Van Dyk, chr. 1743.
Sutveen, Derk, s/o Jan Sutveen and Pieternella Stout, chr. 1743.
Wilmson, Neeltje, s/o Wilm Wilmson and Aaltje Couwenhove, chr. 1743.
Wykhof, Agnietje, d/o Wilm Wykhof and Agnietje Van Doorn, chr. 1743.
Zutveen, Cathrina, d/o Derk Zutveen and Maria Langstraat, chr. 17 June 1739.
Zutveen, Gysbert, s/o Aart Zutveen and Jannetje Van Mattere, chr. 1743.

Van Emburg, Maria, d/o Peregrinus Van Emburg and Cornelia Provoost, chr. 13 Mar. 1743.
Smak, Barent, s/o Barent Smak and Annatje Luister, chr. 20 Mar. 1743.
Van Mettere, Geertie, d/o Jan Van Mettere and Eida Zeedam, chr. 27 Mar. 1743.
Laan, Anna, d/o Abraham Laan and Anna Brouwer, chr. 3 Apr. 1743.
Smit, David, s/o Joseph Smit and Aafje Watson, chr. 17 Apr. 1743.
Van Cleef, Benjamin, s/o Derk Van Cleef and Elisabeth Leek, chr. 29 May 1743.
Forman, Margrietje, d/o Petrus Forman and Neeltje Wilmson, chr. 26 June 1743.
Zeedam, Eva, d/o Hendrik Zeedam and Maria Van Sikkelen chr. 7 Aug. 1743.
Hegens, Maria, d/o Pieter Hegens and Jannetje Thiesse, chr. 21 Aug. 1743.
Sneder, Petrus, s/o Jan Sneder and Aaltje Bennit, chr. 4 Sep. 1743.
Bennit, Jannetje, d/o Abraham Bennit and Jannetje Zedam, chr. 11 Sep. 1743.
Bown, Agnietje, d/o Gysbert Bown and Elisabeth Lement, chr. 18 Sep. 1743.
Dusberry, Wilm Hindrikson, s/o Hindrik Dusberry and Cathrina Hindrikson, chr. 25 Sep.1743.
Clerk, Alexander, s/o Jan Clerk and Antje Doorn, chr. 16 Oct. 1743.
Schenk, Gerrit, s/o Gerrit Schenk and Jannetje Couwenhove, chr. 20 Nov. 1743.
Couwenhove, Jacob, s/o Jacob and Grietje, chr. 27 Nov. 1743.
Couwenhove, Albert, s/o Pieter Couwenhove and Wilmpe Voorhees, chr. 11 Dec. 1743.
Couwenhove, Johannes, s/o Pieter Couwenhove and Neeltje Polhemus, chr. 1744.
Polhemus, Annatje, d/o Cornelis Polhemus and Neeltje Enderson, chr. 1744.
Zeedam, Lucretia, d/o Reik Zeedam and Sara Luister, chr. 1744.
Van De Bilt, Maria, d/o Hindrik Van De Bilt and Nelly Van Cleef, chr. 1744.
Van Doorn, Arie, s/o Jacob Van Doorn and Maria Schenk, chr. 1744.
Laan, Jacob, s/o Mattheus Laan and Cathrina Polhemus, chr. 8 Jan. 1744.
Couwenhove, Daniel, s/o Roelf Couwenhove and Jannetje Hindrickson, chr. 15 Jan. 1744.
Van Mattere, Cornelius, d/o Benjamin Van Mattere and Elisabeth Laan, chr. 26 Mar. 1744.

Dutch Reformed Church - Freehold and Middletown

Van Mattere, Cathrina, d/o Joseph Van Mattere and Sara Schenk, chr. 22 Apr. 1744.
Zutveen, Antje, d/o Abraham Zutveen and Maria Borkloo, chr. 6 May 1744.
Schenk, Hillettie, d/o Luykes Schenk and Lammettie Remse, chr. 14 May 1744.
Polhemus, Tobias, s/o Daniel Polhemus and Margrietje Couwenhove, chr. 3 June 1744.
Langstraat, Jans, s/o Jan Langstraat and Antje Couwenhove, chr. 24 June 1744.
Doorn, Antje, d/o Joseph Doorn and Femmetje Wykhof, chr. 22 July 1744.
Couwenhove, Sara, d/o Roelef Couwenhove and Sara Voorhees, chr. 5 Aug. 1744.
Couwenhove, Gerrit, s/o Wilm Couwenhove and Margrieta Schenk, chr. 16 Sep. 1744.
Schenk, Cornelius, s/o Jan Schenk and Jacomyna Couwenhove, chr. 7 Oct. 1744.
Van Sikkele, Maria, d/o Gysbert Van Sikkele and Annatje Ryder, chr. 12 Oct. 1744.
Schenk, Antje, d/o Jan Schenk and Antje Janson, chr. 28 Oct. 1744.
Smit, Margritie, d/o Joseph Smit and Aafje Watson, chr. 2 Dec. 1744.
Hindrikson, Daniel, s/o Daniel Hindrikson and Catrina Couwenhove, chr. 9 Dec. 1744.
Van Cleef, Cornelius, s/o Benjamin Van Cleef and Helena Couwenhove, chr. 16 Dec. 1744.
Hindrikson, Antje, d/o Hindrik Hiendrikson and Neeltje Schenk, chr. 30 Dec. 1744.
Borklo, Derk, s/o Cornelius Borklo and Jannetje Amak, chr. 1745.
Borkloo, Jannetje, d/o Daniel Borkloo and Antje Luister, chr. 1745.
Emans, Daniel, s/o Daniel Emans and Aaltje Holsart, chr. 1745.
Heyer, Walter, s/o Pieter Heyer and Aaltje Van Pelt, chr. 1745.
Sutveen, Jan, s/o Aart Sutveen and Jannetje Van Mattere, chr. 1745.
Voorhees, Albert, s/o Hindrik Voorhees and Sara Schenk, chr. 1745.
Wykhof, Lea, d/o Wilm Wykhof and Agnietje Van Doorn, chr. 1745.
Zutveen, Abraham, s/o Derk Zutveen and Maria Langstraat, chr. 1745.
Van Cleef, Daniel, s/o Derk Van Cleef and Elisabeth Laak, chr. 13 Jan. 1745.
Thiesson, Johannes, s/o Johannes Thiesson and Sara Goolder, chr. 3 Feb. 1745.
Couwenhove, Sara, d/o Pieter Couwenhove and Lea Schenk chr. 24 Feb. 1745.

Early Church Records of Monmouth County

Schenk, Court, s/o Court Schenk and Maria Couwenhov, chr. 24 Feb. 1745.
Van Noortstrant, Helena, d/o Johannes Van Noortstrant and Helena Wilmson, chr. 10 Mar 1745.
Van Der Veer, Aaltje, d/o Teunis Van Der Veer and Aeltie Schenk, chr. 24 Mar. 1745.
Hindrikson, Maria, d/o Joh. Hindrikson and Sara Mosier, chr. 7 Apr. 1745.
Wilmson, Sara, chr. 29 May 1745.
Laan, Antje, d/o Gerrit Laan and Mayke_ Zutveen, chr. 2 June 1745.
Emans, Johanna, d/o Cornelius Emans and Cornelia Holsart, chr. 9 June 1745.
Wilmson, Sara, d/o Wilm Wilmson and Antje Voorhees, chr. 7 July 1745.
Van Emburg, John, s/o Peregrinus Van Emburg and Cornelia Provoost, chr. 10 Aug. 1745.
Verkerk, Stephanus, s/o Jan Verkerk and Cornelia Van Brakele, chr. 18 Aug. 1745.
Schenk, Jan, s/o Gerrit Schenk and Jannetje Couwenhove, chr. 1 Sep. 1745.
Heyer, Cathrina, d/o Wilm Heyer and Maria Van De Ryp, chr. 27 Oct. 1745.
Bennit, Magdalena, d/o Johannes and Agnietje, chr. 17 Nov. 1745.
Snyder, Petrus, s/o Jan Pieter Snyder and Aaltje Bennit, chr. 2 Nov. 1745.
Van Der Veer, Cornelius, s/o Cornelius Van Der Veer and Marretje Smak, chr. 3 Nov. 1745.
De Neis, Neis, s/o Teunis De Neis and Francyntje Hindrikson, chr. 22 Dec. 1745.
Zutveen, Grietje, d/o Derk Zutveen and Jannetje Voorhees, chr. 29 Dec. 1745.
Clerk, Cornelius, s/o Jan Clerk and Antje Doorn, chr. 1746.
Doorn, Wilmpje, d/o Joseph Doorn and Femmetje Wykhof, chr. 1746.
Couwenhove, Daniel, s/o Elias Couwenhove and Wilmpje Waal, chr. 1746.
Laan, Aaltje, d/o Arie Laan and Sara Couwenhove, chr. 1746.
Zedam, Reik Reikse, s/o Reik Zedam and Sara Luister, chr. 1746.
Couwenhove, Catrina, d/o Roelef Couwenhove and Jannetje Hindrikson, chr. 9 Feb. 1746.
Couwenhove, Maria, d/o Wilm Couwenhove and Elisabeth Van Cleef, chr. 16 Feb. 1746.
Couwenhove, Cornelius, s/o Wilm Couwenhove and Antje Hindrikson,

Dutch Reformed Church - Freehold and Middletown

chr. Apr. 1746.
Thiesse, Sara, d/o Abram Thiesse and Sara Wilmson, chr. 13 Apr. 1746.
Couwenhove, Elisabeth, d/o Albert Couwenhove and Maria Van Doorn, chr. 27 Apr. 1746.
Laan, Maria, d/o Gysbert Laan and Neeltje Smak, chr. 8 May 1746.
Wykhof, Cathrina, d/o Wilm Wykhof and Agnietje Van Doorn, chr. 11 May 1746.
Hervie, Steven, s/o Robert Hervie and Jannetje Amak, chr. 29 June 1746.
Couwenhove, Jacob, s/o Gerrit Couwenhove and Neeltje Schenk, chr. 13 July 1746.
Laan, Daniel, s/o Mattheus Laan and Catrina Polhemus, chr. 24 Aug. 1746.
Laan, Jannetje, d/o Cornelius Laan and Maria Wamsly, chr. 30 Aug. 1746.
Schenk, Sara, d/o Jan Schenk and Jacomyntje Couwenhove, chr. 21 Sep. 1746.
Couwenhove, Arriaantje, d/o Jacob and Margrieta, chr. 25 Sep. 1746.
Couwenhove, Joris, s/o Gerrit Couwenhove and Sara Trophagel, chr. 26 Oct. 1746.
Wilmson, Elbert, s/o David Wilmson and Femmetje Swart, chr. 26 Nov. 1746.
Noortwyk, Aaltje, d/o Adriaan Noortwyk and Rachel Unjart, chr. 7 Dec. 1746.
Heyer, Aafje, d/o Joh. and Elisabeth Heyer, chr. 1747.
Schenk, Johannes, s/o Gerrit Schenk and Neeltje Voorhees, chr. 1747.
Smit, Jan, s/o Joseph Smit and Aafje Watson, chr. 1747.
Van Doorn, Maria, d/o Jacob Van Doorn and Maria Schenk, chr. 11 Jan 1747.
Couwenhove, Neeltje, d/o Peter Couwenhove and Lea Schenk, chr. 8 Feb. 1747.
Van Mattere, Neeltje, d/o Benjamin Van Mattere and Elisabeth Laan, chr. 15 Feb. 1747.
Van Noortstrant, Aaltje, d/o Johannes Van Noortstrant and Helena Wilmson, chr. 8 Mar 1747.
Luister, Johannes, s/o Cornelius Luister and Ariaantje Couwenhove, chr. 15 Mar. 1747.
Slover, Derk, s/o Isaak, chr. 22 Mar. 1747.
Van Mattere, Crein Janze, s/o Joseph Van Mattere and Sara Schenk, chr. 19 Mar. 1747.
Wilmson, Aart, s/o David Wilmson and Geertje Voorhees, chr. 5 Apr. 1747.
Sutphen, Jan, s/o Arie Sutphen and Antje Janson, chr. 3 May 1747.

Early Church Records of Monmouth County

Wilmson, Johannes, s/o Wilm Wilmson and Antje Voorhees, chr. 28 May 1747.
Hindrikson, Sara, d/o Joh. Hindrikson and Sara Mosier, chr. 28 June 1747.
Schenk, Antje, d/o Gerrit Schenk and Jannetje Couwenhove, chr. 23 Aug. 1747.
Langstraat, Elias, s/o Jan Langstraat and Antje Couwenhove, chr. 6 Sep. 1747.
Noordwyk, Rachel, d/o Adriaan Noordwyk and Rachel Unjaart, chr. 27 Sep. 1747.
Hindrikson, Cornelius, s/o Daniel Hindrikson and Cathrina Couwenhove, chr. 11 Oct. 1747.
Heyer, Altje, d/o Pieter Heyer and Aaltje Van Pelt, chr. 1 Nov. 1747.
Couwenhove, Roelef, s/o Gerrit Couwenhove and Neeltje Schenk, chr. 13 Dec. 1747.
Couwenhove, Jannetje, d/o Pieter Couwenhove and Wilmpje Voorhees, chr. 1748.
Doorn, Joseph, s/o Joseph Doorn and Femmetje Wykhof, chr. 1748.
Emans, Jonathan, s/o Daniel Emans and Aaltje Holst, chr. 1748.
Laan, Mattheus, s/o Cornelius Laan and Maria Wamsly, chr. 1748.
Zedam, Sara, d/o Reik Zedam and Sara Luister, chr. 1748.
Van Cleef, Elisabeth, d/o Derk Van Cleef and Elisabeth Laak, chr. 1748.
Wykhof, Wilm, s/o Wilm Wykhof and Agnietje Van Doorn, chr. 1748.
Zutveen, Jan, s/o Jan Zutveen and Jannetje Voorhees, chr. 1748.
Zutveen, Grietje, s/o Derk Zutveen and Jannetje Voorhees, chr. 29 Dec. 1748.
Voorhees, Gerret, s/o Hindrik Voorhees and Sara Schenk, chr. 30 Jan. 1748.
Sutveen, Geertje s/o Aart Sutveen and Jannetje Van Mattere, chr. 14 Feb. 1748.
Thiesse, Abraham, s/o Joh. Thiesse and Sara Goolder, chr. 21 Feb. 1748.
Smak, Maria, d/o Joh. Smak and Elisabeth Couwenhove, chr. 20 Mar. 1748.
Zutveen, Maria, d/o Derk Zutveen and Maria Langstraat, chr. 17 Apr. 1748.
Couwenhove, Aaltje, d/o Elias Couwenhove and Wilempje Waal, chr. 8 May 1748.
De Neis, Daniel, s/o Teunis De Neis and Francyntje Hindrikson, chr. 15 May 1748.
Terheune, Neeltje, d/o Jan Terheune and Neeltje Durjee, chr. 30 May 1748.

Dutch Reformed Church - Freehold and Middletown

Emans, Jonathan, s/o Cornelis Emans and Cornelia Holst, chr. 12 June 1748.
Bennit, Agnietje, d/o Johannes and Agnietje, chr. 3 July 1748.
Borkloo, Stephanus, s/o Cornelius Borkloo and Jannetje Amak, chr. 24 July 1748.
Couwenhove, Wilm, s/o Jacob and Grietje, chr. 31 July 1748.
Laan, Annatje, d/o Mattheus Laan and Cathrina Polhemus, chr. 28 Aug. 1748.
Van Der Veer, David, s/o Teunis Van Der Veer and Aeltie Schenk, chr. 11 Sep. 1748.
Sutveen, Maria, s/o Aart Sutveen and Maria Schenk, chr. 25 Sep. 1748.
Schenk, Geesje, s/o Jan Schenk and Jacomyntje Couwenhove, chr. 9 Oct. 1748.
Van Mattere, Sara, d/o Syrenius Van Mattere and Abigael Lefferson, chr. 23 Oct. 1748.
Clerk, Antje, d/o Jan Clerk and Antje Doorn, chr. 6 Nov. 1748.
Van Emburg, Maria, s/o Peregrinus Van Emburg and Cornelia Provoost, chr. 20 Nov. 1748.
Hindrikson, Wilm, s/o Hindrik Hindrikson and Neeltje Schenk, chr. 27 Nov. 1748.
Janson, Jacobus, s/o Heindert Janson and Annatje Hobbert, chr. 18 Dec. 1748.
Couwenhove, Cathrina, d/o Wilm Couwenhove and Antje Hendrikson, chr. 1749.
Eckman, Petrus, s/o Carel Eckman and Sara Wykhof, chr. 1749.
Heyer, Annatje, d/o Johannes Heyer and Elisabeth Van Dyk, chr. 1749.
Laan, Jannetje, d/o Mattheus Laan and Cathrina Polhemus, chr. 1749.
Schenk, Maria, d/o Gerrit Schenk and Neeltje Voorhees, chr. 1749.
Van Der Bilt, Elsje, d/o Hindrik Van Der Bilt and Neeltje Van Cleef, chr. 1749.
Wilmson, Hindrik, s/o David Wilmson and Geertje Voorhees, chr. 1749.
Schenk, Roelef, s/o Pieter Schenk and Jannetje Hendrickson, chr. 22 Jan. 1749.
Laan, Abraham, s/o Abraham Laan and Antje Brouwer, chr. 26 Mar. 1749.
Schenk, Antje, d/o Gerrit Schenk and Maria Van Siggelen, chr. 27 Mar. 1749.
Couwenhove, Pieter, s/o Pieter Couwenhove and Lea Schenk, chr. 9 Apr. 1749.
Snyder, Chrisstoffer, s/o Jan Pieter Snyder and Aaltje Bennit, chr. 16 Apr. 1749.

Thiesson, Geesje, d/o Joh. Thiesson and Antje Schenk, chr. 21 May 1749.
Heyer, Elsje, d/o Pieter Heyer and Aaltje Van Pelt, chr. 4 June 1749.
Wilmson, Teunis, s/o David Wilmson and Femmetje Swart, chr. 18 June 1749.
Couwenhove, Sara, d/o Gerrit Couwenhove and Neeltje Schenk chr. 30 June 1749.
Couwenhove, Pieter, s/o Cornelius Couwenhove and Annatje Janson, chr. 15 Oct. 1749.
Couwenhove, Jacoba, d/o Gerrit Couwenhove and Neeltje Van Mattere, chr. 3 Dec. 1749.
Schenk, Sara, d/o Gerrit Schenk and Jannetje Couwenhove, chr. 25 Dec. 1749.
Smak, Hindrik, s/o Johannes Smak and Elisabeth Couwenhove, chr. 31 Dec. 1749.
Sutfen, Mayke, d/o Arie Sutfen and Antje Janson, chr. 1750.
Van Cleef, Johannes, s/o Benjamin Van Cleef and Lena Couwenhove, chr. 1750.
Wilmson, Wilm, s/o David Wilmson and Geertje Voorhees, chr. 1750.
Van Noordwyk, Margarita, d/o Adriaan Van Noordwyk and Rachel Unjart, chr. 25 Mar. 1750.
Rempson, Wilm, s/o Jacob Rempson and Cathrina Hindrickson, chr. 16 Apr. 1750.
Couwenhove, Hindrik, s/o Pierter Couwenhove and Wilmpje Voorhees, chr. 6 May 1750.
Leek, Elisabeth, d/o Johannes Leek and Mayke_ Langstratt, chr. 20 May 1750..
Noulen, Sara, d/o Jhon Noulen and Elisabeth Bennet, chr. 3 June 1750.
De Neis, Maria, d/o Teunis De Neis and Francyntje Hindrikson, chr. 29 July 1750.
Couwenhove, Jacobus, s/o Pieter Couwenhove and Cathrina Schenk, chr. 26 Aug. 1750.
Bennit, Geertje, d/o Johannes and Agnitje, chr. 22 Sep. 1750.
Van Emburg, Sara, d/o Peregrinus Van Emburg and Cornelia Provoost, chr. 18 Nov. 1750.
Wykhof, Wilm, s/o Wilm Wykhof and Agnietje Van Doorn, chr. 2 Dec. 1750.
Bennit, Eyda, d/o Jan Bennet and Sara Smak, chr. 1751.
Couwenhove, Daniel, s/o Gerrit Couwenhove and Neeltje Schenk, chr. 1751.
Hervie, Elisabeth, d/o Robert Hervie and Jannetje Amak, chr. 1751.
Heyer, Teunis, s/o Pieter Heyer and Aaltje Van Pelt, chr. 1751.

Dutch Reformed Church - Freehold and Middletown

Piet, Coenraat, s/o Jan Piet and Aaltje Bennet, chr. 1751.
Schenk, Court, s/o Gerrit Schenk and Neeltje Voorhees, chr. 1751.
Thiesson, Jacob, s/o Joh. Thiesson and Antje Schenk, chr. 24 Feb. 1751.
Borkloo, Johannes, s/o Cornelis Borkloo and Jannetje Amak, chr. 24 Mar. 1751.
Couwenhove, Sara, d/o Marten and Wilmpje, chr. 12 May 1751.
Couwenhove, Neeltje, d/o Elias Couwenhove and Wilmpje Waal, chr. 23 May 1751.
Smak, Joris, s/o Johannes Smak and Elisabeth Couwenhove, chr. 26 May 1751.
Couwenhove, Elias, s/o Pieter Couwenhove and Lea Schenk, chr. 9 June 1751.
Couwenhove, Albert, s/o Cornelius Couwenhove and Antje Wilmzon, chr. 21 July 1751.
Schenk, Jannetje, d/o Pieter Schenk and Jannetje Hindrikzon, chr. 28 July 1751.
Van Der Veer, Hindrik, s/o Cornelius Van Der Veer and Marta Smak, chr. 22 Sep. 1751.
Doorn, Antje, d/o Diedlof Doorn and Syntie Van Der Hoeve, chr. 13 Oct. 1751.
Laan, Antje, d/o Cornelius Laan and Maria Wamslie, chr. 3 Nov. 1751.
Zutfen, Neeltje, d/o Aart Zutfen and Maria Schenk, chr. 24 Nov. 1751.
Wilmzon, Jacomyntje, d/o David Wilmzon and Femmetje Swart, chr. 8 Dec. 1751.
Van Cleef, Hundrikje, s/o Derk Van Cleef and Elisabeth Leek, chr. 22 Dec. 1751.
Clerk, Antje, d/o Jan Clerk and Antje Doorn, chr. 1752.
Couwenhove, Antje, d/o Gerrit Couwenhove and Sara Voorhees, chr. 1752.
Couwenhove, Roelef, s/o Pierter Couwenhove and Cathrina Schenk, chr. 1752.
Couwenhove, Jacob, s/o Jan Couwenhove and Maria Van Dorn, chr. 1752.
Noulin, Jannetje, d/o John Noulin and Elisabeth Bennit, chr. 1752.
Van Pelt, Geertje, d/o Christoffer Van Pelt and Aaltje Bennit, chr. 1752.
Wynantze, Geesje, d/o Cornelius Wynantze and Antje Van Brunt, chr. 1752.
Wilmzon, Jacomyntje, d/o Wilm Wilmzon and Antje Voorhees, chr. 5 Jan. 1752.
Thiesson, Sara, d/o Pieter Thiesson and Christina Erkzon, chr. 19 Jan. 1752.

Fenten, Agnietje, d/o Joseph Fenten and Maria Van Dyk, chr. 2 Feb. 1752.
Schenk, Maria, d/o Gerrit Schenk and Jannetje Couwenhov, chr. 23 Feb. 1752.
Hindrikzon, Hindrik, d/o Hindrik Hindrikzon and Sara Tomzon, chr. 3 May 1752.
Van Brunt, Hindrik, s/o Cornelius Van Brunt and Magdalena Fenten, chr. 7 May 1752.
Van Noortwyk, Sinai, s/o Adriaan Van Noortwyk and Rachel Unjart, chr. 7 June 1752.
Couwenhove, Sara, d/o Jacob and Grietje Couwenhove, chr. 17 June 1752.
Wilmson, Jacomyntje, d/o Aart Wilmson and Maria Van Der Veer, chr. 17 June 1752.
Van Der Hoeve, Elisabeth, d/o Cornelius Van Der Hoeve and Elsje Van Kerk, chr. 28 June 1752.
Schenk, Jan, s/o Jan Schenk and Neeltje Bennet, chr. 2 Aug. 1752.
Heyer, Johannes, s/o Walter Heyer and Elisabeth Van Der Bilt, chr. 29 Oct. 1752.
Laan, Maria, d/o Mattheus Laan and Cathrina Polhemus, chr. 12 Nov. 1752.
Bennit, Hindrik, s/o Wilm Bennit and Margarita Smit, chr. 3 Dec. 1752.
Wilmzon, Jannetje, d/o David Wilmzon and Geertje Voorhees, chr. 31 Dec. 1752.
Couwenhove, Benjamin, s/o Gerrit Couwenhove and Neeltje Van Mattere, chr. 1753.
Couwenhove, Wilm, s/o Cornelius Couwenhove and Antje Wilmzon, chr. 1753.
Hindrikson, Johannes, s/o Hindrik Hindrikson and Sara Tamzon, chr. 1753.
Schenk, Antje, d/o Pieter Schenk and Jannetje Hendrikzon, chr. 1753.
Schenk, Petrus, s/o Gerrit Schenk and Neeltje Voorhees, chr. 1753.
Tice, Liedea, d/o Peter Tice and Christina Errickson, chr. 1753.
Hill, Maria, d/o Johannes Hill and Anna Christina Konin, chr. 11 Jan. 1753.
Kouwenhove, Antje, d/o Jan Kouwenhove and Maria Van Doorn, chr. 18 Jan. 1753.
Wendel, Elisabeth, d/o Jacon Wendel and Johanna De Mart, chr. 11 Mar. 1753.
Van Cleef, Margrietje, d/o Benjamin Van Cleef and Helena Couwenhove, chr. 18 Mar. 1753.

Dutch Reformed Church - Freehold and Middletown

Couwenhove, Wilm, s/o Pieter Couwenhove and Lea Schenk, chr. 11 Apr. 1753.
Bennet, Jan, s/o Jan Bennet and Sarah Smack, chr. 31 May 1753.
Willemson, Aert, s/o Elbert Willemson and Willomptje Schenck, chr. 3 June 1753.
Smack, Hendrick, s/o Garret Smack and Jannetie Wikhof, chr. 10 July 1753.
Longstraet, Aaron, s/o John Longstraet and Antye Covenhoven, chr. 22 July 1753.
Kouwenhove, Wilm, s/o Marten and Wilmpje, chr. 29 July 1753.
Van Mattere, Crein Janze, s/o Crein Janze Van Mattere and Maria Zutveen, chr. 5 Aug. 1753.
Van Pelt, Jacob, s/o Christoffer Van Pelt and Aaltje Bennet, chr. 10 Aug. 1753.
Tice, Antje, d/o Jan Tice and Antje Schenk, chr. 19 Aug. 1753.
Couwenhove, Gerrit, s/o Wilm Couwenhove and Elisabeth Amak, chr. 5 Sep. 1753.
Hendrikzon, Cathrina, d/o Daniel Hendrikzon and Cathrina Couwenhove, chr. 9 Sep. 1753.
Vancleeff, Lena, d/o Derrick Vancleef and Elizabeth Leeck, chr. 30 Sep.1753.
Wynantze, Cornelius, s/o Cornelius Wynantze and Antje Van Brunt, chr. 7 Oct. 1753.
Schenk, Crein Janze, s/o Jan Schenk and Neeltje Bennet, chr. 21 Oct. 1753.
Bennet, Joannes, s/o Wilm Bennet and Margarita Smit, chr. 1754.
Vancleeff, Antye, d/o Benjam Vancleef and Rachel Covenhoven, chr. 1754.
Noulen, Elisabeth, d/o John Noulen and Elisabeth Bennet, chr. 1754.
Vanderhooven, Cornelia, d/o Cornelius Vanderhooven and Else Vankerk, chr. 24 Mar. 1754.
Zutphen, Jan, s/o Isaac Zutphen and Jannetje Borkloo, chr. 11 Apr. 1754.
Van Brunt, Cornelius, s/o Cornelius Van Brunt and Magdelena Fenten, chr. 28 Apr. 1754.
Zutphin, Dirrick, s/o Aert Zutphin and Maria Schenck, chr. 30 June 1754.
Willemson, Willem, s/o David Willemson and Fennetye Swart, chr. 20 Oct.1754.
Longstraet, Christina, d/o Christophel Longstraet and Neeltye Schenck, chr. 3 Nov. 1754.
Covenhoven Neeltye, d/o Cornelius Covenhoven and Antye Wellemson, chr. 15 Dec. 1754.

Smock, Joris, s/o Johannes Smock and Elizabeth Covenhoven, chr. 22 Dec. 1754.
Middelswart, Jan, s/o Cornelius and Antye, chr. 25 Dec. 1754.
Covenhoven, Cathriena, d/o Gerrit Covenhoven and Neeltye Van Metere, chr. 1755.
Hendrickson, Aeltye, d/o Hendrik Hendrickson and Sarah Tomson, chr. 1755.
Lane, Willem, s/o Mattheus Lane and Cathriena Polhemus, chr. 1755.
Schenk, Sarah, d/o Gerrit Schenk and Nellie Voorhees, chr. 1755.
Schenk, Gerrit, s/o Albert Schenk and Angenietje Vanbrunt, chr. 1755.
Sutphen, Antye, d/o Adriaen Sutphen and Antje Janson, chr. 1755.
Willemson, Peterius, s/o Elbert Willemson and Willempte Scheck, chr. 1755.
Cowenhoven, Sarah, d/o Peter Cowenhoven and Chatriena Schenck, chr. 12 Jan. 1755.
Cowenhoven, Eleena, d/o Williem Cowenhoven and Elizabeth Amak, chr. 26 Jan 1755.
Willemson, Antje, d/o David Willemson and Geertye Voorhees, chr. 13 Feb.1755.
Zutphen, Jan, s/o Benjamin Zutphen and Eyda Van Mattere, chr. 16 Feb. 1755.
Bennit, Barent, s/o Jan Bennit and Sara Smak, chr. 2 Mar. 1755.
Van Emburg, Cornelia, d/o Peregrinus Van Emburg and Cornelia Provoost, chr. 26 Mar. 1755.
Van Metere, Engeltye, d/o Kreyn Van Metere and Maria Zutphin, chr. 31 Mar. 1755.
Covenhoven, Neeltje, d/o Pieter Covenhoven and Lea Schenk, chr. 13 Apr. 1755.
Wyckhof, Willem, s/o Jacob Wyckhof and Sarah Cowenhoven, chr. 22 Apr. 1755.
Schenk, Willem, s/o Jan Schenk and Neeltje Bennit, chr. 11 May 1755.
Vancleeff, Hendricka, d/o Benjamin Vancleef and Willemptye Voorhees, chr. 15 May 1755.
Vanschoieck, Johannes, s/o William Vanschoieck and Patientie Schenck, chr. 8 June 1755.
Couwenhove, Sara, d/o Jan Couwenhove and Maria Van Doorn, chr. 15 June 1755.
Voorhees, Dirrick, s/o Isaac Voorhees and Helena Berkelow, chr. 22 June 1755.
Janson, Geertruy, d/o Roeloff and Margrieta Janson, chr. 20 July 1755.
Hil, Johannes, s/o Joh. Hil and Anna Christina Konin, chr. 10 Aug. 1755.
Cowenhoven, Jacob, s/o Marten and Willemtye, chr. 24 Aug. 1755.

Dutch Reformed Church - Freehold and Middletown

Van Dooren, Pieter, s/o Jacob Van Dooren and Maria Schenck, chr. 31 Aug. 1755.
Schenk, Leah, d/o Pieter Schenk and Jannetye Hendrikson, chr. 9 Nov. 1755.
Schenk, Courtinus, s/o Albert Schenk and Maria Cowenhoven, chr. 30 Nov. 1755.
Wicoff, Jacob, s/o John Wicoff and Aaltie Berkelow, chr. 28 Dec. 1755.
Borkloo, Jannatje, d/o Cornelis Borkloo and Jannetje Amak, chr. 1756.
Clark, Niclaas, s/o John Clark and Antje Doorn, chr. 1756.
Couwenhove, Gerrit, s/o Dominicus Couwenhove and N._ N., chr. 1756.
Hindrikzon, child of Albert Hindrizson and Johanna Mils, chr. 1756.
Van Der Hoef, Christina, d/o Cornelis Van Der Hoef and Elsje Van Kerk, chr. 1756.
Holzaart, Jaques, s/o Anthonius Holzaart and Maria Berkloo, chr. 1756.
Thiesson, Sara, d/o John Thiesson and Antje Schenk, chr. 1756.
Van Dyk, Elisabeth, d/o Aart Van Dyk and Catharina Schenk, chr. 1756.
Van Mattere, Tryntje, d/o Daniel Van Mattere and Maria Couwenhove, chr. 1756.
Bennit, Cornelius, s/o Johannes and Angenietje, chr. 4 Jan. 1756.
Wtnant, Cornelius, s/o Cornelius Wynant and Engelje Vanbrunt, chr. 15 Jan. 1756.
Hanson, Johannes, s/o Jan Hanson and Maria Amack, chr. 22 Feb.1756.
Brouwer, Joannes, s/o Pieter Brouwer and Antje Van Dyk, chr. 21 Mar. 1756.
Couwenhove, Lea, d/o Pieter Couwenhove and Lea Schenk, chr. 9 May 1756.
Zutphen, Lea, d/o Isaac Zutphen and Jannetje Borkloo, chr. 16 May 1756.
Couwenhove, Albert, s/o Gerrit Couwenhove and Sara Voorhees, chr. 7 June 1756.
Mils, Johanna, chr. 27 June 1754.
Smak, Barent, s/o Johannes Smak and Femmetje Theunisse, chr. 18 July 1756.
Kerl, Judeth, d/o Uriah Kerl and Judith Hun, chr. 25 July 1756.
Bennet, Gerrit, s/o Wilm Bennet and Margrietje Smit, chr. 15 Aug. 1756.
Schenk, Tryntje, d/o Gerrit Schenk and Jannetje Couwenhov, chr. 29 Aug. 1756.
Wilmzon, Jacomyntje, s/o Elbert Wilmzon and Geertje Voorhees, chr. 5 Sep. 1756.
Langstraat, Antje, d/o John Langstraat and Antje Couwenhove, chr. 30 Sep. 1756.
Seddelaar, Elisabeth, d/o Jacob Seddelaar and Catherina Jagere, chr. 3

Oct. 1756.
Couwenhove, Aaltje, d/o Cornelis Couwenhove and Antje Wilmzon, chr. 30 Oct. 1756.
Schenk, Antje, d/o Gerrit Schenk and Neeltje Voorhees, chr. 14 Nov. 1756.
Smak, Neeltje, d/o Joh. Smak and Elisabeth Couwenhove, chr. 21 Nov. 1756.
Van Pelt, Elisabeth, d/o Christoffer Van Pelt and Aaltje Bennit, chr. 28 Nov. 1756.
Brouwer, Helena, d/o Arie Brouwer and Neeltje Couper, chr. 5 Dec. 1756.
Bennit, John, s/o John Bennit and Sara Smak, chr. 1757.
Hendrickson, William, s/o Daniel Hendrickson and Tryntie V Brunt, chr. 1757.
Hendrixson, William, s/o Hendrick Hendrixson and Sartye Tomson, chr. 1757.
Heyer, Hendrick, s/o Walter Heyer and Elisabeth Van Der Bilt, chr. 1757.
Schenk, Eyda, d/o Jan Schenk and Neeltje Bennit, chr. 1757.
Schenk, Catrina, d/o Albert Schenk and Anginietie Van Brunt, chr. 1757.
Smack, Elizabeth, d/o Hanse Smack and Famitie Tunisse, chr. 1757.
Thiesson, Rebecca, d/o Gysbert Thiesson and Rebecca Holmes, chr. 1757.
Teunisse, Cornelis, s/o Cornelis and Antje, chr. 1757.
Van Mattere, Benjamin, s/o Jacob Van Mattere and Neeltje Hindrikzon, chr. 1757.
Van Pelt, Teunis, d/o Hanse Van Pelt and Aan Hyier, chr. 1757.
Van Dorn, Maria, d/o John Van Dorn and Anginietie Schenk, chr. 1757.
Van Oostrant, Johannes, s/o Aart Van Oostrant and Cathrina Van Der Veer, chr. 6 Mar 1757.
Bennit, Johannes s/o Isaak and Geertje, chr. 13 Mar. 1757.
Hindrikzon, Hendrik, s/o Gerrit Hindrikzon and Tryntie De Neis, chr. 20 Mar. 1757.
Couwenhove, Ariaantje, d/o Wilm Couwenhove and Elisabeth Amak, chr. 17 Apr. 1757.
Langstraat, Court, s/o Christoffer Langstraat and Neeltje Schenk, chr. 24 Apr. 1757.
Van Der Bilt, Joannes, s/o John Van Der Bilt and Elisabeth Hindrikzon, chr. 8 May 1757.
Fenten, Rebekka, d/o Benjamin Fenten and Cathrina Peterzen, chr. 15 May 1757.

Dutch Reformed Church - Freehold and Middletown

Van Cleef, Wilm, s/o Benjamin Van Cleef and Helena Couwenhove, chr. 30 May 1757.
Zutveen, Court, s/o Aart Zutveen and Maria Schenck, chr. 12 June 1757.
Wynantze, Tryntie, d/o Cornelius Wynantze and Engeltje Van Brunt, chr. 19 June 1757.
Williamson, Sara, d/o David Williamson and Gertye Voorhees, chr. 26 June 1757.
Van Martyr, Gysbert, s/o Kryn Jonsz Van Martyr and Maria Zutven, chr. 3 July 1757.
Van Dorn, Maria, d/o Jaacob Van Dorn and Maria Schenk, chr. 10 July 1757.
Williamson, John, s/o David Williamson and Famitie Swart, chr. 25 July 1757.
Van Schoyk, Couert, s/o William Van Schoyk and Patience Schenk, chr. 31 July 1757.
Heyer, John, s/o John Heyer and Elisabeth Van Dyk, chr. 9 Aug. 1757.
Holsaart, Aaltie, d/o Peter Holsaart and Willimtie Oostrant, chr. 4 Dec. 1757.
Covenhoven, Antie, s/o Cornelius Covenhoven and Helena Williamsonc, chr. 11 Dec. 1757.
__, Jephta, s/o Perod and Dinaa, chr. 1758.
Amack, Tuinis, d/o Tunis Amack and Arianntie Bennet, chr. 1758.
Bennet, child of William Bennet and Margeritie Smit, 1758.
Brower, Femmitie, d/o Aris Brouwer and Neeltje Couper, chr. 1758.
Van Kleef, Maria, d/o Deryk Van Kleef and Elizabeth Laak, chr. 1758.
Covenhoven, Jan, s/o Peter Covenhoven and Catrana Schanck, chr. 1758.
Hendrickson, Hendrick, s/o Daniel Hendrickson and Catrina Covenhoven, chr. 1758.
Hendrickson, Altye, d/o Albert Hendrickson and Joanna Mills, chr. 1758.
Lamberse, Jan, s/o Rulef, chr. 1758.
Sutfon, Jacobus, s/o Are Sutfon and Ayntie Lamberse, chr. 1758.
Sutfin, Derick, s/o Jan Sutfin and Gerrtie Amack, chr. 1758.
Winant, Maria, s/o Cornelius Winant and Engetye V Brunt, chr. 1758.
Covenhoven, Rulef, s/o Peter Covenhoven and Lea Schenk, chr. 12 Mar. 1758.
Sutfin, Ryk, s/o Benjamin Sutfin and Eyda Van Mattere, chr. 14 Mar. 1758.
Voorhees, Jan, s/o Andreas Voorhees and Antye Sutfin, chr. 26 Mar. 1758.
Vanderveer, Cornelius, s/o Monekus Vanderveer and Janatie Williamson, chr. 9 Apr. 1758.
Luister, Sara, d/o Pieter and Antye, chr. 4 May 1758.

Van Pelt, Antye, d/o Hanse Van Pelt and Aan Hyier, chr. 14 May 1758.
Schenk, Gerret, s/o Gerret Schenk and Neeltye Voorhees, chr. 26 May 1758. Covenhoven, Peter, s/o Marte and Willimtie, chr. 2 June 1758.
Williams, Janitie, d/o Albert Wiliams and Willaimtie Schenck, chr. 2 July 1758.
Tunisse, Cornelis, s/o Neeltie, chr. 3 July 1758.
Hendrickson, Elizabet, d/o Daniel Hendrickson and Tryntie V Brunt, chr. 9 July 1758.
Smack, Sara, d/o Joh. Smack and Elisabet Covenhoven, chr. 16 July 1758.
Bennit, Maria, d/o Hanse and Angienietie, chr. 8 Aug. 1758.
Wicoff, Garret, s/o Garret Wicoff and Patience Williamson, chr. 8 Oct. 1758.
Schenk, Nicolas, s/o Albert Schenk and Angienietie V Brunt, chr. 19 Oct. 1758.
Hulaart, Maria, d/o Peter Hulsaart and Williampie Hanse, chr. 1759.
Heyer, Antye, d/o Walter Heyer and Elisabeth V Der Bilt, chr. 1759.
Mc Cleese, Maria, d/o Cornelius Mc Cleese and Neeltie Tunisse, chr. 1759.
Van Ostrande, Stephanus, d/o John Van Ostrande and Maria Amack, chr. 1759.
Schenk, Neeltie, d/o Pieter Schenk and Janaetije Hendrickson, chr. 1759.
Tyse, Maria, d/o Jan Tyse and Antie_ Schenk, chr. 1759.
Van Pelt, Teunis, s/o Jan Van Pelt and Janitie Hyer, chr. 1759.
V Der Bilt, Aaron, s/o Aert V Der Bilt and Anna Dorsett, chr. 1759.
Hendrixson, Hendrick, s/o Hendrick Hendrixson and Lidia Covenhoven, chr. 18 Feb. 1759.
Kerl, Anna, d/o Uriah Kerl and Judith Hun, chr. 4 Mar. 1759.
Schenk, Sara, d/o Jan Schenk and Neeltye Bennit, chr. 11 Mar. 1759.
Mc Cleese, Rachel Cornelius, d/o Cornelius Mc Cleese and Neeltie Teunisse, chr. 9 May 1759.
Hendrickson, Francyntie, d/o Geerit Hendrickson and Tryntie D Neis, chr. 18 Mar. 1759.
Zutphin, Phebe, d/o Isaac Zutphen and Jannietie Burkeloe, chr. 15 Apr. 1759.
Teunisse, Hendrick, s/o Cornelius and Antie_, chr. 29 Apr. 1759.
Cowenhoven, Janitje, d/o Willem Cowenhoven and Elizabeth Amak, chr. 20 May 1759.
Cowenhoven, Grietje, d/o Willem Cowenhoven and Elizabeth Amak, chr. 20 May 1759.
Pelt, Maria, d/o Christopher V. Pelt and Aaltje Bennet, chr. 31 May 1759.

Dutch Reformed Church - Freehold and Middletown

Covenhoven, Antye, d/o Jacob and Grietye, chr. 17 June 1759.
Laan, Matheus, s/o Mattheus Laan and Catrina Polhemus, chr. 24 June 1759.
Hendrickson, Albert, s/o Hendrick Hendrickson and Sarah Tomson, chr. 8 July 1759.
Hendrickson, Hendrick, s/o Daniel Hendrickson and Catrina Covenhoven, chr. 8 July 1759.
Cowenhoven, Sarah, d/o Cornelius Cowenhoven and Jannitje Denys, chr. 5 Aug. 1759.
Clark, Leah, d/o John Clark and Antje Doorn, chr. 9 Sep. 1759.
Van Mattere, Sara, d/o Daniel Van Mattere and Maria Couwenhove, chr. 16 Sep. 1759.
Brower, Petrus, s/o Pieter Brouwer and Antye Van Dyk, chr. 23 Sep. 1759.
Amak, Stephanus, s/o Teunis Amak and Ann Killy, chr. 23 Dec. 1759.
Amak, Joannis, s/o Teunis Amak and Arianntie Bennit, chr. 1760.
Bolson, Catrina, d/o Willem Bolson and Catrina Philgryn, chr. 1760.
Cowenhoven, Maragrita, d/o Pieter Cowenhoven & Neeltje Polhemus, chr. 1760.
Cowenhoven, Arie, s/o Jan Cowenhoven and Maria Van Doorn, chr. 1760.
Lefferse, Maria, d/o Pieter Lefferse and N._ N. Martyr, chr. 1760.
Pelhemus, Daniel, s/o Johannes Pelhemus and Maria V Martyr, chr. 1760.
Smak, Joanna, d/o Joannis Smak and Femmitie Teunisse, chr. 1760.
Van Cleef, Joseph, s/o Benjamin Van Cleef and Lena Couwenhoven, chr. 1760.
V Pelt, Aaltye, d/o Sander V Pelt and Janitye Mier, chr. 1760.
Vanderveer, Marritje, s/o Dominicas Vanderveer and Janitje Willemze, chr. 1760.
V D Veer, Aaltye, d/o Jacob V D Veer and Aaltye Wicoff, chr. 1760.
Bennit, Kreinjans, s/o Jan Bennit and Sara Smak, chr. 27 Jan. 1760.
Wynant, Nichoas, s/o Cornelius Wynant and Anne Vanbrunt, chr. 24 Feb. 1760.
Sutphen, Antje, d/o Aart Sutphen and Maria Schenck, chr. 2 Mar. 1760.
Schenk, Neeltje, s/o Gerret Schenk and Neeltje Voorhees, chr. 30 Mar. 1760.
Schenk, Hendrick, s/o Albert Schenk and N._ N. Vanbrunt, chr. 6 Apr. 1760.
Brower, Antje, d/o Aaron Brower and Neeltje Cooper, chr. 13 Apr. 1760.
Smak, Catrina, d/o Johannis Smak and Elizabet Cowenhoven, chr. 27 Apr. 1760.

Cowenhoven, Janitje, d/o Martyn and Willemje, chr. 25 May 1760.
Doorn, Micheel, s/o Deatlof Doorn and Styntje V D Hoef, chr. 22 June 1760.
Hendrickson, Abraham, s/o Abraham Hendrickson and Antje Van Kerk, chr. 29 June 1760.
Loogen, Sara, d/o Stophel Loogen and Catherine V. Martyr, chr. 3 Aug. 1760.
Laak, Johannes, s/o Jan Laak and Elsje Lamberse, chr. 10 Aug. 1760.
M Clees, Jan, s/o Cornelius M Clees and Neeltie Tunisse, chr. 17 Aug. 1760.
Luister, Lucretia, d/o Pieter and Antye, chr. 28 Sep.1760.
Van Martyr, Isaac, s/o Creinjanse Van Martyr and Maria Sutphin, chr. 2 Nov. 1760.
V D Veer, Tuenis, s/o Teunis V D Veer and Jannitie Oostrande, chr. 14 Dec. 1760.
Bennet, Increase, s/o Gerrit Bennet and Maria Tiltin, chr. 1761.
Carell, Rebecca, d/o Uriah Carell and Judith Hunn, chr. 1761.
Cowenhoven, Garret, s/o William Cowenhoven and Aaltye Amak, chr. 1761.
Doorn, Petrus, s/o Joseph Doorn and Femmetye Wykoff, chr. 1761.
Hendrickson, Antye, d/o Daniel Hendrickson and Neeltye V Martyr, chr. 1761.
Hendrickson, Willimpje, d/o Hendrick Hendrickson and Lydia Covenhoven, chr. 1761.
Schenk, Albert, s/o Albert Schenk and Aengenietye V Brunt, chr. 1761.
Teunisse, Rebecca, d/o Cornelius and Antye, chr. 1761.
Van Pelt, Maria, d/o Jan Van Pelt and Jannitje Heyer, chr. 1761.
V D Bilt, Jannitie Lydia, d/o Cornelius V D Bilt and Margarietye Lamberze, chr. 1761.
Williamson, Geertye, d/o David Williamson and Femmitye Swart, chr. 1761.
V D Bilt, Hendrick, s/o Cornelius V D Bilt and Margarietye Lamberze, chr. 1761.
Zutphen, Jannitye, d/o Isaac Zutphen and Jannitye Burkalow, chr. 1761.
Hendrickson, William, s/o Daniel Hendrickson and Catrina Van Brunt, chr. 11 Jan. 1761.
Van Der Hoef, Antye, d/o Cornelius Van Der Hoeve and Else Van Kerk, chr. 18 Jan. 1761.
Schenck, Krynjans, s/o John Schenck and Neelje Bennet, chr. 8 Feb. 1761.
Amack, Maria, d/o Teunis Amack and Antye Killey, chr. 22 Feb. 1761.

Dutch Reformed Church - Freehold and Middletown

Amack, Helena, d/o Jacob Amack and Geertye Covenhoven, chr. 22 Mar.1761.
V Derhoven, Cornelius, s/o Michael V Derhoven and Elizabeth Allen, chr. 24 Mar. 1761.
Covenhoven, Antye, d/o Peter Covenhoven and Catrina Schenk, chr. 26 Apr. 1761.
Covenhoven, Tuenis, s/o Cornelius Covenhoven and Jannitye Deneis, chr. 30 Apr. 1761.
Bennit, child of William Bennit and Margerietye Smith, chr. 7 June 1761.
Snyder, Aaltye, d/o Hendrick Snyder and Maria Covenhoven, chr. 2 Aug. 1761.
Van Pelt, Hendrick, s/o Pieter Van Pelt and Neeltye Van Der Bilt, chr. 30 Aug. 1761.
Hendrickson, Aengenietye, d/o Hendrick Hendrickson and Sara Tompson, chr. 6 Sep. 1761.
Tyse, Sara, d/o John Tyse and Antye Schenk, chr. 4 Oct. 1761.
Van Mattere, Neeltye, s/o Jacob Van Mattere and Neeltje Hindrickson, chr. 18 Oct. 1761.
Oostrande, Aart, s/o Hans Oostrande and Maria Amak, chr. 1 Nov. 1761.
Hendrickson, William, s/o Daniel Hendrickson and Catrina Covenhoven, chr. 22 Nov. 1761.
Hendrickson, Rebecca, d/o Albert Hendrickson and Joanna Mills, chr. 29 Nov. 1761.
Swart, Elbert, s/o Hanse Swart and Jacomeintye Luister, chr. 25 Dec. 1761.
Amack, William, s/o Jacob Amack and Geertye Covenhoven, chr. 1762.
Antonides, Nicholaas, s/o Jan Antonides and Sara V Dorn, chr. 1762.
Bennit, William, s/o Jan Bennit and Aaltye Covenhove, chr. 1762.
Brower, Maria, d/o Arison Brower and Neetje Couoper, chr. 1762.
Polhemus, Daniel, s/o Elbert Polhemus and N._ N. V Mattere, chr. 1762.
Leffertze, Krynjans, s/o Pieter Leffertze and N._ M. V Mattere, chr. 1762.
Schenk, Iyde, s/o Garit Schenk and Neeltje Voorhees, chr. 1762.
Sleght, Maria, d/o Abraham Sleght and Geertye Sickely, chr. 1762.
Smack, Sara, d/o Hendrick Smack and Neeltye Van Doorn, chr. 1762.
Sutphen, Maayke, d/o Aart Sutphen and Aane Janse, chr. 1762.
Sutphen, Aaron, s/o Derick Sutphen and Maria Langstraat, chr. 1762.
Van Pelt, Maria, d/o Sander Van Pelt and Catrina Warner, chr. 1762.
Van Der Veer, Tuenis, s/o Jacob Van Der Veer and Aaltye Wicoff, chr. 1762.

Probasco, Christopher, s/o Jan Probasco and Eida Dorlandt, chr. 1 Jan. 1762.
Smack, Cornelius, s/o Hanse Smack and Femmitye Tuenisse, chr. 1 Feb. 1762.
Bennit, Hendrik, s/o Jan Bennit and Sara Smak, chr. 14 Feb. 1762.
Schenk, Jannetje, d/o Pieter Schenk and Jannitye Hendrickze, chr. 7 Mar. 1762.
Amack, Jannitye, d/o Teunis Amack and Ariaantie Bennit, chr. 28 Mar.1762.
Doorn, Nicholas, s/o Nicholas Doorn and Saartye Smittt, chr. 4 Apr. 1762.
Smack, Elizabeth, d/o Hendrick Smack and Elizabeth Covenhoven, chr. 11 Apr. 1762.
Hendrickson, John, s/o Abraham Hendrickson and Anne V Kerk, chr. 1 May 1762.
Van Pelt, Tuenis, s/o Christopher Van Pelt and Aaltye Bennit, chr. 29 May 1762.
Durie, Antje, d/o Simon Durie and Jannitie Van Der Voort, chr. 20 June 1762.
Van Mattere, Benjamin, s/o Cyrenius Van Mattere and Antye Van Doorn, chr. 27 June 1762.
Van Mattere, Grsbert, s/o Daniel Van Mattere and Maria Covenhoven, chr. 26 July 1762.
Covenhoven, Williamtje, d/o Martyn and Willimptie, chr. 22 Aug 1762.
Covenhoven, Martyn, s/o Martyn and Willimptie, chr. 22 Aug 1762.
Sutphen, Elizabeth, d/o Aart Sutphen and Maria Schenk, chr. 29 Aug. 1762.
Sleght, Geertie, d/o Abraham Sleght and Geertye Sickely, chr. 8 Oct. 1762.
Hoogelandt, Maria, d/o N. N. Hoogelandt and Leah Sutphen, chr. 14 Nov. 1762.
Bolzer, Lydia, d/o Wilm and Cathrina, chr. 1763.
Bennit, Eyda, d/o Hendrik Bennit and Neeltie Calwel, chr. 1763.
Janze, Mayke, d/o Jacobus Janze and Antje Van Dyk, chr 1763.
Schenk, Gerrit, s/o Gerrit Schenk and Sara Couwenhov, chr. 1763.
Schenk, Petrus, s/o Jan Schenk and Neeltje Bennit, chr. 1763.
Van Pelt, Wilm, s/o Jan, chr. 1763.
Van Pelt, Geertje, d/o Pieter, chr. 1763.
Vander Hoeve, Elisabeth, d/o Michiel Vander Hoeve and Elisabeth Allen, chr. 1763.
Vander Hoeve, Cornelius, s/o Pieter Vander Hoeve and Maria Bassit, chr. 1763.

Dutch Reformed Church - Freehold and Middletown

Van Veer, Catherina, d/o Jacob Van Veer and Aaltje Wykhof, chr. 1763.
Van Der Veer, child of Gerret Van Der Veer and Jannetje Voorhees, chr. 1763.
Van Mattere, Eyda, d/o Crein Janze Van Mattere and Maria Zutfen, chr. 27 Feb. 1763.
Snyder, Wilm, s/o Hendrick Snyder and Maria Couwenhove, chr. 24 Apr. 1763.
Cretzeler, Cathrina, d/o Christiaan Cretzeler and Antje Parmer, chr. 1 June 1763.
Van Der Veer, Johannes, s/o Teunis Van Der Veer and Jannetje Hanssen, chr. 3 Aug. 1763.
Wykhof, Samuel, s/o Garrit Wykhof and Patiens Wilmzon, chr. 30 Aug. 1763.
Smak, Johannes, s/o Johannes Smak and Elisabeth Couwenhove, chr. 1764.
Aamack, Angeneitie, s/o Tunis Aamack and Arriiantie, chr. 1764.
Aamack, Arriiantie, d/o Jacob Aamack and Geertie Cowenhoven, chr. 1764.
Amack, Johanna, d/o Tunis Amack and Antie_ Killy, chr. 1764.
Antonides, Marya, d/o Johanis Antonides and Sara Van Doorn, chr. 1764.
Bennitt, Johanna, s/o Jan Bennit and Sara Smak, chr. 1764.
Brouwer, Johannes, s/o Arie and Neeltje, chr. 1764.
Brower, Marya, d/o Eelias Brower and Eelesabeth Pertmer, chr. 1764.
Couwenhove, Francyntje, d/o Cornelius Couwenhove and Jannetje De Neis, chr. 1764.
Cowenhoven, Catrena Naeltie, d/o Johanis Cowenhoven and Marya Van Doorn, chr. 1764.
Cretzeler, John, s/o Christiaan Critzinger and Antje Parmer, chr. 1764.
Hanze, Teunis, s/o Jan Hanze and Maria Amak, chr. 1764.
Hanzen, Neeltje, d/o David Hanzen and Antje Hendrickzon, chr. 1764.
Hindrikzon, Jacob, s/o Abraham Hindrikzon and Antje Van Kerk, chr. 1764.
Hindrikzon, Hindrik, s/o Gerrit Hindrikzon and Cathrina De Neis, chr. 1764.
Van Hove, Eelies, s/o Michal Van Hove and Elesabeth Ellen, chr. 1764.
Schenck, Antie, d/o Gerrit Schenck and Sarah Cowenhovn, chr. 1764.
Schenck, Marya, d/o Johonis Schenck and Marya Van Doorn, chr. 1764.
Slaght, Neltie, d/o Abraham and Ghertie, chr. 1764.
Smack, Johanis, s/o Johanes Smack and Feem_metye Tew, chr. 1764.
Tysse, Eelesabeth, d/o Peter Tysse and Eenne Gree, chr. 1764.

Van Matre, Mayke, d/o Daniel Van Matre and Marya Cowenhoven, chr. 1764.
Van Matre, Eelesabeth, d/o Jacob Van Matre and Neeltie Hendrickson, chr. 1764.
Van Matre, Arri, d/o Cerines Van Matre and Antie_ Van Doorn, chr. 1764.
Voorhees, Styntje, d/o Lucas, chr. 1764.
Vande Veer, Cornelius s/o Johanis Vande Veer and Marya Striker, chr. 1764.
Van Der Veer, Johannes, s/o Dominicus Van Der Veer and Jannetje Wilmzon, chr. 1764.
Luister, Johannes, s/o Pieter and Antye, chr. 19 Jan. 1764.
Couwenhove, Aafie, d/o William Couwenhove and Elesebet Aamack, chr. 30 Apr. 1764.
Wilemse, Cornelies, s/o David Wilemse and Femetie Swort, chr. 21 Oct. 1764.
Zutphen, Isac, s/o Isac Zutphen and Janatie Barklow, chr. 9 Nov. 1764.
Amack, Helena, d/o Jacob Amack and Geertruid Covenhoven, chr. 1765.
Bennet, Annanitie, d/o Hendrick Bennet and Neeltie Callewil, chr. 1765.
Bennet, Johannis, s/o Jacob Bennet and Afie Amack, chr. 1765.
Bennet, Elisabeth, d/o Gerrit Bennet and Maria Tilton, chr. 1765.
Bennet, Nathan, s/o Gerrit Bennet and Maria Tilton, chr. 1765.
Covenhoven, Roelef, s/o Cornelius Covenhoven and Janitje Denise, chr. 1765.
Pylhemels, Maria, d/o Albert Pylhemels and Aaltje Van Meter, chr. 1765.
Snyder, Hendrick, s/o Hendrick Snyder and Maria Covenhoven, chr. 1765.
Tison, Antie, s/o John Tison and Antie_ Schenck, chr. 1765.
Van Pelt, Theunis, s/o Petrus Van Pelt and Neeltje Van Derbylt, chr. 1765.
Van Der Byldt, Hendrick, s/o Aart Van Der Byldt and Geertie Van Meter, chr. 20 Jan. 1765.
Smack, Barene, s/o Hendrick Smack and Neeltie Van Doorn, chr. 3 Feb. 1765.
Schenck, Neeltie, d/o Johannis Schenck and Neelie Bennet, chr. 17 Feb. 1765.
Hendrickson, Maria, d/o Daniel Hendrickson and Catharina Van Bront, chr. 17 Mar. 1765.
Van Cleef, Elena, d/o Benjamin Van Cleef and Sara Covenhoven, chr. 14 Apr. 1765.

Dutch Reformed Church - Freehold and Middletown

Login, Yda, d/o Christopher Login and Catharina Van Meter, chr. 21 Apr. 1765.
Probasco, Sara, d/o Abraham Probasco and Neeltje Van Doorn, chr. 28 Apr. 1765.
Bennet, Margarita, d/o Wilm Bennet and Margarita Smit, chr. 16 June 1765.
Vanderveer, Jan, s/o Gerret Vanderveer and Jannitie Voorhees, chr. 16 June 1765.
Van Pelt, Geertje, d/o Jan Van Pelt and Janitje Heyer, chr. 23 June 1765.
Janson, Johannes, s/o Jacobus Janson and Antje Van Dyk, chr. 7 July 1765.
Van Derveer, Gerret, s/o Jacob Van Derveer and Aaltje Wykhof, chr. 15 Sep. 1765.
Hendrickson, Elias, s/o Hendrick Hendrickson and Lydia Covenhoven, chr. 29 Sep. 1765.
Antonides, Jacob, s/o Johannis Antonidis and Sara Van Doorn, chr. 1 Dec. 1765.
Vandiver, Roelef, s/o David Vandiver and Catharine Covenhoven, chr. 15 Dec. 1765.
Covenhoven, Aaltje, d/o William Covenhoven and Elizabeth Amak, chr. 1766.
Gritzinger, Stephanus, s/o Chriatian Gritzinger and Anne Parmer, chr. 1766.
Hendrickson, Cornelia, d/o Abraham Hendrickson and Anne Van Kerk, chr. 1766.
Hubbart, Jacobus, s/o Jacobus Hubbart and Rebeckah Swart, chr. 1766.
Schenck, Roelef, s/o John Schenck and Maria Van Doorn, chr. 1766.
Van Doorn, Jacob, s/o Aron Van Doorn and Gesha Schenck, chr. 1766.
Wynanse, Van_ Brunt, s/o Cornelis Wynanse and Antje Van Brunt, chr. 1766.
Vandiver, David, s/o Teunis Vandiver and Janetje Hans, chr. 26 Jan. 1766.
Van Meter, Neeltje, d/o Cryn Van Meter and Maria Zutphen, chr. 2 Feb. 1766.
Vandiver, Aaltje, d/o Cornelius Vandiver and Maria Covenhoven, chr. 23 Feb. 1766.
Wykhof, Peter, s/o Garret Wykhof and Patience Williamson, chr. 10 Mar. 1766.
Van Mater, Hendrick, s/o Jacob Van Mater and Neeltje Hendrickson, chr. 16 Mar. 1766.
Smak, Sarah, d/o Joannes Smak and Femmetje Teunisse, chr. 13 Apr. 1766.

Van Cleeve, Benjamin, s/o Cornelious Van Cleeve and Anne Leffererson, chr. 8 May 1766.
Pylhemels, Margrietje, d/o Johannis Pylhemels and Maria Van Meter, chr. 11 May 1766.
Smak, Jacomijntje, s/o Cornelis Smak and Aalyje Luister, chr. 18 May 1766.
Logen, Yda, d/o Staufel Logen and Cornelia Van Meter, chr. 19 May 1766.
Clark, Abigeltje, d/o Elexander Clark and Maria Hof, chr. 26 May 1766.
Voorhees, Maria, d/o Isaac Voorhees and Helena Barcalow, chr. 22 June 1766.
Hendrickson, Cyrinus, s/o Daniel Hendrickson and Neeltje Van Meter, chr. 20 July 1766.
Hendrickson, Neeltje, d/o Garret Hendrickson and Catryntje Denise chr. 10 Aug. 1766.
Schenk, Cornelius, s/o Albert Schenk and Agnietje Van Brunt, chr. 17 Aug. 1766.
Voorhees, Neeltje, d/o Albert Voorhees and Maragrietje Zutphen, chr. 17 Aug. 1766.
Van Der Veer, Joannes, s/o Joannes Van Der Veer and Maria Syryker, chr. 7 Sep. 1766.
Sleght, Elizabeth, d/o Abraham Sleght and Geertje Sikelse, chr. 14 Sep. 1766.
Hendrickson, Catrintje, d/o Albert Hendrickson and Joanna Mills, chr. 21 Sep. 1766.
Tyson, John, s/o Peter Tison and Anne Gray, chr. 16 Nov. 1766.
Smak, Sara, d/o Barent Smak and Sara Wilmzon, chr. 1767.
Wilmzon, Jannetje, d/o David Wilmzon and Femmetje Swart, chr. 24 May 1747.
Brouwer, Selvenus, s/o Hendrikus Brower and Abigael Dauty, chr. 21 June 1767.
Swart, Cornelius Gerrit, s/o Johannes Swart and Catrina Teunisse, chr. 17 July 1768.
Hegeman, Magdelena, d/o Cornelius Hegeman and Geesje Van Brunt, chr. 16 Oct. 1768.
Langstraat, Rachel, d/o Gerrit Langstraat and Cathrina Smak, chr. 27 Nov. 1768.
Brouwer, Antje, d/o Benjamin Brouwer and Maria Laan, b. 13 Dec. 1768 and chr. 1770.
Smak, Phebe, d/o Joh. Smak and Femmetje Teunisse, chr. 26 Dec. 1768.
Bennet, Willem, s/o Gerret Bennet and Maria Tilton, b. 16 Aug. 1769 and chr. 1770.

Dutch Reformed Church - Freehold and Middletown

Smak, Roelef, s/o Johannis Smak and Elisabeth Couwenhove, b. 20 Nov. 1769 and chr. 1770.
Antonides, Willem, s/o Johannis Antonidis and Sara Van Doorn, chr. 1770.
Covenhoven, Gerret, s/o Garret Covenhoven and Neeltje Van Mater, chr. 1770.
Hanse, Matje, d/o Aart Hanse and Catharine Van Der Veer, chr. 1770.
Janse, Johannes, s/o Abraham Janse and Maria Zutphen, chr. 1770.
Van De Veer, Jocomyntje, s/o Dominicus Van De Veer and Jannetje Willemse, b. 24 Jan. 1770 and chr. 18 Sep. 1770.
Swart, Jacomymtje, d/o Johannis Swart and Cathrina Teunisse, b. 13 Mar. 1770 and chr. 16 Sep. 1770.
Brouwer, Petrus, s/o Henrik Brower and Abigeltje Hunt, b. 19 Mar. 1770 and chr. 1770.
Gritzenger, Maria, d/o Chriatian Gritzenger and Anne Parmer, chr. 8 Apr. 1770.
Janse, Dirrick, s/o Johannes Janse and Catharina Zutphen, chr. 13 May 1770.
Covenhoven, Jacob, s/o Jacob Covenhoven and Sarah Sedam, chr. 27 May 1770.
Probasco, Christopher, s/o Abraham Probasco and Neeltje Van Doorn, chr. 27 May 1770.
Clark, Willem, d/o Elexander Clark and Maria Hof, chr. 15 July 1770.
Willemson, Willem, s/o Johannis Willemson and Geesje Tyson, chr. 29 July 1770.
Van Der Veer, Anne, d/o Cornelius Van Der Veer and Maria Covenhoven, chr. 12 Aug. 1770.
Schenck, Teunis, s/o John Schenck and Maria Denise, chr. 26 Aug. 1770.
Denise, Richard, s/o Denise_ Denise and Margaret Francis, chr. 18 Nov. 1770.
Walters, John, s/o John Walters and Janitje Schenck, chr. 16 Dec. 1770.
Bennet, Peter, s/o John Bennet and Maria Van Mater, chr. 1771.
Van Brunt, Nycolas, d/o Nycolas Van Brunt and Cathrina Covenhoven, chr. 1771.
Covenhoven, Jan, s/o Jacob and Airantje, chr. 1771.
Schenck, Daniel, s/o John Schenck and Neeltje Bennet, chr. 1771.
Van Mater, Cyrenius, s/o Cornelius and Sarah, chr. 1771.
Vandiver, Tunis, s/o David Vandiver and Catharina Covenhoven, chr. 1771.
Covenhoven, Nelly, d/o Cornelius Covenhoven and Maria Hendrickse, chr. 24 Feb. 1771.
Schencck, Garret, s/o John Schenck and Coboytje Covenhoven, chr. 21

Apr. 1771.
Pylhemels, Cyrinus, s/o Johannis Pylhemels and Maria Van Mater, chr. 28 Apr. 1771.
Du Bois, Maragrietje, d/o Benjamin Du Bois and Phemertje Denise, chr. 5 May 1771.
Wykhof, Aaltje, d/o Auke Wykhof and Sarah Schenck, chr. 26 May 1771.
Van Kerk, Antje, d/o James Van Kerk and Janitje Hansse, chr. 2 June 1771.
Polhemels, Daniel, s/o Tobias Polhemels and Maria Schenck, chr. 21 July 1771.
Lequier, Janitje, d/o Gelliam Lequier and Arriantje Springstien, chr. 4 Aug. 1771.
Janse, Johannes, s/o Johannis Janse and Catharina Zutphen, chr. 11 Aug. 1771.
Balser, William, s/o William Balser and Maria Numen, chr. 1 Sep. 1771.
Van Derveer, Cornelius, s/o John Van Derveer and Maria Stryker, chr. 15 Sep. 1771.
Schenck, Rachel, d/o Albert Schenck and Angenietje Van Brunt, chr. 29 Sep. 1771.
Voorhees, Antje, d/o Albert Voorhees and Maragrietje Zutphen, chr. 3 Nov. 1771.
Antonides, Vancentius, s/o Johannis Antonidis and Sara Van Doorn, chr. 1772.
Denise, Gerret, s/o Denise_ Denise and Catryntje Schenck, chr. 1772.
Provoost, John, s/o John Provoost and Mary Ackland, chr. 1772.
Janse, Maria, d/o Abraham Janse and Maria Zutphen, chr. 22 Feb. 1772.
Provoost, William Turner, s/o William Provoost and Elizabeth Turner, chr. 7 Apr. 1772.
Janson, Antje, d/o Jacobus Janson and Antje Van Dyk, chr. 10 May 1772.
Denise, Gerret, s/o Daniel Denise and Janitje Schenck, chr. 17 May 1772.
Van Mater, Jacob, s/o Cyrineus Van Mater and Cobatje Covenhoven, chr. 19 May 1772.
Vandiver, Aaltje, d/o Teunis Vandiver and Janitje Hans, chr. 24 May 1772.
Willemson, Jacob, s/o Johannis Willemson and Geesje Tyson, chr. 30 May 1772.
Schenck, Sarah, d/o John Schenck and Maria Van Doorn, chr. 5 June 1772.
Schenck, William, s/o John Schenck and Maria Denise, chr. 12 July 1772.

Dutch Reformed Church - Freehold and Middletown

Janse, Fernant, s/o Hendrick Janse and Elizabeth Van Brunt, chr. 6 Sep. 1772.
Probasco, Abraham, s/o Abraham Probasco and Neeltje Van Doorn, chr. 20 Sep. 1772.
Van Derveer, William, s/o Cornelius Van Derveer and Maria Covenhoven, chr. 20 Sep. 1772.
Schenck, Maria, d/o Gerrit Schenck and Sara Covenhoven, chr. 25 Oct. 1772.
Amack, Stephanis, d/o Teunis Amack and Ariantje Bennet, chr. 8 Nov.1772.
Brower, Abigeltje, d/o Hendrick Brower and Abigeltje Hunt, chr. 8 Nov. 1772.
Luyster, Johannis, s/o Cornelius Luyster and Maragrietje Van Der Bylt, chr. 8 Nov. 1772.
Langstraet, Gysbert, s/o Gerret Langstraet and Catrina Smack, chr. 8 Nov. 1772.
Smack, Neeltje, s/o Johannes Smack and Phemertje Teunisse, chr. 8 Nov. 1772.
Smack, Joanna, d/o Cornelius Smack and Aeltje Luyster, chr. 8 Nov. 1772.
Smack, Cornelius, s/o Barent Smack and Neeltje Covenhoven, chr. 8 Nov. 1772.
Brouwer, Henricus, chr. 1773.
Brouwer, Antje, chr. 1773.
Covenhoven, Antje, d/o John Covenhoven and Maria Van Doorn, chr. 1773.
Janse, Abraham, s/o Johannis Janse and Catharina Zutphen, chr.. 1773.
Polhemels, Daniel, s/o Tobias Polhemels and Maria Schenck, chr. 1773.
Clark, John, s/o John Clark and Maria Bennet, chr. 3 Jan. 1773.
Smack, Aaltje, chr. 1773.
Smack, Cornelius, chr.1773.
Zwart, d/o _____, chr. 1773.
Van Mater, Cornelius, s/o Cyrineus Van Mater and Cobatje Covenhoven, chr. 1773.
Amack, Gerret, s/o Jacob Amack and Geertye Covenhoven, chr. 10 Jan.1773.
Springstien, Joost, s/o Jacobis Springstien and Cornelia Voorhees, chr. 21 Feb. 1773.
Van Cleef, Roelef, s/o Benjamin Van Cleef and Sarah Covenhoven, chr. 14 Mar. 1773.
Du Bois, Teunis Denise, s/o Benjamin Du Bois and Phemertje Denise, chr. 28 Mar. 1773.

Schenck, Willem, s/o Albert Schenck and Angenietje Van Brunt, chr. 2 May 1773.
Barcalow, Lucrecea, d/o Dirreck, chr. 17 May 1773.
Van DerBelt, John, s/o Hendrick Van DerBelt and Catharine Snyder, chr. 23 May 1773.
Schenck, Benjamin, s/o John Schenck and Cobaytje Covenhoven, chr. 27 May 1773.
Bennet, Elisabeth, d/o William Bennet and Aaltje Van Mater, chr. 27 June 1773.
Tyse, Sara, d/o Jacob Tyse and Eupheme Francis, chr. 4 July 1773.
Langstraet, Barent, s/o Gerret Langstraet and Catrina Smack, chr. 8 Aug. 1773.
Hendrickse, Aeltje, d/o Abraham Hendrickse and Anne Van Kerk, chr. 15 Aug. 1773.
Provoost, Agnis, d/o William Provoost and Elizabeth Turner, chr. 24 Aug. 1773.
Hendickse, John, s/o Daniel Hendickse and Neeltje Van Brunt, chr. 5 Sep. 1773.
Balser, Maria, d/o William Balser and Maria Numen, chr. 19 Sep. 1773.
Van Der Veer, Gerret, s/o Gerret Van Der Veer and Janitje Voorhees, chr. 26 Sep. 1773.
Covenhoven, Peggy, d/o Cornelius Covenhoven and Janitje Denise, chr. 21 Dec. 1773.
Bennet, Willem, s/o Jacob Bennet and Afia Amack, chr. 1774.
Clark, Joseph, s/o John Clark and Maria Bennet, chr. 1774.
Janse, Jacobus, s/o Jacobus Janse and Antje Van Dyk, chr. 1774.
Smack, Barent, s/o Barent Smack and Neeltje Covenhoven, chr. 1774.
Smack, Antje, d/o Johannis Smack and Phemertje Teunisse, chr. 23 Jan. 1774.
Schenck, Maria, d/o Gerret Schenck and Sara Covenhoven, chr. 6 Feb. 1774.
Schenck, Jacob, s/o John Schenck and Maria Van Doorn, chr. 13 Feb. 1774.
Bennet, Hendrick, s/o Hendrick Bennet and Meeltje Colwill, chr. 3 Apr. 1774.
Janse, David, s/o Johannis Janse and Catharine Zutphen, chr. 17 Apr. 1774.
Van Brunt, Antje, d/o Nycolas Van Brunt and Cathrina Covenhoven, chr. 8 May 1774.
Willemse, Anne, d/o William Willemse and Lena Brewer, chr. 12 May 1774.

Dutch Reformed Church - Freehold and Middletown

Janse, Antje, d/o Abraham Janse and Maria Zutphen, chr. 29 May 1774.
Denise, Tryntje, d/o Daniel Denise and Janitje Schenck, chr. 12 June 1774.
Tyson, Peter, s/o Peter Tison and Anne Gray, chr. 19 June 1774.
Antonides, Petrus, s/o Johannis Antonidis and Sara Van Doorn, chr. 26 June 1774.
Pylhemels, Neeltje, d/o Johannis Pylhemels and Maria Van Mater, chr. 17 July 1774.
Schenck, Johannis, s/o Johannis Schenck and Maria Denise, chr. 1 Aug. 1774.
Sedam, Willem, s/o Sara Sedam, chr. 14 Aug. 1774.
Brower, Cornelius, s/o Benjamin Brower and Maria Laen, chr. 9 Oct. 1774.
Prest, Elena, d/o Richard Prest and Jenny Van Der Rype, chr. 30 Oct. 1774.
Van Cleef, Benjamin, s/o Benjamin Van Cleef and Sara Covenhoven, chr. 13 Nov. 1774.
Bennet, John Van Matter, s/o William Bennet and Aaltje Van Mater, chr. 18 Dec. 1774.
Karny, Joseph, s/o Catharine, chr. 1775.
Hendrickse, Yda, d/o Gerret Hendrickse and Lena Van Leeuwe, chr. 1775.
Probasco, Isaack, s/o Abraham Probasco and Neeltje Van Doorn, chr. 1775.
Van Deveer, Janitje, s/o David Van Deveer and Tryntje Covenhoven, chr. 1775.
Wykhof, Janitje, d/o Auke Wykhof and Sarah Schenck, chr. May 1775.
Covenhoven, Elizabeth, d/o William Covenhoven and Elizabeth Amak, chr. 15 Jan. 1775.
Covenhoven, Peter, s/o Albert and Petience, chr. 19 Mar. 1775.
Hubbart, Teunis, s/o Jacobus Hubbart and Rebeckah Swart, chr. 9 Apr. 1775.
Brouwer, Henrik, s/o Henrik Brouwer and Abigeltje Hunt, chr. 13 Apr. 1775.
Disbrow, Henry, s/o Henry Disbrow and Catharine Van mater, chr. 13 Apr. 1775.
Shepherd, Sarah, d/o Elisha Shepherd and Aeltje Smack, chr. 21 Apr. 1775.
Schenck, Mary, d/o John Schenck and Neeltje Bennet, chr. 14 May 1775.
Denise, Margaret, d/o Denise_ Denise and Catharine Schenck, chr. 21 May 1775.
Van Brunt, Maria, d/o Nycolas Van Brunt and Cathrina Covenhoven,

chr. 25 June 1775.
Lefferse, Margaret, d/o Auke Lefferse and Sarah Schenck, chr. 16 July 1775.
Thorn, William Brasier, s/o Thomas Thorn and Catharine Brasier, chr. 18 Sep. 1775.
Schenck, Rachel, d/o John Schenck and Maria Van Doorn, chr. 15 Oct. 1775.
Schenck, Peter Vorhees, s/o Koert Schenck and Sarah Voorhees, chr. 26 Nov. 1775.
Cowenhoven, Anne, d/o William Cowenhoven and Yda Schenck, chr. 10 Dec. 1775.
Du Bois, Sophia, d/o Benjamin Du Bois and Phemertje Denise, chr. 17 Dec. 1775.
Covenhoven, Peter, s/o Roelef Covenhoven and Aeltje Voorhees, chr. 1776.
Harber, Willem, s/o James Harber and Elizabeth Covenhoven, chr. 1776.
Holmes, Adrian Banker, s/o Josia Holmes and Maria Banker, chr. 1776.
Schenck, Denise, s/o John Schenck and Maria Denise, chr. 1776.
Snyder, Antje, d/o Christophel Snyder and Sarah Lyster, chr. 1776.
Van Derveer, John, s/o Cornelius Van Derveer and Maria Covenhoven, chr. 14 Jan. 1776.
Langstraet, Gerret, s/o Gerret Langstraet and Catrina Smack, chr. 6 Feb. 1776.
Tyse, Catherine Morris, d/o Jacob Tyse and Eupheme Francis, chr. 11 Feb. 1776.
Covenhoven, Neeltje, d/o Cornelius Covenhoven and Janitje Denise, chr. 18 Feb. 1776.
Covenhoven, Martha, d/o Benjamin Covenhoven and Abigel Buckalew, chr. 10 Mar. 1776.
Schenck, Ellenor, d/o John Schenck and Coboytje Covenhoven, chr. 10 Mar. 1776.
Janse, Jacobus, s/o Johannis Janse and Catharina Zutphen, chr. 28 Apr. 1776.
Denise, Teunis, s/o Daniel Denise and Janitje Schenck, chr. 2 June 1776.
Barcalow, Dirrick, d/o Daniel Barcalow and Lydia Stilwell, chr. 9 June 1776.
Van Der Byldt, Aron, s/o Aart Van Der Byldt and Geertje Van Mater, chr. 16 June 1776.
Janse, Ellenor, d/o Abraham Janse and Maria Zutphen, chr. 23 June 1776.
Van Cleef, Janitje, d/o John Van Cleef and Lea Schenck, chr. 23 June 1776.

Dutch Reformed Church - Freehold and Middletown

Polhemes, Janitje, d/o Tobias Polhemes, chr. 7 July 1776.
Clark, Anne, d/o John Clark and Maria Bennet, chr. 21 July 1776.
Bennet, Albert, s/o William Bennet and Aaltje Van Mater, chr. 28 July 1776.
Van Mater, Gerret, s/o Cyrineus Van Mater and Cobatje Covenhoven, chr. 25 Aug. 1776.
Pylhemels, John, s/o Johannis Pylhemels and Maria Van Mater, chr. 22 Sep. 1776.
Smack, Cornelius, s/o Barent Smack and Neeltje Covenhoven, chr. 3 Nov. 1776.
Cowenhoven, Nelly, d/o William Cowenhoven and Yda Schenck, chr. 1777.
Heyer, Maria, d/o Walter Heyer and Elisabeth Brewer, chr. 1777.
Heyer, Teunis, s/o Teunis Heyer and Catharine Van Pelt, chr. 1777.
Holmes, Hannah, d/o Josia Holmes and Maria Banker, chr. 1777.
Shepherd, Elisha, d/o Elisha Shepherd and Aeltje Smack, chr. 1777.
Clark, Benjamin, s/o Ellexander Clark and Aaltje Hendrickse, chr. 3 Feb. 1777.
Hendrickse, Nelly, d/o Albert Hendrickse and Joanna Mills, chr. 3 Feb. 1777.
Hendrickse, John, s/o Albert Hendrickse and Joanna Mills, chr. 3 Feb. 1777.
Hendrickse, William, s/o Albert Hendrickse and Joanna Mills, chr. 3 Feb. 1777.
Van Kerk, John Nelly, d/o James Van Kerk and Janitje Hanse, chr. 16 Mar. 1777.
Little, Theophilus, s/o Theophilus Little and Maria Polhemels, chr. 23 Mar. 1777.
Schenck, Gerret, s/o Koert Schenck and Sarah Voorhees, chr. 4 May 1777.
Hendrickse, Daniel, s/o Gerret Hendrickse and Lena Van Leuwe, chr. 1 June 1777.
Van Pelt, Janitje, d/o Jan Van Pelt and Janitje Heyr, chr. 8 June 1777.
Clark, Mary, d/o Elizabeth Clark, chr. 22 June 1777.
Petit, John, s/o William Petit and Hannah Morrel, chr. 24 Aug. 1777.
Van Der Bylt, Elizabeth, d/o John Van Der Bylt and Anne Covenhoven, b. 4 Nov. 1777 and chr. 15 Feb. 1778.
Lot, Abraham, s/o Philip Lot and Mary Karny, chr. 16 Nov. 1777.
Lefferse, Nelly, d/o Auke Lefferse and Sarah Schenck, chr. 23 Nov. 1777.
Van Der Veer, Aeltje, d/o David Van Der Veer and Tryntje Covenhoven, chr. 7 Dec. 1777.

Van Brunt, Hendrick, s/o Nicolaus Van Brunt and Cathrina Covenhoven, chr. 1778.
Clark, Benjamin, s/o Nicolas and Sarah, chr. 1778.
Clark, Hendrick, Ellexander Clark and Aaltje Hendrickse, chr. 1778.
Forman, Gerrit, s/o William Forman and Francynte Hendrickse, chr. 1778.
Harber, Isaack, s/o James Harber and Elizabeth Covenhoven, chr. 1778.
Van Cleef, Lena, d/o John Van Cleef and Lea Schenck, chr. 1778.
Du Bois, Daniel, s/o Benjamin Du Bois and Phemertje Denise, b. 23 Feb. 1778 and chr. 15 Mar. 1778.
Van Pelt, Nelle, d/o Peter Van Pelt and Nelle Van Der Bylt, chr. 8 Mar. 1778.
Schenck, Roelef Covenhoven, s/o Gerrit Schenck and Sara Covenhoven, chr. 5 Apr. 1778.
Willemse, David, s/o William Willemse and Lena Brewer, chr. 12 Apr. 1778.
Brewer, Joseph, s/o Hendrick Brewer and Abigeltje Hunt, chr. 19 Apr. 1778.
Van Der Veer, David, s/o Gerret Van Der Veer and Janitje Voorhees, chr. 3 May 1778.
Van Mater, Elizabeth, d/o Cyrineus Van Mater and Cobatje Covenhoven, chr. 10 May 1778.
Janse, Aron, s/o Johannis Janse and Catharina Zutphen, chr. 17 May 1778.
Shepherd, Elizabeth, d/o Elisha Shepherd and Aeltje Smack, chr. 26 July 1778.
Schenck, Isaack, s/o Albert Schenck and Angenietje Van Brunt, chr. 19 July 1778.
Mc Night, Charles Daniel, s/o Richard Mc Night and Elizabeth Hendrickse, chr. 16 Oct. 1778.
Van Der Veer, David, s/o Cornelius Van Der Veer and Maria Covenhoven, chr. 18 Oct. 1778.
Covenhoven, Lydia, d/o Cornelius Covenhoven and Maria Hendrickse, chr. 20 Dec. 1778.
Antonides, Maria, d/o John Antonidis and Sarah Van Doorn, chr. 1779.
Barber, Nathaniel Eells, s/o Thomas Barber and Mary Darrall, chr. 1779.
Clark, Benjamin, s/o Andrew Clark and Henrica Van Cleef, chr. 1779.
Hartshorn, William, s/o Richard, chr. 1779.
Hendrickse, Maria, d/o Gerret Hendrickse and Lena Van Leuwe, chr. 1779.

Dutch Reformed Church - Freehold and Middletown

Hubbert, Sameul, s/o Jacobus Hubbart and Rebeckah Swart, chr. 1779.
Lane, Rachel, d/o Abraham Lane and Hanna Horn, chr. 1779.
Petit, William, s/o William Petit and Hanna Moral, chr. 1779.
Teunisse, Philip, s/o Cornelius and Rebecka, chr. 1779.
Burrowes, Catharine, d/o John Borrowes and Margeret Forman, chr. 10 Jan. 1779.
Schenck, Daniel, s/o John Schenck and Maria Denise, chr. 14 Feb. 1779.
Covenhoven, Jane, d/o Albert and Patience, chr. 19 Mar. 1779.
Wool, Mary, d/o Isiah Wool and Margeret Witlock, chr. 23 Mar. 1779.
Van Mater, Jacob, s/o Benjamin and Sarah, chr. 4 Apr. 1779.
Hulse, David, s/o William Hulse and Maragrietje Zutphen, chr. 13 Apr. 1779.
Wykhof, William, s/o Auke Wykhof and Sarah Schenck, chr. 2 May 1779.
Hun, Mary, d/o Thomas Hun and Catharine Van Emburgh, chr. 20 May 1779.
Brower, Jan, d/o Benjamin Brower and Maria Laen, chr. 13 June 1779.
Bennet, Cyrineus, s/o William Bennet and Aaltje Van Mater, chr. 22 Aug. 1779.
Covenhoven, John, s/o Roelef Covenhoven and Aeltje Voorhees, chr. 29 Aug. 1779.
Langhstraet, Anne, d/o Aaron Langhstraet and Willempje Hendrickse, chr. 5 Sep. 1779.
Van Noortwyk, Nelly, d/o Martinus Van Noortwyk and Nelly Van Pelt, chr. 26 Sep. 1779.
Ledyard, Benjamin, s/o Benjamin Ledyard and Catharine Furman, chr. 22 Oct. 1779.
Little, Tobias, s/o Theophilus Little and Maria Polhemus, chr. 19 Sep. 1779.
Van Cleef, Nelly, d/o John Van Cleef and Lea Schenck, chr. 7 Nov. 1779.
Denise, William, s/o Denise_ Denise and Catharine Schenck, chr. 19 Dec. 1779.
Allen, William, s/o Jacob Allen and Grietje Covenhoven, chr. 1780.
Clark, Susannah, d/o Ellexander Clark and Aaltje Hendrickse, chr. 1780.
Covenhoven, William, s/o Albert and Petience, chr. 1780.
Denise, William, s/o Daniel Denise and Janitje Schenck, chr. 1780.
Heyer, Koert, s/o John Heyer and Neeltje Zutphen, chr. 1780.
Janse, Phebe, d/o Abraham Janse and Maria Zutphen, chr 1780.
Janse, Joseph, s/o Johannis Janse and Catharina Zutphen, chr. 1780.
Provoost, David, s/o John and Mary, chr. 1780.
Shepherd, Neltje, d/o Elisha Shepherd and Aeltje Smack, chr. 1780.

Smack, Johannis, s/o Jores Smack and Sarah Covenhoven, chr. 1780.
Snyder, Caty, d/o Harmanus Snyder and Polly Golder, chr. 1780.
Van Mater, Abigael, d/o Cornelius and Sarah, chr. 1780.
Van Mater, Polly, d/o Cyrineus Van Mater and Cobatje Covenhoven, chr. 1780.
Van Pelt, Agnis, s/o Jacob Van Pelt and Mary Brooks, chr. 1780.
Willemse, Genny, d/o William Willemse and Lena Brower, chr. 1780.
Johnson, Thomas Bown, s/o George Johnson and Elizabeth Bowne, chr. 9 Jan. 1780.
Johnson, Gorge, s/o George Johnson and Elizabeth Bowne, chr. 9 Jan. 1780.
Bennet, Logen, s/o John Bennet and Sarah Logan, chr. 23 Jan. 1780.
Van Mater, Isaack, d/o John Van Mater and Lena Hans, chr. 13 Feb. 1780.
Schenck, Anne, d/o William Schenck and Mary Tysse, chr. 27 Feb. 1780.
Van Doorn, Jacob, s/o Peter Van Doorn and Janitke Willemse, chr. 26 Mar. 1780.
Du Bois, Benjamin, s/o Benjamin Du Bois and Phemertje Denise, chr. 2 Apr. 1780.
Lefferse, Benjamin, s/o Auke Lefferse and Sarah Schenck, chr. 16 Apr. 1780.
Covenhoven, Janite, d/o Cornelius Covenhoven and Janitje Denice, chr. 23 Apr. 1780.
Van Brunt, Daniel Covenhoven, s/o Nycolas Van Brunt and Cathrina Covenhoven, chr. 30 Apr. 1780.
Pees, Jane, d/o Samuel Pees and Mary Galledat, chr. 7 May 1780.
Holmes, Josia, s/o Josia Holmes and Maria Bancker, chr. 14 May 1780.
Heyer, Aaltje, d/o Walter Heyer and Elisabeth Brewer, chr. 28 May 1780.
Van Brunt, Lydia, d/o Hendrick Van Brunt and Sarah Bown, chr. 20 June 1780.
Ramse, Catharine, d/o William Ramse and Agness Covenhoven, chr. 8 Oct. 1780.
Van Aarsdalen, Isaac, chr. 15 Oct. 1780.
Schenck, Gerret s/o Gerret Schenck and Sara Covenhoven, chr. 29 Oct. 1780.
Van De Veer, Sarah, d/o David Van De Veer and Catharine Covenhoven, b. 2 Nov. 1780 and chr. 4 Mar. 1781.
Antonides, Jacob, s/o Johannis Antonidis and Sarah Van Doorn, chr. 12 Nov. 1780.
Denise, Anne, d/o Jaques Denise and Neeltje Hans, chr. 17 Dec. 1780.
Willemse, David, s/o Hendrick Willemse and Neeltje Covenhoven, chr.

Dutch Reformed Church - Freehold and Middletown

24 Dec 1780.
Barber, Jonathan, d/o Thomas Barber and Mary Darrall, chr. 1781.
Hun, Catharine d/o Thomas Hun and Catharine Van Emburgh, chr. 1781.
Lane, Abraham, s/o Abraham Lane and Hanna Horn, chr. 1781.
Langhstraet, Lydia, d/o Aron Langhstraet and Willempje Hendrickse, chr. 1781.
Petit, Sarah, d/o William Petit and Hannah Moral, chr. 1781.
Reed, Maria Helena, d/o Samuel Reed and Maria D. Garrison, chr. 1781.
Schenck, De_Lefayette, s/o John Schenck and Maria Denise, chr. 1781.
Schenck, Koertinus, s/o William Schenck and Mary Tye, chr. 1781.
Shepherd, Hendrick, s/o Elisha Shepherd and Aeltje Smack, chr. 1781.
Wool, Deborah, d/o Isiah Wool and Margeret Witlock, chr. 1781.
Brees, Abigael, d/o Samuel Brees and Elizabeth Arthur, chr. 13 Feb. 1781.
De Graef, Maragrietje, d/o Johannis De Graef and Sarah Covenhoven, chr. 18 Feb. 1781.
Covenhoven, Samuel, s/o Sarah Covenhovene, chr. 11 Mar. 1781.
Van Der Bylt, Sarah, d/o John Van Der Bylt and Antje Covenhoven, chr. 25 Mar. 1781.
Polhemels, Maragrietje, d/o Tobias Polhemels and Maria Schenck, chr. 13 May 1781.
Forman, Aron, s/o Lewis Forman and Afia Van Emburgh, chr. 20 May 1781.
Barcalow, Cornelius, s/o Direck Barcalow and Sarah Covenhoven, chr. 3 June 1781.
Johnson, Sarah Helena, d/o George Johnson and Elizabeth Bowne, chr. 8 July 1781.
Johnson, Lewis Bown, s/o George Johnson and Elizabeth Bowne, chr. 8 July 1781.
Tyse, Anne, d/o Jacob Tyse and Euphame Fransis, chr. 22 July 1781.
Van Mater, Nelly, d/o Cyrineus Van Mater and Cobatje Covenhoven, chr. 9 Sep. 1781.
Heyer, Elizabeth, d/o John Heyer and Neeltje Zutphen, chr. 30 Sep. 1781.
Smack, Johannis, s/o Hendrick Smack and Sarah Lane, chr. 4 Nov. 1781.
Bennet, Sarah, d/o John Bennet and Sarah Logan, chr. 7 Nov. 1781.
Schenck, Peter, s/o Peter Schenck and Mary Covenhonen, chr. 25 Nov. 1781.
Brewer, Benjamin, s/o Benjamin Brewer and Maria Laen, chr. 1782.
Clark, Cornelius, s/o Andrew Clark and Henrica Van Cleef, chr. 1782.
Clarke, Elexander Bennett, s/o John Clarke and Mary Bennet, 1782.
Clark, Cornelius, s/o Andrew Clark and Henrica Van Cleef, chr. 1782.
Covenhoven, Sarah, d/o Albert and Petience, chr. 1782.

Covenhoven, Maria, d/o Jacob Covenhoven, chr. 1782.
Hendrickson, Caty, s/o Hendrick Hendrickson and Francyntje Covenhoven, chr. 1782.
Heyer, Abraham, s/o Walter Heyer and Elisabeth Brewer, chr. 1782.
Johnson, Mary, d/o John Johnson and Catharine Zutphe, chr. 1782.
Lefferson, Genny, d/o Auke Lefferson and Sarah Schenck, chr. 1782.
Pees, Abigael, d/o Samuel Pees and Mary Galledet, chr. 1782.
Stymets, Polly Stilwill, d/o Johannis Stymets and Aaltje Simonson, chr. 1782.
Van Duyn, Willem, s/o Hendrick, chr. 1782.
Hubbert, Elias, s/o Jacobus Hubbert and Rebeckah Swart, chr. 27 Jan. 1782.
Swart, Phemertje, d/o Cornelius Swart and Maragrietje Witlock, chr. 14 Mar. 1782.
Swart, Rebecka, d/o Cornelius Swart and Maragrietje Witlock, chr. 14 Mar. 1782.
Swart, Johannis, s/o Cornelius Swart and Maragrietje Witlock, chr. 14 Mar. 1782.
Ledyard, Samuel, s/o Benjamin Ledyard and Catharine Furman, chr. 17 Mar. 1782.
Du Bois, Carharine, d/o Benjamin Du Bois and Phemertje Denise, chr. 7 Apr. 1782.
Smack, Arie, s/o Jores Smack and Sarah Covenhoven, chr. 12 May 1782.
Van Brunt, Anne, d/o Nicolaus Van Brunt and Adriantje Tyse, chr. 26 May 1782.
Denise, John, s/o Denise_ Denise and Catharine Schenck, chr. 2 June 1782.
Covenhoven, William Hendrick, s/o Cornelius Covenhoven and Maria Hendricse, chr. 20 June 1782.
Brewer, Aaris, d/o Hendrick Brewer and Abigeltje Hunt, chr. 23 June 1782.
Carrall, Ann, d/o John Carrall and Mary Van Aalstyn, chr. 30 June 1782.
Covenhoven, William, s/o Wlliam Covenhoven and Yda Schenck, chr. 14 July 1782.
Ramson, Harriet, d/o William Ramson and Agnis Covenhoven, chr. 11 Aug. 1782.
Denise, Janitje, d/o Daniel Denise and Janitje Schenck, chr. 6 Oct. 1782.
Brower, Elias, chr. 9 Oct. 1782.
Van Der Bylt, Elizabeth, d/o John Van Der Bylt and Anne Covenhoven, b. 15 Oct. 1782 and chr. 24 Nov. 1782.
Chew, Phebe, d/o Richard Chew and Rachel Ball, chr. 1783.
Chew, William, s/o Richard Chew and Rachel Ball, chr. 1783.

Dutch Reformed Church - Freehold and Middletown

Chew, John, s/o Richard Chew and Rachel Ball, chr. 1783.
Chew, Hanna, d/o Richard Chew and Rachel Ball, chr. 1783.
Covenhoven, Stephen, s/o Teunis Covenhoven and Hanna Van Brakel, chr. 1783.
Hall, Mary, d/o Moses Hall and Ellis_ Easlick, chr. 1783.
Hall, Charlotte, d/o Moses Hall and Ellis_ Easlick, chr. 1783.
Lane, Nelly, d/o Hendrick Lane and Catharine Covenhoven, chr. 1783.
Lane, Sarah, d/o Gorge Lane and Nelly Covenhoven, chr. 1783.
Loyd, Catharine, d/o David Loyd and Jane Lane, chr. 1783.
Mc Dannel, Mary, d/o Benjamin Mc Dannel and Mary Easlick, chr. 1783.
Spargo, Elizabeth, d/o Gorge Spargo and Lena York, chr. 1783.
Spargo, Mary, d/o Gorge Spargo and Lena York, chr. 1783.
Van Cleef, Lena, d/o Joseph Van Cleef and Nelly Schenck, chr. 1783.
Van Mater, Catharine, d/o Cyrenius Van Mater and Cobatje Covenhoven, chr. 1783.
Van Mater, Daniel, s/o Benjamin and Sarah, chr. 1783.
Wool, James, s/o Isiah Wool and Margeret Witlock, chr. 1783.
Woolley, Mary, d/o Joseph Woolley and Catharine Vonk, chr. 1783.
Wykhoof, Nelly, d/o William Wykhoof and Lidia Bown, chr. 1783.
Forman, Hellen, d/o Jonathan Forman and Polly Ledyard, chr. 8 Feb. 1783.
Vonk, Alida, d/o Peter Vonk and Mary Rogers, chr. 10 Feb. 1783.
Vonk, Lidia, d/o Peter Vonk and Mary Rogers, chr. 10 Feb. 1783.
Vonk, Sarah, d/o Peter Vonk and Mary Rogers, chr. 10 Feb. 1783.
Van Brunt, William, s/o Cornelius Van Brunt chr. 7 Mar. 1783.
Van Brunt, Joseph, s/o Cornelius Van Brunt chr. 7 Mar. 1783.
Van Brunt, Mary, d/o Cornelius Van Brunt chr. 7 Mar. 1783.
Schenck, Nelly, d/o Garret Schenck and Sarah Covenhoven, chr. 16 Mar. 1783.
Mc Dannel, Sarah, d/o Benjamin Mc Dannel and Mary Easlick, chr. 6 Apr. 1783.
Clark, Johanna, d/o Alexander Clark and Aaltje Hendrickse, chr. 17 Apr. 1783.
Borrows, John, s/o John Borrows and Margeret Forman, chr. 22 May 1783.
Covenhoven, Cornelius, s/o Cornelius Covenhoven and Jane Denise, chr. 8 June 1783.
Rue, Mary Tomson, d/o Matthew Rue and Sarah Voorhees, chr. 15 June 1783.
Schenck, David, s/o John Schenck and Maria Denise, chr. 6 July 1783.

Schenck, Edmon Harris, s/o John Schenck and Cobatje Covenhoven, chr. 13 July 1783.
De Graef, Peter, s/o Johannis De Graaf and Sarah Covenhoven, chr. 27 July 1783.
Clark, David, s/o Nicolaus and Sarah Clark, chr. 10 Aug. 1783.
Provoost, Catharine Johanna, d/o James Provoost, chr. 28 Aug. 1783.
Van Brunt, Sarah Wykhof, d/o Nicolaus Van Brunt and Catharine Covenhoven, chr. 28 Sep. 1783.
Allen, Garret, s/o Jacob Allen and Margaret Covenhoven, b. 30 Nov. 1783 and chr. 1784.
Johnson, Joseph, s/o Abraham Johnson and Maria Zutphen, chr. 5 Oct. 1783.
Smock, Aaron, s/o Hendrick Smock and Sarah Lane, chr. 12 Oct. 1783.
Schenck, Nelly, d/o William Schenck and Sarah Covenhoven, chr. 26 Oct. 1783.
Schenck, John, s/o William Schenck and Sarah Covenhoven, chr. 26 Oct. 1783.
Van Cleef, Caty, d/o John Van Cleef and Lea Schenck, chr. 16 Nov. 1783.
Hendrickse, Anne, d/o Garret Hendrickse and Lena Van Leuwe, chr. 7 Dec.1783.
Lane, Elizabeth, d/o Matthew Lane and Catharine Smack, chr. 1784.
Covenhoven, Mary, d/o Albert and Petience, chr. 11 Jan. 1784.
Schenck, John, s/o William Schenck and Mary Tyse, chr. 5 Feb. 1784.
Shepherd, Jacob, s/o Elisha Shepherd and Aeltje Smack, chr. 4 Apr. 1784.
Van Doorn, Williampje, d/o Peter Van Doorn and Jane Williamse, chr. 20 June 1784.
Van Der Bylt, John, s/o John Van Der Bylt and Anne Covenhoven, b. 9 July 1784 and chr. 29 Aug. 1784.
Covenhoven, Elizabeth, d/o Jacob Covenhoven and Nelly Smack, chr. 11 July 1784.
Smack, Mary, d/o Gorge Smack and Sarah Covenhoven, chr. 18 July 1784.
Ledyard, Isaac, s/o Benjamin Ledyard and Catharine Furman, chr. 25 July 1784.
Williamson, Peter, s/o Hendrick Williamson and Nelly Covenhoven, chr. 15 Aug. 1784.
Van Der Bylt, Elizabeth Maria, d/o Jacob Van Der Bylt and Mary Ackland, chr. 29 Aug. 1784.
Rue, Joseph, s/o Matthew Rue and Mary Schuyler, chr. 12 Sep. 1784.

Dutch Reformed Church - Freehold and Middletown

Denise, Sarah Schenck, d/o Daniel Denise and Janitje Schenck, chr. 28 Nov. 1784.
Aamack, Mary, d/o Agnis Aamack, chr. 1785.
Byse, Adam, s/o Patty, chr. 1785.
Brewer, Mary, d/o Benjamin Brewer and Mary Lane, chr. 1785.
Clarke, Elizabeth, d/o John Clarke and Mary Bennet, chr. 1785.
Covenhoven, Maria, d/o William Covenhoven and Yda Schenck, chr. 1785.
Pees, John, s/o Samuel Pees and Mary Galledat, chr. 1785.
Schenck, John, s/o Koert Schenck and Sarah Voorhees, chr. 1785.
Van Cleef, Margaret, d/o John Van Cleef and Lea Schenck, chr. 1785.
Van Cleef, Anne, d/o Joseph Van Cleef and Nelly Schenck, chr. 1785.
Van Mater, Anne, d/o Aaron Van Mater and Mary Polhemes, chr. 1785.
Wykhof, Garret, s/o William Wykhof and Lydia Bown, chr. 1785.
Wykhoof, John, s/o Cornelius Wykhoof and Aeltje Covenhoven, chr. 1785.
Denise, Sidney, s/o Denise_ Denise and Catharine Schenck, chr. 3 Jan. 1785.
Tyse, Eupheme, d/o Jacob, chr. 3 Feb. 1785.
Forman, Mary Ledyard, d/o Jonathan Forman and Mary Ledyard, chr. 31 Mar. 1785.
Dubois, Elizabeth, d/o Benjamin Dubois and Phebe Denise, chr. 3 Apr. 1785.
Bennet, Logen, s/o John Bennet and Sarah Logan, chr. 10 Apr. 1785.
Antonides, Anne, d/o John Antonidis and Sara Van Doorn, chr. 17 Apr. 1785.
Hendrickson, Daniel, s/o Cornelius Hendrickson and Lydia Van Der Bylt, chr. 5 May 1785.
Lefferson, Mary, d/o Auke Lefferson and Sarah Schenck, chr. 16 May 1785.
Shepherd, Amelia, d/o Elisha Shepherd and Aeltje Smack, chr. 12 June 1785.
Brewer, Helena, d/o Hendrick Brewer and Abigael Hunt, chr. 19 June 1785.
Clark, John, s/o Andrew Clark and Henrica Van Cleef, chr. 26 June 1785.
Schenck, Polly, d/o John Schenck and Maria Denise, chr. 10 July 1785.
Clarke, Nancy, d/o Nicolaus and Sarah, chr. 7 Aug. 1785.
Covenhoven, Reolof, s/o Teunis Covenhoven, chr. 25 Sep. 1785.
Smack, Elizabeth, d/o Hendrick Smack and Sarah Lane, chr. 5 Nov. 1785.
Schenck, Polly, d/o William Schenck and Mary Tyse, chr. 1 Dec. 1785.

Van Duyn, Lena, d/o Hendrick, chr. 15 Dec. 1785.
Van Mater, Anne, d/o John Van Mater and Elizabeth Carle, chr. 20 Dec. 1785.
Van Mater, Elizabeth, d/o John Van Mater and Elizabeth Carle, chr. 20 Dec. 1785.
Ball, Mary, d/o Rachel Ball (relict of Richard Chew), chr. 1786.
Tyse, James Carny, s/o Jacob Tyse, chr. 1786.
Voorhees, William, s/o John Voorhees and Maria Laquear, chr. 1786.
Mc Clochen, John, s/o Micael Mc Clochen and Leah Clark, chr. 1 Jan. 1786.
Longstreet, Hendrick, s/o Aaron Longstreet and Willempje Hendrickse, chr. 12 Feb. 1786.
Longstreet, Nelly, d/o Aaron Longstreet and Willempje Hendrickse, chr. 12 Feb. 1786.
Smock, Sarah, d/o Hendrick Smock and Sarah Lane, chr. 25 Feb. 1786.
Wooly, John Throckmorton, s/o Joseph Wooly and Catharine Vonk, chr. 26 Feb. 1786.
Van Cleef, Lydia Williamson, d/o Joseph Van Cleef and Nelly Schenck, chr. 11 Mar. 1786.
Van Brunt, William Covenhoven, s/o William Van Brunt and Elizabeth Hankinson, chr. 18 Mar. 1786.
Willemse, Jane, d/o Hendrick Willemse and Nelly Covenhoven, chr. 19 Mar. 1786.
Snyder, Margaret, d/o Hendrick Snyder and Elizabeth Zutphen, chr. 16 Apr. 1786.
Willemse, Sarah, d/o William Willemse and Lena Brewer, chr. 7 May 1786.
__, Sarah, chr. 25 May 1786.
Springsteen, James, s/o John Springsteen and Catherine Van Pelt, chr. 4 June 1786.
Vander Bylt, Micael Field, s/o John Vander Bylt and Anne Covenhoven, b. 10 July 1786 and chr. 10 Sep. 1786.
Johnson, Sarah, d/o Abraham Johnson and Maria Zutphen, chr. 13 Aug. 1786.
Van Brunt, Peter, s/o Nicolaus Van Brunt and Adriantje Tyse, chr. 3 Sep. 1786.
Ledyard, Caleb, s/o Benjamin Ledyard and Catharine Furman, chr. 7 Oct. 1786.
Van Mater, Peter, s/o Cyrenius Van Mater and Cobatje Covenhoven, chr. 15 Oct. 1786.
Clark, Ellenor, d/o Ellexander Clark and Aaltje Hendrickse, chr. 22 Oct. 1786.

Dutch Reformed Church - Freehold and Middletown

Denise, Ursuls White, d/o Daniel Denise and Jane Schenck, chr. 5 Nov. 1786.
Schenck, Sarah Covenhoven, d/o Garret Schenck and Sarah Covenhoven, chr. 12 Nov. 1786.
Johnson, John Bown, s/o Gorge, chr. 23 Nov. 1786.
Johnson, Mary Stilwell, s/o Gorge, chr. 23 Nov. 1786.
Barcalow, Mathias, s/o Dirreck Barcalow and Sarah Covenhoven, chr. 1787.
Clark, Betsy, d/o Nicolaus and Sarah Clark, chr. 1787.
Pees, Peter Elisha, s/o Samuel Pees and Mary Galledat, chr. 1787.
Schenck, Hellenor, d/o Koert Schenck and Sarah Voorhees, chr. 1787.
Allen, Elizabeth, d/o Jacob Allen and Margaret Covenhoven, b. 11 Jan. 1787 and chr. 1794.
Covenhoven, Nelley, d/o Daniel Covenhoven and Mary Wykhof, chr. 27 Jan. 1787.
Hendrickse, William, s/o Hendrick Hendrickse and Francyntje Covehoven, chr. 17 May 1787.
Van Der Veer, David, s/o David Van Der Veer and Catharine Covenhoven, chr. 24 June 1787.
Schenck, Catharine, d/o John Schenck and Maria Denise, chr. 22 July 1787.
Lane, Mary, d/o George Lane and Nelly Covenhoven, chr. 26 Aug. 1787.
Hendrickson, Garret, s/o Denise_ Hendrickson and Anne Schenck, chr. 9 Sep. 1787.
Shepherd, Hellenor, d/o Elisha Shepherd and Aeltje Smack, chr. 16 Sep. 1787.
Lequeer, Genny, d/o John Lequeer and Mary Acker, chr. 23 Sep. 1787.
Byse, Jenny, d/o Patty, chr. 30 Sep. 1787.
Schenck, Anne, d/o William Schenck and Sarah Covenhoven, chr. 28 Oct. 1787.
Van Brunt, Daniel Covenhoven, s/o Nicholaus Van Brunt and Catharine Covenhoven, chr. 18 Nov. 1787.
Voorhees, Lena, d/o John Voorhees and Maria Laquear, chr. 2 Dec. 787.
Ame, Hannah, d/o David Ame and Elizabeth Van Derhoof, chr. 1788.
Hendrickson, Margeret, d/o Cornelius Hendrickson and Lydia Van Der Bylt, chr. 1788.
Lane, John, s/o Abraham Lane and Hannah Horn, chr. 1788.
Mac Kenney, Elizabeth, d/o William Mac Kenney and Catharine Geren, chr. 1788.
Hendrickson, Catharine, d/o Cornelius Hendrickson and Lydia Van Der Bylt, chr. 1788.

Snyder, Jacob Covenhoven, d/o Hendrick Snyder and Elizabeth Zutphen, chr. 1788.
Van Der Bylt, Nancy, d/o Hendrick Van Der Bylt and Elizabeth Combs, chr. 1788.
Van Duyn, Hendrick, s/o Hendrick, chr. 1788.
Joste, Charels, s/o Christopher Joste and Rebeckah Hymns, chr. 1788.
Van Doorn, John, d/o Peter Van Doorn and Jane Williamse, chr. 20 Jan. 1788.
Covenhoven, Anne, d/o Jacob Covenhoven and Nelly Smock, chr. 27 Jan. 1788.
Schenck, Peter, s/o William Schenck and Mary Tyse, chr. 21 Feb. 1788.
Van Mater, Gilbert, s/o Benjamin and Sarah, chr. 23 Mar. 1788.
Van Brunt, Peter, s/o Nicholaus Van Brunt and Adriantje Tyse, chr. 25 Feb. 1788.
Woolly, Petrus, s/o Joseph Wooly and Catharine Vonk, chr. 4 May 1788.
Lefferson, Arther, s/o Auke Lefferson and Sarah Schenck, chr. 18 May 1788.
Clark, Lena, d/o Andrew Clark and Henrica Van Cleef, chr. 16 June 1788.
States, Elizabeth, d/o John States and Agnis Aamack, chr. 19 June 1788.
Denise, Catharine Schanck, d/o Denise_ Denise, chr. 22 June 1788.
Provoost, Ann Reed, d/o Jemes Provoost, chr. 27 July 1788.
Smith, Elizabeth, d/o John Smith and Frances Williams, chr. 23 Sep. 1788.
Ellison, John, s/o Daniel Ellison and Elizabeth Manly, chr. 3 Aug. 1788.
Laqueer, John, s/o John Laqueer and Catharine Van Pelt, chr. 24 Aug. 1788.
Wykhoof, Samuel, s/o William Wykhoof and Lidia Bown, chr. 14 Sep. 1788.
Brewer, William, s/o Hendrick Brewer and Abigael Hunt, chr. 19 Oct. 1788.
Schenck, James, s/o Gerret Schenck and Jane Van Kerk, chr. 7 Dec. 1788.
Van Der Bylt, Joseph, s/o Aart Van Der Bylt and Geertie Van Meter, chr. 16 Dec. 1788.
Van Der Bylt, Jeremiah, s/o Aart Van Der Bylt and Geertie Van Meter, chr. 16 Dec. 1788.
Schenck, Koert, d/o John Schenck and Cobatje Covenhoven, chr. 1789.
Schenck, John, s/o Garret Schenck and Mary Covenhoven, chr. 1789.
Shepherd, Gorge, s/o Elisha Sheepherd and Aeltje Smock, chr. 1789.
Snyder, Elizabeth Pees, d/o William, chr. 1789.

Dutch Reformed Church - Freehold and Middletown

Wykhoof, Nelly, d/o Cornelius Wykhoof and Aeltje Covenhoven, chr. 17895.
Van Mater, Anne Van Doorn, d/o Benjamin and Elizabeth, chr. 11 Jan. 1789.
Lane, John, s/o Matthew Lane and Catharine Smock, chr. 25 Jan. 1789.
Wykhoof, Patience, s/o Samuel Wykhoof and Sarah Van Cleef, chr. 29 Mar. 1789.
Van Der Bylt, Jacob, s/o John Van Der Bylt and Anne Covenhoven, b. 27 Jan. 1789 and chr. 17 May 1789.
Van Brunt, Elizabeth, d/o William Van Brunt and Elizabeth Hankinson, chr. 8 Feb. 1789.
Clark, Mary, d/o Alexander Clark and Aeltje Hendrickse, chr. 12 Apr. 1789.
Brewer, Hendrick, s/o John Brewer and Nelly Hendrickson, chr. 3 June 1789.
Van Cleef, Benjamin, s/o Joseph Van Cleef and Nelly Schenck, chr. 7 June 1789.
Lidyard, Catharine, d/o Benjamin Ledyard and Catharine Furman, chr. 25 June 1789.
Covenhoven, Eliazbeth, d/o Teunis Covenhoven, chr. 5 July 1789.
Schenck, Jane, d/o John Schenck and Maria Denise, chr. 9 July 1789.
Smock, Garret, s/o Hendrick Smock and Sarah Lane, chr. 26 July 1789.
Pees, Samuel, s/o Samuel Pees and Mary Galledet, chr. 16 Aug. 1789.
Covenhoven, Mary, d/o Daniel Covenhoven and Margeret Resoe, chr. 23 Aug. 1789.
Covenhoven, Gorge, s/o Daniel Covenhoven and Mary Wykhoof, chr. 4 Oct. 1789.
Upson, Ellenor, d/o Ashbel Upson and Mary Munson, chr. 18 Oct. 1789.
Upson, Erastus, s/o Ashbel Upson and Mary Munson, chr. 18 Oct. 1789.
Upson, Anne, d/o Ashbel Upson and Mary Munson, chr. 18 Oct. 1789.
Hulst, Hannah, d/o John Hulst and Mary Pelhemels, b. 27 Nov. 1789 and chr. 1789.
Schenck, Catharine, d/o Koert Schenck and Sarah Voorhees, chr. 6 Dec. 1789.
Ame, John, s/o David Ame and Elizabeth Van Derhoof, chr. 1790.
Covenhoven, Elizabeth, d/o Garret and Mary, chr. 1790.
Fryer, William, s/o Matthew Fryer and Susannah Kerl, chr. 1790.
Van Derhoof, Patty, d/o Cornelius Van Derhoof, chr. 1790.
Leffertson, Anne, d/o Auke Leffertson and Sarah Schenck, chr. 1790.
Van Noortwyk, Nelly, d/o Simion Van Noortwyk and Rebeckah Hendrickson, chr. 1790.
Pelhemes, William, s/o Daniel Pelhemes and Micha_ Van Mater, chr.

1790.
Seguin, James, s/o John Seguin and Ann Baty, chr. 1790.
Van Meter, Maria, d/o Benjamin and Sarah, chr. 1790.
Van Pelt, Ellse, d/o William Van Pelt and Catherine Seguin, chr. 1790.
Ward, Anne, d/o John, chr. 1790.
Covenhoven, Teunis, s/o Roelef Covenhoven and Sarah Van Der Veer, chr. 10 Jan. 1790.
Covenhoven, Hendrick Smock, s/o John Covenhoven and Anne Smock, chr. 7 Feb. 1790.
Van Horn, Abraham, s/o Abraham C. Van Horn and Anne Covenhoven, chr. 7 Feb. 1790.
Heyer, Aron, s/o Walter Heyer and Elisabeth Brewer, chr. 9 Feb. 1790.
Heyer, Catharine, d/o Walter Heyer and Elisabeth Brewer, chr. 9 Feb. 1790.
Heyer, Nelly, d/o Walter Heyer and Elisabeth Brewer, chr. 9 Feb. 1790.
Dubois, Mary, d/o Benjamin Dubois and Phebe Denise, chr. 28 Feb. 1790.
States, Ellenor, d/o John States and Agnis Aamack, chr. 25 Mar. 1790.
Covenhoven, Nelly, d/o Jacob Covenhoven and Nelly Schenck, chr. 5 Apr. 1790.
Van Mater, Sarah, d/o Cyrenius Van Mater and Cobatje Covenhoven, chr. 11 Apr. 1790.
Hulst, Lena, d/o John Hulst and Mary Pelhemels, b. 19 Apr. 1790 and chr. 1798.
Van Doorn, William, s/o Peter Van Doorn and Jane Williamson, chr. 2 May 1790.
Wykhoof, Garret, s/o Samuel Wykhoof and Sarah Van Cleef, chr. 8 May 1791.
Allen, Jacob, s/o Jacob Allen and Margaret Covenhoven, b. 10 May 1790 and chr. 1794.
Schenck, Ellener, d/o Garret Schenck and Jane Van Kerk, chr. 27 June 1790.
Van Cleef, Maria, d/o Joseph Van Cleef and Nelly Schenck, chr. 8 Aug. 1790.
Smock, Nelly, d/o Barent Smock and Junis_ West, chr. 6 Oct. 1790.
Smock, Archible, s/o Barent Smock and Junis_ West, chr. 6 Oct. 1790.
Smock, Anne, d/o Gorge Smock and Sarah Covenhoven, chr. 17 Oct. 1790.
Schenck, William Bennet, s/o William Schenck and Sarah Covenhoven, chr. 24 Oct. 1790.
Williamson, Catherine, d/o Hendrick Williamson and Nelly Covenhoven, chr. 31 Oct. 1790.

Dutch Reformed Church - Freehold and Middletown

Clark, Jane, d/o Nicolaus and Sarah Clark, chr. 1791.
Heyer, John, s/o Walter Heyer and Elisabeth Brewer, chr. 1791.
Mac Kenney, Benjamin, s/o William Mac Keney and Catharine Amey, chr. 1791.
Robenson, Genny Stymats, d/o George Robenson and Lena Aamack, chr. 1791.
Shepherd, Clemens, s/o Elisha Shepherd and Aaeltje Smack, chr. 1791.
Van Horn, William, s/o Cornelius Van Horn and Nelly Covenhoven, chr. 1791.
Wykhof, Peter, s/o Cornelius Wykhof and Aaltje Covenhoven, chr. 1791.
Yoest, John, s/o Christopher, chr. 22 Mar. 1791.
Covenhoven, Toiley, s/o Daniel Covenhoven and Margeret Resoe, chr. 3 Apr. 1791.
Van Brunt, Nelly, d/o William Van Brunt and Elizabeth Hankinson, chr. 15 May 1791.
Hulst, Thomas, s/o Hannah Hulst (spouse of Thomas Smith), chr. 31 May 1791.
Hulst, Debora, d/o Hannah Hulst (spouse of Thomas Smith), chr. 31 May 1791.
Hulst, Samuel, s/o Hannah Hulst (spouse of Thomas Smith), chr. 31 May 1791.
Hulst, Hanna, d/o Hannah Hulst (spouse of Thomas Smith), chr. 31 May 1791.
Hulst, Mary, d/o Hannah Hulst (spouse of Thomas Smith), chr. 31 May 1791.
Van Pelt, Peter, s/o John Van Pelt and Yda Van Der Bylt, chr. 24 July 1791.
Forman, Margeret, d/o Catharine Forman, spouse of Benjamin Lydyerd, chr. 25 July 1791.
Lyster, Williampe, s/o John Lyster and Anne Covenhoven, chr. 7 Aug. 1791.
Aamack, Mary, d/o John Aamack and Sarah Van Der Veer, chr. 21 Aug.1791.
Schenck, Hendrick Van Brunt, s/o John Schenck and Maria Denise, chr. 28 Aug. 1791.
Lane, Ellenor, d/o George Lane and Nelly Covenhoven, chr. 11 Sep. 1791.
Lane, Catharine, d/o George Lane and Nelly Covenhoven, chr. 11 Sep. 1791.
Hendrickson, Polly, d/o Hendrick Hendrickson and Phebe Van Mater, chr. 30 Oct. 1791.

Covenhoven, Mary, d/o Tunis Covenhoven and Matje Vanderhoof, chr. 4 Dec. 1791.
Van Mater, Henry, s/o Benjamin and Sarah, chr. 11 Dec. 1791.
Smock, Jane, d/o Hendrick Smock and Sarah Lane, chr. 26 Dec. 1791.
Covenhoven, Mary, d/o Cornelius and Elizabeth Covenhoven, chr. 1792.
Harris, Margeret, d/o Isaac Harris and Gesha Schenck, chr. 1792.
Snyder, Mary, d/o William, chr. 1792.
Van Cleef, Margeret, d/o Joseph Van Cleef and Nelly Schenck, chr. 1792.
Van Mater, Crynjans Bennet, s/o William Van Mater and Yda Bennet, chr. 1792.
Van Der Bylt, Ellenor Field, d/o John Van Der Bylt and Anne Covenhoven, 1792.
Covenhoven, John Wykoof, s/o Daniel Covenhoven and Mary Wykhoof, chr. 26 Feb. 1792.
Schenck, Harmen, s/o Garret Schenck and Mary Covenhoven, chr. 8 Apr. 1792.
Hendrickson, Genny, d/o Hendrick Hendrickson and Francyntje Covenhoven, chr. 22 Apr. 1792.
Van Doorn, Isaac, s/o Peter Van Doorn and Jane Williamse, chr. 29 Apr. 1792.
Brewer, Garret, s/o John Brewer and Nelly Hendrickson, chr. 5 May 1792.
Woolly, Joseph, s/o Joseph Wooly and Catharine Vonk, chr. 6 May 1792.
Wikoof, Lenah, d/o Samuel Wikoof and Sarah Van Cleef, b. 8 Aug. 1792 and chr. 1799.
Schenck, Garret, s/o Garret Schenck and Jane Van Kerk, chr. 20 May 1792.
Schenck, Ephraim Loree, s/o Koert Schenck, chr. 22 May 1792.
Fransis, Phebe, d/o Catherine Fransis, spouse of Cornelius Smock, chr. 17 June 1792.
Van Der Veer, Arther, s/o Cornelius and Aaltje, chr. 12 July 1792.
Lane, Aaron, s/o Matthew Lane and Catherine Smack, chr. 12 Aug. 1792.
Vander Hoof, Cornelius, s/o John Vander Hoof and Patty Byse, chr. 19 Aug. 1792.
Roads, Cathy, d/o Michael Roads and Ledia Mount, b. 25 Aug. 1792 and chr. 18 Nov. 1802.
Brewer, Charles, s/o Anne Brewer (spouse of Isaac Morris), b. 3 Sep. 1792 and chr. 18 Nov. 1792.
Smith, Adaline, d/o James Smith and Ida Bennet, b. 17 Sep. 1792 and chr. 1813.

Dutch Reformed Church - Freehold and Middletown

Smock, Peter, s/o Gorge Smock and Sarah Covenhoven, chr. 30 Sep. 1792.
States, Yoanne, d/o John States and Agnis Aamack, chr. 11 Oct. 1792.
Schenck, Catherine, d/o John Schenck and Cobatje Covenhoven, chr. 14 Oct. 1792.
Van Brunt, Sarah, d/o Nicolaus Van Brunt and Adriantje Tyse, chr. 1793.
Van Brunt, Elisha, d/o Nicolaus Van Brunt and Adriantje Tyse, chr. 1793.
Dun, Ann, d/o James Dun and Catherine Carl, chr. 1793.
Van Derhoof, Rebecka, d/o Cornelius Van Derhoof, chr. 1793.
Heyer, Cortenus, s/o Walter Heyer and Elisabeth Brewer, chr. 1793.
Lefferson, Garret, s/o Auke Lefferson and Sarah Schenck, chr. 1793.
Tomson, John, s/o Abraham Tomson and Rebecka Carl, chr. 1793.
Van Pelt, Peter, s/o Peter Van Pelt and Mary Hyer, chr. 1793.
Van Pelt, Getty, d/o John Van Pelt and Yda Van Der Bylt, chr. 1793.
Van Der Bylt, John Combes, s/o Hendrick Van Der Bylt and Elizabeth Combes, chr. 1793.
Voorhees, Adriantje, d/o John Voorhees and Maria Laqueer, chr. 1793.
Voorhees, Mary, s/o John Voorhees and Maria Laqueer, chr. 1793.
Yoest, Gorge Hymes, s/o Christopher Yoest and Rebecka Hymes, chr. 1793.
Zutphen, James, s/o Micha Zutphen (relict of Thomas Boyd), chr. 1793.
Zutphen, John, s/o Micha Zutphen (relict of Thomas Boyd), chr. 1793.
Zutphen, Jane, d/o Micha Zutphen (relict of Thomas Boyd), chr. 1793.
Van Brunt, Catherine, d/o William Van Brunt and Elizabeth Hankenson, chr. 13 Jan. 1793.
Seguin, Ann, d/o John Seguin and Ann Baty, chr. 28 Jan. 1793.
Seguin, Ellis, s/o John Seguin and Ann Baty, chr. 28 Jan. 1793.
Bennet, John, s/o Barns Bennet and Geertje Williamson, chr. 10 Mar. 1793.
Brewer, West, s/o Sylvenus Brewer and Yda West, chr. 13 Mar. 1793.
Smock, Sarah Schenck, d/o Garret Smock and Jane Schenck, chr. 24 Mar. 1793.
Van Der Bylt, Mary Combs, d/o Hendrick Van Der Bylt and Elizabeth Combs, b. 28 Mar. 1793 and chr. 1794.
Van Mater, John, s/o Cyrenius Van Mater and Cobatje Covenhoven, chr. 1 Apr. 1793.
Snyder, Peter Lyster, s/o Christopher Snyder and Sarah Lyster, 14 Apr. 1793.
Aamack, Mary, d/o Lena Aamack, b. 16 Apr. 1793 and chr. 20 Mar. 1794.

Van Kerk, Margeret, d/o Anne Van Kerk (spouse of Daniel Peecock), b. 25 Apr. 1793 and chr. 20 Oct. 1793.
Shepherd, Barns Smock, s/o John Shepherd and Anne Covenhoven, chr. 21 May 1793.
Snyder, Aart Zutphen, s/o Hendrick Snyder and Elizabeth Zutphen, chr. 6 June 1793.
Springsteen, Elexander, s/o John Springsteen and Catherine Van Pelt, chr. 13 June 1793.
Springsteen, William, s/o John Springsteen and Catherine Van Pelt, chr. 13 June 1793.
Williamson, Aart, s/o Hendrick Williamson and Nelly Covenhoven, chr. 16 June 1793.
Covenhoven, Nelly, d/o Garret Covenhoven and Mary Schenck, chr. 7 July 1793.
Brewer, Abigael, d/o John Brewer and Nelly Hendrickson, chr. 21 July 1793.
Clark, Andrew, s/o Elexander Clark and Aaltje Hendrickson, chr. 28 July 1793.
Clark, Maria, d/o Jane Clark (spouse of Obadiah Harber), b. 30 July 1793 and chr. 22 Sep. 1793.
Hendrickson, Abraham, s/o Matthias Hendrickson, b. 20 Sep. 1793 and chr. 1794.
Van Der Bylt, Samuel Broom, s/o John Van Der Bylt and Anne Covenhoven, b. 20 Sep 1793 and chr. 27 Mar. 1794.
Forman, Jonathen Denice, s/o Catharine Forman, spouse of Benjamin Ledgerd, chr. 5 Oct. 1793.
Hendrickson, Garret, s/o Hendrick Hendrickson, chr. 13 Oct. 1793.
Van Mater, Ellenor, d/o Benjamin and Sarah, b. 21 Oct. 1793 and chr. 9 Mar. 1794.
Van Der Veer, Benjamin, s/o Teunis Van Der Veer and Margeret Du Bois, b. 15 Nov. 1793 and chr. 1794.
Aamack, Teunis, s/o John Aamack and Sarah Van Der Veer, chr. 22 Dec.1793.
Hulst, Maria, d/o John Hulst and Mary Pelhemels, b. 24 Dec. 1793 and chr. 1798.
Pees, William, s/o Samuel Pees and Mary Galledet, chr. 1794.
Schenck, David Forman, s/o Garret Schenck and Jan_ Van Kerk, chr. 1794.
Van Der Veer, Daniel, s/o David Van Der Veer and Catherine Denise, chr. 1794.
Schenck, Elisha Shephard, s/o Peter Schenck and Sarah Shephard, b. 4 Jan. 1794 and chr. 1794.

Dutch Reformed Church - Freehold and Middletown

Schenck, Catherine, d/o Teunis Schenck and Aaltje Van Der Veer, b. 12 Jan. 1794 and chr. 1794.

Van Der Veer, Jacob, s/o Cornelius and Aeltje, chr. 19 Jan. 1794.

Schenck, Ellenor, d/o Garret Schenck and Mary Covenhoven, b. 9 Feb. 1794 and chr. 22 June 1794.

Van Mater, Betsy, d/o William Van Mater and Yda Bennet, b. 16 Feb. 1794 and chr. 13 July 1794.

Lane, Anna, d/o George Lane and Nelly Covenhoven, b. 25 Feb.1794 and chr. 20 Apr. 1794.

Schenck, John, s/o Daniel Schenck and Catherine Smock, b. 26 Feb. 1794 and chr. 18 May 1794.

Smock, Anne, d/o Hendrick Smock and Sarah Lane, b. 28 Feb. 1794 and chr. 6 Apr. 1794.

Kerl, Anne, d/o Uria, chr. 2 Mar. 1794.

Van Pelt, Mary, d/o Peter Van Pelt and Mary Hyer, b. 2 Mar. 1794 and chr. 8 Apr. 1794.

Morris, Mary, d/o Isaak Morris and Anne Brewer, b. 4 Mar. 1794 and chr. 4 May 1794.

Van Doorn, Pater, s/o Peter Van Doorn and Jane Williamse, b. 15 Apr. 1794 and chr. 7 June 1794.

Williamson, William, s/o William Williamson and Lena Brewer, b. 24 May 1794 and chr. 12 Oct. 1794.

Van Nortwyk, John, s/o Simion Van Nortwyk and Rebecka Hendrickson, b. 7 June 1794 and chr. 1794.

Wikoof, Euphame, d/o Pater Wikoof and Catherine Tyse, b. 19 June 1794 and chr. 20 July 1794.

Covenhoven, William, s/o Teunis Covenhoven and Matje Vanderhoof, b. 24 July 1794 and chr. 31 Aug. 1794.

Bennet, Maria, d/o Peter Bennet and Margeret Swart, b. 25 July 1794 and chr. 25 Dec. 1794.

Heyer, John, s/o William Heyer, chr. b. 21 Aug. 1794 and chr. 1794.

Clark, Benjamin, s/o Jane Clark (spouse of Obadia Harber), b. 4 Sep. 1794 and chr. 23 Nov. 1794.

Wikoof, Sarah, d/o Samuel Wikoof and Sarah Van Cleef, b. 11 Sep. 1794 and chr. 1799.

Logen, William, s/o Mary Logen, b. 13 Sep. 1794 and chr. 1795.

Covenhoven, John, s/o Garret Covenhoven, b. 17 Sep. 1794 and chr. 8 Dec. 1794.

Snyder, Aaltie, d/o William, b. 17 Sep. 1794 and chr. 19 July 1795.

Shepherd, Thomas, s/o Aeltje Shepherd, b. 20 Sep. 1794 and chr. 1795.

Van Kleef, John Kovenhoven, s/o Joseph Van Kleef and Nelly Schenck, b. 29 Oct. 1794 and chr. 1794.

Brewer, Elias, s/o Issack Brewer and Christina Van Brunt, b. 3 Nov. 1794 and chr. 1795.
Van Kerk, Jane, d/o Anne Van Kerk (spouse of Daniel Peecock), b. 25 Nov. 1794 and chr. 19 Apr. 1795.
States, Jane, d/o John States and Agnis Aamack, b. 3 Dec. 1794 and chr. 27 Jan. 1795.
Brewer, Catherine, d/o John Brewer and Nelly Hendrickson, chr. 1795.
Lane, Cornelius, s/o Cornelius. chr. 1795.
Denise, Jane, d/o Garret Denise and Nelly Schenck, b. 11 Jan. 1795 and chr. 24 May 1795.
Denise, Daniel, s/o Daniel Denise and Jane Schenck, b. 22 Jan. 1795 and chr. 1795.
Schenck, Maria, d/o Chrineyonce Schenck and Peggy Polhemus, b. 2 Feb. 1795 and chr. 1795.
Lane, Mary, d/o Matthew Lane and Catherine Smock, chr. 8 Feb. 1795.
Van Mater, Yda, d/o Joseph Van Mater and Yda Hendrickson, b. 20 Mar. 1795 and chr. 30 May 1795.
Schenck, Maria, d/o Teunis Schenck and Aaltje Vanderveer, b. 12 Apr. 1795 and chr. 1796.
Shepherd, Sarah, d/o Thomas Shepherd, b. 25 June 1795 and chr. 25 Oct. 1795.
Polhemus, Jacob, s/o Daniel Polhemus and Elizabeth Van Mater, chr. 28 June 1795.
Vander Veer, Elias, s/o Cornelius and Aeltje, b. 6 July 1795 and chr. 23 Oct. 1796.
Lyster, Sarah, d/o John Lyster and Anne Covenhoven, b. 12 July 1795 and chr. 23 Aug. 1795.
Schenck, Ellener, d/o Koert Schenck and Sarah Voorhees, b. 10 Aug. 1795 and chr. 6 Dec. 1795.
Hendrickson, William Herd, s/o Hendrick Hendrickson, b. 22 Sep. 1795 and chr. 29 Nov. 1795.
Covenhoven, William, s/o Garret Covenhoven and Mary Schenck, b. 12 Oct. 1795 and chr. 22 Nov. 1795.
Wykhoof, John, s/o Aukey Wykhoof and Mary Antonidis, b. 19 Oct. 1795 and chr. 1795.
Wykhoof, Roelef, s/o Aart Wykhoof and Nelly Covenhoven, chr. 8 Nov. 1795.
Covenhoven, Elizabeth, d/o Daniel Covenhoven and Margeret Rezeau, b. 9 Nov. 1795 and chr. 29 Dec. 1795.
Rees, Nancy, d/o Samuel Rees and Mary Galledet, chr. 1796.
Denise, Daniel, s/o Garret Denise and Elizabeth Davis, b. 15 Jan. 1796 and chr. 24 July 1796.

Dutch Reformed Church - Freehold and Middletown

Covenhoven or Schecck, Betsy, d/o Garret Schenck and Mary Covenhoven, b. 23 Jan. 1796 and chr. 5 Feb. 1804.
Clark, Susannah, d/o Jane Clark (spouse of Obadia Harber), b. 24 Feb. 1796 and chr. 29 May 1796.
Wykhoof, John, s/o Garret Wykhoof and Elizabeth Vanhorn, b. 29 Feb. 1796 and chr. 5 May 1796.
Covenhoven, Elizabeth, d/o Garret Covenhoven, chr. 28 Mar. 1796.
Wykhoof, Sarah Ann, d/o Peter Wykhoof and Catherine Tyse, chr. 17 Apr. 1796.
Vanderveer, Sarah Van Mater, d/o Albert Vanderveer and Phila Howlin, b. 30 July 1796 and chr. 5 June 1796.
Lane, Aletta, d/o George Lane and Ellenory Covenhoven, b. 14 Sep. 1796 and chr. 30 Oct. 1796.
Denise, John Schanck, s/o Daniel Denise and Jane Schaenck, b. 30 Sep. 1796 and chr. 31 Mar. 1797.
Schenck, Jane, d/o Garret Schenck and Jane Van Kerk, chr. 2 Nov. 1796.
Shumway, John Tyse, s/o Nehemia Shumway and Sarah Tyse, b. 10 Nov. 1796 and chr. 5 Mar. 1797.
Wykhoof, Samuel Covenhoven, s/o Cornelius Wykhoof and Aeltje Covenhoven, b. 29 Feb. 1796.
Brewer, Styje, d/o Isaac Brewer and Styntje Van Brunt, chr. 1797.
Schenck, Sarah, d/o Teunis Schenck and Aaltje Vanderveer, chr. 1797.
Williamson, Mary, d/o William Williamson and Lena Brower, b. 26 Jan 1797 and chr. 1798.
Van Cleef, Ellenor Schench, d/o Joseph Van Cleef and Nelly Schenck, b. 6 Feb. 1797 and chr. 26 Mar. 1797.
Bennet, Cornelius, s/o Peter Bennet and Margeret Swart, b. 7 Feb. 1797 and chr. 21 May 1797.
Snyder, Catharine, d/o Christopher Snyder and Sarah Lyster, b. 2 Mar. 1797 and chr. 7 May 1797.
Peecock, Sarah Vankerk, d/o Daniel Peecock and Anne Vankerk, b. 20 Mar. 1797 and chr. 4 June 1797.
Covenhoven, Hellena, d/o Teunis Covenhoven and Matje Van Derhoof, b. 30 Mar. 1797 and chr. 14 May 1797.
Smith, Cyrenius, s/o James Smith and Anne Van Mater, chr. 13 Apr. 1797.
Smith, Sally Ann, d/o James Smith and Anne Van Mater, chr. 13 Apr. 1797.
Snyder, Hendrick, s/o William Snyder and Elizabeth Pees, b. 19 Apr. 1797 and chr. 8 Oct. 1797.
Schenck, Sarah, d/o Peter Schenck and Sarah Shephard, b. 30 Apr. 1797 and chr. 18 June 1797.

Lane, Hendrick, s/o Matthew Lane and Catherine Smock, b. 24 May 1797 and chr. 9 July 1797.

Harber, William, s/o Obadia Harber and Jane Clarke, b. 1 June 1797 and chr. 1797.

Gorge, Aletta, d/o David Gorge and Aaltje Sherherd, b. 1 June 1797 and chr. 13 Aug. 1797.

Schenck, John, s/o Chrineyonce Schenck and Peggy Polhemus, b. 2 June 1797 and chr. 20 Aug. 1797.

Antonides, Jane, d/o Peter Antonidis and Mary Loyd, chr. 12 June 1797 and chr. 30 July 1797.

Williamson, John, s/o Hendrick Williamson and Nelly Covenhoven, b. 17 June 1797 and chr. 20 May 1798.

Covenhoven, Ellenor, d/o Albert Covenhoven and Elizabeth Shepherd, b. 22 June 1797 and chr. 3 Sep. 1797.

Wykhoof, Patience, d/o Aart Wykhoof and Nelly Covenhoven, b. 28 June 1797 and chr. 27 Aug. 1797.

Pelhemels, Catherine, d/o Daniel Pelhemels and Catherine Covenhoven, b. 16 July 1797 and chr. 1797.

Vandoorn, Arther, s/o Peter Vandoorn and Jane Williamse, b. 29 July 1797 and chr. 30 Apr. 1798.

Allen, Jane, d/o Jacob Allen and Margaret Covenhoven, chr. 23 July 1797.

Smock, Hendrick, s/o Hendrick Smock and Sarah Lane, b. 22 Aug. 1797 and chr. 26 Nov. 1797.

Lyster, Lucretia, d/o John P. Lyster and Anne Covenhoven, b. 25 Aug. 1797 and chr.15 Oct. 1797.

Van Mater, William, s/o Cornelius Van Mater and Orpha Tayler, b. 21 Sep. 1797 and chr. 1798.

Covenhoven, Anne, d/o Garret Covenhoven, chr. 26 Sep. 1797.

Hubbert, Cornelius Covenhoven, s/o Teunis Hubbert and Margaret Covenhoven, b. 30 Sep. 1797 and chr. 28 Oct. 1797.

Little, James Seabrook, s/o Daniel Little and Nelly Covenhoven, b. 23 Oct. 1797 and chr. 1798.

Shepherd, Catherine Voorhees, d/o Elisha Shepherd and Nelly Van Kerk, b. 25 Oct. 1797 and chr. 1798.

Denise, John, s/o Garret Denise and Elener Schenck, b. 11 Nov. 1797 and chr. 25 Mar. 1798.

Statesir, Isaac, s/o John Statesir and Agness Aamack, b. 15 Nov. 1797 and chr. 22 July 1798.

Smock, Elizabeth, d/o Garret Smock and Jane Schenck, b. 26 Nov. 1797 and chr. 7 Jan. 1798.

Dutch Reformed Church - Freehold and Middletown

Hendrickson, Elenor, d/o Hendrick Hendrickson and Phebe Van Mater, b. 7 Dec. 1797 and chr. 9 May 1798.
Vanderveer, Anne, d/o Garret Vanderveer and Jane Grigs, b. 16 Dec. 1797 and chr. 8 Apr. 1798.
Pelhemus, Abbe, s/o Daniel Pelhemus and Elizabeth Vanmater, b. 19 Dec. 1797 and chr. 1797.
Bennet, Aaltje, d/o John Bennet and Elizabeth Van Mater, chr. 1798.
Springsteen, Catherine, d/o William, chr. 1798.
Vander Veer, Anna, d/o Joseph Vander Veer and Sarah Tyse, chr. 1798.
Laqueer, William, s/o Jacobus Laqueer, b. 27 Jan. 1798 and chr. 1 Apr. 1798.
Vanderveer, John, s/o Cornelius and Aaltje, b. 14 Feb. 1798 and chr. 6 May 1798.
Wykhooff, Alette Williamse, d/o Auke Wykhooff and Mary Antonidis, b. 18 Feb. 1798 and chr. 1798..
Hendrickson, Jehannah, d/o William Hendrickson and Elizabeth Vanderype, b. 8 Mar. 1798 and chr. 1798.
Snyder, William, s/o Hendrick Snyder and Elizabeth Zutphen, b. 31 Mar. 1798 and chr. 1798.
Van Brunt, Keneth Hankinson, s/o William Van Brunt and Elizabeth Hankinson, b. 8 Apr. 1798 and chr. 24 June 1798.
Covenhoven, Ellener, d/o Peter Covenhoven and Sophia Du Bois, chr. 3 May 1798.
Smock, John, s/o Rulef Smock and Mary Van Doorn, b. 9 June 1798 and chr. 19 Aug. 1798.
Bennet, Caty Logen, d/o John Bennet and Sarah Logan, b. 1 July 1798 and chr. 14 July 1798.
Herbert, John Sebrook, s/o Obadia Herbert and Jane Clark, b. 3 Sep. 1798 and chr. 29 Sep. 1799.
Van Aarstdalen, Semion, s/o Jacob Van Aarstdalen and Sarah Smack, b. 7 Nov. 1798 and chr. 21 Feb. 1799.
Schenck, Arintha, d/o Schyler Schenck and Margeret Covenhoven, b. 24 Nov. 1798 and chr. 21 Feb. 1799.
Denise, Ann, d/o Garret Denise and Elizabeth Davis, b. 12 Sep. 1798 and chr. 16 Dec. 1798.
Bennet, Jane, d/o Ida Bennet (spouse of James Smith), b. 5 Oct. 1798 and chr. 25 Mar. 1799.
Schenck, Anna, d/o John Schenck and Mich_ Vanhuys, b. 10 Oct. 1798 and chr. 4 Nov. 1798.
Schenck, David Vandeveer, s/o Teunis Schenck and Aaltje Vanderveer, b. 1 Nov. 1798 and chr. 3 Feb. 1799.

Shepherd, Ida, d/o John Shepherd and Anne Covenhoven, b. 6 Nov. 1798 and chr. 31 Mar. 1799.
Wikoff, Margeret, d/o Samuel Wikoff and Sarah Van Cleef, b. 18 Nov. 1798 and chr. 2 Dec. 1799..
Covenhoven, Clementine Loyd, d/o Albert Covenhoven and Elizabeth Shepherd, b. 19 Dec. 1798 and chr. 7 Apr. 1798.
Peacock, John, s/o Daniel Peacock and Anne Van Kerk, chr. 1799.
Schenck, John, s/o Garret Schenck and Jane Van Kerk, chr. 1799.
Schenck, Sarah, d/o Roelef Schenck and Sarah Bennet, chr. 1799.
George, Rachel, d/o David George and Aaltje Shepherd, b. 4 Jan. 1799 and chr. 1799.
Schenck, Benjamin, s/o Garret Schenck and Mary Covenhoven, b. 9 Mar. 1799 and chr. 10 Apr. 1808.
Covenhoven, Micael, s/o Teunis Covenhoven and Matje Vanderhoof, b. 23 Mar. 1799 and chr. 19 May 1799.
Van Doorn, Jannete, d/o Peter Van Doorn and Jane Williamse, b. 30 Apr. 1799 and chr. 8 July 1799.
Lane, Anna, d/o Matthew Lane and Catharine Smock, chr. b. 5 May 1799 and chr. 19 July 1799.
Covenhoven, Sally Schenck, d/o Garret Covenhoven and Mary Schenck, b. 13 June 1799 and chr. 4 Aug. 1799.
Morris, Benjamin, s/o Isaak Morris and Anne Brewer, b. 29 June 1799 and chr. 25 Aug. 1799.
Brewer, Elizabeth, d/o Hendrick Brewer and Ledia Hendrickson, b. 1 July 1799 and chr. 2 June 1805.
Lane, John, s/o George Lane and Nelly Covenhoven, b. 16 July 1799 and chr. 1799.
Antonides, John, s/o Peter Antonidis and Mary Loyd, b. 19 July 1799 and chr. July 1799.
Schenck, Sally, d/o Garret Schenck and Nelly Covenhoven, b. 19 July 1799 and chr. 1799.
Schenck, Eliza, d/o Crynjans Schenck and Margeret Pelhemels, chr. 11 Aug. 1799.
Schenck, Ellenor, d/o Crynjans Schenck and Margeret Pelhemels, chr. 11 Aug. 1799.
Schenck, Garret, s/o Denise_ Schenck and Margeret Pelhemels, b. 14 Aug. 1799 and chr. 6 Oct. 1799.
Morrel, John, s/o Jacobus Morrel and Mary Hyer, b. 16 Aug. 1799 and chr. 1799.
Schenck, William, s/o Koert Schenck and Sarah Voorhees, b. 21 Aug. 1799 and chr. 1799.

Dutch Reformed Church - Freehold and Middletown

Lefferson, Lefford, s/o Auke Lefferson and Sarah Schenck, chr. 1 Sep. 1799.

Covenhoven, Margeret, d/o Garret Covenhoven and Nelly Myer, chr. 12 Oct. 1799.

Covenhoven, John, s/o Cornelius and Elizabeth Covenhoven, b. 10 Nov. 1799 and chr. 6 July 1800.

Brewer, David, s/o Cornelius Brewer and Jane Williamse, b. 16 Nov. 1799 and chr. 1799.

Brewer, Joseph, s/o Isaac Brewer and Styntje Van Brunt, chr. 17 Nov. 1799.

Vanderveer, John, s/o Garret Vanderveer and Jane Grigs, b. 26 Nov. 1799 and chr. 2 Feb. 1800.

Laqueer, Abraham Derunde, s/o Jacobus Laqueer, b. 1 Jan. 1800 and chr. 1800.

Bennet, Anne, d/o John Bennet and Elizabeth Van Mater, b. 21 Jan. 1800 and chr. 1800.

Heyer, William, s/o William Heyer and Margeret Hill, b. 26 Jan. 1800 and chr. 1803.

Hendrickson, Garret, s/o Hendrick Hendrickson and Phebe Van Mater, b. 21 Feb. 1800 and chr. 27 Apr. 1800.

Bennet, John, s/o Peter Bennet and Margeret Swart, b. 22 Feb. 1800 and chr. 1800.

Vanderveer, David, s/o Tunis D. Vanderveer and Jane Grigs, b. 7 Mar. 1800 and chr. 20 Apr. 1800.

Van Mater, John, s/o Benjamin and Anne, chr. 8 Mar. 1800 and chr. 1800.

Hubbert, William Henery, s/o Teunis Hubbert and Margeret Covenhoven, b. 28 Mar. 1800 and chr. 4 May 1800.

Shepherd, Elisha, s/o Elisha Shepherd and Nelly Vankerk, b. 4 Apr. 1800 and chr. 14 June 1801.

Covenhoven, Ellener, d/o Cornelius Covenhoven and Margeret Hans, b. 22 Apr. 1800 and chr. 25 May 1800.

Covenhoven, Daniel D., s/o Peter Covenhoven and Jane Denise, b. 24 Apr. 1800.

Van Mater, Cyrenius, s/o Cornelius Van Mater and Orpha Taylor, b. 6 May 1800 and chr. 13 July 1800.

Covenhoven, Barns Smock., s/o John Covenhoven and Anne Smock, b. 11 May 1800.

Covenhoven, Benjamin Du Bois, s/o Peter Covenhoven and Sophia Du Bois, b. 20 May 1800 and chr. 1800.

Denise, Ursula, d/o Garret Denise, b. 1 June 1800 and chr. 7 Dec. 1800.

Van Brunt, Richard, s/o Necolas Van Brunt and Elizabeth Jaques, b. 18

July 1800 and chr. 7 Sep. 1800.

Snyder, Phebe, d/o William Snyder and Elizabeth Pees, b. 14 Aug. 1800 and chr. 2 Sep. 1802.

Wykhoff, John, s/o William Wykhoff and Nelly Van Mater, b. 29 Feb. 1796 and b. 20 Aug. 1800 and chr. 2 Nov. 1800.

Schenck, Annah Mariah, d/o John Schenck and Mich_ Vanhuys, b. 21 Sep. 1800 and chr. 19 Oct. 1800.

Harbert, Ruben Brown, s/o Obadia Harbert and Jane Clark, b. 8 Oct. 1800 and chr. 18 Oct. 1801.

Covenhoven, Daniel, s/o Daniel Covenhoven and Margeret Rezeau, b. 10 Oct. 1800 and chr. 30 Nov. 1800.

Bennet, Barns, s/o Barns Bennet and Geertje Williamson, b. 21 Nov. 1800 and chr. 2 Aug. 1801.

Morrel, Elizabeth Brower, d/o Jacobus Morrel and Maty Hyer, b. 8 Dec. 1800 and chr. 1801.

Schenck, Jane, d/o Denise_ Schenck and Margeret Pelhemels, b. 8 Dec. 1800 and chr. 8 Mar. 1801.

Schenck, Garret, s/o Roelef Schenck and Sarah Bennet, b. 16 Dec. 1799 and chr. 1801.

CHRIST CHURCH AT SHREWSBURY
Baptisms: 1733-1800

_____, Aaron, s/o Peter a p--- negro, 4 July 1760
_____, Abraham, a negro boy with Mr. Samuel Leonard, 22 May 1749
Abraham, James, s/o Jas. Jr. and _____, 27 May 1764
Abraham, James, 25 May 1766
Abraham, John, s/o James and Gavut, 3 Aug 1735
Abraham, John, s/o James Jr. and _____, 3 June 1759
Abraham, Latitia, d/o James and _____, 25 May 1766
Abraham, Lydia, d/o James Jr. and _____, 11 July 1762
Abraham, Phoebe, d/o John and Abigail, 8 June 1766
Abraham, Rebecca, d/o James and Ann, 15 Aug 1756
Abraham, Ruhannah, d/o James and _____, 30 Aug 1767
Abraham, Samuel, s/o James and Ann, 28 Aug 1757
Akin, Mary, adult, 3 Apl 1758
Akin, Rachel, d/o Timothy and _____, 2 Apl 1758
Allen, Catharine, adult, 11 July 1756
Allen, Mary, d/o William and Elizabeth, 25 Dec 1763
Allen, Mary, adult, 20 Apl 1740
Amey, Elisha, s/o John and Agnes, 14 Apl 1741
Amey, Hannah, d/o John and Elizabeth, 9 Aug 1764
Amey, William, s/o John and Agnes, 14 Apl 1748
Anderson, Ann, d/o Jonathan and _____, 27 Aug 1749
Anderson, Joseph, s/o Jonathan and _____, 27 Aug 1749
Anderson, Timothy, s/o James and _____, 5 Oct 1735
Andruvat, Rebecca, 30 Oct 1763
_____, Anthony, Negro child belonging to Mrs. Jane Forman, __ Sep 1749
Applegate, Hannah, d/o John and _____, 14 May 1753
Applegate, Rebecca, d/o John and Hannah, 7 Mar 1750
Applegate, Samuel, s/o John and Hannah, 25 Mar 1747-8
Applin, Thomas, s/o Thomas and _____, 15 June 1735
Arvey, David, s/o John and _____, 14 June 1749
Ash, Ann, d/o Gilbert and _____, 6 May 1753
Ashfield, Catharine, d/o Lewis Morris and Elizabeth, 27 Nov 1757
Ashfield, Euphemia, d/o Lewis Morris and Elizabeth, 7 Jan 1754
Ashfield, Elizabeth, d/o Lewis Morris and Elizabeth, 30 Nov 1755
Ashfield, Isabella, d/o Lewis Morris and Elizabeth, 7 Jan 1750
Ashfield, Mary, d/o Lewis Morris and Elizabeth, 16 Aug 1752
Ashfield, Lydia, d/o Lewis Morris and Elizabeth, 30 Nov 1755

Ashfield, Redford, s/o Lewis Morris and Elizabeth, 17 Mar 1751
Ashley, Cornelius, s/o Dennis and Mary, 25 Jan 1746-7
Audrey, Jacob, s/o Audrey and _____, 3 Feb 1750
Bainbridge, Hannah, 9 Nov 1812
_____, Smelziel, d/o Henry and Maria
Bainbridge, Maria Reid, d/o Henry and Maria, 9 Nov 1812
Bailey, Edward, s/o Rose O.W., 9 June 1751
Ball, Lydia, 24 July 1768
Ballman, Gersham, s/o Thomas and Ann, 18 June 1752
_____, Barbara, d/o 1 Nov 1761
Barclay, Catharine, d/o Peter and Jane, 30 July 1758
Barclay, Elizabeth, d/o John and Catharine, 19 Sep 1752
Barclay, Lydia, d/o David and Catharine, 20 July 1766
Barclay, Jane, d/o David and Catharine, 15 Feb 1767
Barclay, Samuel, s/o John and _____, 14 May 1753
Barwick, Benjamin, s/o John and Deborah, 22 Apl 1739
Barwick, Deborah, w/o John, 22 Apl 1739
Barwick, Robert, s/o John and Deborah, 22 Apl 1739
Bartley, Peter, s/o James and Catharine, 28 Aug 1735
Bartley, William, s/o John and Catharine, 20 Sep 1747
Bates, Agnus, d/o Richard and _____, 17 May 1757
Bates, Ann, d/o Richard and _____, 4 Apl 1746
Bates, Andrew, s/o Richard and _____, 14 Apl 1748
Bates, Catharine, d/o Richard and _____, 27 Apl 1766
Bates, James, s/o Richard and _____, 14 May 1755
Bates, John, s/o Richard and _____, 8 Nov 1752
Bates, Mary, d/o Richard and _____, 15 Apl 1750
Bates, Richard, s/o Richard and _____, 12 Dec 1762
Bates, Sarah, d/o Richard and Agnes, 3 July 1760
Bearney, Ann, d/o John and Ann, 6 Mar 1747
Beckerer, Catharine, d/o John and Mary, 25 June 1755
Beddel, Bethesda, d/o Benaiah and Sarah, 21 July 1751
Bell, Deborah, w/o Thomas, 27 Oct 1760
Bell, Jacob, s/o Thomas and Deborah, 29 July 1764
Bell, James, s/o Thomas and _____, 22 Sep 1754
Bell, James, s/o Thomas and _____, 3 Oct 1756
Bell, Jeremiah, s/o Thomas and Leah, 3 June 1748
Bell, Theodosia, d/o Thomas and Deborah, 5 Apl 1767
Bell, Thomas, s/o Thomas and Deborah, 4 July 1762
Bell, — s/o Thomas and Deborah, 27 Oct 1760
_____, Bella, d/o Rachel a negro belonging to Miss Isabella Kearney, 6 May 1756

Christ Church at Shrewsbury

Benjamin, Leah, 17 Apl 1768
_____, Benjamin, a negro belonging to Capt Robert Troup, 1 Nov 1764
_____, Benjamin, a black belonging to John Croes Jr., 12 Oct 1819
Bennett, Ann, 14 Jan 1823
Bennett, Sarah, d/o Edward and _____, 11 June 1809
_____, Bethana, d/o Tom a free negro, 28 July 1765
_____, Bethsheba, d/o Robin and Elizabeth, 27 Aug 1751
Betts, Jane Gamage, d/o _____ and Jane, 11 Oct 1771
Bishop, Rachel, d/o Rachel and Thomas, 7 May 1750
Bizzard, Eleanor, d/o David and _____, 29 Apl 1756
Blain, Anna, d/o Thomas and Alice, 22 May 1754
Bodine, Anna, d/o Vincent and _____, 11 June 1764
Bodine, James, s/o Vincent and _____, 8 May 1757
Bodine, Mary, d/o John and Dorethy, 24 Mar 1751
Boggs, Elizabeth, d/o Dr. James and Mary, 3 Apl 1768
Boggs, James, s/o James and Mary, 7 May 1769
Boggs, Rebecca, d/o Dr. James and Mary, 20 June 1773
Boggs, Robert, s/o James and Mary, 14 Dec 1766
Boggs, Thomas, s/o Dr. James and Mary, 10 Aug 1771
Boughker, Abraham, s/o Stephen and _____, 20 Sep 1749
Boughker, Mary, d/o Widow Boughker, 20 Apl 1749
Boughker, Sarah, d/o Widow Boughker, 20 Apl 1749
Boune, William, s/o Mr. Boune and his wife, 7 Mar 1750
Bowie, William, s/o Gerhsam and Elizabeth, 29 June 1747
Bowde, John, s/o Peter and Frances, 20 Apl 1749
Bowde, Peter, s/o Peter and Frances, 20 Apl 1749
Bowman, Elizabeth, d/o Edward and _____, 4 Feb 1753
Boyles, Daniel, s/o Charles and Mary, 1 Nov 1764
Boyles, Michael, s/o Charles and Mary, 1 Nov 1764
Boyles, Margaret, d/o Charles and Mary, 1 Nov 1764
Boyles, Mary, w/o Charles, 1 Nov 1764
Boyles, Patience, d/o Charles and Mary, 1 Nov 1764
Bradsbury, Jacob, s/o James and Elizabeth, 13 Mar 1742-3
Bradsbury, Hannah, d/o James and Elizabeth, 25 Jan 1740-1
Bradshaw, Ann, d/o James and _____, 24 Sep 1758
Bradshaw, Henry, s/o James and _____, 27 Apl 1749
Bradshaw, James, s/o James and _____, 21 Apl 1751
Bradshaw, Mary, d/o James and _____, 13 Apl 1755
Bradshaw, Margaret, d/o James and Mary, 31 May 1747
Brewer, Rachel, 10 May 1750
Brian, Rhoda, d/o Willam and Rachel, 8 July 1750
Brooks, Mary, d/o _____, 3 Oct 1756

Brown, Abram, 10 May 1751
Brown, Agnes, d/o John and Barary, 25 Feb 1747-8
Brown, Isabella, d/o Arthur and _____, 26 June 1754
Brown, James, s/o Andrew and Sarah, 24 Feb 1771
Brown, Jane, d/o Arthur and Jane, 18 June 1752
Brown, Jane, d/o John and Barbary, 25 May 1750
Brown, Josiah, s/o William and Mary, 21 Mar 1762
Brown, Mary, d/o Arthur and Jane, 25 Feb 1747-8
Brown, Mary, d/o John and _____, 4 Apl 1746
Brown, Martha, w/o Abram, 10 May 1751
Brown, Richard, s/o Abram and Martha, 10 May 1751
Brown, Rosseau, s/o William and Catharine, 8 June 1766
Brown, Samuel, s/o Abram and Martha, 10 May 1751
Brown, Sarah, d/o Caleb and Phebe, 4 Nov 1753
Buckennes, Jane, d/o John and Isabel, 28 Aug 1735
Buckelow, Isabella, d/o John and _____, 23 May 1757
Buckelow, Isaac, s/o John and Esther, 11 June 1764
Buckelow, Jane, d/o John and Esther, 30 Oct 1763
Buckelow, Jennet, d/o John and Elizabeth, 30 July 1746
Buckelow, John, s/o Abraham and _____, 23 May 1757
Buckulow, John, s/o Thomas and Mary, 2 Aug 1753
Buckulow, Mary, d/o Thomas and Mary, 2 Aug 1753
Buckolow, Sarah, d/o John and Esther, 30 Oct 1763
Bullman, Ann, d/o Thomas and Ann, 17 Aug 1751
Bullman, Gertrude, d/o Thomas and _____, 27 Aug 1766
Bullman, Joseph, s/o Thomas and Ann, 17 Aug 1751
Bullman, Rose, d/o Thomas and Ann, 17 Aug 1751
Bullman, Sarah, d/o Thomas and Ann, 17 Aug 1751
Bullman, Sussannah, d/o Thomas and Ann, 17 Aug 1751
Bullman, Thomas, s/o Thomas and Ann, 17 Aug 1751
Bullock, John, s/o John and _____, 5 Oct 1735
Bunnel, Edward, s/o Moses and Alice, 14 Sep 1752
Bunnel, Joseph, s/o Edward and Margaret, 14 Sep 1752
Burden, Amey, d/o Joseph and _____, 8 Apl 1750
Burdoigne, Aphy, d/o Frances and Abigal, 5 Aug 1750
Burdoigne, Joel, s/o Frances and Abigal, 27 Oct 1745
Burdoigne, John, s/o Frances and Abigal, 27 Dec 1747
Burg, William, 12 Nov 1749
Burger, Catharine, d/o Elias and _____, 23 Sep 1753
Burger, Sussana, d/o Elias and _____, 23 Sep 1753
Burns, Elizabeth, d/o John and Mary, 28 June 1747
Caffrey, Hannah, d/o John and _____, 17 Mar 1744-5

Christ Church at Shrewsbury

Cahall, Lawrence, s/o William and Mary, 5 Sep 1756
Cahart, Lord, s/o Philip son of William and Phebe, 3 Aug 1735
Cahart, William, s/o Philip son of William and Phebe, 3 Aug 1735
Caley, Catharine, d/o Henry and Christian, 5 Sep 1756
Caley, John, s/o John and _____, 5 Sep 1756
Caley, Rebecca, d/o John and _____, 5 Sep 1756
Campbell, John and Rachel, 13 July 1756
Campbell, Andrew, s/o Robert and _____, 22 July 1764
Campbell, Duncan, s/o John and Rachel, 10 June 1753
Campbell, Collin, s/o Alexander and _____, 21 Mar 1762
Campbell, Eleanor, d/o John and Rachel, 1 Feb 1756
Campbell, Elizabeth, d/o John and Rachel, 23 Apl 1758
Campbell, Isabella, d/o Robert and _____, 11 July 1762
Campbell, George, s/o John and Rachel, 17 Apl 1748
Campbell, John, s/o John and Rachel, 7 Apl 1751
Campbell, Jane, d/o Robert and Mary, 25 Mar 1757
Campbell, Mary, w/o Robert, 25 Mar 1757
Campbell, Mary, d/o Robert and _____, 27 Apl 1766
Campbell, Mathias, s/o Robert and _____, 27 Sep 1759
Campbell, William, s/o Robert and Frances, 9 Feb 1746
Carman, Samuel, 6 Nov 1748
Carpenter, Sarah, 19 Sep 1813
_____, Catharine, d/o William and Lucy _____
Carrigan, John, s/o William and Ann, 1 Dec 1749
_____, Catharine, negro child belonging to Widow Forman, 23 Aug 1752
Chamberlain, Ann, d/o John and Mary, 9 May 1750
Chamberlain, Catharine, d/o of the widow, 8 May 1748
Chamberlain, Derick, s/o William and Catharine, 18 May 1748
Chamberlain, James, 6 May 1750
Chamberlain, Lydia, 9 May 1750
Chamberlain, Mary, w/o John, 9 May 1750
Chamberlain, Thomas, 21 May 1748
Chamberlain, Valena, 21 May 1748
Chamberlain, William, 18 May 1748
Chamberlain, William, Sev..., 26 May 1749
Chamberlain, Zelphia, d/o William and _____, 28 May 1749
Chambers, Elizabeth, 9 Mar 1739-40
Chapman, Catharine, d/o Catharine, 9 Apl 1746
_____, Chloe, a negro belonging to Mrs. Isabella Kearney, 31 Aug 1766
Clark, Alexander, s/o Richard and _____, 25 Aug 1751
Clark, Catharine, w/o John, 14 Feb 1773

Clark, Job, s/o Richard and _____, 23 Aug 1761
Clark, John, s/o John and Catharine, 6 Feb 1773
Clark, John, s/o John and Catharine, 9 May 1773
Clark, Moses, s/o Richard and _____, 19 June 1757
Clarke, Richard, s/o Richard and _____, 26 May 1754
Clayton, Ann, 11 May 1735
Clayton, David, 11 May 1735
Clayton, Hannah, 11 May 1735
Clayton, Isabel, 11 May 1735
Clayton, John, 11 May 1735
Clayton, Jonatha, 11 May 1735
Clayton, Mary, 11 May 1735
Cline, Frances M, adult, 19 Aug 1821
Cline, Mary Mott, adult, 25 Dec 1822
Colvill, Elizabeth, d/o Thomas and Elizabeth, 9 Aug 1764
Colvil, Thomas, s/o Thomas and _____, 3 July 1760
Colwell, Eleanor, d/o Thomas and Elizabeth, 25 Feb 1747-8
Colwell, John, s/o Thomas and Elizabeth, 9 May 1749
Colwell, Jedau, d/o Thomas and _____, 14 May 1755
Colwell, Mary, d/o Thomas and _____, 23 Oct 1751
Colwell, Martha, d/o Thomas and Elizabeth, 25 Feb 1747-8
Colwell, William, s/o Thomas and Elizabeth, 25 Feb 1747-8
Combs, Ann, d/o John and Mary, 28 Aug 1757
Combs, Ann, d/o John and Sarah, 28 Aug 1757
Combs, Hannah, adult, 22 June 1766
Combs, Jane, d/o John and _____, 2 Sep 1764
Combs, John, s/o John and Mary, 28 Aug 1757
Combs, Phebe, d/o Joseph and _____, 26 Nov 1752
Compton, Ann, d/o John and _____, 28 May 1757
Connor, James, adult, 22 July 1764
Cooper, David, s/o Philip and _____, 19 Mar 1775
Cooper, Elizabeth, d/o Philip and _____, 11 Mar 1764
Cooper, George, s/o George and Barbara, 16 Aug 1752
Cooper, George, s/o Philip and _____, 19 Mar 1775
Cooper, Henry, s/o Henry and Ann, 17 Mar 1754
Cooper, Jasper, s/o Philip and _____, 5 Oct 1755
Cooper, Lena, d/o John and Mary, 5 Nov 1752
Cooper, Michar, s/o Philip and _____, 19 Mar 1775
Cooper, Sarah, d/o Philip and _____, 19 Mar 1775
Cooper, William, s/o Henrick and _____, 5 Oct 1755
Cook, Abraham, s/o Lilas and _____, 20 May 1750
Cook, Hannah, d/o Lilas and Sarah, 24 May 1752

Christ Church at Shrewsbury

Cook, Mary, d/o Lilas and _____, 14 May 1758
Cook, Nathaniel, 20 Aug 1748
Cook, Sarah, d/o Lilas and Mary, 11 Oct 1747
Cook, Uriah, s/o Lilas and Mary, 13 June 1756
Cooke, Annastatia, d/o Samuel and Graham, 21 Mar 1771
Cooke, Grace, d/o Samuel and Graham, 25 Aug 1765
Cooke, Isabella, d/o Samuel and Graham, 19 July 1767
Cooke, Lydia, d/o Samuel and Graham, 9 Apl 1769
Cooke, Mary, d/o Samuel and Graham, 23 Apl 1758
Cooke, Michael, s/o Samuel and Graham, 30 Oct 1763
Cooke, Sarah, d/o Samuel and Graham, 27 Apl 1760
Cooke, Thomas, s/o Samuel and Graham, 7 Sep 1761
Cotes, Rebecca, d/o John and Mary, 25 Oct 1761
Cotterly, James, s/o John and Elizabeth, 11 Oct 1747
Couper, Benjamin, adult, 24 July 1768
Couper, Ezekiah, s/o John and Mary, 3 Aug 1746
Couper, James, s/o Joseph and Deborah, 20 Feb 1746
Couper, John, s/o John and Mary, 29 July 1750
Couper, Mary, w/o John, 29 July 1750
Couper, Mary, d/o Hendrick and Ann, 14 Apl 1751
Couper, Phebe, adult, 24 July 1768
Couper, Samuel, s/o John and Mary, 29 July 1750
Couper, William, s/o John and Mary, 6 May 1746
Cowen, Anna, d/o John and Mary, 27 May 1753
Cox, Thomas, s/o Thomas and Elizabeth, 14 Apl 1751
Cox, William, s/o Longfield and Ann, 17 Dec 1752
Craddock, Arabella, d/o   - and Mary, 15 July 1739
Craddock, Elizabeth, adult, 20 Apl 1740
Craddock, Elizabeth, d/o John and _____, 10 Jan 1771
Craddock, John, s/o John and Ann Martha, 22 Sep 1745
Craddock, John, s/o John and _____, 10 Jan 1771
Craddock, Margaret, d/o John and _____, 31 July 1774
Craddock, Sarah, d/o John and _____, 10 Jan 1771
Craddock, Thomas, s/o John and _____, 10 Jan 1771
Craddock, William, s/o John and _____, 10 Nov 1771
Craddock, — , s/o William and _____, 15 June 1740
Crafts, Ann, d/o Thomas and _____, 25 Mar 1746
Crafts, Catharine, d/o Thomas and Elizabeth, 1 Jan 1737-8
Crafts, Elizabeth, d/o Thomas and _____, 25 Mar 1746
Crafts, Mary, d/o Thomas and _____, 24 Apl 1746
Crafts, Margaret, d/o Thomas and _____, 24 Apl 1746
Crain, Azro Amander, s/o Samuel and Nancy, 9 Mar 1823

Crain, Amanda Esther, d/o Samuel and Nancy, 9 Mar 1823
Crain, Nancy, adult, 16 Feb 1823
Crain, Oscar Valverde, s/o Samuel and Nancy, 9 Mar 1823
Crain, Orlando, s/o Samuel and Nancy, 9 Mar 1823
Crain, Samuel, s/o Samuel and Nancy, 9 Mar 1823
Crain, Samuel, adult, 16 Feb 1823
Cravat, Aaron, 21 Apl 1752
Crawford, Andrew, s/o James and Margaret, 6 Sep 1761
Crawford, Hannah, d/o James and Margaret, 18 Sep 1758
Crawford, Peter, s/o James and Margaret, 16 Oct 1763
Crawford, Thomas, s/o James and Margaret, 8 June 1766
Crips, Richard, s/o William and Sarah, 2 Apl 1758
Croes, Anna Theodosia, d/o Rev. John and Eleanor, 12 Oct 1879
Croes, Cath.Van Mater, d/o Rev. John and Eleanor, 31 Oct 1813
Croes, Charlotte Martha, d/o Rev. John and Eleanor, 31 Oct 1815
Croes, Eleanor Rattoone, d/o Rev. John and Eleanor, 10 Sep 1821
Croes, Ralph Van Mater, s/o Rev. John and Eleanor, 30 Sep 1817
Crossland, Elizabeth, d/o George and Elizabeth, 3 Mar 1749
Crossland, George, s/o George and Elizabeth, 3 Mar 1749
_____, Daniel, negro belonging to Mrs. Isabella Kearny, 31 Aug 1766
Darbe, John, s/o John and Eleanor, 3 Dec 1749
Dassigny, Judith, d/o Benjamin and _____, 6 May 1755
Debow, John, adult, 26 May 1822
Debole, Christian, s/o Christian and Mary, 18 Dec 1763
Dehart, Elizabeth, d/o Mauritz and _____, 28 Mar 1766
Dennis, Amelia, d/o Benjamin and _____, 26 Aug 1764
Dennis, Anthony, s/o Jacob and _____, 5 May 1765
Dennis, Anthony, s/o Jacob and Clement, 28 Nov 1735
Dennis, Benjamin, s/o Jacob and Clement, 27 July 1740
Dennis, Benjamin, s/o Jacob and Clement, 13 Aug 1738
Dennis, Clement, d/o Anthony and _____, 18 Apl 1773
Dennis, Clement, w/o Jacob, 28 Nov 1735
Dennis, Elizabeth, d/o Jacob and Clement, 28 Nov 1735
Dennis, Gordon, s/o Jacob and Mary, 27 May 1799
Dennis, Hannah, d/o Anthony and Clemence, 14 June 1812
Dennis, Hannah, d/o Jacob and Clement, 28 Nov 1735
Dennis, Increase, d/o Jacob and Clement, 28 Nov 1735
Dennis, Increase, d/o Jacob and Clement, 30 Jan 1742-3
Dennis, Isaac, s/o Jacob and _____, 1 Feb 1747
Dennis, Jacob, s/o Benjamin and _____, 1 Oct 1766
Dennis, Jacob, s/o Jacob and Clement, 28 Nov 1735
Dennis, James S, s/o Jacob and _____, 17 Mar 1744-5

Christ Church at Shrewsbury

Dennis, John Ellsworth, s/o Woodward and Hilah, 27June 1824
Dennis, John, s/o Benjamin and _____, 2 Oct 1768
Dennis, Joseph, s/o Jacob Jr and _____, 25 Oct 1762
Dennis, Lewis, s/o Samuel and Ann, 22 May 1738
Dennis, Littleton, s/o Jacob Jr and _____, 4 Apl 1768
Dennis, Margaret, d/o Jacob Jr and _____, 9 May 1773
Dennis, Margaret, d/o Samuel and Ann, 11 July 1736
Dennis, Mary, d/o Jacob and _____, 28 Oct 1770
Dennis, Mercy, d/o Benjamin and _____, 14 Nov 1773
Dennis, Samuel, s/o Jacob and Clement, 28 Nov 1735
Dennis, Samuel, s/o Jacob and Clement, 13 Aug 1738
Dennis, Samuel, s/o Jacob Jr and _____, 22 Feb 1756
Dennis, Sarah, d/o Jacob and Clement, 28 Nov 1735
Dennis, Thomas, s/o Benjamin and _____, 17 Oct 1771
Dennis, William, s/o Anthony and Clemence, 14 June 1812
Dennis, Zilpha, w/o Joseph, 9 Dec 1822
Derriskill, John, s/o Dennis and _____, 22 July 1764
Derriskill, Sarah, d/o Dennis and _____, 22 July 1764
Desbourere, Mary, d/o Peter and Jane Roger, 31 Jan 1746-7
Dey, Andrew, s/o James and Sarah, 3 Jan 1749
Dey, Angeline, d/o James Jr. and _____, 12 Apl 1756
Dey, Catharine, d/o James and _____, 10 Aug 1760
Dey, Dinah, d/o William and Hannah, 1 Nov 1761
Dey, John, s/o Lawrence and _____, 24 Feb 1751
Dey, John, s/o William and Hannah, 9 June 1765
Dey, Joseph, s/o James and Margaret, 2 Oct 1763
Dey, Lewis, s/o James Jr. and _____, 7 May 1758
Dey, Margaret, d/o James and Margaret, 19 Aug 1753
Dey, Mary, d/o James and Margaret, 1 Nov 1761
Dey, Rebecca, d/o William and Hannah, 21 June 1767
Dey, Sarah, d/o James and Sarah, 13 Nov 1750
_____, Diego, negro belonging to Jos Throngmorton Jr., 23 Aug 1752
_____, Dinah, negro belonging to Mrs. Isabella Kearny, 31 Aug 1766
Dixon, Jane, adult, 1 Jan 1758
Dorcey, Elizabeth, d/o William and _____, 9 Aug 1764
Dorcey, Mary, d/o William and _____, 9 Aug 1764
_____, Dorothy, Negro belonging to Capt Robert Troup, 1 Nov 1764
Doughan, Cornelius, s/o Patrick and _____, 3 June 1750
Doughan, John, s/o Patrick and Margaret, 7 June 1747
Doughan, Mary, d/o Patrick and _____, 11 Sep 1748
Doughan, Patrick, s/o Patrick and _____, 1 June 1755
Dressgill, Isabella, d/o Dennis and Hannah, 30 Mar 1768

Dressgill, Joseph, s/o Dennis and Hannah, 30 Mar 1768
Drugan, Eleanor, d/o Patrick and Margaret, 22 Aug 1756
Drugan, William, s/o Patrick and _____, 28 May 1758
Dunham, Thankful, Adult, 26 May 1771
Dye, Ann, d/o James and Sarah, 30 July 1746
Dye, Catharine, d/o Joseph and Martha, 20 Apl 1749
Dye, Dinah, d/o James Jr. and Margaret, 28 July 1751
Dye, Elizabeth, d/o James and Sarah, 25 Mar 1748
Dye, Elizabeth, d/o Lawrence and Sarah, 23 Aug 1747
Dye, Mary, d/o James Jr. and _____, 4 Apl 1735
Dye, Phebe, d/o James and Sarah, 27 May 1750
Dye, Phebe, d/o Joseph and Martha, 20 Apl 1749
Eatton, Joanna, 12 May 1761
Eaton, John, s/o Joseph and _____, 26 Apl 1752
Eaton, Margaret, Adult, 16 Apl 1752
Eaton, Thomas, s/o Dr. Jos Eaton, 30 Nov 1755
Early, Catharine, d/o Patrick and _____, 8 Feb 1747
Early, Elizabeth, d/o Patrick and _____, 8 Feb 1747
Early, Mary, d/o Patrick and _____, 14 June 1749
Eastleek, Alice, d/o John and _____, 7 Nov 1756
Eastleek, Alexander, s/o John and _____, 25 Feb 1753
Eastleek, John, s/o John and _____, 8 May 1768
Eastleek, Mary, d/o John and _____, 29 Aug 1750
Eastleek, Sarah, d/o John and _____, 8 May 1768
Eastleek, Stephen, s/o John and _____, 8 May 1768
Eastleek, Stephen, s/o John and _____, 4 July 1756
_____, Eda, negro girl, 15 Oct 1766
Edwards, Philip, s/o Philip and Elizabeth, 7 June 1739
Egbert, Abraham, s/o John and _____, 23 Aug 1747
Egbert, John, s/o John and Margaret, 21 Apl 1752
Egbert, William, s/o John and Margaret, 7 Mar 1750
Egbert, William, s/o John and _____, 16 Oct 1753
Elimens, Mareviasteot, d/o Henrichus and Anna Maria, 2 June 1754
_____, Elizabeth, negro woman belonging to Mrs. Morford, 4 Oct 1751
_____, Elizabeth, d/o Thomas and Elizabeth, 15 Jan 1751
_____, Elizabeth, a mulatto belonging to Mr. Cox, 5 Oct 1750
_____, Elizabeth, a negro servant, 25 July 1746
_____, Elizabeth, negro women belonging to Widow Forman, 23 Aug 1752
Emmonds, Ann, d/o Abraham and _____, 19 Aug 1753
Emmonds, Abraham, s/o Abraham and Margaret, 24 Aug 1760
Emmonds, Abraham, 30 June 1751

Christ Church at Shrewsbury

Emmonds, Isaac, s/o Abraham and Margaret, 14 July 1751
Emmonds, Isaac, s/o Isaac and Jane, 27 June 1765
Emmonds, John, s/o Abraham and Margaret, 15 Aug 1756
Erickson, Lydia, d/o Thomas and Margaret, 1 May 1763
Eshile, Margaret, d/o Joseph and Mary, 30 June 1746
Estle, Thomas Little, s/o William and Abigail, 25 Dec 1814
Evaut, Agnes, d/o Bernard and _____, 3 Aug 1766
Everingham, John, s/o Joseph and Amey, 8 Apl 1750
Felmore, David, s/o Christian and Margaret, 23 Oct 1763
Felmore, Jacob, s/o Christian and Margaret, 23 Oct 1763
Felmore, Moses, s/o Christian and Margaret, 2 Oct 1768
Fennil, John, s/o John and Jane, 24 Nov 1751
Ferrymore, Thomas, s/o Thomas and _____, 18 Dec 1743
Fenton, Ann, d/o Thomas and Margaret, 5 June 1747
Fenton, Charlotte, d/o John and Sarah, 7 June 1818
Fenton, William, s/o Thomas and Margaret, 5 June 1747
Ferril, James, s/o James and _____, 12 Apl 1756
Ferril, Jane, d/o James and Mary, 19 Sep 1752
Ferril, Mary, d/o James and _____, 22 May 1754
Finemore, Edith, d/o Edith and Jos West, 28 Oct 1749
Fisher, Hannah, d/o John and Avicia, 3 June 1747
Fisher, Sarah, d/o John and Avicia, 13 Sep 1747
Fisher, Zephanaih, s/o John and Avicia, 13 Sep 1747
Fetz Randolph, Isaac, s/o Isaac and Hannah, 8 July 1750
Fetz Randolph, Mary, d/o Isaac and Hannah, 8 July 1750
Flin, Catharine, d/o Peter and Charity, 26 May 1811
Forman, Ann, d/o John and Jane, 9 Feb 1746
Forman, Catharine, d/o John and _____, 14 Sep 1755
Forman, Dennis, s/o John and _____, 6 May 1759
Forman, Elizabeth Ann, d/o Denise I and Elizabeth, 17 Apl 1814
Forman, Emelina, d/o Denise I and Elizabeth, 8 July 1810
Forman, James, s/o John and Jane, 5 May 1748
Forman, Jane, d/o John and _____, 19 Aug 1753
Forman, John, s/o John and _____, 19 Apl 1761
Forman, John, s/o Jonathan Jr. and Sarah, 14 June 1747
Forman, Jonathan, s/o Jonathan and Sarah, 11 Mar 1753
Forman, Mary, d/o John and _____, 1 Feb 1767
Forman, Mary, d/o Jonathan and Sarah, 9 Nov 1755
Forman, Margaret, d/o Jonathan and Sarah, 27 May 1750
Forman, Samuel, s/o John and _____, 18 Sep 1763
Fortune, Henry, Negro servant of Mr. Leonard, 18 Sep 1748
Fortune, William, Negro servant of Tunis Denis, 19 Aug 1750

Francis, Adonijah, d/o John and Mary, 19 Sep 1752
Francis, Allen, s/o John and Mary, 19 Sep 1752
Francis, Elizabeth, Adult, 25 Sep 1758
Francis, Euphemia, d/o Richard and _____, 8 May 1757
Francis, James, s/o Richard and _____, 10 Apl 1754
Francis, John, s/o Richard and Sarah, 3 May 1752
Francis, Letitia, d/o — and Sarah, 25 May 1746
Francis, Margaret, Adult, 25 Sep 1758
Francis, Margaret, d/o Mr and Sarah, 25 Feb 1747-8
Francis, Rachel, d/o Richard and Sarah, 14 Nov 1749
Francis, Valerea, Adult, 25 Sep 1758
_____, Francis, Negro child belonging to Widow Forman, 23 Aug 1752
_____, Frederic, s/o 22 Feb 1756
French, Abigail, d/o John and _____, 20 May 1750
French, Ann, Adult, 22 May 1754
French, Samuel, s/o Thomas and _____, 17 July 1757
Frees, Patience, d/o James and _____, 15 June 1735
Frost, Esther, w/o John, 1 Apl 1768
_____, Gabriel, Negro child belonging to Widow Forman, 23 Aug 1752
Gang, Anthony, s/o John and _____, 12 Sep 1756
Gang, Henry, s/o John and _____, 12 Sep 1756
Gang, Mathias, s/o John and _____, 12 Sep 1756
Gang, Sarah, d/o John and _____, 12 Sep 1756
_____, George, s/o — 24 Oct 1756
Gifford, Anna, d/o Jos and _____, 3 Dec 1752
Gifford, Ananias, s/o Joshua and Hannah, 23 Sep 1755
Gillpatrick, Ann, d/o Thomas and Ann, 22 Dec 1734
Gillpatrick, Frances, d/o Thomas and Ann, 3 Apl 1740
Gordon, Agisyles, s/o Thomas and Margaret, 28 May 1747
Gordon, Ann, d/o John and _____, 6 May 1753
Gordon, Sarah, d/o John and _____, 6 May 1753
Gordon, Thomas, s/o John and _____, 6 May 1753
Gordon, William, s/o John and _____, 6 May 1753
Grandin, Eleanor, d/o Philip and Eleanor, 11 Oct 1767
Grandin, Jane, d/o Philip and Eleanor, 18 June 1758
Grandin, Mary, d/o Philip and _____, 17 Aug 1755
Grandine, Mary, d/o Daniel and Sarah, 8 Nov 1751
Grandine, Sarah, d/o Amos and Patience, 11 May 1735
Grandine, William, s/o Daniel and Sarah, 8 Mar 1751
Grant, Ann, w/o John, 25 Nov 1810
Grant, Catharine, d/o John and Ann, 8 Nov 1818
Grant, Edward Wellington, s/o John and Ann, 10 Dec _____

Christ Church at Shrewsbury

Grant, John, s/o John and Ann, 10 Dec _____
Grant, Martha Wait, d/o John and Ann, 25 Nov 1810
Grant, Thos Walker, s/o John and Ann, 11 June 1809
Grigs, Elizabeth, d/o John and Jane, 18 June 1752
Grigs, Margaret, d/o John and _____, 14 May 1755
Griffith, Mary, d/o Samuel and Catharine, 17 June 1748
Grimes, Ann, d/o Richard and Mary, 8 Apl 1750
Grinsted, John, 29 Mar 1752
Gyford, Ann, d/o Joshua and Hannah, 24 Nov 1750
Gyford, Jos, s/o Joshua and Hannah, 24 Nov 1750
Gyford, Joshua, 24 Nov 1750
Gyford, Hannah, w/o Joshua, 24 Nov 1750
Gyford, William, s/o Joshua and Hannah, 24 Nov 1750
Hadgson, Thomas, s/o John Nathan and Magdaline, 2 Jan 1734
_____, Hagar, Colored servant of Capt Osburne, 11 Sep 1751
_____, Hagar, a free negro wench, 1 Nov 1764
Haggarty, Anthony Holmes, s/o Taylor and Clemence, 10 Oct 1813
Hagerty, Mary Catharine, d/o Taylor and Clemence, 5 May 1816
Halsted, Ann, d/o Timothy and _____, 21 Mar 1756
Halsted, Christopher, s/o Daniel and Sarah, 9 Feb 1752
Halsted, Josiah, s/o Timothy and _____, 22 Nov 1759
Halsted, Margaret, d/o Josiah and Zilpha, 18 Aug 1752
Halstead, Mirtilla, d/o Josiah and Anna, 30 Sep 1759
Halstead, Rebecca, d/o Timothy and Zilpha, 31 Dec 1770
Halstead, Sarah, d/o Josiah and _____, 25 Dec 1757
Halstead, Sarah, d/o Timothy and Zilpha, 31 Dec 1770
Halsted, Slyvia, d/o Timothy and _____, 21 Mar 1756
Halsted, Zilpha, d/o Josiah and Anna, 8 Aug 1756
Handlin, Matthew, 27 June 1762
Handlin, Margaret, 27 June 1762
Hankinson, Helena, d/o Kenneth and _____, 4 June 1758
Hankinson, Hannah, d/o Kenneth and _____, 22 Mar 1761
Hankinson, James, s/o Kenneth and _____, 1 May 1763
Hankinson, Joseph, s/o Thomas and Hannah, 23 Aug 1752
Hankinson, — d/o James and _____, 15 May 1763
Harbert, Elizabeth, d/o Samuel and Elizabeth, 24 June 1750
Harding, Mary, d/o Francis and Ann, 18 June 1752
Harding, Rebecca, d/o Luke and Mary, 30 June 1746
Harding, Robert, s/o Francis and _____, 10 Apl 1754
Harding, Sarah, d/o Luke and Mary, 30 June 1746
Harding, Thomas, s/o Valentine and Ann, 4 Oct 1748
Harris, Abraham, s/o William and _____, 15 Feb 1767

Harris, William, s/o William and _____, 30 Mar 1766
Harrison, Ann, d/o William and _____, 21 Apl 1754
Harrison, John, s/o George and Hannah, 22 Jan 1751
Harleton, Elizabeth, d/o Jervis and Ann, 20 May 1748
Harleton, James, s/o Jervis and Ann, 20 May 1748
Hart, Catharine, d/o Dr. Hart, 28 Dec 1755
Hartman, Edward, adult, 31 May 1823
Hasselton, Mary, d/o Jervis and Ann, 7 May 1750
Hasset, Daniel, s/o James and Elienor, 11 May 1746
Haviland, John, s/o Stephen and _____, 23 Aug 1761
Haydin, Charlotte, d/o William and Lydia, 9 Oct 1774
_____, Helena, d/o _____, 24 Apl 1775
Hengins, Daniel, s/o _____ and Martha, 23 Sep 1745
Hengins, Lewis, s/o _____ and Martha, 23 Sep 1745
Hengins, Martha, 23 Sep 1745
Hengins, Sarah, d/o _____ - and Martha, 23 Sep 1745
Henry, Martha, d/o John and _____, 5 Nov 1759
_____, Henry, s/o 22 Sep 1754
_____, Henryetta, a negro servant of Mr. Ashfield, 5 Dec 1750
Herbert, John, s/o John and Easter, 14 Apl 1734
Herbert, Thomas, s/o Daniel and Susanna, 11 Aug 1734
Hevlon, Patience, d/o Stephen and _____, 20 June 1756
Hevlon, Stephen, s/o Stephen and _____, 19 Aug 1753
Hewitt, Abigail, d/o Thomas and _____, 6 June 1762
Hewlett, Catharine, d/o William and Abigail, 21 Oct 1764
Hewlett, Elizabeth, d/o William and Abigail, 12 Oct 1766
Hewlett, Isaac, s/o William and Abigail, 29 May 1768
Hewlet, Susannah, 28 Aug 1748
Hewlet, William, 28 Aug 1748
Heyden, Christopher, s/o Christopher and _____, 31 Oct 1756
Heyden, Enoch, s/o William and _____, 31 Oct 1756
Heyden, John, s/o William and _____, 31 Oct 1756
Heyden, Hosea, s/o William and Lydia, 16 Oct 1757
Heyden, Noah, s/o William and _____, 31 Oct 1756
Heyden, Nicodemus, s/o Christopher and _____, 31 Oct 1756
Heyden, Rhoda, d/o Christopher and _____, 31 Oct 1756
Heyden, Stephen, s/o William and _____, 31 Oct 1756
Highland, Joseph, s/o Catharine O.W., 24 Apl 1746
Hildyard, John, s/o Nathaniel and Mary, 7 Mar 1750
Hill, William, 28 Aug 1748
Hoar, Catharine, d/o John and _____, 9 May 1756
Holman, Samuel, s/o Francis and Catherine, 3 Jan 1749

Christ Church at Shrewsbury

Holman, Joseph, Adult, 19 Oct 1760
Holmes, Abraham, s/o Jacob and Ann, 26 May 1771
Holmes, Abraham, s/o Abraham and Jerusha, 10 Oct 1813
Holmes, Abraham Russel, s/o Jacob and Eleanor, 23 May 1819
Holmes, Ann Eliza, d/o Jacob Jr and Eleanor, 9 Jan 1812
Holmes, Ann Eliza, d/o Josiah and Mary Ann, 21 Feb 1823
Holmes, Anthony, s/o Josiah and Hannah, 26 Oct 1760
Holmes, Benjamin, s/o Josiah and Hannah, 12 Feb 1764
Holmes, Clement, s/o Josiah and Hannah, 29 Mar 1752
Holmes, Clementina, d/o Josiah and Mary Ann, 20 Dec 1823
Holmes, Easter, d/o Josiah and Hannah, 15 July 1739
Holmes, Ellen, d/o Jacob Jr and Eleanor, 23 Feb 1814
Holmes, Hannah, d/o Thomas and Eleanor, 1807
Holmes, Hannah, d/o Josiah and Hannah, 22 Feb 1740-1
Holmes, Hannah Lambert, d/o Abraham and Jerusha, 18 May 1817
Holmes, Jacob, s/o Josiah and Hannah, 1 June 1745
Holmes, Jacob, s/o Abraham and Jerusha, 1807
Holmes, John, s/o Abraham and Jerusha, 8 Jan 1811
Holmes, John Garrison, s/o Josiah and Hannah, 3 Sep 1758
Holmes, Josiah, s/o Josiah and Hannah, 5 May 1754
Holmes, Lydia, w/o Anthony, 1 Mar 1812
Holmes, Mary, d/o Jacob and Eleanor, 16 June 1816
Holmes, Mary Ann, w/o Josiah, 25 Dec 1822
Holmes, Matilda, d/o Jacob and Eleanor, 27 June 1824
Holmes, Michael, s/o Josiah and Mary Ann, 21 Feb 1823
Holmes, Samuel, s/o Josiah and Hannah, 13 June 1756
Holmes, Sarah Clark, d/o Thomas Jr and Ellen, 16 Oct 1814
Holmes, Thomas, s/o Josiah and Mary Ann, 21 Feb 1823
Holmes, Thomas, s/o Josiah and Hannah, 19 Nov 1749
Holmes, Thomas, s/o Josiah and Hannah, 14 Aug 1743
Holmes, William, s/o Josiah and Hannah, 29 Oct 1747
Holsted, Abigail, Adult, 25 Dec 1738
Holsted, Abigail, d/o Daniel and Sarah, 1 Apl 1750
Holstead, Abigal, d/o Josiah and Zilpha, 6 May 1744
Holsted, Bell Fame, d/o Josiah and Zilpha, 22 Apl 1750
Holsted, Daniel, Adult, 25 Dec 1738
Holsted, Daniel, s/o Timothy and Elizabeth, 15 Sep 1748
Holsted, Joshua, Adult, 25 Dec 1738
Holsted, Margery, Adult, 25 Dec 1738
Holsted, Margaret, d/o Josiah and Zilpha, 4 Mar 1753
Holsted, Pearson, Adult, 25 Dec 1738
Holsted, Rebecca, d/o Josiah and Zilpha, 8 Aug 1742

Holsted, Sarah, d/o Timothy and Elizabeth, 10 Oct 1747
Holsted, Timothy, 19 Nov 1749
Holsted, Timothy, s/o Josiah and Zilpha, 11 July 1747
Hopmire, Armenia, d/o Samuel and Mary, 24 May 1752
Hopmire, Deborah, d/o Samuel and Mary, 24 May 1752
Hopmire, Elizabeth, d/o Samuel and Mary, 24 May 1752
Hopmire, Lydia, d/o Samuel and Mary, 24 May 1752
Hopmire, Margaret, d/o Samuel and Mary, 9 Sep 1753
Hopmire, Peter s/o Samuel and Mary, 24 May 1752
Hopmire, Susanna, d/o Samuel and Mary, 9 Sep 1753
Hopmire, William, s/o Samuel and Mary, 24 May 1752
Horn, Elizabeth, d/o Nathaniel and _____, 1 July 1750
Horn, Esther, d/o Nathaniel and _____, 1 July 1750
Hortwick, Thomas, s/o George and _____, 2 Dec 1753
Hoskins, Susannah, d/o John and Mary, 5 Sep 1736
Howel, Richard, s/o Thomas and _____, 2 June 1765
Howell, Robert, s/o Thomas and Ann, 8 May 1763
Howel, Thomas, s/o Thomas and _____, 2 June 1765
Hubbs, Sarah, Miss. an adult, 8 May 1757
Hulet, Elizabeth, d/o Thomas and Sarah, 26 Dec 1748
Hulet, Sarah, w/o Thomas, 26 Dec 1748
Hulet, Lydia, d/o William and Abigail, 9 Dec 1770
Hulet, Samuel, s/o William and Abigail, 1 Aug 1775
Hume, James, at Mr. Blains, 13 Nov 1750
Hunt, Ashfield, s/o Samuel and Isabella, 29 June 1755
Hunt, Elizabeth, d/o Samuel and Elizabeth, 5 June 1763
Hunt, Elizabeth, d/o Mr. Hunt and Isabel, 21 Dec 1749
Hunt, Euphemia, d/o Samuel and Isabella, 30 Oct 1768
Hunt, Isabella, d/o Samuel and Isabella, 9 Sep 1753
Hunt, Isaac Willet, s/o Samuel and Isabella, 19 Mar 1759
Hunt, Lydia, d/o Samuel and Isabella, 6 Dec 1757
Hunt, Mary, d/o Samuel and Isabella, 10 Aug 1751
Hunt, Obadiah, s/o Obadiah and _____, 19 Mar 1751
Hunt, Richard, s/o Samuel and Isabella, 26 Jan 1766
Hunt, Samuel, s/o Samuel and Isabella, 10 May 1761
Husband, Lewis, 11 July 1747
Hutchins, John, s/o John and Mary, 18 Sep 1748
Hutchinson, Ann, d/o Thomas and Mary, 20 May 1750
Hyssong, Catharine, d/o Christopher and Abalon, 4 Sep 1757
Hyssong, Elizabeth, d/o Christopher and _____, 25 Oct 1762
Hyssong, John, s/o Christopher and _____, 28 July 1765
Hyssong, Sarah, d/o Christopher and _____, 8 July 1759

Christ Church at Shrewsbury

Irving, June, d/o Ebenezer and Elizabeth, 1 Oct 1819
Irving, Julia, d/o Ebenezer and Elizabeth, 1 Oct 1819
Irving, Sarah, d/o Ebenezer and Elizabeth, 1 Oct 1819
____, Isaac, s/o Hagar, 1 Nov 1764
Isteton, John, s/o Robert and ____, 24 June 1759
Jackson, Elizabeth, Adult, 22 Apl 1739
Jackson, Margaret, Adult, 17 Dec 1767
____, Jacob, s/o Sussex and Judith, 14 July 1771
____, Jacob, 30 Sep 1759
____, Jacob, s/o 15 May 1757
Jaques, John Oglivie, s/o 15 May 1768
Jaques, Mary, d/o Dr. Richard and ____, 15 May 1768
Jaques, Peter Lott, Adult, 12 Jan 1823
Jaques, Peter Lott, s/o Richard and ____, 15 June 1766
Jarvis, Amelia, Adult, 18 Jan 1821
Jarvis, Cornelia, d/o Amelia, 18 Jan 1821
Jenison, Jacob, s/o Jacob and ____, 5 Oct 1735
Jewel, Ann, d/o James and Mary, 7 Mar 1750
Jewel, Joseph, s/o Joseph and Martha, 20 Mar 1751
Jewel, Mary, d/o Widow Jewel, 14 May 1753
____, James, s/o William and ____, 2 Oct 1763
____, Jane, a negro belonging to Mr. Tole, 12 Feb 1764
____, Joan, d/o____, 7 May 1767
Jobs, Lewis, s/o James and Barsheba, 11 June 1764
____, John, s/o 21 Jan 1759
____, John, s/o ____, 15 Dec 1754
____, John, s/o ____, 28 Nov 1756
____, John, s/o ____, 17 Nov 1754
____, John, a negro servant of Mr. Guzebert Van Martin, 19 Aug 1750
____, John, a negro servant to Mr. T Clayton, 5 Aug 1746
____, John, s/o Sussex and Judith, 14 July 1771
Johnson, Mary, d/o John and ____, 13 Jan 1733
Johnson, John, s/o John and Rachel, 4 July 1736
Johnson, Sarah, d/o Rachel Widow, 9 Apl 1746
Johnson, William, s/o Mathias and ____, 11 Aug 1751
Jolly, Catharine, Adult, 16 Sep 1764
Jolly, Lydia, d/o William and Hannah, 16 Sep 1764
Jolly, Phebe, d/o William and Hannah, 16 Sep 1764
Jolly, William, Adult, 11 Nov 1759
____, Jonathan, a Free negro child, 7 Aug 1768
Jones, Edward Holms, s/o Robert and Ann, 8 Mar 1747
Jones, Mary, d/o Robert and ____, 19 May 1765

_____, Joseph, Negro child belonging to Widow Forman, 23 Aug 1752
_____, Joseph, Negro boy belonging to Capt Osbourn, 15 Sep 1752
Journey, Audery, d/o Peter and Audery, 23 Nov 1750
Journey, Catharine, d/o Peter and Audery, 23 Nov 1750
Journey, Elizabeth, d/o Peter and Audery, 23 Nov 1750
Journey, James, s/o Peter and Audery, 23 Nov 1750
Journey, Joseph, s/o Peter and Audery, 23 Nov 1750
_____, Judith, w/o Sussex, 14 July 1771
Kerns, Catharine, d/o Patrick and _____, 15 June 1735
Kerns, John, s/o Patrick and _____, 15 June 1735
Kerns, Sarah, d/o Patrick and _____, 15 June 1735
Kearney, Annastatia, d/o Edmund and Ann, 3 Sep 1816
Kearney, Catharine, d/o Edmund and Ann, 3 Sep 1816
Kearney, Catharine, d/o John and _____, 2 Feb 1734-5
Kearney, Catharine, d/o James and Margaret, 5 Nov 1752
Kearney, James, s/o Thomas and _____, 17 Sep 1755
Kearney, Maria Theresa, d/o Thomas and _____, 17 Sep 1755
Kearney, Michael, s/o James and Margaret, 20 Feb 1765
Kearney, Philip, s/o Ravaud and Ann, 24 Oct 1767
Kelham, Lucy, 13 Nov 1750
Kemble, Elizabeth, d/o Peter and _____, 10 Feb 1754
Ketchen, Daniel Littleton, s/o Daniel, 5 Oct 1735
Kilpatrick, Ann, d/o Thomas and Ann, 10 June 1765
Kilpatrick, Jane, d/o Thomas and _____, 8 Nov 1748
Kilpatrick, Jane, d/o Thomas and Ann, 10 June 1765
King, Mary, d/o Robert and Margaret, 13 Sep 1761
King, Susanna, d/o Robert and _____, 24 June 1759
Lake, Sarah, w/o Thomas, 21 Sep 1749
Lambertson, Cornelius, s/o James and Sarah, 3 Sep 1749
Lambertson, Deborah, d/o James and Sarah, 24 Aug 1746
Lane, Sarah, d/o Elizabeth, 26 Aug 1759
Larzeline, Jacob, s/o Jacob and Alice, 9 Oct 1774
Lawrence, Ann, d/o James and _____, 26 June 1748
Lawrence, Elisha, s/o Elisha and _____, 1 Jan 1746-7
Lawrence, Elizabeth, d/o Elisha and Elizabeth, 22 Sep 1734
Lawrence, George, s/o James and _____, 9 May 1756
Lawrence, Lucy, d/o Elisha and _____, 24 Dec 1749
Lawrence, Margaret, Adult, 15, Oct 1814
Lee, Eleanor, d/o John and Alice, 13 May 1810
Lee, Elizabeth, d/o Robert and Rachel, 8 June 1741
Lee, Giles, s/o Robert and Rachel, 22 May 1738
Lee, Jane, d/o John and Alice, 13 May 1810

Christ Church at Shrewsbury

Lee, John, s/o Robert and Mary, 18 Aug 1750
Legget, Ann, d/o John and Hannah, 18 Sep 1758
Leonard, Anastatia, d/o Samuel and Mary, 7 May 1749
Leonard, Ann Frances, d/o Joseph and Magdalen, June 1770
Leonard, Deborah, d/o Samuel and Mary, 7 Dec 1746
Leonard, Elizabeth, d/o Samuel and Mary, 9 Feb 1746
Leonard, Elizabeth, Widow, 27 Apl 1749
Leonard, Henry, s/o Joseph and Magdalen, 25 Dec 1774
Leonard, John, s/o Joseph and Magdalen, 6 Apl 1773
Leonard, Henry, s/o Henry and _____, 21 Dec 1755
Leonard, Joseph, Adult, 10 Nov 1760
Leonard, Lucy, d/o Samuel and Mary, 19 May 1751
Leonard, Lydia, 11 Oct 1747
Leonard, Margaret, 27 June 1762
Leonard, Mary, w/o Thomas, 8 May 1757
Leonard, Mary, 4 Aug 1751
Leonard, Robert Morris, s/o Henry and Bellfame, 17 Sep 1753
Leonard, Susanna, d/o Samuel and Mary, 27 Jan 1754
Leonard, Susanna, d/o Henry and _____, 26 Aug 1759
Leonard, Samuel, s/o Samuel and Mary, 3 Apl 1756
Leonard, Samuel, s/o Samuel and Mary, 13 June 1756
Leonard, William, s/o Joseph and Magdalen, 19 June 1768
Leonard, —, w/o Capt Leonard, 13 Apl 1750
Letts, Ann, d/o Francis and Sarah, 27 Dec 1747
Letts, Rachel, d/o Francis and Sarah, 27 Dec 1747
Letts, Zerucah, s/o Francis and Catherine, 27 Dec 1747
Linch, Lena, d/o Patrick and Elizabeth, 9 Apl 1746
Lippincott, Mary Ann, Adult, 3 Nov 1822
Little, Abigail, Adult, 19 Feb 1812
Livings, Dorothy, d/o Richard and _____, 25 Mar 1757
Lloyd, Eleanor Forman, d/o William and Rachel, 25 Mar 1810
Lloyd, Henrietta, d/o Cabel and Martha Ann, 11 Aug 1811
Lloyd, Louisa Matilda, d/o Cabel and Martha, 2 June 1816
Lloyd, Susan Parker, d/o William and Rachel, 4 July 1813
Lolwell, Elizabeth, w/o Thomas, Nov 1749
Longstreet, Ann, d/o Derick and _____, 17 June 1748
Longstreet, Derrick, s/o Derick and _____, 13 Dec 1745
Loyd, Mary, d/o Thomas and Sarah, 30 June 1746
Lynes, Ann, d/o Thomas and _____, 24 Sep 1752
Maccurtain, Ann, d/o John and _____, 16 Oct 1753
Maccurtain, James, s/o John and _____, 16 Oct 1753
Maccurtain, John, s/o John and _____, 16 Oct 1753

Mackerferty, John, s/o Joseph and _____, 26 Apl 1752
Mackdowel, Eleanor, d/o Robert and _____, 19 Nov 1752
Macknichol, Catharine, d/o Widow Macknichol, 24 Nov 1751
Maddock, Hannah, w/o Mr Maddock, 26 Aug 1747
Marsh, Sarah Cornhill, d/o Richard and _____, 30 Nov 1766
_____, Margaret, d/o, 17 Apl 1759
_____, Margaret, d/o Rachel a negro of Mrs. Isabella Kearney, 6 May 1756
_____, Mary, servant of Mr Osburn, 23 Nov 1750
_____, Mary, 30 Sep 1759
_____, Mary, Negro belonging to Mr. S. Leonard, 17 July 1759
_____, Mary, Negro belonging to Mrs. Martin, 20 Oct 1757
_____, Mary, d/o Rachel a negro of Mrs. Isabella Kearney, 6 May 1756
Masterson, Gabriel, s/o Michael and _____, 20 Nov 1757
Masterson, Salathiel, s/o Michael and _____, 20 Nov 1757
Masterson, Uriel, s/o Michael and _____, 20 Nov 1757
Matchet, Huldah, d/o Richard and Mary, 11 June 1764
Matchet, John, s/o Richard and Mary, 11 June 1764
Matchet, Margaret, d/o Richard and Mary, 11 June 1764
Matchet, Mary, d/o Richard and Mary, 11 June 1764
Matchet, William, s/o Richard and Mary, 11 June 1764
Mathew, Elizabeth, d/o Evert and Ann, 18 Nov 1739
Mathew, s/o Evert Mathew, 30 June 1741
McCafferty, Elizabeth, d/o John and _____, 5 Aug 1759
McCafferty, Hannah Holmes, d/o John and _____, 29 July 1764
McCafferty, William, s/o John and _____, 23 July 1749
McClease, Catharine, d/o John and Catharine, 11 Apl 1746
McClease, Catharine, w/o John, 28 Aug 1746
McClease, James, s/o John and Catharine, 10 Sep 1746
McClease, John, s/o John and Catharine, 10 Sep 1746
McConolly, Andrew, 11 June 1764
McConolly, Neale, 11 June 1764
McDaniel, Alexander, s/o Daniel and Catharine, 2 Oct 1768
McDaniel, Catharine, d/o Daniel and Catharine, 8 Dec 1771
McDaniel, John, s/o Daniel and Catharine, 21 Nov 1773
McElwe, Elizabeth, 27 June 1762
McFall, Hugh, 27 June 1762
McGee, Samuel, 3 July 1766
McMullin, Daniel, s/o Neale and _____, 27 June 1762
McMullin, James, s/o Neale and _____, 22 July 1764
McMullin, John, s/o Neale and _____, 27 June 1762
McMullin, Margaret, d/o Neale and _____, 22 July 1764

Christ Church at Shrewsbury

Mercer, Anthony, s/o Dr. Mercer and Lucy, 28 May 1757
Mercer, Lawrence, s/o Dr. Mercer and Lucy, 22 July 1753
_____, Meridin, d/o Hagar, 1 Nov 1764
_____, Merrin, a negro belonging to Duncan Robinson, 18 June 1752
Michaels, Alexander, s/o Jacob and Rachel, 13 Dec 1818
Miller, John, s/o John and Mary, 11 Dec 1763
Miller, Sarah, d/o John and Mary, 25 Feb 1767
Millar, Mary, d/o Paul and _____, 23 May 1757
Millar, Sarah, d/o Paul and _____, 11 June 1764
Mills, Hannah, d/o Richard and Phebe, 11 Oct 1747
Mills, Richard, s/o Richard and Phebe, 12 Jan 1746
Mills, Phebe, d/o Richard and Phebe, 12 Jan 1746
Mitton, Elizabeth, Adult, 17 June 1753
Mitton, Joseph, Adult, 9 Sep 1753
Morfith, Hannah, d/o Thomas and Hannah, 17 Nov 1734
Morford, Augustus Wing, s/o Thomas and Rebecca, 2 May 1818
Morford, Catharine, Adult, 10 Sep 1821
Morford, George Taylor, Adult, 28 July 1765
Morford, Hannah, w/o Thomas, 25 Dec 1738
Morford, Hannah, d/o Widow Morford, 15 Sep 1765
Morford, Hernnaby, Garret and Catharine, 10 Sep 1821
Morford, Hannah, d/o Thomas and Hester, 12 May 1771
Morford, Joseph, s/o Thomas and Hannah, 18 June 1738
Morford, Lydia, d/o Joseph and _____, 15 Nov 1761
Morford, Meribah, d/o Thomas and Rebecca, 1815
Morford, Rebecca, w/o Garret, 18 June 1748
Morford, Sarah, d/o Thomas and Hester, 24 Mar 1769
Morford, Thomas, s/o Garret and Catharine, 10 Sep 1821
Morford, William, s/o Joseph and _____, 27 May 1764
Moore, Garrat, s/o Henry and _____, 14 May 1753
Morrell, John, s/o Samuel and Margaret, 13 Dec 1760
Morrell, Samuel, s/o Samuel and Margaret, 18 Sep 1758
Morris, Amelia, d/o John and Sarah, 29 Jan 1775
Morris, Burrough, s/o William and _____, 4 Sep 1749
Morris, Edward, s/o John and Mary, 30 July 1758
Morris, John, s/o John and Sarah, 20 Aug 1772
Morris, John, s/o Widow Morris, 5 May 1765
Morris, John, s/o John and _____, 1 Jan 1737
Morris, Joseph, s/o Widow Morris, 5 May 1765
Morris, Mary, d/o Lewis and _____, 31 May 1748
Morris, Mary, d/o Widow Morris, 5 May 1765
Morris, Sarah, d/o John and Sarah, 24 July 1774

Morris, Thomas, s/o John and _____, 18 Aug 1754
Morris, William, s/o Widow Morris, 8 June 1766
Morrison, John, s/o John and Mary, 8 July 1750
Morrison, Mary, d/o John and Mary, 26 Nov 1752
Motsoon, Jacob, s/o Felix and _____, 2 Apl 1758
Mounson, Andrew, s/o John and Mary, 20 Apl 1749
Mount, Ann, d/o James and Patience, 29 Dec 1770
Mount, Abigail, Adult, 8 June 1823
Mount, Cynthia, Adult, 8 June 1823
Mount, James, s/o James and Patience, 29 Dec 1770
Mount, Joseph, s/o James and Patience, 29 Dec 1770
Mount, Joseph, s/o Joseph and Sarah, 27 May 1799
Mount, Littleton, s/o James and Patience, 9 May 1775
Mount, Margaret, d/o James and Patience, 29 Dec 1770
Mount, Mary, d/o James and Patience, 29 Dec 1770
Mount, Michael Price, s/o James and Patience, 29 Dec 1770
Mount, Patience, w/o James, 29 Dec 1770
Mount, Patience, d/o James and Patience, 29 Dec 1770
Murry, Alsee, d/o George and _____, 15 June 1735
Mytton, Ann, 3 July 1748
Newel, Mary, d/o James and _____, 9 May 1756
Newton, Ann, d/o Joseph and _____, 24 Sep 1758
Newton, Hannah, d/o Joseph and _____, 24 Sep 1758
Newton, Hannah, d/o Joseph and _____, 14 Oct 1748
Newton, Joseph, Jr., 30 Oct 1748
Newton, Thomas, 10 June 1750
Nicholson, Catharine, d/o Christian and Mary, 14 June 1737
Niper, Mary, d/o James and _____, 5 Oct 1735
Nixon, James, s/o Widow Nixon, 27 May 1753
Nixon, Jane, d/o Widow Nixon, 27 May 1753
Nixon, Sarah, d/o Widow Nixon, 27 May 1753
Norris, Catharine, d/o William and Mary, 4 June 1738
Norris, Mary, w/o William, 14 Aug 1748
O'Brian, Ellen, d/o Dennis and Catharine, 3 Dec 1749
O'Brian, John, s/o William and Rachel, 26 Apl 1747
O'Brian, John, s/o Daniel and _____, 3 Apl 1758
O'Brian, Mary, d/o Daniel and _____, 3 Apl 1758
O'Hara, Hugh, s/o Felix and Martha, 3 May 1761
_____, Olive, Negro belonging to Mr. Samuel Leonard, 30 Mar 1752
_____, Oliver, a Negro boy, 27 July 1766
_____, Oliver, a Negro servant of Mr. J. Througmorton, 9 June 1747
_____, One adult person, 22 Apl 1750

Christ Church at Shrewsbury

Osburn, Catharine, d/o James and _____, 23 Nov 1750
Osburn, Samuel, s/o James and Ann, 6 Apl 1735
Palmer, Hannah, d/o Isaac and Mary, 26 Apl 1747
Palmer, Henry, s/o Isaac and Mary, 27 July 1746
Palmer, John, s/o Isaac and Mary, 27 July 1746
Palmer, Lydia, d/o Elizabeth   O.W., 9 Feb 1751
Palmer, Susanna, d/o John and Sarah, 17 June 1753
Parker, Hannah, d/o Jacob and _____, 1 May 1768
Parker, Jacob, s/o Jacob and _____, 22 July 1770
Parker, Nathaniel, 22 Sep 1745
Parker, Martha, d/o Peter and Mary, 2 Sep 1746
Parker, Mary, d/o Nathaniel and Hannah, 1 Mar 1747
Parker, —, d/o Nathaniel and Ann, 22 Sep 1745
Parker, Elizabeth, d/o Isaac and _____, 27 Oct 1751
Parr, Samuel, s/o Isaac and Mary, 8 Apl 1750
Parr, Ann, d/o James and Rebecca, 9 Apl 1746
Patten, Catharine, w/o John, 9 Apl 1746
Patten, Elizabeth, d/o Thomas and Margaret, 3 Apl 1740
Patten, Esther, d/o John and Catharine, 9 Apl 1746
Patten, Hugh, s/o John and Catharine, 9 Apl 1746
Patten, James, s/o James and Rebecca, 28 Aug 1749
Patten, John, s/o John and Catharine, 9 Apl 1746
Patten, Mary, d/o William and Mary, 20 Apl 1740
Patten, Mary, d/o James and Rebecca, 9 Apl 1746
Patten, Rebecca, d/o James and Rebecca, 19 Aug 1753
Patten, William, s/o William and Mary, 28 July 1734
Pege, Adam, 27 June 1762
Pege, Ann, 27 June 1762
Pege, Cornelius, Adult, 27 Sep 1759
Pege, Cornelius, s/o   -- and Ann, 10 June 1765
Pege, David, s/o Cornelius and Elizabeth, 27 Sep 1759
Pege, David, 27 June 1762
Pege, Elizabeth, w/o Cornelius, 27 Sep 1759
Pege, Jonathan, 27 June 1762
Pege, Rebecca, 27 June 1762
Pege, William, s/o Cornelius and Elizabeth, 24 Aug 1760
Perine, Catharine, d/o John and Rebecca, 27 July 1746
Perine, Elizabeth, d/o James and Mary, 30 July 1746
Perreine, Hannah, d/o John and Mary, 4 Aug 1765
Perrine, Henry, s/o Nathaniel and _____, 25 Aug 1751
Perrine, Hester, d/o Matthew and Hannah, 1 July 1810
Perrine, James, s/o Peter and Margaret, 28 Aug 1735

Perrine, James, s/o Henry and _____, 29 Oct 1752
Perrine, John, s/o Mr. Perrine, 10 Nov 1751
Perine, John, s/o Henry and Abigail, 19 Oct 1760
Perine, Joseph, s/o Henry and Martha, 3 Jan 1749
Perreine, Joseph, s/o Joseph and Margaret, 28 Sep 1766
Perine, Kenneth, s/o Mathew and Isabel, 31 May 1747
Perreine, Lewis, s/o Henry and Abigail, 13 Aug 1758
Perrine, Martha, d/o Henry and Martha, 13 Nov 1750
Perreine, Mathew, s/o William and _____, 21 June 1767
Perrine, Rebecca, d/o Matthew and Hannah, 1 July 1810
Perreine, Robert, s/o John and _____, 2 Sep 1764
Perreine, Sarah, d/o Daniel and _____, 16 Aug 1761
Perreine, Sarah, d/o Henry and Abigail, 15 May 1763
Perine, William, s/o Henry and Martha, 28 Sep 1746
Perrine, William, s/o Helena, 22 July 1764
Perrine, William Holmes, s/o Matthew and Hannah, 1 July 1810
Perkins, Amey, d/o John and Elizabeth, 8 May 1750
Perkins, Elizabeth, d/o John and Jane, 8 May 1750
Perkins, James, s/o John and Jane, 8 May 1750
Perkins, Jemima, d/o John and Jane, 8 May 1750
Perkins, Jonathan, s/o John and Jane, 8 May 1750
Perkins, Joseph, s/o John and Jane, 8 May 1750
Perkins, Rachel, d/o John and Jane, 8 May 1750
Perkins, Sarah, d/o John and Elizabeth, 8 May 1750
Perkins, William, s/o John and Elizabeth, 8 May 1750
_____, Peter, a free negro living with Mr. Devile, 13 June 1749
_____, Peter, a negro servant of Mr. Samuel Osburn, 15 Oct 1749
_____, Peter, a negro child of Capt Osburne, 11 Sep 1751
_____, Peter, a black belonging to Mr. Samuel Pintard, 15 Apl 1819
Petshine, Franscina, d/o Peter and _____, 9 Sep 1764
Petshine, Isabella, d/o Peter and _____, 9 Sep 1764
Petshine, James, s/o Peter and _____, 27 Sep 1759
Petshine, Peter, s/o Peter and _____, 27 Sep 1759
Petshine, Priscilla, d/o Thomas and _____, 27 Nov 1768
Pharess, Andrew, s/o Robert and _____, 16 Aug 1761
_____, Phebe, a Negro wench, 9 Oct 1746
_____, Phebe, d/o Sussex and Judith, 14 July 1771
_____, Phebe, a Negro belonging to James and Patience Mount, 29 Dec 1770
_____, Phillis, a Negro belonging to Mrs. Isabella Kearney, 31 Aug 1766
_____, Phillis, Negro child belonging to Thomas Leonard, 5 Jan 1762
_____, Phillip, s/o, — 10 June 1759

Christ Church at Shrewsbury

Philips, Eugenie, w/o Mr. Philips, schoolmaster, 27 Nov 1748
Philips, Joyce, d/o Mr. Philips and Eugenie, 27 Nov 1748
Philips, Thomas, s/o William and Ann, 11 Dec 1763
Pintard, Amey, d/o William and _____, 1 Dec 1765
Pintard, Ann, d/o Samuel and Ann, 12 May 1745
Pintard, Catharine, d/o Samuel and Ann, 18 May 1740
Pintard, Catharine, Adult, 27 Apl 1823
Pintard, Deborah, Adult, 21 Oct 1821
Pintard, Deborah, w/o Samuel, 9 Dec 1810
Pintard, Elizabeth, d/o Samuel and Ann, 18 Apl 1742
Pintard, Eliza, Adult, 27 Apl 1823
Pintard, Glencross, s/o William and _____, 26 Oct 1767
Pintard, Hannah, Adult, 6 July 1823
Pintard, John Lewis, s/o Samuel and Ann, 13 Aug 1738
Pintard, John Legourge, s/o Samuel and Ann, 8 May 1747
Pintard, Joseph, s/o John Legorge and _____, 9 Aug 1772
Pintard, Marsdin, Adult, 26 Aug 1821
Pintard, Samuel Holmes, s/o William and Lydia, 9 Jan 1812
Pintard, Samuel, s/o William and Hannah, 25 Oct 1762
Pintard, Samuel, s/o Samuel and Ann, 27 July 1735
Pintard, Susan, Adult, 27 Apl 1823
Pintard, William, s/o Samuel and Ann, 14 Apl 1733
Pitcher, William, s/o William and Elizabeth, 22 Sep 1765
Plentze, Jacob, s/o Leonard and Margaret, 21 July 1751
Powel, Samuel, s/o John and _____, 21 Jan 1759
Preston, Ann, d/o Thomas and Jane, 26 July 1752
Preston, Mary, d/o Thomas and _____, 22 May 1754
Price, Ann, d/o Joseph and Abigail, 24 May 1772
Price, Amey, 13 Mar 1747-8
Price, Ophelia, 1 Sep 1751
Price, Catharine, 8 May 1748
Price, Margaret, d/o Joseph and Mary, 1 Jan 1737-8
Price, Margaret, d/o Joseph Jr and _____, 13 Dec 1767
Price, Mary, d/o Joseph and Abigail, 8 May 1763
Price, Perrine, s/o Joseph and Mary, 1 Jan 1737-8
Price, Phebe, 1 Sep 1751
Price, Zilpha, d/o Joseph and _____, 25 Dec 1764
_____, Primus, a free negro, 11 Feb 1753
Quinn, Mary, d/o Thomas and Catharine, 2 Aug 1753
_____, Rachel, d/o Thomas a free negro, 4 July 1762
_____, Rachel, Negro belonging to Miss Isabella Kearney, 16 May 1756
_____, Rachel, d/o Robin and Elizabeth, 27 Aug 1751

Randal, Elizabeth, w/o Benjamin, 10 May1751
Randall, Stephen, s/o Thomas and _____, 31 July 1755
Ransom, Henry, s/o Robert and _____, 2 Aug 1753
Reid, John, s/o Noble and Abigail, 12 Dec 1811
Reed, Mary, d/o John and _____, 12 Apl 1754
Reed, Theadeus, d/o John and Mary, 17 June 1739
Reed, Euphemia, d/o John and Mary, 27 July 1735
Reid, Margaret, d/o John and Margaret, 21 Jan 1759
Reid, Samuel Noble, s/o Noble and Abigail, 12 Dec 1811
Reila, John, s/o John and Hannah, 23 May 1757
Rice, Catharine, d/o James and Christian, 2 Mar 1734-5
Riddle, John, s/o Thomas and Elizabeth, 1 June 1737
Riddle, Mary, d/o Thomas and Elizabeth, 17 Apl 1739
Ritcheker, John, s/o Hans and Mary, 11 July 1756
Ritcheker, Mary, d/o Hans and Mary, 8 Aug 1756
_____, Robert Johnson, s/o Rachel negro belonging to Miss Isabella Kearney, 6 May 1756
Robertson, Jane, d/o Patrick and _____, 17, May, 1757
Robbins, Rebecca, Adult, 1820
Robinson, Christian, d/o Patrick and Mary, 29, Oct 1750
Robinson, Deborah, d/o Patrick and Mary, 25, June, 1755
Robinson, Duncan, s/o William and Mary, 3, Sep, 1749
Robinson, Isabella, d/o Patrick and Mary, 3, July, 1760
Robinson, Mary, d/o Patrick and Mary, 18, June, 1752
Robinson, Mary, d/o William and Mary, 25, Feb, 1747-8
Robinson, Mary, d/o David and Mary, 5, May, 1751
Robinson, Patrick, s/o Patrick and _____, 9, Aug, 1764
Robinson, Phebe, d/o David and _____, 9, May, 1749
Robinson, William, s/o David and Phebe, 14, May, 1748
Rockhills, Eliza, Adult, 1, Aug, 1824
Rogers, Elizabeth, d/o Othiniel and Elizabeth, 22, Mar, 1766
Rogers, Elizabeth, w/o Othiniel, 1, Sep, 1751
Rogers, Henry, s/o Othiniel and Elizabeth, 16, Aug, 1752
Rogers, James, s/o Othiniel and Elizabeth, 1, Sep, 1751
Rogers, John, s/o Othiniel and Elizabeth, 1, Sep, 1751
Rogers, John, s/o William and Rebecca, 6, Mar, 1751
Rogers, Leonard, s/o Othiniel and Elizabeth, 30, Aug, 1761
Rogers, Lewis, s/o Othiniel and Elizabeth, 25, Oct, 1756
Rogers, Lydia, d/o Othiniel and _____, 15, Dec, 1754
Rogers, Mary, d/o Samuel and Mary, 22, Sep, 1734
Rogers, Othineil, s/o Othiniel and Elizabeth, 30, Aug, 1761
Rogers, Raymond, s/o Othiniel and Elizabeth, 30, Aug, 1768

Christ Church at Shrewsbury

Rogers, Thomas, s/o Othiniel and _____, 30, Sep, 1759
Rose, Elizabeth, d/o Samuel and Ann, 8, May, 1750
Rose, Martha, d/o Samuel and Ann, 8, May, 1750
Rose, William, s/o Samuel and Ann, 8, May, 1750
Roris, Catharine, d/o John and _____, 8, July, 1759
Ruckles, Lydia, w/o Thomas, 27, Dec, 1823
Russel, William, s/o John and _____, 8, July, 1759
Rice, Ann Johnson, d/o John and _____, 222, May, 1754
Rue, Catharine, d/o John and _____, 3, May, 1761
Rue, Catharine, d/o Joseph and _____, 19, June, 1754
Rue, Elizabeth, d/o John and Mary, 30, Sep, 1764
Rue, Henry, s/o John and _____, 26, Aug, 1759
Rue, Henry, s/o Joseph Jr and _____, 23, May, 1757
Rue, Jane, d/o Mathew and _____, 29, Apl, 1748
Rue, Margaret, d/o Samuel and _____, 3, Aug, 1755
Rue, Margaret, d/o Mathew and _____, 30, Sep, 1750
Rue, Mary, d/o Joseph and Sariah, 23, Aug, 1747
Rue, Mary, d/o William and _____, 3, July, 1757
Rue, Mathias, s/o William and Elizabeth, 28, June, 1749
Rue, Mathew, d/o William and _____, 28, Oct, 1750
Rue, Mathias, s/o Mathew and, 14, June, 1752
Rue, John, s/o Matthew and _____, 15, Sep, 1754
Rue, Joseph, s/o Joseph and _____, 14, July, 1751
Rue, Joseph, s/o Joseph Jr and Ann, 4, Aug, 1754
Rue, Rachel, d/o William and _____, 29, Oct, 1752
Rue, Rebecca, d/o John and _____, 16, Aug, 1761
Rue, Sarah, d/o Joseph and _____, 17, Aug, 1755
Rue, Lyntyche, d/o John and _____, 22, May, 1754
Rue, William, s/o Joseph and _____, 31, Dec, 1749
Russel, Abigail, d/o James and Abigail, 27, Sep, 1761
Russel, Abraham, s/o James and _____, 17, Feb, 1746
Russel, Abraham, s/o James and Abigail, 17, Sep, 1745
Russel, Ann, d/o James and Abigail, 1, Jan, 1743-4
Russel, Benjamin, s/o James and _____, 13, Mar, 1747-8
Russel, Elizabeth, d/o John and Hannah, 8, Feb, 1767
Russel, Hannah, d/o James and Abigail, 16, May, 1742
Russel, James, s/o James and Abigail, 27, Sep, 1761
Russel, James, s/o John and Hannah, 19, Nov, 1752
Russel, John, s/o John and Hannah, 20, Mar, 1757
Russel, Josiah, s/o James and _____, 16, Apl, 1758
Russel, John, s/o James and _____, 22, Apl, 1750
Russel, Lydia, d/o John and _____, 28, Dec, 1755

Russel, Mary, d/o John and Hannah, 2, Dec, 1750
Russel, Richard, s/o John and Hannah, 27, Sep, 1761
Russel, Timothy, s/o James and _____, 22, Oct, 1752
Savage, Hannah, d/o Mr. Savage and Wife, 9, May, 1749
Savage, Patrick, s/o Robert and Hannah, 17, Apl, 1739
Savage, Thomas, s/o Robert and Hannah, 18, June, 1752
Scandler, Sarah, d/o Darby and _____, 13, Nov, 1750
Scoby, John, Adult, 16, Sep, 1764
Scoby, Margaret, d/o, 15, July, 1759
Seaman, Richard, s/o Benjamin and Catharine, Feb, 1821
Sears, Mary, w/o William, 11, Oct, 1771
Seers, Ann, d/o John and Greezel, 1, Jan, 1737-8
Seers, James, s/o John and Greezel, 1, Jan, 1737-8
Seers, William, s/o John and Greezel, 1, Jan, 1737-8
Sellon, Latrobe Rosevelt, s/o John and Lucy, 9, June, 1821
Seryeant, John, s/o Samuel and _____, 13, May, 1759
Shaddock, Ann, Adult, 3, July, 1738
Shaddock, Ann, d/o John and Anna Martha, 23, Oct, 1756
Shaddock, Anna, d/o Thomas and _____, 14, Feb, 1773
Shaddock, Francis, s/o John and Anna Martha, 25, Sep, 1745
Shaddock, Jeremiah, s/o John and Anna Martha, 25, Oct, 1756
Shaddock, John, Adult, 2, July, 1738
Shaddock, Martha, Adult, 2, July, 1738
Shaddock, Mary, d/o John and Anna Martha, 25, Oct, 1756
Shaddock, Samuel, s/o John and Anna Martha, 25, Sep, 1745
Shaddock, Sarah, Adult, 16, July, 1738
Shaddock, William, s/o John and _____, 15, July, 1739
Shaddock, William, s/o John and Martha, 16, July, 1738
_____, Sharper, Negro child belonging to Widow Forman, 23, Aug, 1752
Sharrock, Francis, s/o John and _____, 25, Nov, 1745
Sharrock, John, s/o John and _____, 25, Nov, 1745
Sharrock, Sarah, d/o John and _____, 12, Mar, 1747-8
Shepard, Amelia, d/o John and _____, 12, Aug, 1753
Shepard, Benoni, s/o Amelia, 1, Nov, 1772
Shepard, Clemens, d/o Thomas and _____, 20, Apl, 1755
Shepard, Jacob, s/o Thomas and Sarah, 28, Nov, 1756
Shepard, John, s/o Elisha and _____, 6, June, 1773
Shepard, Sarah, d/o Thomas and Sarah, 30, June, 1763
Shepard, Thomas, s/o Elisha and _____, 30, Dec,
Sherrock, Elizabeth, d/o John and _____, 19, Mar, 1746
Sherrock, Thomas, s/o John and Martha, 15, July, 1750
Shreve, William, Adult, 6, Oct, 1823

Christ Church at Shrewsbury

Shutter, Catharine, d/o Felix and _____, 16, Aug, 1761
Simpson, James, s/o John and _____, 4, Feb, 1753
Simpson, Lydia, d/o Robert and _____, 20, Apl, 1755
Skinner, Cortland, s/o Cortland and Elizabeth, 28, Nov, 1766
Skinner, Gertrude, d/o Cortland and _____, 13, May, 1759
Skinner, John, s/o Cortland and Elizabeth, 1, Dec, 1761
Smith, Ann Treyphena, d/o Francis and Lucy, 7, June, 1818
Smith, Hannah, d/o William and Ellen, 4, July, 1736
Smith, Lydia, d/o John and _____, 25, Oct, 1756
Smith, Mary, d/o Bryant and Frances, 23, June, 1765
Smith, Mary, d/o Tunis and Margaret, 22, May, 1753
Smith, Peter, s/o Thomas and Lydia, 27, Nov, 1763
Smith, Susanna, d/o Bryant and Frances, 23, June, 1765
Smith, Thomas, s/o ― and Jane, 27, Dec, 1747
Southern, Phebe, d/o Abraham and Susannah, 12, May, 1751
Speedwell, Hannah, a mullato, 6, Mar, 1747-8
Staateser, Elizabeth, d/o Christopher and Christeen, 16, May, 1756
Steel, James, s/o John and Jane, 30, July, 1746
Steel, Margaret, d/o John and Jane, 30, July, 1746
Steel, Mary, d/o John and Jane, 30, July, 1746
Stelle, Elizabeth, Adult, 26, Jan, 1734-5
Stelle, Thomas Gordon, s/o Gabriel and Mary, 24, Oct, 1734
Stephens, John, s/o Thomas and Mary, 3, Aug, 1735
Stephens, Mary, d/o Thomas and Mary, 3, Aug, 1735
Stephens, Mary, w/o Thomas, 3, Aug, 1735
Stephens, Thomas, s/o Thomas and Mary, 3, Aug, 1735
Stetcher, William, s/o David and Margaret, 17, May, 1755
Stevens, Catharine, d/o Deborah, a widow, 28, Aug, 1768
Stevens, June, d/o Deborah, a widow, 28, Aug, 1768
Stevens, Joseph, s/o Deborah, a widow, 28, Aug, 1768
Stevens, Mary, d/o Deborah, a widow, 28, Aug, 1768
Stevens, William, s/o Deborah, a widow, 28, Aug, 1768
Stevenson, Hannah, d/o John and Elizabeth, 31, Jan, 1755
Stevenson, Robert, s/o John and Elizabeth, 11, Apl, 1756
Stevenson, William, s/o John and Elizabeth, 23, Oct, 1760
Stewart, William, s/o John and Elizabeth, 15, June, 1735
Stillwell, Ann, d/o John and _____, 7, July, 1765
Stillwell, James, s/o James and Elizabeth, 28, Nov, 1773
Stillwell, John, s/o James and Elizabeth, 7, July, 1765
Stillwell, Joseph, s/o Capt and _____, 9, Aug, 1747
Stillwell, Rebecca, d/o James and Elizabeth, 28, Nov, 1773
Stillwell, Rebecca, w/o Jeremiah, 12, Oct, 1735

Stit, John, s/o John and Margaret, 9, Feb, 1752
Stout, Ann, d/o David and Catharine, 1, Nov, 1761
Stout, David, Adult, 1, Nov, 1761
Stout, Elizabeth, d/o David and Catharine, 1, May, 1763
Stout, John Barclay, s/o David and Catharine, 9, Dec, 1764
Stout, Jonathan, 11, Nov, 1759
Stout, Leah, w/o Jonathan, 11, Nov, 1759
Stout, Rebecca, d/o Jonathan and Leah, 18, July, 1762
Stout, Robert, Adult, 31, Oct, 1773
Sullivan, Mary, 11, June, 1764
_____, Susanna, 20, Nov, 1763
_____, Sussex, Mullato, 14, July, 1771
Sutton, Charles, Adult, 27, Oct, 1752
Sutton, Kezid, d/o Charles and _____, 29, Oct, 1752
Sutton, Margaret, d/o Charles and _____, 22, May, 1754
Taylor, Elisha, s/o Mrs. Taylor, 9, Feb, 1746
Taylor, George, Adult, 5, May, 1765
Taylor, John, s/o Mrs. Taylor, 9, Feb, 1746
Taylor, Morford, s/o Mrs. Taylor, 9, Feb, 1746
Taylor, Nathaniel, s/o Mrs. Taylor, 9, Feb, 1746
_____, Thomas, s/o Thomas a free negro, 6, July, 1760
_____, Thomas, Negro servant of Mr. Samuel Osburn, 15, Oct, 1749
Thomas (?), Davis, s/o Enoch Thomas, 27, Apl, 1766
Thomas, James, s/o Enoch and Elizabeth, 4, Apl, 1762
Thomas, Lydia, d/o Enoch and Elizabeth, 15, July, 1759
Thomas, Mary, d/o Enoch and Elizabeth, 28, Aug, 1757
Thomson, Joseph, s/o Samuel and Sarah, 10, Sep, 1821
Thompson, Catharine, d/o Lewis and Cornelia, 21, Oct, 1810
Thompson, Edgar, s/o Catharine O.W., 26, Dec, 1818
Thompson, Elizabeth, d/o Lewis and Anne, 18, Oct, 1810
Thompson, Frances, s/o Lewis and Anne, 18, Oct, 1810
Thompson, Franklin, s/o Lewis and Anne, 18, Oct, 1810
Thompson, Jane Forman, d/o Samuel and Sarah, 29, Aug, 1824
Thompson, John, s/o Joseph and Mary, 23, June, 1816
Thompson, Joseph, s/o Samuel and Sarah, 18, May, 1819
Thompson, Mary, d/o Samuel and Elizabeth, 27, Sep, 1747
Thompson, Mary, w/o Joseph, 14, Dec, 1813
Thompson, Mary Ann, d/o Thomas and Sarah, 8, Mar, 1812
Thompson, Thomas, s/o Samuel and Sarah, 18, May, 1819
Thompson, Thomas, s/o Joseph and Mary, 14, Dec, 1813
Thompson, William, s/o Lewis and Anne, 18, Oct, 1810
Thompson, William Craig, s/o Thomas and Sarah, 25, Mar, 1810

Christ Church at Shrewsbury

Thorn, John, s/o Widow Thorn, 1, July, 1753
Thorn, Sarah, d/o John and _____, 25, Dec, 1752
Throughmorton, Ann, d/o Job and _____, 14, Apl, 1754
Throckmorton, Ann Matilda, d/o Forman and Elizabeth, 7, June, 1818
Throckmorton, Aaron Rhea, s/o Thomas and Elizabeth, 23, Oct, 1818
Throckmorton, Barbarie, s/o Thomas and Elizabeth, 4, July, 1813
Throckmorton, Charles Forman, s/o Forman and Elizabeth, 16, June, 1816
Throckmorton, Catharine, d/o Forman and Elizabeth, 19, Aug, 1822
Throckmorton, David, s/o Job and Frances, 11, May, 1735
Throckmorton, Elizabeth, w/o Forman, 3, July, 1814
Throughmorton, Elizabeth, d/o Job and Hannah, 9, Feb, 1746
Throckmorton, Frances Eliza, d/o Thomas and Elizabeth, 1, Sep, 1811
Throckmorton, Gertrude Eliza, d/o Joseph and Mary Ann, 25, Oct, 1818
Throughmorton, Hannah, w/o Job, 28, Mar, 1746
Throckmorton, Hannah, d/o Job and _____, 25, Dec, 1758
Throughmorton, Hartness, s/o Samuel and Mary, 28, Aug, 1735
Throckmorton, Holmes, s/o John and _____, 22, Apl, 1759
Througmorton, James, s/o Joseph and Alice, 3, Aug, 1735
Throckmorton, James, s/o Joseph Jr and Mary, 4, Aug, 1754
Throckmorton, James, s/o Thomas and Elizabeth, 25, Mar, 1810
Throughmorton, James, s/o John and Sarah, 10, Nov, 1751
Throughmorton, Jane, d/o Joseph Jr and Mary, 11, Mar, 1750
Throckmorton, Jane, d/o Forman and Elizabeth — 1820
Througmorton, Jane, d/o Joseph and Mary, 30, May, 1748
Throckmorton, Jane, d/o Forman and Elizabeth, 19, Aug, 1822
Througmorton, Jemima, d/o Job and Mary, 31, Mar, 1749
Throgmorton, Job, s/o Job and _____, 23, Aug, 1761
Througmorton, Job, s/o Job Senr and Frances, 9, Feb, 1746
Througmorton, John, s/o John and Sarah, 24, Oct, 1750
Througmorton, John, s/o Samuel and Mary, 7, Oct, 1747
Througmorton, John, s/o Joseph and _____, 9, Feb, 1746
Througmorton, John, s/o Joseph and Mary, 14, June, 1752
Throckmorton, John Fisher, s/o Samuel and Catharine, 8, Oct, 1758
Throckmorton, Joseph Forman, s/o Joseph and Mary, 8, May, 1757
Througmorton, Joseph, s/o Job Senr and Frances, 26, Aug, 1746
Throckmorton, Julian, s/o Thomas and Elizabeth, 23, June, 1816
Througmorton, Lewis, s/o Job Senr and Frances, 9, Feb, 1746
Throckmorton, Margaret, Widow of Joseph, 1, Mar, 1812
Througmorton, Mary, w/o Samuel, 28, Aug, 1746
Througmorton, Mary, d/o Joseph and _____, 9, Feb, 1746
Througmorton, Mary, d/o Job and Mary, 14, July, 1751

Througmorton, Mirtilla, d/o John and _____, 11, Aug, 1753
Througmorton, Rebecca, d/o Job Senr and Frances, 9, Feb, 1746
Througmorton, Rebecca, d/o John and _____, 26, May, 1754
Throckmorton, Richard, s/o Samuel and Catharine, 10, Aug, 1760
Throckmorton, Samuel, s/o Joseph and Mary, 28, Jan, 1759
Througmorton, Samuel, s/o Samuel and Mary, 7, Oct, 1747
Throckmorton, Sarah Forman, d/o Forman and Elizabeth, 10, Oct, 1813
Througmorton, Sarah, d/o John and Sarah, 30, June, 1746
Throckmorton, Sarah, d/o Samuel and Catharine, 12, Apl, 1767
Througmorton, Sarah, d/o Job, 22, June, 1746
Throckmorton, Sarah, d/o John and _____, 6, Nov, 1757
Throckmorton, Susanna, d/o Forman and Elizabeth, 14, July, 1822
Throckmorton, Susanna, d/o Job and _____, 18, July, 1756
Throckmorton, Thomas, s/o Joseph and Mary, 15, Sep, 1764
Throckmorton, William, s/o Joseph and Mary, 5, Apl, 1761
Throckmorton, William, s/o Forman and Elizabeth, 3, July, 1814
Tillier, John, s/o William and Martha, 30, July, 1746
Tillier, Thomas, s/o William and Martha, 30, July, 1746
Tilton, Mary Ann, Adult, 21, Oct, 1821
Tilton, Mersey, Adult, 28, Mar, 1823
Tilton, Rebecca, d/o Samuel and _____, 2, July, 1749
Tison, Alice, d/o Rarnt and Mary, 8, Jan, 1811
Tison, Mary, d/o Rarnt and Mary, 8, Jan, 1811
Titus, Lydia, d/o Ephram and _____, 6, June, 1775
Tole, Joseph, s/o Richard and Sarah, 4, July, 1762
Van Dam, Isaac, s/o Isaac and Isabel, 4, Apl, 1736
Van Dam, Rip, s/o Isaac and Isabel, 6, Jan, 1733
Van Dam, John, s/o Isaac and Isabel, 22, May, 1738
Vanderife, Jane, Adult, 25, Mar, 1757
Vanderife, Martha, d/o Mathias and Mary, 25, Mar, 1757
Vanderife, Mary, w/o Mathias, 25, Mar, 1757
Vanderife, Mary, d/o Mathias and Mary, 15, July, 1759
Vanderife, Mathias, Adult, 25, Mar, 1757
Van Hoist, Richard, s/o Richard and _____, 13, May, 1759
Van Mater, Aaron Schenk, s/o Joseph and Ann, 1815
Van Marter, Eleanor, Adult, 16, Sep, 1812
Vanort, Eleanor, d/o Joseph and _____, 31, Oct, 1762
Vanort, Frances Kilpatrick, 29, Nov, 1769
Vanpelt, Catharine, d/o Walter and Mary, 4, Oct, 1748
_____, Violeta, negro child belonging to Capt Troup, 3, Mar, 1767
Voorhees, Ann, d/o Joseph and Hannah, 1804
Voorhees, Eleanor, d/o Joseph and Hannah, 1807

Christ Church at Shrewsbury

Voorhees, Hannah, d/o Joseph and Hannah, 18, Oct, 1812
Voorhees, Jacob, s/o Joseph and Hannah, 25, Dec,
Voorhees, Peter, s/o Joseph and Hannah, 1805
Wainwright, Nicholas, 7, May, 1750
Wall, James, s/o Joseph and Elizabeth, 11, Oct, 1812
Wall, John, s/o Joseph and Elizabeth, 11, Oct, 1812
Wall, William, s/o Joseph and Elizabeth, 11, Oct, 1812
Walsh, David, s/o Walter and Alice, 4, Oct, 1747
Wamsley, Leah, Adult, 31, May, 1772
Wardell, John, s/o Henry and Lucy, 23, Feb, 1775
Wardell, Sarah, Adult, 29, Dec, 1770
Wardle, Ameline, d/o Richard and Margaret, 27, May, 1799
Warne, Benjamin, s/o Thomas and Hannah, 2, Aug, 1753
Warne, Deborah, d/o Thomas and Hannah, 15, June, 1735
Warne, Hezekias, s/o Joshua and Elizabeth, 28, Oct, 1750
Warne, James, s/o Joshua and ____-, 13, June, 1749
Warne, Job, s/o Joshua and ____-, 17, May, 1757
Warne, Joseph, s/o Joshua and Elizabeth, 10, Apl, 1754
Warne, Joshua, s/o Thomas and Mary, 13, Dec, 1760
Warne, Richard, s/o Thomas and Hannah, 14, June, 1747
Warne, Thomas, s/o Samuel and Hannah, 18, Sep, 1758
Warne, William, s/o Joshua and Elizabeth, 12, July, 1747
Warne, Mary, d/o Joshua and Elizabeth, 3, Aug, 1735
Warne, Samuel, s/o Thomas and Hannah, 8, July, 1750
Warne, Thomas, s/o Samuel and ____, 25, June, 1766
Warner, Kezia, d/o Samuel and Margaret, 8, May, 1746
Warner, Lewis, s/o Thomas and Mary, 8, July, 1764
Warner, Thomas, s/o Joshua and Helena, 20, July, 1764
Weatherhill, Vincent, s/o ---- and Ann, 24, Apl, 1749
Webbley, Audery, d/o John and ____, 24, May, 1747
Webbley, Catharine, d/o John and ____, 21, May, 1747
Webbley, Mary, d/o John and ____, 21, May, 1747
Webley, Margaret, d/o John and ____, 8, May, 1748
Webley, Mary, d/o John and ____, 8, May, 1748
Webley, Sarah, d/o Thomas and Elizabeth, 21, Nov, 1747
Welsh, Elizabeth, d/o Walter and Mary, 20, Jan, 1752
West, Abigail, d/o Stephen and —, 15, Aug, 1750
West, Ann, d/o Joseph and Audrey, 4, Feb, 1750
West, Ann, d/o Webley, 25, Dec, 1734
West, Asher, s/o Joseph and Audrey, 21, June, 1747
West, Audrey, d/o James and Ann, 28, Aug, 1768
West, Audrey, w/o Joseph, 14, June, 1747

West, Beriah, s/o Joseph and Audrey, 21, June, 1747
West, Catharine, d/o James and Ann, 28, Aug, 1768
West, Catharine, Adult, 19, July, 1768
West, Catharine, d/o Joseph and Audrey, 21, June, 1747
West, Daniel, s/o Daniel and Mary, 15, June, 1773
West, Deborah, d/o Joseph and Audrey, 21, June, 1747
West, Edmund, Adult, 2, May, 1818
West, Elizabeth, d/o Asher and Anna, 28, Aug, 1768
West, Elizabeth, d/o Webley West, 5, Oct, 1746
West, Euphemia, d/o Asher and Anna, 28, Aug, 1768
West, Gabriel, Adult, 2, May, 1818
West, James, s/o Joseph and Audrey, 21, June, 1747
West, James, Adult, 2, May, 1818
West, Jane, d/o Joseph and Audrey, 21, June, 1747
West, John Leonard, s/o George and Catherine, 3, Aug, 1760
West, John, s/o James and Ann, 21, June, 1752
West, John, s/o Joseph and Audrey, 21, June, 1747
West, John, Adult, 2, May, 1818
West, Joseph, s/o Webley and Clenicas, 9, July, 1746
West, Joseph, s/o Joseph and Audrey, 14, June, 1747
West, Joseph, 14, June, 1747
West, Joseph, s/o Joseph and Mary, 26, Apl, 1752
West, Lewis, s/o Joseph and Audrey, 16, May, 1756
West, Mary, Adult, 11, Aug, 1734
West, Mary, d/o William and ____, 15, Feb, 1761
West, Matthew, s/o Joseph and Audrey, 5, May, 1754
West, Meribah, w/o John, 2, May, 1818
West, Moses, s/o George and Catherine, 1, Aug, 1762
West, Rebecca, w/o Webley, 26, Dec, 1748
West, Revo, Adult, 2, May, 1818
West, Samuel, s/o Joseph and Audrey, 21, June, 1747
West, Sarah, d/o Robin and ____ Mullato, 24, July, 1751
West, Sarah, d/o James and Ann, 14, Apl, 1751
West, Stephen, s/o Joseph and Audrey, 5, May, 1754
West, Stephen, 30, May, 1748
West, Susanna, Adult, 19, July, 1768
West, Webley, Junr, 21, May, 1750
West, Zilphia, Adult, 15, July, 1739
West, ____, w/o Stephen, 30, May, 1748
White, Abigail, d/o Jacob and Abigail, 21, Oct, 1821
White, Albert, s/o John and Nancy, 17, Jan, 1819
White, Charles, s/o Lyttleton and Nancy, 23, Feb, 1814

Christ Church at Shrewsbury

White, Cordelia, d/o Lyttleton and Nancy, 1, Oct, 1819
White, Eleanor, d/o Jacob and Abigail, 8, Jan, 1811
White, Elizabeth, d/o Thomas and Hannah, 19, June, 1812
White, Emeline, d/o Jacob and Abigail, 18, Dec, 1814
White, Frances Margaret Hart, d/o John and Nancy, 17, Jan, 1819
White, George Haggerty, s/o Thomas and Hannah, 24, June, 1812
White, Hannah Voorhes, d/o Jacob and Abigail, 18, June, 1817
White, Henry, s/o Thomas and Hannah, 14, June, 1812
White, Jacob, s/o Lyttleton and Nancy, 26, May, 1822
White, Jacob, Adult, 27, Dec, 1813
White, John, s/o Robert Hood and Ellen White O.W., 26, Jan, 1751
White, John Henry Hobart, s/o John and Nancy, 17, Jan, 1819
White, Lucy, d/o Jacob and Abigail, 20, Dec, 1812
White, Mary Ann, d/o Jacob and Abigail, 8, Oct,
White, Robert Holmes, s/o Lyttleton and Nancy, 5, May, 1816
White, Russel, s/o Lyttleton and Nancy, 10, May, 1812
White, William, s/o Robert Hood and Ellen White O.W., 23, July, 1751
Wildes, John, s/o Robert and Elizabeth, 1, Jan, 1746-7
Wildes, Richard, s/o Robert and _____, 17, Oct, 1748
Wiles, Joseph, s/o Robert and _____, 9, May, 1756
Wilkie, Deborah, d/o George and Mary, 2, May, 1751
Wilkie, George, s/o George and Mary, 2, May, 1751
Wilkie, Sarah, d/o George and Mary, 2, May, 1751
Wilson, Ann, d/o Joseph and Margaret, 19, May, 1754
Wilson, Daniel, s/o James and Margaret, 15, Aug, 1756
Wilson, Elizabeth, d/o Joseph and Margaret, 19, Sep, 1756
Wilson, Elizabeth, d/o Thomas O.W., 8, Apl, 1771
Wilson, Henry, s/o James and Margaret, 3, Dec, 1758
Wilson, James, s/o Joseph and _____, 13, Oct, 1751
Wilson, Susan, d/o Benjamin and Elizabeth, 1, Dec, 1811
Wilson, William, s/o Benjamin and Elizabeth, 1, Dec, 1811
William, John, s/o James and Elizabeth, 12, Dec, 1762
_____, William, s/o a Mullato O.W., 13, Sep, 1747
_____, William, s/o_____, 25, Aug, 1765
Wildes, John, s/o John and Margaret, 29, Sep, 1746
Willis, Ophelia, d/o John and Margaret, 4, Sep, 1748
Willis, Patience, d/o John and Margaret, 29, June, 1746
Willis, Rebecca, d/o John and Margaret, 29, June, 1746
Willson, Henry, s/o James and Mary, 15, June, 1735
Willson, John, s/o James and Margaret, 30, July, 1746
Wilson, John, s/o Joseph and Margaret, 4, Feb, 1751
Willson, Mary, d/o Joseph and Margaret, 4, Feb, 1751

Willson, Sarah, d/o Joseph and Margaret, 4, Feb, 1751
Willson, Susannah, d/o Joseph and Margaret, 4, Feb, 1751
Wing, Ann, 11, Oct, 1747
Witherill, Ann, d/o John and _____, 15, June, 1735
Wright, Abigail, d/o Edward and Mary, 15, Mar, 1747
Wright, Ann, d/o Edward and _____, 27, June, 1742
Wright, Edward, s/o Edward and Mary, 15, Mar, 1747
Wright, Increase, d/o Edward and Mary, 15, Mar, 1747
Wright, Mary, d/o Edward and Mary, 15, Mar, 1747
Wright, William, s/o Edward and Mary, 13, Aug, 1738
Wood, Ezekial, 20, May, 1748
Wood, John, s/o Erick and Sarah, 7, May, 1750
Wood, Obediah, s/o George and _____, 9, Feb, 1766
Wood, Phebe, d/o John and Sarah, 7, May, 1750
Wood, Susannah, 20, May, 1748
Wood, Susanna, d/o George and _____, 31, July, 1768
Woolly, Content, d/o George and _____, 25, June, 1749
Woolley, Joseph, s/o Daniel and _____, 30, Sep, 1759
Worthley, Ann, d/o John and Lydia, 1, Apl, 1750
Worthley, John, Adult, 11, Oct, 1771
Worthley, John, s/o John and Grazel, 1, June, 1737
Worthley, Lydia, w/o John, 17, Dec, 1749
Worthley, Obadiah, s/o John and Grazel, 1, June, 1737
_____, Zebulon, s/o a Mullato called Black Robin, 8, Sep, 1749

Heritage Books by Anna Miller Watring:

Accomack County, Virginia, Marriage References and Family Relationships, 1620–1800

*Bucks County, Pennsylvania, Church Records of the 17th and 18th Centuries,
Volume 2: Quaker Records: Falls and Middletown Monthly Meetings*
Anna Miller Watring and F. Edward Wright

*Bucks County, Pennsylvania, Church Records of the 17th and 18th Centuries,
Volume 3: Quaker Records: Wrightstown, Richland, Buckingham,
Makefield And Solebury Monthly Meetings*

Civil War Burials in Baltimore's Loudon Park Cemetery

Early Church Records of Monmouth County, New Jersey

*Early Quaker Records of Philadelphia, Pennsylvania,
Volume 1: 1682–1750*

*Early Quaker Records of Philadelphia, Pennsylvania,
Volume 2, 1751–1800*

*King George County, Virginia, Marriage References
and Family Relationships, 1721–1800*
Anne M. Watring and F. Edward Wright

Loudon Park Caretaker Records, A–B, 1853–1986
Anna M. Watring, E. Charles Miller, and R. Scott Johnson

*New Jersey Bible Records:
Volume 1, Atlantic, Burlington, Cape May
and Gloucester Counties*

*New Jersey Bible Records:
Volume 2, Salem and Cumberland Counties*

www.ingramcontent.com/pod-product-compliance
Lightning Source LLC
Chambersburg PA
CBHW070732160426
43192CB00009B/1406